PERSUASION AND SOCIAL MOVEMENTS

THIRD EDITION

CHARLES J. STEWART
Purdue University

CRAIG ALLEN SMITH
The University of North Carolina at Greensboro

ROBERT E. DENTON, JR.
Virginia Polytechnic Institute and State University

WAVELAND
PRESS, INC.
Prospect Heights, Illinois

For information about this book, write or call:

Waveland Press, Inc.
P.O. Box 400
Prospect Heights, Illinois 60070
(708) 634-0081

Printed in the United States of America

7 6 5 4 3 2

Preface

Ever since neanderthals thought their tribe's "system" needed alterations, social movements have directly or indirectly provided the impetus for almost all important socio-political changes. In just over a century in our country alone, social movements have contributed to the freeing of the slaves, the end of child labor, the suffrage of blacks, women, and 18–20 year olds, the eight-hour workday and forty-hour week, direct election of U.S. Senators, the graduated income tax, social security, collective bargaining, prohibition of alcoholic beverages, the end of prohibition, and desegregation of public facilities and schools.

Nevertheless, only recently have people begun to regard social movements as more than nuisances to be harshly corrected. Studies of social movements were encouraged in the field of communication as early as 1923, and they received periodic attention from such writers as Donald C. Bryant, Dallas Dickey, and Bower Aly. The first serious discussion of *how* one should study the persuasive efforts of social movements did not appear until 1947 when S. Judson Crandell discussed social movement patterns developed by social psychologists and offered suggestions to the prospective rhetorical analyst. Five years later, Leland Griffin's "The Rhetoric of Historical Movements" presented a rudimentary "rhetorical" pattern for movement studies and a workable approach to the analysis of social movements. The 1950s and 1960s witnessed an increased interest in the persuasive dimensions of social movements, but the intellectual advances were modest. Many studies fell into the ruts left by generations of rhetorical analysts. For example, some authors spent most of their time trying to demonstrate that the "public speaking" in a movement was all important — at the expense of other kinds of communication. Other authors could not avoid pursuing the worst kind of "neo-Aristotelian" criticism. A 1964 master's thesis about the women's suffrage movement, for example, asked whether the speakers were formally trained and whether their speeches were consistent with the classical teachings of invention, disposition, memory, style, and delivery. These early studies investigated few topics with the thoroughness needed either for theory building or for the understanding of complex historical events.

The state of affairs began to change rapidly with the dawn of the 1970s, undoubtedly in part because social movements had become commonplace on most college campuses and could no longer be avoided or ignored. Three publications more than any others helped us turn an intellectual corner. Herbert Simons' "Requirements, Problems, and Strategies: A Theory of Persuasion for Social Movements," published in 1970, was the first methodological statement since Griffin's 1952 article. Simons synthesized the notions of social-psychological resources, situational tasks, and rhetorical adaptation into an emphasis upon the social movement's management of its persuasive resources—a leader-centered approach to social movements. *The Rhetoric of Agitation and Control*, by John Bowers and Donovan Ochs appeared the next year. It was the first book about persuasion and social movements that was not primarily a collection of speeches and the first to focus on the methods used by institutions to counter the persuasive efforts of social movements. Then in 1972 Simons wrote "Persuasion in Social Conflicts: A Critique of Prevailing Conceptions and a Framework for Future Research," arguing that most previous research had reflected an establishment bias by focusing on persuasive tactics more appropriate for the drawing room than for the streets.

The contributions of these three works are evident in both the quantity and quality of social movement studies since the early 1970s. Issues of many communication journals have included at least one "movement" study, and in 1980 and 1991 entire issues of the *Central States Speech Journal* and *Communication Studies* were devoted to the study of persuasion and social movements. Literally hundreds of articles and book chapters have generated thought-provoking results, research approaches, and controversies. Many students of persuasion and social movements—whether undergraduates, graduates, or professors—have experienced difficulties in understanding and using these results and approaches and in resolving the controversies that have often appeared in brief and highly sophisticated journal articles. We conceived this book, in part, as a solution to this state of affairs. Our purpose was threefold: to synthesize, extend, and apply many of the findings, theories, and approaches generated since the 1960s in the fields of sociology and social psychology as well as communication.

Chapters 1 through 4 focus on the role of persuasion in social movements and include topics that explore the characteristics of social movements, the social movement from a social systems perspective, the persuasive functions of social movements, and the typical life cycle of social movements. Chapters 5 and 6 focus on the sources of leadership and how social movements address the needs of members, particularly democratic and authoritarian character structures. Chapters 7 and 8 focus on the strategies social movements employ to attain legitimacy and the strategies institutions use to resist social movements. Chapters 9, 10, and 11 focus on the symbolism and symbolic acts of social movements, particularly the theories of Kenneth Burke, language strategies, and the persuasive functions of protest music. Chapters 12, 13, and 14 focus on the argumentative strategies of social movements and counter-movements, including types of argument, argument from narrative vision, and argument from transcendence. Chapter 15 serves as a summary of the major principles and findings of this book.

We have approached this book with five fundamental assumptions. The first assumption is that since persuasion is inherently practical, we can study it most profitably by examining the functions of persuasive acts. Second, we presume that even apparently irrational acts make sense to the actor—the trick is discovering the reasoning behind the act. Third, people create and comprehend their world through symbols, and it is people who create, use, ignore, or act upon these symbolic creations. Fourth, public speeches are an important form of social movement persuasion, but they are neither the most prevalent nor necessarily the most effective form. And fifth, we can rarely explain social movement as mere instances of orneriness, perversion, or ignorance. Someone once wryly observed that a rebel who loses is a traitor, while a rebel who wins is a patriot and founder. These assumptions may strike some readers as heresy and still others as "old-hat." We hope this revised, restructured, and up-dated edition strikes a similar balance.

Charles J. Stewart
Craig Allen Smith
Robert E. Denton, Jr.

Table of Contents

Chapter One
The Social Movement as a Unique Collective Phenomenon

The second half of the twentieth century may well be called "the age of the social movement" in America. African Americans, Hispanic Americans, native Americans, women, gays, college students, prison inmates, and workers from the vineyard to the university campus have demanded rights, equality, identity, and a fair share of the American dream. Organizations have formed to protest American involvement in military conflicts, destruction of the environment, nuclear power plants, violence and sex on television, legalized abortion, marijuana laws, abuse of animals for research and profit, centralized power in corporate, governmental, and educational bureaucracies, and revolutionary changes in American social structures, norms, and values. For every movement created to bring about change, a countermovement determined to resist change with all available resources also appears.

Social movements, of course, did not arrive upon the American scene with the advent of the 1950s. A great many colonists came to America to escape persecution for their beliefs and their fledgling social movements in England and Europe. The American Revolution began as a social movement before it evolved into a full-scale military conflict. And the nineteenth century witnessed great struggles to free the slaves, improve working conditions and compensation, reduce (and later to prohibit) the selling of alcoholic beverages, gain equal rights for women, and return religion to the fundamentals of the Bible.

In our efforts to understand, explain, and manage the bewildering variety of demands, protests, events, and changes that have affected American lives during the past half-century, and the lives of our ancestors during the previous centuries of American history, we tend to call them *movements* whether they are internal changes within established groups, protest organizations, campaigns, uprisings, riots, violent revolutions, civil wars, trends, fads, or crazes. Since many of these *movements* have obvious differences, we often attach modifiers such as social,

1

political, religious, historical, rhetorical, reform, revisionary, nationalistic, resistance, conservative, and individualistic. If we are suspicious or fearful of movements—or downright hostile—we may call them radical, reactionary, revolutionary, repressive, or fanatical. Some groups may call themselves movements to claim size, importance, and influence far beyond reality.[1] The result leads to confusion rather than to an understanding of movements.

This book focuses on the persuasive efforts of one unique collective phenomenon designed to bring about or resist change, the *social movement*. What is a social movement? How is it similar to and different from other collective phenomena called movements? Attempts to define the term have often added to rather than lessened confusion and disagreement. For example, some writers have proposed "collective action definitions." William Bruce Cameron says "a social movement occurs when a fairly large number of people band together in order to alter or to supplant some portion of the existing culture or social order."[2] Malcolm Sillars, in an attempt to "cast the widest net," defines social movements as "collective actions which are perceived by a critic."[3] These definitions appear to encompass all collective actions and do not distinguish the social movement from presidential campaigns, political action committees (PACs), United Way campaigns, or petition drives to prevent sexual orientation clauses from being added to municipal human rights ordinances.

Others have developed "social psychological" definitions. For example, John Wilson writes that a social movement is "a conscious, collective, organized attempt to bring about or to resist large-scale change in the social order by noninstitution-alized means."[4] Herbert Simons defines social movements as "struggles on behalf of a cause by groups whose core organizations, modes of action, and/or guiding ideas are not fully legitimated by the larger society."[5] Social psychological definitions address more precisely *what* a social movement *is* and *is not*, but they do not address *how* this collective phenomenon achieves its goals or differs from civil wars, revolutions, or lobbying groups.

Other theorists have developed "rhetorical" definitions of social movements. Charles Wilkinson, for instance, defines social movements as "languaging strategies by which a significantly vocal part of an established society, experiencing together a sustained dialectical tension growing out of moral (ethical) conflict, agitate to induce cooperation in others, either directly or indirectly, and thereby affecting the status quo."[6] Wilkinson's definition addresses more precisely *how* a social movement achieves its goals but not precisely *what* a social movement is and is not. For instance, is a large and vocal group of Christians demanding the right to display a nativity scene on the courthouse lawn at Christmas time a social movement? Robert Cathcart's definition comes closer to identifying both how and what: "A social movement can be said to emerge when the languaging strategies of a change-seeking collective clash with the languaging strategies of the establishment and thereby produce the perception of a group's operating outside the established social hierarchy."[7]

If we are to comprehend the persuasive efforts of social movements, then we must be able to determine if the particular phenomenon under investigation is a social movement or at least a portion of a social movement. Current collective action, social psychological, and rhetorical definitions make important but partial contributions to this comprehension. In this chapter, we attempt to identify the essential characteristics of social movements and the pervasiveness of persuasion in such efforts to bring about or resist change.

An Organized Collectivity

A social movement has at least minimal organization. If we cannot identify leaders (spokespersons), membership (followers or believers), and organizations, the phenomenon under study is a trend, a fad, or unrest, not a social movement.[8] A phenomenon such as the current "men's movement," in which groups of men attend weekend retreats to pour out their hearts and to seek comfort in brotherhood, may eventually develop into a full-fledged social movement if organizations develop, leaders other than poets and writers emerge, and memberships develop.[9] The degree of organization, visibility of leaders, and nature of membership varies from movement to movement. For instance, Martin Luther King, Jr. of the Southern Christian Leadership Conference, Roy Wilkins of the National Association for the Advancement of Colored People (NAACP), and Malcolm X of the Black Muslims were internationally known leaders of the black rights movement. Although it would be difficult for most of us to name a single leader or organization of the gay rights or environmental movements, two highly visible and active social movements in the 1990s, they do exist, have sizeable memberships, and are essential for the continued existence and progress of each movement. Leaders, members, and organizations that stage frequent public demonstrations and media events, such as pro-life's Operation Rescue and environmentalism's Greenpeace, are more visible than ones that operate primarily through the courts, in small groups, or within the social movement community such as the National Right to Life Committee and the Sierra Club. All must have at least minimal organization to qualify as social movements.

The mass media, as James Chesebro and Roger Howe have noted, may create the illusion of a social movement by treating "relatively isolated, but similar, rhetorical situations throughout the nation . . . as a single, dynamic and interrelated phenomenon."[10] For example, the "death of God theology" attracted a great deal of media coverage and attention of religious leaders in the late 1970s and early 1980s and appeared to be a booming social movement when, in fact, no leaders, membership, or organization existed.[11] The same can be said for the "secular humanist conspiracy" seen as a powerful, demonic social movement by Christian fundamentalists in the 1980s and 1990s. Although they could point to writings of self-styled secular humanists and to Secular Humanist Manifestos I and II issued by small groups of philosophers in 1933 and 1973, the secular changes continuing in the United States are decades-old trends.[12] There is no evidence of organizations, leaders, demonstrations, or campaigns urging teenagers to have sex, husbands and wives to divorce, or God-fearing people to stop attending churches and synagogues. Thus, a secular movement but not a secular humanist social movement has apparently altered norms and values in American life during the twentieth century.

Social movements and campaigns are often confused, partly because social movements employ campaigns to achieve specific goals. For instance, the Clamshell Alliance in New Hampshire conducted numerous campaigns to keep the Seabrook Nuclear Power Plant from being constructed and operated; Earth First! has conducted many campaigns to stop logging operations in the northwest.[13] Although campaigns and social movements share similarities, they have significant differences.[14] Social movements tend to be organized from the bottom up while campaigns tend to be organized from the top down.[15] A leader of a social movement usually rises from a protest group as it develops and discovers the need for such a person, often an evolutionary process. A campaign leader, on the other hand, is usually a manager designated by an organization's decision makers; the manager in turn selects and organizes a staff and runs the campaign. Campaigns, whether run by a social movement organization, political party, corporation, political action committee, or university development office, have managers with assigned roles, organizational charts, chiefs of staff, schedules of operations, specific goals, and known end-points such as election day or the date a fund or membership drive is to "go over the top." For example, native American movement organizations organize protests when the Atlanta Braves or Washington Redskins play in the World Series or Super Bowl, but these protests (brief social movement campaigns) end when the sports events end. By contrast, social movements may last for decades, must change as circumstances change, rarely maintain tight control over memberships, and often alter and add to goals as they proceed. No social movement knows when, if ever, it will achieve its ends and disband.

Social movement organizations are often confused with social movements. The National Organization for Women (NOW), the American Indian Movement (AIM), People for the Ethical Treatment of Animals (PETA), and Greenpeace are social movement organizations, not social movements. Each is *one* organization of several striving for equality for women, native American rights, humane treatment of wild and domestic animals, and protection of the environment. To fully understand the persuasive efforts of the animal rights movement, for instance, we must analyze the messages of all the organizations of the movement, including the Friends of Animals, the Animal Protection Institute of America, Beauty Without Cruelty International, Trans-Species Unlimited, the Animal Welfare Institute, Humans Against Rabbit Exploitation (HARE), and PETA. Thus, while one or more organizations are a necessary component for a collective action to qualify as a social movement, a single organization is *not* synonymous with the movement.

Although minimal organization is a hallmark of social movements, it frequently never expands to a higher level of organization. The reality is that social movements never proceed in orderly step-by-step fashion, contain one supreme leader who controls *the* organization, appeal to a single target audience, have a carefully defined and identifiable membership, or strive to attain a single, well-defined goal through the employment of one persuasive strategy.

An Uninstitutionalized Collectivity

A social movement is an uninstitutionalized collectivity. No social movement or social movement organization is part of an established order that governs and changes social, political, religious, or economic norms and values.[16] "Movements" by the Roman Catholic hierarchy to alter its liturgy, members of Congress to reform its ethical standards, bankers to revise lending policies, or the United Auto Workers Union to gain a better contract with Ford Motor Company are not social movements.[17] These are establishments changing themselves and striving for goals through institutionalized means and procedures. Primary impetus for change comes from within rather than from without.

In efforts to comprehend the persuasive efforts of complex social movements, we have too often assumed they are no different from the collective actions of political parties, PACs, legislatures, religious organizations, and corporations. Social movements operate from *outside* of established institutions. Social movements often attempt to persuade members of established orders (legislators, governors, judges, bishops, trustees, industrialists, actors and actresses) to change or to support programs for change, but they cease to be social movements if they become part of an established order.

The "outsider" or uninstitutionalized nature of social movements, according to Herbert Simons and others, presents leaders with "extraordinary rhetorical dilemmas" in requirements they must fulfill, problems they face, and strategies they may adopt to meet these requirements.[18] David Zarefsky counters this position by arguing that "establishment movements" such as President Lyndon Johnson's "War on Poverty" have rhetorical careers identical to that of a social movement and that major rhetorical dilemmas "are not unique to persuasive campaigns mounted by uninstitutionalized collectivities."[19] After discussing three "establishment movements," Zarefsky concludes that "officially sanctioned organizations do not always have controls to assure effectiveness."

Although success is never assured for any persuasive effort, a comparison of the situations uninstitutionalized social movements and institutionalized established orders confront suggests the social movements do indeed encounter unique persuasive requirements and handicaps. Social movements are always "out-groups" viewed by society as illegitimate.[20] They are criticized for not handling conflicts and controversies through normal, proper channels and procedures, even when these channels and procedures are denied them. Social movements have virtually no powers of reward and punishment beyond personal recognition or expulsion, and expulsion often leads to competing organizations created by the exiled. They have neither legislative nor enforcement powers and no assured means of financial support. Monetary funds are fractions of those available to established governments, churches, political parties, labor unions, and corporations.

Uninstitutionalized leaders survive only as long as they perform the necessary tasks well, and when new tasks or abilities are required, leaders may be unceremoniously discarded. Leaders have minimal control over single factions or fragile coalitions of movement organizations and none over important establishments such as courts, investigative agencies, and boards of trustees. Rarely can they bring most of a social movement's resources to bear on a single event, let alone a persuasive campaign. The mass media devote little space or air time to social movements, are rarely favorable toward them (unless success appears near), are rarely controlled by social movements (although some social movements are adept at manipulating media to attain coverage), and provide exposure only when a social movement does something spectacular or stupid. Social movement organizations rarely have the money to purchase significant space or air time to present their cases directly to the American people. Persuasion is the sole means available to most social movements to accomplish such functions as transforming perceptions of reality, prescribing courses of action, and mobilizing the discontented.

The institutionalized group, on the other hand, is always an "in-group" viewed by society as legitimate. It strives to maintain at least the appearance of dealing with conflicts and controversies through normal, proper channels and procedures. Most institutions have immense powers of reward and punishment since they control law enforcement agencies, investigative groups, regulatory agencies, legislative bodies, political parties, tax authorities, courts, prisons, lucrative positions, church hierarchies, and bureaucracies. They may keep disgruntled people in line by enhancing their economic well-being, threatening their membership status, amending pieces of legislation, or granting or withholding contracts or licenses. Leaders may serve guaranteed terms of from two years to life, enjoy the support of organized and well-financed groups, and have opportunities to advance within corporate, political, or church hierarchies. Funding is much less a problem for institutionalized groups. Legislatures have access to millions or billions of tax dollars; political parties and PACs can raise millions of dollars through computerized mailings; chambers of commerce may raise dues; and large corporations such as Mobil Oil have vast resources to counter environmentalists.[21] Institutionalized groups and leaders are newsworthy and demand attention of the media. They may command multiple network and front page coverage of trivial as well as consequential speeches, press conferences, conventions, announcements, meetings of stockholders or bishops, ceremonies, and events. The president's cat or dog may draw more media attention than a social movement's demonstration. At the same time, institutions may stifle uncooperative or unfriendly media by threatening not to provide certain reporters or networks with seats on campaign planes, access to leaders, or entry into restricted areas, by threatening to unleash regulatory agencies (such as the FCC) or to create new regulations and restrictions, and by threatening to withdraw advertising. The president may gain international attention merely by strolling through the White House rose garden, visiting a "typical" American family, or attending a baseball game. All major networks and newspapers are owned by institutionalized groups devoted to maintaining societal norms and values and making a profit, and whatever support they give social movements is likely to be implicit rather than explicit.

Zarefsky may be correct in arguing that "establishment movements," or more accurately establishment campaigns, follow rhetorical careers similar to social movements. However, it is difficult to believe that the president of the United States or the public relations arm of Mobil Oil, even when following similar rhetorical patterns, have no advantages over the loosely knit social movement and, indeed, face identical persuasive requirements and dilemmas. H. Ross Perot demonstrated effectively during the 1992 presidential campaign what an American billionaire can accomplish in a few months with institutional connections, unlimited funds, and access to long blocks of uninterrupted, primetime television. No social movement has such connections, funds, or access to the media. Efforts to bring about changes through institutions—as seen in efforts of African Americans, women, and gays—have proven fragmentary, slow, and ephemeral. The gay rights movement, for example, is now experiencing a backlash that threatens many of the gains it has made over the past twenty years.[22] Hundreds of provisions of environmental laws, passed after years of agitation by environmental groups, were simply set aside from 1988 to 1992 by Vice President Dan Quayle's secretive Council on Competitiveness to eliminate "unnecessary and burdensome" government regulations that were allegedly making American companies noncompetitive.[23]

Large in Scope

A Social Movement is large in scope. The social movement must be large enough—in terms of geographical area, time, events, and participants—to achieve its goals.[24] Scope alone distinguishes social movements from most pressure groups, religious cults, lobbies, PACs, campaigns, and protests. Unlike these phenomena, social movements are usually national or international in scope, sustain efforts for years, select many leaders, create many organizations, conduct many membership drives, design many campaigns, expand and constrict ideologies, set and alter many goals, and employ many strategies.

Social movements in the United States cannot afford to be characterized as "small" because small ventures tend to be seen as insignificant or dangerous and therefore to be ignored, ridiculed, or suppressed. The tragic end of Ranch Apocalypse in Waco, Texas in 1993, in which eighty-five Branch Davidians died in a fiery inferno with leader David Koresh after a fifty-one-day stand-off with government authorities, illustrates what might happen when a small, seemingly dangerous group confronts institutions. Oliver and Marwell note that "One person marching for a thousand hours is not the same as a thousand people marching for one hour."[25] Institutions and their supporters went to great length in the 1960s to characterize the anti-war, student rights, and black power movements as small groups of radicals, sex perverts, traitors, cowards, racists, and degenerates clearly not representative of the great "silent majority" of citizens, students, and blacks. The native American movement, small in number and isolated in scattered, remote regions of the country, has experienced difficulty in attracting attention, maintaining media and governmental interest, and persuading audiences to take it seriously. It has resorted to takeovers of Alcatraz Island in San Francisco Bay, Wounded Knee in South Dakota, and the Bureau of Indian Affairs in Washington, D.C. to gain national attention. But the *Wall Street Journal* dismissed the occupation of the Bureau of Indian Affairs, for example, as "an exercise in play-acting—an effort by a relative handful of militants claiming to speak for the broader Indian community."[26] Forces on both sides of the abortion conflict have portrayed one another as vocal minorities and handfuls of people.[27] It is little wonder that virtually every social movement claims to be a "great grassroots movement." Whenever social movements stage "mass demonstrations," estimates of turnout vary drastically between establishment and social movement because each side has a stake in the size game. A recent survey that found only 1 percent of men considered themselves to be exclusively homosexual, contrary to the long-standing claim of 10 percent, prompted *Time* to headline a report, "The Shrinking Ten Percent: A New Survey Claiming that Only 1 percent of Men Are Gay Has Put the Movement Off Stride."[28]

Since changes in social structures, norms, and values usually take decades and sometimes centuries to bring about, established orders have time on their side. They may wait until a social, economic, and political crisis passes; a war ends; or protestors graduate. Establishment leadership changes occurring through normal processes of election, retirement, resignation, or discharge may remove favorite rhetorical targets of agitators. The public may become disenchanted with and intolerant of protest and disorder, and the mass media and audiences become bored with an issue, event, or strategy (particularly a boycott or takeover) that seems to drag on endlessly. Movement leadership changes as a result of power struggles, deaths, or assassinations may weaken social movements or lead to the dissolution of social movement organizations, and both leaders and followers may grow weary of the struggle or become disillusioned by lack of real progress. If social movement leaders and followers do not tire, they may become desperate and resort to extreme methods that allow established orders to discredit or to suppress their movements.

A few victories or events do not guarantee success. Even spectacular events such as the 1963 civil rights march on Washington that drew over 250,000 persons and ended with Martin Luther King's famous "I Have a Dream" speech are soon forgotten. "What's next?" is asked by friend and foe. Social movements and the media have insatiable appetites for "rhetorical happenings," but few social movements have adequate leaders, members, energy, and funds to satisfy these appetites wisely over long periods of time while fending off counterefforts of other movements and established orders. The radical environmentalist group Earth First! used every tactic it could copy or invent during the 1980s and 1990s to defend Mother Earth from the logging industry and those who would pollute her streams and eliminate her wildlife. Earth Firsters! used "guerilla" theatre, non-violent civil disobedience, confrontations, destruction of property and machinery (called monkeywrenching, ecotage, or ecodefense), cemented themselves into roadblocks and chained themselves to trees and logging equipment, sat in the tops of eighty-foot trees for up to forty days at a time, dropped a three-hundred-foot roll of black plastic from the top of the Glen Canyon Dam to simulate a crack in the dam, and draped a huge banner across the face of George Washington at Mount Rushmore reading "We The People Say No to Acid Rain."[29] Yet its efforts and name have largely disappeared from the media, and logging, development, and pollution in the northwest have continued.

Proposes or Opposes Change in Societal Norms and Values

A social movement proposes or opposes a program for change in societal norms, values, or both. Programs include prescriptions for what must be done, who must do it, and how it must be accomplished. We can identify three general types of social movements by the nature of the changes they advocate or oppose. An *innovative* social movement seeks to replace existing norms or values with *new* ones.[30] Examples of innovative social movements are women's liberation, civil rights, socialism, gay liberation, and animal rights. A *revivalistic* social movement seeks to replace existing norms or values with ones from a *venerable, idealized past*.[31] Examples of revivalistic social movements are the native American, Back to Africa, pro-life, environmental, and a host of religious movements. A *resistance* social movement seeks to block changes in norms or values because it perceives nothing to be wrong with the status quo, at least nothing that cannot and will not be resolved in due time by established institutions. Examples of resistance social movements are the anti-women's liberation, anti-civil rights, anti-gay rights, pro-war, and pro-choice movements.[32]

Social movements are both valuistic *and* normative because changes in values alter norms and changes in norms alter values. For instance, guaranteeing African Americans and women equal employment opportunities or busing children to create diversity in schools, basically normative changes, have affected values of equality, fairness, and justice. Most social movements also have both reform-oriented (demanding partial change) and revolutionary-oriented (demanding total change) elements, and their ideologies, leaders, members, and organizations develop and change. The student movement, for example, began in the 1950s as a reform-oriented free speech movement at American universities that traditionally restricted who could speak, when, and where on campuses. The movement evolved into demands for removal of strictures on where students could live, hours they could stay out at night, and clothes they could wear. Eventually on some campuses, the movement became revolutionary with demands that students determine courses offered, course content, course requirements, graduation standards, appointments of administrators, and investment of endowments.[33] We might place a social movement along a reform-to-revolution continuum, but where we might place it at a particular time depends upon our perceptions. One may view the animal rights movement, for example, as merely a reform movement aimed at assuring the humane treatment of animals, while a second person may see the movement as a revolutionary attempt to alter the relationships of humans to animals and the rights of hunters and those who raise livestock for a living. While one person's "radical" movement is another's "moderate" movement, most social movements contain both radical and moderate elements. Organizations of the women's liberation movement ranged from the National Organization for Women to the Women's International Terrorist Conspiracy from Hell and the Society for Cutting Up Men (SCUM). Terms such as moderate and radical best describe types of strategies or arguments rather than types of social movements, a point we will develop in chapter 12.

The nature of social movement ideologies or belief systems preclude precise classification. They tend to be strange mixtures of vagueness and precision; they tend to borrow from old systems while espousing the new; they are both static and ever-changing; they are both consistent and contradictory. Some social movements have one ideology for true believers and a somewhat different one for public consumption. In addition, as Hans Toch writes, "Each person joins a somewhat different social movement," often "for reasons far removed from the central concerns of the movement."[34] We tend to perceive a movement's demands, goals, strategies, and potential outcomes from our unique perspectives. One of us may join a group protesting the proliferation of nuclear power plants to save the environment, a second to protect children, a third to protect property values, a fourth to fight giant corporations, a fifth for self-protection, a sixth to stop electric rate hikes, and a seventh for the fellowship of the group.

The diversity, flexibility, and fluid nature of social movement belief systems or programs for change set them apart from other collectives. Most religious, political, social, and pressure groups have a single set of principles that remain relatively constant and goals that are fairly precise: convert unbelievers to a particular faith, elect a party's nominees, maintain subsidies for milk producers, elect candidates favorable toward public school funding, stop gun control legislation. In contrast, even a fairly focused social movement such as pro-life has a wide variety of organizations that espouse positions ranging from no abortions under any circumstances to some abortions in particular situations, strategies ranging from legal actions to violence, and goals ranging from protection of the unborn to protection of the unborn, disabled, infirm, and aged.

Moral in Tone

A social movement's rhetoric is moral in tone. Whether a social movement's leaders and members are striving to bring about or to resist changes in social norms and values and whether those changes pertain to people (constitutional rights or right to life), things (nuclear power plants or alcoholic beverages), or animals (medical experiments or fur coats), they assume the power to distinguish right from wrong, good from evil, and ethical from unethical motivations, purposes, characters, choices, and actions. Each social movement believes that it alone constitutes an ethical, virtuous, principled, and righteous force with a "moral obligation" to raise the consciousness of "the people" and thus to reveal the moral, intellectual, and coercive bankruptcy of the opposition."[35] Kenneth Burke and Leland Griffin conclude that "all movements are essentially moral—striving for salvation, perfection, the 'good.' "[36]

The moral stance or tone of a social movement's rhetoric is critical to its claim of legitimacy as an uninstitutionalized force. Anthony Oberschall writes that a movement's legitimacy rests upon an "elaboration of systems of belief and moral ideas," while Herbert Simons notes that a movement establishes "its legitimacy by representing its cause as one that any virtuous individual may endorse."[37] A leaflet by PETA states the case for the animal rights movement's claim to the moral high ground.

> All species fear injury and death, and all species fight for life and freedom. How can one species, ours, consider it has the right to deny others their basic interests of liberty and life? Just as we denied these rights to other human beings in the past for arbitrary reasons, such as skin color, we now deny these basic rights to others because they happen not to be of our own species.
>
> We do not need animals' fur, skin or flesh to survive. But we have come to like the feel, look and taste of these pieces of animals and we are loathe to give them up, even though to do so means a healthier existence for us all.
>
> What gives human beings the right to kill other animals who have lives of their own to live?
>
> Truly, history will judge the worth of our "civilization" less by our technological accomplishments than by the way we treat our fellow beings.[38]

As with most individuals or collectives who place themselves upon a moral pedestal—particularly ones striving for the mantle of legitimacy—a social movement's rhetoric often magnifies its righteousness. Delegates to the 1900 American Federation of Labor convention were welcomed with these words:

> Upon you rests the dawn of a new century, and may the record made here shine forth during the years to come as does now the Declaration of Independence. Your work is a noble and holy one, and when accomplished will be but the realization of our Savior's mission on earth—the uplifting and elevation morally and socially of all humanity.[39]

Herbert Simons, Elizabeth Mechling, and Howard Schreier note that "Most ideological messages" of social movements "tend to exaggerate the strength, unity, and intellectual and moral legitimacy of the movement."[40]

Encounters Opposition

A social movement is countered by institutions. As a social movement develops or resists a program for change from a moral perspective and lays claim to legitimacy, members become frustrated to the point of disaffection with the established order and institutional means of change and control. They are willing to devote their lives—on occasion to sacrifice their lives—to attain victory in the moral struggle between good and evil. Innovative and revivalistic social movements see institutions as unaware of, disinterested in, or openly resistant to necessary changes. Resistance movements see institutions as unwilling or unable to respond to grievous threats to social norms and values and, perhaps, as actively compromising norms and values.

Robert Cathcart contends that the social movement must create a "drama or agonistic ritual which forces response from the establishment commensurate with the moral evil perceived by movement members."[41] It does not take long for a social movement to pose a threat an established order can no longer ignore, and some theorists claim that a social movement at the national level spawns immediate organized opposition.[42] Perceived threat and confrontational strategies eventually produce, according to Cathcart, a "dialectical tension growing out of moral conflict" and provokes a clash between the social movement and the threatened establishment.[43] The struggle between institutional and uninstitutional forces becomes a "true moral battle for power and for the legitimate right to define the true order."[44] During the 1980s, groups of students and faculty on hundreds of American college campuses launched protests against the brutal apartheid policies of South Africa. They created shanty towns, distributed facsimiles of pass books blacks were required to carry in South Africa, and gave speeches emphasizing the reality of life for blacks in South Africa. They also demanded that university administrators divest endowment investments in companies doing business in South Africa. At first, administrations distributed press releases explaining why they could not or would not divest, made modest changes in their investment policies, and met with protesting groups. As protestors gained media attention, began to embarrass administrations, and refused to stop demonstrations or remove their shanty towns at prescribed deadlines, many were arrested and shanties were destroyed. Administrations came to see the anti-apartheid demonstrations as threats to their powers and legitimate right to determine college rules and investment policies.[45] "Social conflict," Herbert Simons writes, is "a clash over incompatible interests in which one party's relative gain is another's loss."[46] Thus, if the Gray Panthers pressure legislatures into allocating more money for social security, medicare, medicaid, or tax breaks for "senior citizens," younger taxpayers, companies, and the medical establishment will lose money, income, and control. Social movements always seem to play a zero-sum game.

Institutions, often portraying themselves as goaded into action by dangerous, fanatical, irresponsible, unreasonable threats to legitimate social order, counter social movements directly and indirectly through agencies, agents, and beneficiaries.

1. *Agencies*: legislative bodies, executive and administrative groups, courts, police, armed forces, tribunals, councils, committees, task forces, regulatory

bodies, tax authorities, communication media, investigative groups, and so on.

2. *Agents*: legislators, presidents, governors, mayors, bishops, judges, police officers, soldiers, owners of communication media, editors, reporters, commentators, committee or council chairpersons, investigators, and so on.

3. *Beneficiaries*: most of the above plus corporations, business owners and operators (including farmers), colleges and universities, churches, patriotic and civic groups, the "silent majority" of citizens, and so on.

Ralph Smith and Russell Windes argue that not all social movements clash with established orders.[47] Innovative movements, according to Smith and Windes, try to prevent dialectical tensions by stressing common ground between themselves and established orders and by avoiding confrontational strategies and tactics. During their analysis of the Sunday school movement as an innovative movement, however, they remark:

> Sunday schools were described as an "entering wedge to a union of church and state." This threat became especially salient when Ezra Styles Ely, a leading Presbyterian minister, urged from the pulpit a "Christian Party in Politics" which could "govern every public election in this country." Throughout the nation came charges that Sunday schools would train the young to abandon the religion of their sectarian fathers in favor of an established evangelical church.

The Sunday school movement, whether intentionally or unintentionally, had created a dialectical tension and was being countered by an established order—sectarian religious leaders and followers. Confrontation was not the essence of this reform-oriented innovative movement, but neither was it absent. John Wilson writes:

> Such is the hold of custom and tradition on men and women and such is the power of those already in authority positions to perpetuate their privileges, that a great deal of the impetus for change must be looked for in the noninstitutionalized sector of society.[48]

Institutions, no matter how tolerant they may seem, are willing to accept only minor challenges to norms and values and ones that can be assigned to or co-opted by task forces, committees, think tanks, or professional associations. They cannot sustain a "relative loss" to the noninstitutionalized sector and, at the same time, maintain authority, credibility, and control over constituencies.

Persuasion Is Pervasive

Persuasion is pervasive in social movements. Social movements must satisfy a number of requirements if they are to *become* and to *remain* significant forces for changes in societal norms and values. For instance, they must transform perceptions of reality, prescribe and sell courses of action, mobilize the disaffected, and sustain the movement over time.

Theoretically, social movements may attempt to satisfy requirements through a combination of three strategies: coercion, bargaining, and persuasion. *Coercion* is the "manipulation of the target group's situation in such fashion that the pursuit of any course of action other than that sought by the movement will be met by considerable cost or punishment." *Bargaining* may occur when the "movement has control of some exchangeable value that the target group wants and offers some of that value in return for compliance with demands."[49] Persuasion is a communication process by which a social movement seeks through the use of verbal and nonverbal symbols to affect audience perceptions and thus to bring about changes in ways of thinking, feeling, and/or acting. In reality, however, social movements discover that inherent constraints deny them free selection and use of these three interrelated strategies.

The typical uninstitutionalized, minimally organized social movement enjoys few means of reward or punishment necessary either to coerce people to join or to remain loyal to a cause or to coerce an established order to capitulate to all or some of its demands. Institutions, with little to gain and much to lose, resist "bargaining" with social movements whose leaders and followers they have stigmatized as dangerous social degenerates. Michael Lipsky notes that "People in power do not like to sit down with rogues."[50] Mere association with a social movement's leaders may grant an undesired degree of legitimacy to the social movement and its cause. In addition, as Lipsky, writes, established orders doubt the capability of movements to bargain effectively:

> Protest oriented groups, whose primary talents are in dramatizing issues, cannot credibly attempt to present data considered "objective" or suggestions considered "responsible" by public officials. Few can be convincing as both advocate and arbitrator at the same time.

Social movements often have little or nothing to exchange in bargaining sessions. Ralph Turner and Lewis Killian comment, for instance, that "the difficulty that constantly besets black movements is that they have nothing to offer whites in a bargaining exchange to match their disruptive potential."[51] Institutions pressure one another not to "give in" to demands of protestors. During the mid-1980s when students and faculties on campuses throughout the United States were protesting the apartheid policies of South Africa and demanding that their colleges divest of holdings in corporations doing business in South Africa until such policies ended, the *Wall Street Journal* commented:

> But a surprising number of colleges have caved in to protest and announced divestment. This cowardice, too, promotes the kind of disruption going on this week on campuses across the nation, and undermines the institutions the administrations and trustees are supposed to protect.[52]

Social movements are equally loathe to bargain with the devil—the established order—when they are morally correct in their portrayals of reality and demands for change and have often suffered grievous mental, economic, social, and physical abuse for their beliefs and protests. Talking to, let alone compromising with, established orders seen as corrupt and oppressive may be deemed a moral outrage by a movement's true believers. Thus, the invited party and the constituencies of both parties are likely to perceive bargaining offers as signs of weakness, desperation, deception, or "selling out."[53]

Social movements can satisfy only a few major requirements through bargaining and coercive strategies. For example, bargaining may help to mobilize for action by uniting disparate movement elements into coalitions, and it might exert pressure on established orders to meet with collectives seemingly willing to discuss potential compromises. In so doing, an establishment may grant a degree of legitimacy to a group and a few minor concessions. Bargaining cannot, however, transform perceptions of history or society, prescribe courses of action, or justify setbacks. Coercion is limited mainly to pressuring the opposition or transforming perceptions of society by goading an established order into excessive repression. Although a social movement may "unmask" an establishment and gain some sympathy by provoking violent suppression, the public may just as easily perceive the suppression as an "unfortunate but inevitable" result of dangerous radicalism.[54] Social movements often splinter into factions over the issue of employing coercion (particularly violent acts such as bombings, assassinations, destruction of property, and disruptions) to achieve ends. Thus, because of numerous constraints under which uninstitutionalized, social movements must operate, *persuasion* is the primary agency for satisfying requirements.

Bargaining includes elements of persuasion. For instance, a social movement attempting to bargain must *convince* both the support and the opposition within and outside of the movement that it is serious and that it has something of value to exchange for concessions. On the other hand, persuasion may preclude bargaining as a strategy. Lipsky notes that "admission to policymaking councils is frequently barred because of the angry, militant rhetorical style adopted by protest leaders."[55]

Coercion also includes elements of persuasion. Turner and Killian observe that "nonviolence always couples persuasive strategy to coercion."[56] For example, sit-ins, mass demonstrations, and disobeying laws claimed to be unjust have persuasive elements such as speeches, signs, and symbolic acts, but they also threaten institutions. Simons uses the phrase "coercive persuasion" to emphasize that "all acts of influence are rhetorical in at least some respects." He argues that:

> The trouble with the persuasion-coercion dichotomy is that it cannot be applied reliably to the real world, and especially to most conflict situations. Although the criteria used to distinguish persuasion and coercion enable us to identify different elements within a given act, and although there are a great many cases of "pure" persuasion which are free of coercive elements, by these same criteria, acts conventionally labelled as "coercive" are almost never free of persuasive elements."[57]

Are *any acts* devoid of symbolic value and thus *instances* of pure coercion? The Supreme Court has ruled that "coercive" acts such as marches, sit-ins, boycotts, demonstrations, and articles of clothing such as armbands and uniforms constitute "symbolic speech" and are entitled to First Amendment protection. The Berrigan brothers' seizure and destruction with napalm of draft records from the Selective Service office in Catonsville, Maryland was a coercive and yet highly symbolic protest act during the Vietnam War.[58] So also are pro-life's "sidewalk counseling" (screaming "Don't kill your baby" at patients attempting to enter abortion clinics) and animal rights activists throwing blood on women wearing fur coats. Parke Burgess argues that persuasion is essential when social movements *threaten* to use coercive tactics:

> The victim must be convinced that dire consequences are likely, not to say certain, *before* he can feel coerced to comply, just as he must become convinced of the coercer's probable capacity and intent to commit the act of violence *before* he can conclude that the act is likely to follow noncompliance.[59]

Are any acts pure bargaining and devoid of persuasion and coercion? When two antagonists sit down to bargain, they attempt to convince one another that they are sincere, have something of value to offer, are operating from a position of strength, and can and will break off negotiations (and resort to force) if all does not proceed as desired.

Are any acts pure persuasion and devoid of bargaining or any hint of the carrot or the stick? Malcolm X's famous speech "The Ballot or the Bullet," by definition persuasion, opens with attempts to appease the followers of Elijah Muhammad (founder of the Black Muslims), Christians in the audience, and followers of Martin Luther King, Jr.—bargaining; proceeds with a lengthy appeal for black capitalism—persuasion; and ends with thinly, veiled threats to resort to the bullet if the ballot is unavailable or ineffective—coercion.[60] Robert Doolittle reveals that some people perceived the riots of the 1960s as inherently symbolic, others conceded that the riots were potentially symbolic, and some viewed them as lawless and totally lacking in symbolism.[61] News reports of the 1992 riot in Los Angeles that followed the acquittal of the police who attacked Rodney King indicate that people interpreted this event much the same as they had the riots of the 1960s.[62] James Andrews suggests that persuasion may be most effective when established orders "accept the harsh reality that they may be coerced."[63]

Clearly, persuasion permeates social movements and is the primary agency available for satisfying essential requirements. The role of persuasion distinguishes social movements from two, often closely related, collective actions: civil wars and revolutions. In social movements, persuasion is pervasive while violence is incidental and often employed for symbolic purposes. In civil wars and revolutions, violence is pervasive while persuasion is incidental.

To say that persuasion is pervasive in social movements and that it is the primary means for satisfying major requirements is *not* to suggest that persuasion *alone* can bring ultimate success to social movements. Social movements must have skilled leaders, dedicated followers, effective organizations, a social system that tolerates protest, and a climate conducive to change. Pivotal events such as the nuclear power plant accidents at Three Mile Island in Pennsylvania and Chernobyl in the Ukraine, the advent of AIDS in this country, *Brown v. Board of Education* that overturned the "separate but equal" interpretations that had made segregation of races legal, and the withdrawal of American troops from Vietnam are critical to the progress and dissolution of social movements. However, such events would disappear into the pages of history if social movements did not employ persuasion to interpret them, focus attention upon them through the mass media, and bring them back to audiences in demonstrations, ceremonies, speeches, songs, and anniversary celebrations. Persuasion alone grows stale without the urgency events inject into protest.

Conclusions

A social movement, then, is an organized, uninstitutionalized, and large collectivity that emerges to bring about or to resist a program of change in societal norms and values, operates primarily through persuasive strategies, and encounters opposition in a moral struggle. This definition addresses both *what* a social movement is and *how* it attempts to achieve its program for change or resistance to change. Persuasion is a pervasive element and is not restricted to a particular audience, purpose, requirement, strategy, or stage of a movement's life cycle. No other phenomenon called a "movement" shares all of these characteristics. A trend or fad, for example, is unorganized and contains no "program" for change. A revolution relies primarily upon violence rather than persuasion. A PAC or lobbying group tends to be institutionalized (licensed), small in size, and created for limited, pragmatic ends rather than a moral struggle for changes in societal norms and values. A religious cult tends to be small, centered upon a single, all-powerful leader who created the cult, and is fearful of contacts with the "outside world." A campaign tends to be highly organized to achieve a specific goal within a specified, brief time.

Our attempt to define the *social movement* as a unique collective phenomenon is designed to provide a clear focus for the chapters that follow and to inform readers of the underlying premises upon which this book is based. Our definition is not designed to place rigid limitations on "movement" or "campaign studies," and we recognize that "movements" occur within established institutions, describe changes in academic fields of study and voting trends, and determine our personal appearance, habits, actions, and tastes. The debate over whether social movements are unique or exist beyond our imaginations seems analogous to the study of campaigns.[64] Researchers analyze political, sales, advertising, recruiting, and military campaigns, and they recognize that campaigns share some common characteristics. They do not, however, claim that each is totally unique or that because they share some characteristics, they should all be called "political campaigns," "sales campaigns," or "rhetorical campaigns." The same is true of movements. As David Zarefsky has pointed out, establishment or institutional movements share many characteristics with social movements. These shared characteristics, however, do not make them identical twins, and a few campaigns do not constitute a social movement. Thus, we are using the word "social" to identify a particular type of movement and see such words as institutional, political, and historical as identifying similar but different collective phenomena.

Endnotes

1 Michael C. McGee, "'Social Movement': Phenomenon or Meaning," *Central States Speech Journal* 31 (Winter 1980), 233–244.

2 William Bruce Cameron, *Modern Social Movements: A Sociological Outline* (New York: Random House, 1966), 7.

3 Malcolm O. Sillars, "Defining Movements Rhetorically: Casting the Widest Net," *Southern Speech Communication Journal* 46 (Fall 1980), 30.

4 John Wilson, *Introduction to Social Movements* (New York: Basic Books, 1973), 8.

5 Herbert W. Simons, "On the Rhetoric of Social Movements, Historical Movements, and 'Top-Down' Movements: A Commentary," *Communication Studies* 42 (Spring 1991), 100.

6 Charles A. Wilkinson, "A Rhetorical Definition of Movements," *Central States Speech Journal* 27 (Summer 1976), 91.

7 Robert S. Cathcart, "Defining Social Movements by Their Rhetorical Form," *Central States Speech Journal* 31 (Winter 1980), 269.

8 Herbert W. Simons, "Requirements, Problems, and Strategies: A Theory of Persuasion for Social Movements," *Quarterly Journal of Speech* 56 (February 1970), 1–11; Wilson, 156–166.

9 "Drums, Sweat, and Tears" and " Heeding the Call of the Drums," *Newsweek*, June 24, 1991, 46–51 and 52–53.

10 James W. Chesebro, "Cultures in Conflict—A Generic and Axiological View," *Today's Speech* 21 (Spring 1973), 12.

11 Roger W. Howe, "The Rhetoric of the Death of God Theology," *Southern Speech Communication Journal* 37 (Winter 1971), 150.

12 Paul Kurtz, ed., *Humanist Manifestos I and II* (Buffalo, NY: Prometheus Books, 1973).

13 Brant Short, "Earth First! and the Rhetoric of Moral Confrontation," *Communication Studies* 42 (Summer 1991), 172–188.

14 Herbert W. Simons, James W. Chesebro, and C. Jack Orr, "A Movement Perspective on the 1972 Presidential Campaign," *Quarterly Journal of Speech* 59 (April 1973), 168–179.

15 Herbert W. Simons, Elizabeth W. Mechling, and Howard N. Schreier, "The Functions of Human Communication in Mobilizing from the Bottom Up: The Rhetoric of Social Movements," *Handbook of Rhetorical and Communication Theory*, Carroll C. Arnold and John W. Bowers, eds. (Boston: Allyn and Bacon, 1984), 792–867.

16 Simons, "Requirements, Problems, and Strategies," 3; and Neil J. Smelser, *Theory of Collective Behavior* (New York: Free Press, 1962), 110 and 129–130.

17 At one time labor organizations such as the United Auto Workers, Teamsters, and the AFL-CIO were clearly social movement organizations. Today, however, they are parts of the established order that controls workers and production. The teamsters, for example, have openly opposed non-established labor groups such as the Cesar Chavez-led United Farm Workers.

18 Simons, "Requirements, Problems, and Strategies," 11.

19 David Zarefsky, "President Johnson's War on Poverty: The Rhetoric of Three 'Establishment' Movements," *Communication Monographs* 44 (November 1977), 352–373.

20 Joseph R. Gusfield, *Protest, Reform, and Revolt: A Reader in Social Movements* (New York: John Wiley & Sons, 1970), 310.

21 See for example, Mobile Corporation, "Target: environmental excellence," *Time*, June 10, 1991, 4.

22 "Gays Under Fire," *Newsweek*, September 14, 1992, 35–40.

23 Arthur E. Rowse, "Deregulatory Creep: Dan Quayle Clears the Way for Industry," *The Progressive*, May 1992, 28–32.

24 Wilkinson, 92–93; Carol McClurg Mueller, "Building Social Movement Theory," *Frontiers in Social Movement Theory*, Aldon D. Morris and Carol McClurg Mueller, eds. (New Haven, CT: Yale University Press, 1992), 9.

25 Pamela E. Oliver and Gerald Marwell, "Mobilizing Technologies for Collective Action," *Frontiers in Social Movement Theory*, 258.

[26] *Wall Street Journal*, November 16, 1972, 26.

[27] "Five Ways to Prevent Abortion (And One Way That Won't)," Lafayette, Indiana *Journal and Courier*, September 8, 1985, A-15; "In 1982, If You Have a Miscarriage You Could Be Charged with Murder," Lafayette, Indiana *Journal and Courier*, May 26, 1981, B-4.

[28] *Time*, April 26, 1993, 27.

[29] Jonathan I. Lange, "Refusal to Compromise: The Case of Earth First!" *Western Journal of Speech Communication* 54 (Fall 1990), 473–494.

[30] Other names for innovative social movements are revisionary, alternative, redemptive, and transformative.

[31] Other names for revivalistic social movements are reactionary, regressive, and nationalistic.

[32] Other names for resistance social movements are conservative and counter.

[33] James R. Andrews, "Confrontation at Columbia: A Case Study in Coercive Rhetoric," *Quarterly Journal of Speech* 55 (February 1969), 9–16; Donald E. Phillips, *Student Protest, 1960–1970: An Analysis of the Speeches and Issues* (Lanham, MD: University Press of America, 1985; James Miller, *"Democracy Is in The Street": From Port Huron to the Siege of Chicago*. New York: Simon & Schuster, 1987.

[34] Hans Toch, *The Social Psychology of Social Movements* (Indianapolis: Bobbs-Merrill, 1965), 21–26.

[35] R. R. McGuire, "Speech Acts, Communicative Competence and the Paradox of Authority," *Philosophy and Rhetoric* 10 (Winter 1977), 33; Herbert W. Simons, "Persuasion in Social Conflicts: A Critique of Prevailing Concepts and a Framework for Future Research," *Speech Monographs* 39 (November 1972), 233.

[36] Leland M. Griffin, "A Dramatistic Theory of the Rhetoric of Movements," *Critical Responses to Kenneth Burke*, William Rueckert, ed. (Minneapolis: University of Minnesota Press, 1969), 456.

[37] Anthony Oberschall, *Social Conflict and Social Movements* (Englewood Cliffs, NJ: Prentice-Hall, 1973), 188; Simons, "Persuasion in Social Conflicts," 235.

[38] PETA, *Animal Rights*, n.d.

[39] William H. Higgins, "Welcoming Address," *Report of the Proceedings of the American Federation of Labor* (1900), 13.

[40] Simons, Mechling, and Schreier, 797.

[41] Robert S. Cathcart, "Movements: Confrontation as Rhetorical Form," *Southern Speech Communication Journal* 43 (Spring 1978), 242.

[42] John D. McCarthy and Mark Wolfson, "Consensus Movements, Conflict Movements, and the Co-optation of Civic and State Infrastructures," *Frontiers in Social Movement Theory*, 275.

[43] Cathcart, "Movements," 242; Robert S. Cathcart, "New Approaches to the Study of Movements: Defining Movements Rhetorically," *Western Speech* 36 (Spring 1972), 87.

[44] Cathcart, "Movements," 246.

[45] "Shanty Raids," *Wall Street Journal*, April 9, 1986, 32; "PU Police Arrest 22 Anti-Apartheid Supporters," *The Purdue Exponent*, April 7, 1986, 1; "Berkeley Police Arrest 120 Protestors in Violent Campus Shantytown Dispute," *The Purdue Exponent*, April 4, 1986, 1; "Purdue Defends Apartheid Stance," Lafayette, Indiana *Journal and Courier*, April 15, 1986, 1.

[46] Herbert W. Simons, *Persuasion: Understanding, Practice and Analysis* (Reading, MA: Addison-Wesley, 1976), 18.

[47] Ralph R. Smith and Russell R. Windes, "The Innovational Movement: A Rhetorical Theory," *Quarterly Journal of Speech* 61 (April 1975), 140–143.

[48] Wilson, 4.

[49] These definitions of coercion and bargaining appear in Ralph H. Turner and Lewis M. Killian, *Collective Behavior* (Englewood Cliffs, NJ: Prentice-Hall, 1972), 291.

[50] Michael Lipsky, "Protest as Political Resource," *The American Political Science Review* 52 (December 1968), 1154.

[51] Turner and Killian, 421.

[52] *Wall Street Journal*, April 9, 1986, 32.

[53] James R. Andrews, "Reflections of the National Character in American Rhetoric," *Quarterly Journal of Speech* 57 (October 1971), 316–324; Lipsky, 1153–1157.

[54] Kurt W. Ritter, "Confrontation as Moral Drama: The Boston Massacre in Rhetorical Perspective," *Southern Speech Communication Journal* 42 (Winter 1977), 114–136.

[55] Lipsky, 1154.

[56] Turner and Killian, 298.

[57] Simons, *Persuasion*, 43–44; Simons, "Persuasion in Social Conflict," 232.

[58] John H. Patton, "Rhetoric at Catonsville: Daniel Berrigan, Conscience, and Image Attraction," *Today's Speech* 23 (Winter 1975), 3–12.

[59] Parke G. Burgess, "Crisis Rhetoric: Coercion vs. Force," *Quarterly Journal of Speech* 59 (February 1973), 69.

[60] Malcolm X, "The Ballot or the Bullet," *The Sixties Papers: Documents of a Rebellious Decade* (New York: Praeger, 1984), 126–132.

[61] Robert J. Doolittle, "Riots as Symbolic: A Criticism and Approach," *Central States Speech Journal* 27 (Winter 1976), 310–317.

[62] "The Overture: The Fire This Time" and "Violence: Los Angeles in a Fury," *Time*, May 11, 1992, 18–25 and 26–29; "Days of Rage," *U.S. News and World Report*, May 11, 1992, 20–26.

[63] James R. Andrews, "The Rhetoric of Coercion and Persuasion: The Reform Bill of 1812," *Quarterly Journal of Speech* 56 (April 1970), 195.

[64] McGee, 233–244; David Zarefsky, "A Skeptical View of Movement Studies," *Central States Speech Journal* 31 (Winter 1980), 245–254.

Chapter Two

The Social Movement from a Social Systems Perspective

History is social, and all social acts have implicit and explicit rhetorical or persuasive dimensions. Over the centuries, human communication theorists have found it useful to create models or paradigms which metaphorically compare communication to other familiar phenomena to understand the persuasive dimensions inherent in social acts. The most popular of these models is the "systems model." B. Aubrey Fisher suggests four tenets of systems theory: the principle of nonsummativity; the role of structure, function, and evolution; the principle of openness; and hierarchical organization.[1] Let us begin by reviewing each of these tenets and its relevance to persuasion and social movements.

Systems Theory and Communication

Characteristic 1: Nonsummativity

A system is comprised of interdependent components, and the "principle of nonsummativity" holds that this interdependence makes the whole something other than merely the sum of its parts. Individual items in a pile, heap, or aggregation do not noticeably affect one another; usually, one piece can be removed from the pile without directly altering other individual pieces. But the interdependence among system components means that a change in any one component can produce changes in other components as well as changes in the overall system. Because of the effects of this interaction, we may enjoy a rally against mistreatment of research animals more (or less) than we enjoy the company of individual rally members. The interdependent relationships among components of a system serve as a catalyst that fosters the creation of a whole which behaves differently from its individual components. As these individual components interact

21

they become a group, usually with its own identity such as MADD (Mothers Against Drunk Driving), the National Gay and Lesbian Task Force, and PETA (People for the Ethical Treatment of Animals). Thus, just as auto parts can be put together to form a Mercedes, a Cavalier, or a Model T Ford, similar people interacting differently can create noticeably different human groups each with its own identity, behavioral tendencies (syntality), needs, and energy for survival (synergy). It is communication that transforms a "heap of individuals" into a group. The principle of nonsummativity is important to understanding social movements because a movement collectivity is something more (or less) than the sum of its parts. In fact, Fisher illustrates nonsummativity by contrasting labor unions with "all left-handed people:"

> There is simply little or no consistent effect of one left-handed person on another because of their left-handedness. But the labor union does function as a whole in many significant ways. Its members go on strike as a whole. They all go to work, perform assigned jobs, and in other ways honor the labor contract as a whole. In short, the actions of one affect the actions of others.[2]

The interaction between individuals—their communication—serves as a catalyst for the creation of something other than an "aggregate" or "heap" of individuals.

Students of social movement persuasion must pay close attention to the communication opportunities and activities that transform individuals into groups. Fisher's "left-handed people" constitute a heap only because they have yet to interact on the basis of their shared concerns about left-handedness. Conversely, the labor union is a system only because individual workers interacted over the years to develop a sense of "usness." In his autobiography, American Federation of Labor founder Samuel Gompers reflected upon the opportunities for interaction among the cigarmakers:

> It gave education in such a way as to develop personality, for in no other place were we so wholly natural. The nature of our work developed a camaraderie of the shop such as few workers enjoy. It was a world in itself—a cosmopolitan world. Shopmates came from everywhere—some had been nearly everywhere. When they told us of strange lands and peoples, we listened eagerly.[3]

Other social movement organizations come into being because of shared concerns over abortion, nuclear power plants, and the environment. Some of these interactions have developed into the "consciousness-raising" sessions of the women's liberation, gay rights, and fledgling men's liberation movements. In each case, individuals discover common experiences, aspirations, problems, and solutions through communication. Identification with a cause or social movement can emerge from the development of a communication system, a social movement organization.

Characteristic 2: Function-Structure-Evolution

The second axiom of systems theory is that interdependent relationships can be explained in terms of function, structure, and evolution. Behavior and action are purposeful because they fulfill needs or "functions" for individuals and collectivities. When a function regularly recurs (such as seasonal greetings, monthly bill payments, and the selection of government representatives), we develop behavioral "structures" that assure their performance (Christmas cards, household budgets, and elections). Most of these structures perform the function imperfectly, and we continue to quibble and tinker along the same lines to enhance the performance of the function. Sometimes we create a structure that performs the function so nicely that new needs and functions that had been obscured from view become apparent. At this point, we "evolve" into a phase guided by the new functional necessities and the search for fresh behavioral structures. Thus, the interplay of functional behaviors leads to evolutionary change as the system moves from the performance of one hierarchy of functions to another.

The structure of a social movement can refer to its membership profile, its organizational structure, or its strategic efforts. The anti-Vietnam War movement needed dedicated workers during its early phases, but it needed a plurality of voters in 1968 and 1972. The A.F. of L. organized skilled tradesmen and excluded unskilled industrial workers, a tactic that worked until the increasing industrialization of America led to the formation of the Industrial Workers of the World and, later, the Congress of Industrial Organizations. David Duke's branch of the Ku Klux Klan moved from the old Klan's cross-burnings and lynchings to recruitment of Catholic and women members and the use of television and radio talk shows. The pro-life movement began with emphasis on elections and the passage of a constitutional amendment, but it turned more toward direct actions such as Operation Rescue when elections and legislative action and inaction did not reduce or stop abortions. Chapter 3 identifies and illustrates the persuasive functions of social movements and the ways in which persuasive communication fulfills these needs. The point is that social movements evolve structures to perform functions, thereby altering the pattern of functions remaining to be performed. This process is continuous—every aspect of a system has evolved from and will evolve to something else; hence beginnings and endings are purely relative. We rarely know when a social movement begins and ends, only that it has evolved.

Characteristic 3: Hierarchical Organization

The third axiom is that all systems have hierarchical organization. It is possible to locate each system (e.g., a social movement) within an encompassing "supra-system" (the society) and to ascertain "sub-systems" (individual organizations and individual persons) within each system. All systems are influenced both by their sub-systems and by their supra-systems. However, the precise distinction between sub-system, system, and supra-system is generally a matter of the observer's perspective (one could reasonably consider the movement as the supra-system, an organization as the system, and the individual as the sub-system). Once we have identified the hierarchical structure of systems, the level of analysis is largely a matter of choice.

The "nesting" of systems in other systems is important for understanding social movements. It is not uncommon for social movements led by major figures, enjoying institutional support, or having widespread support, to fail. Eugene V. Debs' American Railway Union won several major victories in 1893 leading to vast increases in membership which created an uncontrollable, undisciplined organization that was promptly and permanently demolished only months later in the Pullman Strike. The white citizens councils and the Ku Klux Klan in the south delayed but failed to stop the civil rights movement.

An energetic social movement can change the behavior of the supra-system by changing the larger system's functional needs. The civil rights movement raised American society's concerns about discrimination, poverty, and voting rights by demonstrating that all was not well in America. The War on Poverty, the Civil Rights Act of 1964, the Voting Rights Act of 1965, and other changes were responses to a restructured set of American functional priorities derived from black Americans' demands for justice and white Americans' discomfort over these demands. In 1964 the Democratic party had little need for black support to defeat Barry Goldwater and the Republicans. But by 1988, the Democrats sorely needed Jesse Jackson and his multitude of new voters to contest the presidential election, and President Clinton could not have won without strong support from African Americans. As the institution's functional needs change, so does party structure. With the Dukakis-Jackson-Carter convention in Atlanta and Jackson's historic convention address, the civil rights movement took its rhetorical place alongside the labor and women's movements as institutionalized pillars of the Democratic party, not challengers at the convention gate.

Characteristic 4: The Degree of Openness

Fisher's fourth axiom of systems theory is that any system can be described on the basis of its "openness"—the permeability of its boundaries. We can assess a system with respect to the freedom of exchange between the system and its environment and thereby classify it as "open" or "closed." Open systems have boundaries that permit the interaction of system and environment, whereas closed systems are entirely self-contained. Degree of openness is important because open and closed systems are governed by different principles.

Closed systems, according to Fisher, are governed by the principle of "equilibrium"—"the final state of the closed system is determined by the initial state" because a self-contained system must balance without any help from the outside. Thus, a closed system always returns to its initial starting point. Conversely, open systems are governed by the principle of "equifinality" which states that "the same final state may be reached from different initial conditions and in different ways . . . [and] different open systems with the same initial condition could well achieve different final states.''[4] Put differently, you can get anywhere in an open system from anywhere, and you can get there by a variety of paths.

The difference between the equilibrium of closed systems and the equifinality of open systems derives from the principle of ''entropy,'' an irreversible process of disintegration. Closed systems can only respond to entropy by exerting a counter-force (negentropy) to slow that disintegration. But once slowed, the disintegration is not reversed. As Fisher observes, ''The balanced state of homeostasis . . . does not suggest an increase in order or structure, only a slowing down or stoppage of the disintegrative process.''[5] The rights of African Americans, women, gays, and even animals have expanded in spite of Herculean efforts by institutions and resistance movements.

Open systems, capable of exchange with their environment, can combat entropy either by adding new information from the environment or by generating their own original or novel information. In this sense, open systems take stock of their environment and adjust to it. The net result is that open systems can increase order over the original state and grow stronger because of a more equal sharing of rights, duties, and rewards.

Even in the natural sciences there are few truly closed systems, and human or social systems are considered open. Nevertheless, theorists have found it useful to draw upon the similarities between persons and machines to explain the process of human communication. Therefore, all systems models of communication emphasize that the whole is more than the sum of its parts because of the interaction of persons, that communication systems evolve as structures perform functions, that each system is comprised of subsystems while itself constituting part of a supra-system both of which influence and are influenced by it, and that each system is to some degree capable of exchange with its environment. Having said this, let us consider the differences between ''mechanical'' and ''social'' systems as models of human communication.

Mechanical vs. Social Systems

People employ a mechanical systems model to describe communication every time they mention transmission, reception, feedback, noise, barriers, breakdowns, leverage, being pushed around, or being on the same wavelength. They tend to think of communication as a process of mechanical adjustment. This thesis pervades the works of Norbert Wiener and the team of Shannon and Weaver who observe parallels between human communication and mechanical systems.[6] Indeed, a *closed* system does measure its environment and adjust to it. Wiener's study of ''cybernetics'' suggests that people can be profitably compared to self-regulating machines like thermostats. Yet a thermostat has only one pattern of reaction—when it detects too low a temperature, it begins to heat, only to stop when a satisfactory temperature is reached. Unlike a person, the thermostat cannot decide whether to offer you a sweater, close the windows, or build a fire; it simply performs its specified function for the system. The thermostat cannot choose; it can only execute. Even the most sophisticated computer can only execute programs provided by a human programmer.

Dennis Smith challenges the mechanical view of human communication when he notes that our study of communication is too heavily influenced by the engineering sciences. He argues that the differences between human communication and mechanical systems are more important than the similarities. Smith specifically challenges the concept of "communication breakdown" on the grounds that it teaches four fallacies about communication:

1. *The Fallacy of Linearity* presumes that communication is a straight line of actions from one person to another, rather than an interdependent process in which people anticipate and build upon one another's (and even outsiders') behaviors to create meaning.

2. *The Fallacy of Mechanism* mistakenly treats persons as machines rather than humans, thereby omitting consideration of biological, psychological, and sociological influences.

3. *The Fallacy of Noncommunication* presumes that communication involves purely what is said or written, and overlooks the communicative significance of interpretation.

4. *The Fallacy of Reification* presumes that unsatisfactory communication results from a "thing" (breakdown) which can be removed or fixed, rather than from interpretive behavior.[7]

We would add a fifth fallacy to Smith's list. *The Fallacy of Success* presumes that communication will be satisfactory and effective unless something goes wrong (i.e., the breakdown). Much communication is fairly difficult (e.g., asking for a grade change, complimenting a friend's unattractive outfit, interviewing for a job), and effective or satisfying communication is more often the exception than the rule. It is more productive to approach communication as a constructive, adaptive process at which people sometimes succeed and often fail. All of our conflicts are not due to "failures to communicate" or "communication breakdowns" because many derive from deep-seated, irreconcilable differences between subsystems. Too often references to "ineffective communication" or a "breakdown in communication" distract us from more important issues.

Smith's critique of communication breakdowns illustrates the implications of choosing inappropriate metaphoric models for explaining human communication. Like Smith and Fisher, we find mechanical models inappropriate for the explanation of human communication in general and social movement persuasion in particular because of their omission of human choice and creativity from the process. However, the concept of system need not be discarded simply because mechanical metaphors are inappropriate to social systems.

Social Systems

An alternative is a "social systems model" of communication that differs markedly from the "mechanical systems model." Brent D. Ruben summarizes the four propositions of a social or "living" systems approach as follows:

1. People, like other animals, are instances of living systems.
2. Living systems are structural and functional units (individual and social) which maintain themselves (and grow, change, and deteriorate) only through interactions with their environment.
3. Environmental interaction[s] are of two types: (a) transactions which involve the transformation of matter-energy, which may be termed biophysical metabolism; and (b) transactions which involve the transformation of data-information, which may be termed informational-metabolism or communication.
4. The functional goal [of the behavior] of all living systems is adaptation with the environment.[8]

First, Ruben differentiates living systems which grow and change only through interaction with their environments from both mechanical systems (which only deteriorate) and from closed systems (which cannot interact with their environments). Elaborating upon the characteristics of living systems, Ruben concurs with Smith that "communication is both continual and inevitable. There are no 'breakdowns in communication'; there is no option to be in communication with the environment so long as the system is alive." Indeed, silence itself is a means of adapting to the environment.

Second, Ruben observes that an organism adapts to its environment, and adapts its environment to it. Thus, one should be encouraged neither to ask with Lloyd Bitzer how a persuader responds to a rhetorical situation, nor to ask with Richard Vatz how the persuader created the rhetorical situation through language.[9] Instead, we should search for both in the mutual adaptation of system with environment.

Third, adaptation occurs as "discrepancies between the needs and capacities of the system and those of the environment emerge, and the system, acting on the discrepancy, strives to close the gap." From a social systems perspective, the natural, healthy state of affairs involves people actively adapting to their environment by creating alternatives and choosing among them. This creative choosing leads us into new eras of human progress.

Views of Influence, Conflict, and Relationships

The choice between social and mechanical systems models of communication rests upon our preferred conceptions of human influence, human conflict, and human relationships.

Conceptions of Human Influence

Influence in mechanical systems is highly manipulative. A persuader examines the persuasive landscape and ascertains (1) the auditor's susceptibility to influence and (2) the persuader's resources for influence, so that (3) the persuader can construct or apply a formula or equation which creates the necessary and sufficient stimuli for the auditor to respond in accordance with the persuader's intent. Mechanical conceptions of influence are therefore analogous to an automobile engine. If we know (1) the automobile's susceptibility to misfire, and (2) that such misfiring is influenced by sparkplugs, timing, and fuel mixture, then we can (3) manipulate sparkplugs, timing, and fuel mixture to produce a necessary and sufficient change in the system to cause the engine's proper operation. The parallel assumption in persuasion is that we can structure message variables to produce consistently the desired auditor behavior. The key to mechanistic persuasion is knowing the right set of equations for a particular "target" audience.

Influence in social systems is adaptive behavior. An organism will adapt to its environment in diverse ways (the principle of equifinality): by attempting to change its environment, by attempting to change itself, or by attempting to escape from the environment through selective attention, selective perception, and selective retention. The metaphor here is not the car on the garage rack, but the driven automobile. The driver chooses to ignore speed limits or road conditions, drive faster or slower, take dubious creative shortcuts, or devote adequate attention to maintenance of the car's mechanical operation. No matter how many speed limit signs the driver sees, he or she can always choose to ignore them. Sometimes, as when the driver chooses to pay the cost of a CB radio or a radar detector for the benefit of an additional 5 to 10 miles per hour, the adaptive choice is not purely rational.

Adaptive humans have often confounded mechanical systems theorists. Sensing that someone has concocted a formula to influence them, auditors can feel that their essential human ability to choose is endangered. These concerned humans may refuse to comply by imposing new conditions, misunderstanding the message, and/or reconstructing the relationship and its ground rules. While mechanistic theorists revise their equation to account for this erratic behavior, the social systems theorists recognize it as the kind of adaptive behavior that is central to communication studies.

Mechanical systems models are particularly ill-suited to the study of persuasion and social movements because movements need to be creative and unusual. Any social movement that responds predictably to the establishment will not long survive, since the establishment creates and enforces all of the rules. Organizer Saul Alinsky succinctly recommends that:

> Radicals must be resilient, adaptable to shifting political circumstances, and sensitive enough to the process of action and reaction to avoid being trapped by their own tactics and forced to travel a road not of their own choosing. In short, radicals must have a degree of control over the flow of events.[10]

A social movement must adapt in a manner that retains its freedom and independence from the established order, which seems to render equations for influence almost useless.

Additionally, it is very difficult to predict the effectiveness of a tactic. An assassination may end a movement or perpetuate it by creating a needed martyr (perhaps even removing an unpopular leader). Nonviolence worked well for Gandhi in India and Martin Luther King, Jr. in America, but it failed horribly for Jews in Nazi Germany (whether from their lack of organization or the society's lack of moral sensitivity is arguable). Human influence in social movements, then, is by necessity highly adaptive and does not conform to manipulative mechanical laws.

Conception of Human Conflict

Mechanistic systems view conflict as imbalances (barriers or breakdowns) that should be either prevented or repaired. At best, imbalance is prevented and the system hums along, quietly disintegrating under the law of entropy. When imbalance does occur, balance can only be restored after considerable upheaval (negentropy). When a car breaks down, it is out of commission until Mr. Goodwrench pronounces it "as good as new" (the principle of equilibrium). The return to normal is attained only through financial setback, children waiting at school, the cat stranded at the vet's, and a strong sense of frustration. In systems terminology, negentropy has been introduced to restore equilibrium. Nothing is ever gained in mechanical systems. Thus, we should strive for preventive maintenance of our mechanical systems lest they "break down."

Social systems see conflict as creating the opportunity for growth and progress. Discrepancies between the needs and capacities of the system and the needs and capacities of the environment challenge the organism. If the organism fails to resolve the discrepancy, it dies; if it meets the challenge adequately, it survives and grows or evolves into a new phase of life. As Alinsky observes, "In the politics of human life, consistency is not a virtue. To be consistent means, according to the Oxford Universal Dictionary, 'standing still or not moving.' Men [women] must change with the times or die."[11] Of course, this discrepancy simultaneously creates an opportunity for destruction—that is the nature of equifinality. The important fact is that unlike the mechanical systems model, the social systems model views conflict and controversy as potentially constructive or creative, if somewhat troublesome. The difference is that upheaval can lead to an enhanced state of order rather than simply slowed disintegration and temporarily restored order. Let us return to our example of the automobile.

Whereas an automobile with a broken fan belt can only be restored to its antecedent state, the drivers who adapt to the environment by fixing it can improve themselves. Conceivably, they are proud to become self-reliant, able fixers of fan belts. Each person has "grown" as a result of the conflict and will never again be quite as awed by the prospect of car troubles (of course, equifinality also dictates that it can lead to long hours on the side of the road and intense exasperation). Thus, while mechanical conflict is purely disruptive, social systems conflict leads to evolutionary change. Now, if human conflict mirrors mechanical conflict, it should be avoided on the grounds that it is purely wasteful. Since the establishment functions to maintain systemic order, no study rooted in mechanical premises should ever sanction the creation of conflict. Indeed, rhetorical studies of agitation reflected just this kind of establishment bias until Herbert Simons attacked it and suggested a "dual perspective" (establishment and social movement). In so doing, Simons revealed this weakness in our mechanist assumptions.[12]

If human conflict is more nearly social than mechanical, then controversy and conflict are our only means for progress. If this is the case, then we should employ models which encourage consideration of multiple conflicting viewpoints and focus on the process of ongoing adaptation. Simons' works on social movements broke important theoretical ground in the early 1970s, but he did not go far enough. No model based upon mechanical assumptions can admit the equivalence of both agitator and establishment perspectives since mechanical systems models assume that (1) no good can come from imbalance, (2) the establishment is empowered to maintain balance, and (3) agitators and social movements function to create imbalance.

The various subsystems of a social system attempt to close the discrepancy in different ways. The establishment usually minimizes the discrepancy in favor of the prior state of affairs (in which it gained its authority), while one or more parts of the system strive to resolve it in other directions. After the U.S. Supreme Court's *Brown v. Board of Education* decision in 1954 ruled segregation unconstitutional, for example, civil rights activists highlighted for us the discrepancy between the law and our practices; southern politicians such as Ross Barnett raised the possibility that states could ignore the federal law; and the federal government wrestled with the problem of satisfying all of its constituent subsystems. The important point is that all parts work in their own ways to adjust their system with the environment. Therefore, all of their efforts deserve comparable attention. Conversely, it would be counterproductive to favor the establishment's effort to maintain balance, since that effort could or would restrain the system's adaptive capabilities.

Conception of Human Relationships

The third issue is systemic maturation. Mechanical systems are at their prime when new or almost new (some require a brief "break-in" period). All mechanical systems experience friction, deterioration, and general wear. With proper maintenance, this process of deterioration (entropy) can be slowed, but it can never be reversed; even if the price of a Rolls-Royce appreciates with age, its mechanical system nevertheless deteriorates. Such an approach to human communication is depressing at best and frightening at worst. It implies that relationships begin at or near their zenith and can only be slowed in their deterioration.

But a social systems approach presumes that relationships develop from initial encounters. Whether we choose to nurture or to ignore them, past experiences influence future conversations. From this perspective, experience and practice become important. Having fixed one broken fan belt is no guarantee that you can fix another, but you expect the experience to prove useful. Similarly, a first date may be the best, or it may simply be the start of a growing relationship, depending upon the parties' willingness and abilities to build upon their encounter for the process of mutual accommodation. The social systems view suggests that one is likely to find the more successful relationships among the longer ones, while admitting that some may have developed quickly and yet others may have persisted unhappily.

When studying social movement persuasion, the mechanical systems theorist is concerned with stability, while the social systems theorist is concerned with change. And since social systems (governed by equifinality) can develop from any state into any other through any means, the study of social systems emphasizes the process by which subsystems emerge and adapt by creating alternatives and choosing among them. Our country is very different today from what it was in the 18th century. While not all of these changes have been improvements, neither have they all been disintegrative. Most, if not all, of these changes have been adaptive efforts by humans not yet born in 1776 to adapt to environments not yet existing in 1776. In this light, the American Revolution, the Civil War, women's suffrage, agrarianism, labor and civil rights, and environmental movements have led us into new eras of life in America which could not be satisfactorily explained as a return to equilibrium, because each of these movements created novel alternatives. Just as we study American history developmentally, a social systems approach to social movement persuasion views the relationship between the movement and society developmentally. The frequent intransigence of some labor unions today, for example, can be better understood in terms of management's parental behavior during labor's infancy and adolescence.

While people will probably continue to use the jargon of mechanical systems to describe human communication, we hope they will become aware of the implications of their metaphors. To conceptualize communication mechanically is to conceive of conflict and change as disruptive, influence as manipulative, and relationships as disintegrative. We believe it is more accurate, realistic, and therefore productive to conceive of conflict as adjustive and evolutionary, influence as accommodative, and relationships as integrative. Toward this end, we need to formulate approaches to communication that embody these assumptions so we can ascertain the relative explanatory powers of the mechanical and social systems approaches.

Social Systems and the Study of Social Movements

Chapter 1 discussed the pervasiveness of persuasion in social movements, and this chapter has stressed the importance of thinking about human activities as growing and changing social systems. But we have yet to set forth a theoretical framework that can help us find answers to the basic questions about social movement persuasion. We will explain the interpretive systems model of political communication and then offer a framework for analyzing social movements.

The Interpretive Systems Approach to Political Communication

The interpretive systems model begins with four involuntary "personal interpretive processes" through which each person arrives at a personally useful conception of the world.[13] Through these four processes, people need, symbolize, reason, and prefer. Because humans never stop revising their personal inventories of needs, symbols, reasons, and preferences, it is useful to discuss these processes as needing, symbolizing, reasoning, and preferencing. *Needing* is the process through which individuals (re)formulate their needs and goals. *Symbolizing* is the process of (re)formulating semantic relationships among meanings and images. *Reasoning* is the process of (re)formulating explanatory accounts that lend coherence to one's needs and symbols. It is the process of "making sense." Finally, *preferencing* is the process of (re)formulating one's personal hierarchy of needs, symbols, and reasons so that some become more important than others. These processes are independent. We learn new words when we need them and forget them when we do not. We sometimes reason our way to a preference, but we often muster reasons to rationalize an existing preference. We are often attracted to persons who think like us, but we often learn to think like persons to whom we are attracted.

Parents, teachers, clergy, and others teach and reinforce the "right" ways of needing, symbolizing, reasoning, and preferencing with the result that each of us acquires a personally efficient way of interpreting the world around us. Because each of us has different parents, teachers, clergy, and lessons, we develop personal ways of interpreting life. At home, in school, and through public discourse, each of us is exposed to multiple ways of interpreting life's ebb and flow. Each of us discovers that things that make sense to us may make no sense to others. This is because each of them has also developed a personally useful interpretation of the world.

We cannot isolate ourselves from other people, so we need to coordinate our behavior with theirs. We do this by developing "social interpretive structures" as ways to coordinate our personal needing, symbolizing, reasoning, and preferencing processes with those of others. People construct "languages" to coordinate their symbolizing, "logics" to coordinate their reasoning, "ideologies" to coordinate their preferencing, and "laws" to coordinate their need fulfillment activities. We use laws to guide our personal behavior, but few of us are students of the law and we all tend to interpret and apply society's laws in ways that are personally useful. Similarly, we use languages, logics, and ideologies to guide our daily behavior, and because few of us are students of language, logic, or ideology, most of us use them in ways that are personally useful.

The persons who subscribe to a social interpretive structure are an "interpretive community." They are bound together, and separated from others, by their agreement to coordinate their personal interpretive behaviors. Thus, people who speak the same language are a linguistic community, those who share rules of reasoning are a logical community, those who share ways of establishing their preferences are an ideological community, and those who coordinate their needing with a set of laws are a legal community.

Each of us is born into an array of interpretive communities, and we soon learn to use their interpretive structures. Sometimes we merge multiple interpretive structures into one, perhaps by blending the economic logic of capitalism, the ideology of Christianity, and the laws of popular sovereignty. Social movements often try to separate these fused structures. As we go through life, we encounter other people and their interpretive structures. We window shop a good deal, trying on new and old needs, words, reasons, and preferences to see how they fit. Over time we change the importance of our interpretive communities, and sometimes we change communities.

Interpretive communities are not congruent, and social and political stability require some kind of interpretive coalition. Liberals and conservatives, for example, disagree about many things, but they share a commitment to the established order that distinguishes them from radicals and reactionaries. The established order by definition legitimizes a dominant language, logic, ideology, and law (such as the Constitution). It emphasizes the importance of "working within the system," "following procedures," and "not rocking the boat," and, indeed, that is how most changes come about.

Sooner or later, incongruent interpretive communities come into conflict. Language, logic, ideology, and laws are interdependent. As elections, appointments, and rulings empower interpretive communities they also empower their languages, logics, and ideologies. The language of the interpretive community in power necessarily disadvantages members of its competing communities, as when they define words such as patriotic, right, and America. The temporarily dominant ideology frames the nation's problems and solutions, such that the outgoing community's solutions often become the incoming community's problems. And the logic of the temporarily dominant interpretive community defines the rationality of policies, as when they tackle deficits by cutting taxes and spending, by increasing taxes and spending, or by increasing the one and cutting the other. The establishing of one interpretive structure as legitimate necessarily disadvantages people who do not share it. Moreover, it poorly equips people who use it to coordinate their perceptions with all those people who do not use it. Thus, the people with the most severe grievances are generally least able to voice them in the ways that the established order either understands or recognizes as legitimate. The movements toward and against bilingual education are examples of conflicting linguistic communities struggling over laws, while the pro-life and pro-choice movements are examples of conflicting languages, logics, and ideologies.

Politics consists of the struggle among interpretive communities to establish their own interpretive structures as legitimate so as to define social and political realities for everybody else. When an interpretive community feels that it can be effective within the system, it plays by the rules. But when individuals or communities lose confidence in the responsiveness of institutions, they begin to mobilize from the bottom up. They step outside the legitimate laws, language, logic, and ideology to challenge them. They become social movements.

The interpretive systems model is an integrative framework that can help us to see that controversies arise because different people have incongruent needs, preferences, and verbal constructions of reality, each of which makes perfect sense to its own people. Moreover, it helps us to see that these interpretive structures are created and learned through communication. Thus, the interpretive systems model helps us to understand politics as communication.

The interpretive systems approach to social movements enables us to see that individuals form relationships and groups on the basis of their needs, symbols, reasons, and preferences. Agitators use language to articulate their potential followers' needs and to critique the established order. They frequently must avoid the dominant language and ideology because figures of speech are figures of thought that can trap the protestor in the web of established modes of thinking. Later chapters will explore some of the ways in which social movements use nontraditional rhetorical forms such as music, slogans, ridicule, and obscenities to introduce new ways of thinking about persistent sources of dissatisfaction.

Those who study the persuasive efforts of social movements can use an interpretive or social systems perspective by pursuing the question, "Which individuals, conceiving themselves to be what 'people' in what environment, use what relational patterns and what adaptive strategies with what evolutionary results?" Let us examine each part of this question.[14]

Which Individuals? Since persuasion is a human activity, we must ascertain precisely which people create the system's adaptive effort. This means locating prominent individuals, their demographic traits, and their personality or character traits. We must devote more attention to the discovery of similarities and differences among the people who come to share particular rhetorical visions or self-conceptions. Discovering that a particular social movement is largely comprised of people with a low tolerance of ambiguity, a familiarity with crime and violence, and/or a common regional, racial, or religious experience may help us understand better their susceptibility to one characterization of their environment and their aversion to others. Thus, biological, sociological, and psychological information can help us to understand the movement, the hierarchy, and their interdependence.

Information about leaders is easily found in biographies, autobiographies, movement studies, journalistic accounts, histories, and single-speaker rhetorical studies. The social systems approach does not equate a leader's background or behavior with the movement, but instead seeks to understand the leadership subsystem as a means of understanding the social movement system. It helps, for example, to study the theological development of Martin Luther King, Jr. and Malcolm X before studying their persuasion. It is also helpful to know that John Birch Society founder Robert Welch wrote a primer on salesmanship, that socialist labor leader Eugene V. Debs originally opposed strikes, and that neighborhood organizer Saul Alinsky held a Ph.D. in psychology. Much helpful information about major movement figures and their rhetoric can be found in two reference books on *American Orators* by Bernard Duffy and Halford Ross Ryan and *Free at Last? The Civil Rights Movements and the People Who Made it* by Fred Powledge.[15]

If studying the leadership subsystem requires biographical materials, studying the membership subsystem requires social-psychological data. This kind of scientific research is rare in communication literature. One exception is Michael J. Hogan's study of the people participating in rallies for former Alabama Governor George Wallace.[16] Consequently, the social systems critic will often need to draw upon surveys and studies from other disciplines, such as political scientist Fred Grupp's survey of John Birch Society members in 1964. His data suggested that Birchers were unrepresentative of the American population in several respects, and he was able to identify four types of Birch Society members based upon their reasons for joining: "informed" who joined for educational benefits, "likeminded" who wanted to associate with people who "thought like them," "politically committed" who wanted an outlet for their political activities, and "ideological" who wanted something in which to believe.[17] Chapter 6 will explore further the role of personality in the adaptive behavior of John Birch Society members. For the present, it should be apparent that Grupp's study provides valuable information about Birch members' needs, motives, and preferences which helps explain their enthusiasm for an otherwise unpopular set of beliefs. Our first task, then, is to identify the influential leaders and their followers: who are they? what are their demographic, experiential, sociological, psychological, and political traits? This first step tells us something about the people from whom the social movement develops. With this information we can better predict and explain the leaders' and members' adaptive choices. But unfortunately, it is not enough to identify individuals' traits or tendencies since systems theory is based on the principle of nonsummativity.

Conceiving Themselves to Be What 'People.'   In an old joke, the "faithful Indian companion Tonto" exemplifies our ability to adapt self-conception to environmental discrepancy:

Lone Ranger: Well, Tonto, the Indians have us surrounded. It looks like we're done for.

Tonto: What do you mean "We," Paleface?

Having ascertained who people are and what they are like, it remains for us
to discover who they think they are. Michael C. McGee, Aaron Gresson, and
others have described the processes by which "peoples" arise through their shared
myths and pasts.[18] In the final analysis, real people, not rhetorical creations, take
action. In this sense, then, we need to be concerned with the movement's and
the institutional hierarchy's self-conceptions. We should ascertain who they think
they are, the degree to which this self-image corresponds with our appraisal of
who they really are, and the psychological/sociological reasons for their rhetorical
susceptibility to these particular characterizations.

When "you" and "I" create an "us," we begin to see something beyond our
individuality (which we call "usness"). This "us" is the relational system created
as you and I adapt to our environments (including each other's). Tonto adapted
to his environment by transforming his relational bonds—his native American
heritage became more salient for him than his friendship with the Lone Ranger.
Tonto did not physically become "more Indian," but his perceptions changed
significantly. He conceived himself as "Indian" rather than "kimosabe." When
the labor movement song asks "Which Side Are You On?" the listener faces
a choice much like Tonto's.

The self-conceptions of movement leaders and members are not always
consistent with demographic or experiential profiles. Well-heeled labor leaders
are often seen on television complaining about inadequate wages as they prepare
to be chauffeured back to labor headquarters. Religious groups believe they serve
God by throwing bombs in Lebanon or Belfast or by enacting a mass suicide in
Guyana or Waco. The interpretive or social systems analyst wants to know how
these people see themselves and how they develop that self-conception (in light
of their objective characteristics) through communication.

In What Environment.   "In what environment" draws our attention to the world
in which the organism must survive. Just as the organism develops, so does the
environment—partly in response to the organism's adaptive behavior. But the
environment contains other social and mechanical systems as well as the
movement, all of which mitigate an organism's ability to adapt effectively to its
environment. The social systems analyst needs to pursue factual materials about,
for example, labor conditions or discriminatory practices against which to compare
complaints of women, African Americans, and gays.

We are not solely interested in the objective environment because humans
interpret their environment. Our experiences (direct and vicarious) and our
relationships help us construct vocabularies and logical frameworks which we
use to "make sense" of the world. We interpret people and events through these
frameworks whenever possible and renovate them whenever they prove
dysfunctional (the interpretive roles of authoritarian and democratic personalities
are discussed further in chapter 6). We therefore must consider characterizations
or depictions of the environment. For example, the discrepancies which concern
people most are instances of "relative deprivation:" they are denied something
to which they feel entitled. These deprivations may be as blatant and specific

as a wage cut, denial of the right to vote, expulsion from the Navy for being gay, or imprisonment. The perceived deprivation may be more subtle. The important point, as sociologist John Wilson notes, is that "the individuals involved come to feel that their expectations are reasonable" and are being denied.[19] A frequent complaint of protestors is that they are losing their status or self-respect. In testimony before the Senate in 1883, a machinist emphasized dehumanization and limited horizons:

> Well, the trade has been subdivided . . . so that a man never learns the machinist's trade now. . . . It has a very demoralizing effect upon the mind. . . . When I first went to learn the trade a machinist considered himself more than the average workingman; in fact he did not like to be called a workingman. Today he recognizes that he is simply a laborer the same as the others.[20]

The native American movement addresses the lost status and self-respect of tribes that were well-developed and established centuries before Europeans arrived to take their lands and their lives and subject them to meager existences on barren plantations. Women, African Americans, Hispanics, and gays demand status and self-respect and to be able to rise above the "glass ceiling" that permits them to view yet also prevents them from assuming significant leadership roles in American society.

Persuasion is important to the development of a sense of relative deprivation because people must realize that they have been short-changed. How is the environment perceived by both the social movement and institutional hierarchy? Real things do happen to real people which constitute an objective reality (a bloodied nose, a picket line, a limit on how high they can rise on the corporate ladder, and a wage cut are more than perceptual "tricks of the mind"). But these "real" events are perceived, experienced, and understood in diverse ways, leading to diverse realities. Thus, we should focus on the competing characterizations of the environment and the discrepancies among them.

Use What Relational Patterns. "Use what relational patterns" reminds us that not all social movement persuasion is the product of an orator on a soapbox. Who establishes and maintains communicative systems with whom? Such relationships are important for several reasons. First, they indicate the audiences persuaders consider to be capable of resolving the problem. Second, relational patterns suggest the persuader's conception of the auditor's importance to both the social movement (system) and the larger society (supra-system). Third, these relational choices suggest the persuader's working assumption that the auditors either are, or should be, involved in the process of systemic adaptation.

Attention to relationships, then, may help us distinguish functional differences between animal rights demonstrations at the meat packing plant (which seek to influence local implementation), on the steps of the Capitol (which seek to influence national legislation by drawing national attention), and on Main Street (which enhance solidarity and recruiting while polarizing the demonstrators from their opposition). Similarly, it should focus our attention on the hierarchy's response to acts of protest, particularly to the differences between meetings with demonstrators, meetings with representatives of demonstrators, arrests of demonstrators, and press conferences which reassure public and press that the demonstrators are "simply a handful of troublemakers."

In "The Rhetorical Situation," Lloyd Bitzer explains an audience as one or more people capable of resolving an exigence or problem. Too rarely do we take the time to ascertain the relationships between persuader and audience, or audience and exigence. Thus, relational systems and their evolution are important elements of a social systems approach to social movement persuasion that deserve careful study. The important point is not that social movements use different "channels" (the mechanistic theorist's conveyor belts for meaning). The channel used for transmission may matter, or it may not. Rather, the important point is how relational patterns include and exclude potential supporters and critics, foster or preclude the sense of transformation from individuals to group, and reinforce or contradict adaptive efforts.

And What Adaptive Strategies. "And what adaptive strategies" directs our attention to the ongoing, thoughtful process of adjustment as individuals and groups, perceiving a discrepancy between their experienced and preferred environments, create instrumental techniques to minimize that discrepancy. Again, we should look for links between individual characteristics, self-conceptions, relationships, and environment. Immigrant workers at the turn of the century who shared no common language marched rather than spoke; reactionary groups with a fundamentalist strain preached; while African Americans in the South expecting to be brutalized by white authorities, opted for a Gandhian approach to dramatize the system's inhumanity.

Unlike the dichotomy between a "rhetoric of agitation" and a "rhetoric of control," we should search for adaptive, evolutionary patterns in which choices reflect the attempts of individuals to adapt to the system as they try to help their system adapt to its environment.[21] This should produce a richer understanding of social movements and their strategies.

"What adaptive strategies" leads us to the classic Aristotelian focus of "discovering the available means of persuasion." Rather than simply cataloguing strategies, we must view these strategies from the larger perspective of unfolding adaptations—what others have done and what they may be expected to do in response to one's own adaptive efforts.

With What Evolutionary Results. "With what evolutionary results" is our measure of movement growth. The social systems approach is developmental and disdains the notion that adaptations are permanent (since the environment and other organisms are themselves constantly adapting). We can therefore look for evolutionary phases in this developmental process like the typical life cycle presented in chapter 4. These may be changes in the movement's people or their self-conception, changes in the environment or their characterizations of it, changes in their relational patterns or their adaptive strategies. In any case, we need to know how the change facilitated the organism's adaptation with its environment. Did the system adapt effectively? Did it adapt too late to a discrepancy which was otherwise resolved? Did attempted adaptation exacerbate the initial discrepancy? Did the organism appear to enter a new evolutionary phase? We can compare any social movement to the normative life cycle. The answers to such questions should enable us to understand more fully the rhetorical (i.e., adaptive, accommodative) functions of movements in society.

Emphasizing evolutionary results requires an examination of the system-environment fit at a minimum of two points in the adaptive process. These points are a matter of critical judgment and may be chosen in either of two ways. The more traditional method historically ascertains transitions in the social movement's life cycle and studies the role of persuasion in that transition. Although this is a reasonable historical approach, it raises the possibility that persuasive evolution and historical evolution may be "out of synch." The second approach is closer to Fisher and Hawes' interpersonal approach. It involves the careful analysis of persuasion over time for the purpose of ascertaining shifts in recurrent patterns. This is an effective method for finding shifts in argument (segregationists' shift from white supremacy to states' rights), audience (the Communist party's shift from workers to intellectuals), relational patterns (the John Birch Society's shift from study sessions to the Goldwater campaign and back again), self-conceptions (the emergence of the notion of Black Power and Black Is Beautiful), or exigence (pro-life's shift from opposing the legalization of abortion to supporting an anti-abortion amendment to the Constitution).

Regardless of the method employed, we should watch for signs that the social movement and its environment are entering a qualitatively different evolutionary phase. Since change is unavoidable, we are looking for empirically discernible changes in the system-environment fit, not mere changes in the movement, the hierarchy, the environment, or in rhetorical strategy. To the disappointment of many Americans, Richard Nixon's succession to the presidency after Lyndon Johnson only marginally changed the system-environment fit; despite the change in personnel, both the anti-Vietnam War movement's argument and the government's response remained essentially the same.

Many parts of our original question (Which individuals, conceiving themselves to be what "people" in what environment, use what relational patterns and what adaptive strategies with what evolutionary results?) are frequently asked in similar ways. A successful analysis deemphasizes the parts in favor of their interrelationship. It is not sufficient to know only which people were active in a social movement or which symbols pervaded the social movement's rhetoric. We need to know why certain symbolic behaviors proved useful (or futile) for certain people in a particular environment—how all aspects of a social movement worked together to arrive at a particular stage.

Conclusions

Stemming from Aristotle's attention to speaker, audience, message, and occasion, the elements of communication have often been emphasized rather than the interdependence and interaction of these variables. In recent years, we have increasingly noticed that an understanding of the pieces fails to explain the whole of human communication. At the same time, we have seen a growth in social systems models of interpersonal communication that suggest an approach to communication as the efforts of parties in a relationship adapting to one another and their environment.

This chapter has developed a social systems approach to the persuasive activities of social movements that provides a framework for bringing analysis of societal communication into line with our knowledge of interpersonal communication. This perspective not only permits but encourages us to examine people and events not always classified as "social movements," to incorporate insights from interpersonal and organizational communication, and to turn to individual orator and event studies.

We must find and share better ways of understanding and handling adaptation. We must understand that conflict is not simply to be avoided; it is unavoidable. Conflict is a sign of system-environment adaptation. Agitation, exhortations and threats of violence are signs that the system is not adapting satisfactorily with its environment. We must recognize that the system-environment relationship is not a thing but a process and that restraining or retarding that process often increases the trauma of adaptation when it ultimately comes. In the final analysis, we must remember that persuasion is not something that one does to another or has done to oneself. It is a process of mutual adjustment in which people and societies engage.

The mechanical systems approach to social movement persuasion implicitly requires that we adopt a movement-establishment stance. The critic proceeding from that base learns only about interconnected components. The social systems model presented here seeks to discover and to explain the interdependent, adaptive, growing nature of the social organism. The model is predicated on the notion that all of us—Black Panthers, Gray Panthers, Nazis, Klansmen, radical feminists, populists, environmentalists, gays, Democrats, Republicans, presidents, legislators, and the Great Silent Majority—are part of the same socio-political-rhetorical system. A full understanding of who we are, why we are as we are, and how we got this way requires that we take a holistic, developmental perspective.

Endnotes

[1] Unless otherwise noted, all references to the axioms of systems theory are taken from B. Aubrey Fisher, *Perspectives on Human Communication* (New York: Macmillan, 1978), 196–204.

[2] Fisher, 197–198.

[3] Samuel Gompers, *Seventy Years of Life and Labor*, vol. I (New York: Augustus M. Kelly, 1967), 69–70.

4 Ludwig von Bertalanffy, *General Systems Theory: Foundations, Development, Applications* (New York: George Braziller, 1968), 40 cited by Fisher, 201.

5 Fisher, 201.

6 Norbert Wiener, *The Human Use of Human Beings: Cybernetics and Society* (Boston: Houghton Mifflin, 1954); and Claude Shannon and Warren Weaver, *The Mathematical Theory of Communication* (Urbana, IL: University of Illinois Press, 1949).

7 Dennis R. Smith, "The Fallacy of the Communication Breakdown," *Quarterly Journal of Speech* 56 (December 1970), 343–346.

8 Brent D. Ruben, "Communication and Conflict: A Systems-Theoretic Perspective," *Quarterly Journal of Speech* 64 (April 1978), 205.

9 Bitzer argues that rhetorical acts are responses to the situation, while Vatz argues that the persuader defines that situation through language. See Lloyd Bitzer, "The Rhetorical Situation," *Philosophy and Rhetoric* 1 (Winter 1968), 1–14; and Richard E. Vatz, "The Myth of the Rhetorical Situation," *Philosophy and Rhetoric* 6 (Summer 1973), 154–161.

10 Saul D. Alinsky, *Rules for Radicals: A Practical Primer for Realsistic Radicals* (New York: Vintage, 1971), 6–7.

11 Alinsky, 21–32.

12 Herbert W. Simons, "Persuasion in Social Conflicts: A Critique of Prevailing Conceptions and a Framework for Future Research," *Speech Monographs* 39 (November 1972), 239.

13 This chapter is based on a significant revision of the interpretive systems model published in Craig Allen Smith and Kathy B. Smith, *The White House Speaks: Presidential Leadership as Persuasion* (Westport, CT: Praeger, 1994). The model was first presented in Craig Allen Smith, *Political Communication* (San Diego: Harcourt Brace Jovanovich, 1990), 1–77. It was later used to suggest an approach to the college course in political communication and to using the C-SPAN materials in the classroom, respectively, "Interpretive Communities in Conflict: A Master Syllabus for Political Communication," *Communication Education* 41 (October 1992), 415–428; and "The Interpretive Systems Approach to Teaching Political Communication," *C-SPAN in the Classroom: Theory and Applications*, Janette K. Muir, ed. (Annandale, VA: Speech Communication Association, 1992), 21–34.

14 For an example of social systems criticism see Craig Allen Smith, "An Organic Systems Analysis of John Birch Society Discourse, 1958–1966," *Southern Speech Communication Journal* 50 (Winter 1984), 155–176.

15 Bernard K. Duffy and Halford Ryan Ross, (eds.) *American Orators of The Twentieth Century* (Westport, CT: Greenwood, 1987); Fred Powledge, *Free at Last? The Civil Rights Movement and the People Who Made It* (Boston: Little Brown and Company, 1991).

16 Michael Hogan, "Wallace and the Wallaceites: A Reexamination," *Southern Speech Communication Journal* 50 (Fall 1984), 24–48.

17 Birchers responding to the survey were younger, better educated, and better off financially than the American norm of that period. Most were white-collar Republicans whose education was disproportionately in the natural sciences and engineering, who became politically aware during or after World War II, and lived in states with rapidly fluctuating populations. Fred W. Grupp, Jr., "The Political Perspectives of John Birch Society Members," *The American Right Wing*, Robert A. Schoenberger, ed., (Atlantic: Holt, Rinehart, and Winston, 1969), 83–118.

18 Michael C. McGee, "In Search of 'The People': A Rhetorical Alternative," *Quarterly Journal of Speech* 61 (October 1975), 235–249; and Aaron D. Gresson, III, "Phenomenology and the Rhetoric of Identification—A Neglected Dimension of Communication Inquiry," *Communication Quarterly* 26 (Fall 1978), 14–23.

19 John Wilson, *Introduction to Social Movements* (New York: Basic Books, 1973), 70.

20 Testimony of John Morrison (excerpted), Leon Litwack, ed., *The American Labor Movement* (Englewood Cliffs, NJ: Prentice-Hall, 1962), 10–12.

21 John Waite Bowers, Donovan J. Ochs, and Richard J. Jensen, *The Rhetoric of Agitation and Control*, 2/E (Prospect Heights, IL: Waveland Press, 1993).

Chapter Three
The Persuasive Functions of Social Movements

As discussed in chapters 1 and 2, persuasion is the primary *agency* through which social movements perform *functions* that enable them to come into existence, to satisfy requirements, to meet oppositions, and, perhaps, to succeed in bringing about or resisting change. Functions are the indispensable processes that contribute to the success or maintenance of social movements.[1] For instance, Richard Gregg has explored the ego-function of the protest rhetoric of black power, student rights, and women's liberation movements. Dale Leathers has discovered that the persuasive efforts of the John Birch Society were "highly functional for the maintenance of in-group solidarity."[2] Michael McGee concludes his essay, "In Search of 'The People': A Rhetorical Alternative," by suggesting that the "analysis of rhetorical documents should not turn inward, to an application of persuasive, manipulative techniques, but outward to functions of rhetoric."[3]

What functions, then, must persuasion fulfill for social movements? In his effort to provide a "leader-centered conception of persuasion for social movements," Herbert Simons writes that social movements "must fulfill the same rhetorical requirements as more formal collectives. These imperatives constitute *rhetorical requirements* for the leadership of a movement."[4] He discusses these functions or requirements under three broad headings:

1. They must attract, maintain, and mold workers (followers) into an efficiently run unit.
2. They must secure adoption of their product by the larger structure (the external system, the established order).
3. They must react to resistance generated by the larger structure.

Bruce Gronbeck develops a more inclusive list of persuasive functions in his study of the Black Action Movement at the University of Michigan in the spring of 1970. He writes that rhetorical or persuasive "forces function as a set of skills

able to create, sustain, and terminate movements by uniting the other forces.''[5]
Gronbeck lists six functions that are tied to a chronological series of stages:

1. Defining: Somebody or some group takes the first step. A problem is defined and a solution is urged.
2. Legitimizing: Legitimizers can lend positive authority, a regional or national presence to a budding movement.
3. In-gathering: The movement builds a power-base, a group of adherents ready to talk, march, and fight for the cause.
4. Pressuring: The movement also mounts a campaign urging reform or revolution.
5. Compromising: After direct confrontation, usually some sort of compromise must be worked out.
6. Satisfying: Leaders must be able to return to the masses of their movement, proclaiming victory, even if only partial gains have been made.

With these functions in mind, according to Gronbeck, we should ask three questions when analyzing the persuasion of social movements: (1) What functions are fulfilled by persuasive discourse? (2) With what substance are these functions fulfilled? And (3) in what form does that substance appear? While Gronbeck's list of functions is more inclusive than Simons' three broad rhetorical requirements, it is best suited for studying a social movement campaign or action in which a single social movement organization has attempted to fulfill all six functions in a fairly brief time.

Building upon the foundation laid by previous writers, we have developed a more inclusive scheme of interrelated general and specific functions that emphasize the importance of audience perceptions.[6]

1. Transforming perceptions of reality
   a. Altering perceptions of the past
   b. Altering perceptions of the present
   c. Altering perceptions of the future
2. Altering perceptions of society
   a. Altering perceptions of the opposition
   b. Altering self-perceptions
3. Prescribing courses of action
   a. Prescribing what must be done
   b. Prescribing who must accomplish the task
   c. Prescribing how the task must be accomplished
4. Mobilizing for action
   a. Organizing the united and discontented
   b. Pressuring the opposition
   c. Gaining sympathy and support from opinion leaders or legitimizers

5. Sustaining the social movement
   a. Justifying setbacks and delays
   b. Maintaining viability of the movement
   c. Maintaining visibility of the movement

Several caveats are in order before we explain and illustrate each function in this scheme of persuasive functions.

First, although the functions listed are essential to the existence and success of social movements, they are not unique to social movements. As we argued in chapter 1, social movements differ from institutionalized collectivities—not principally in terms of the functions their persuasive efforts must perform but in terms of the constraints placed upon the fulfillment of these functions. The uninstitutionalized nature of movements greatly limits their powers and access to the mass media and hence their strategic options.[7]

Second, while social movements must perform all of these functions, their fundamental programs for change (innovative, revivalistic, or resistance), the degree of change desired (reform to revolutionary), the rhetorical situation, and the stage of the movement or movement organization will determine which functions assume greater prominence at a particular time. Our functional scheme is not intended to be chronological or related to a specific series of progressive stages. No social movement will perform any function once and then proceed to another. Although some functions may dominate the persuasion of a social movement at a given time (transforming perceptions of reality during an early stage or pressuring the opposition and gaining support of legitimizers during a later stage), most functions demand attention on a continual basis.

Third, focus on persuasive functions encourages studies of entire social movements, but we may study the persuasive efforts of a portion of a social movement, a social movement organization, or a social movement campaign. For example, we may study one or more *general functions* such as transforming perceptions of reality. Alternatively, we may choose to focus on a *specific function* such as altering perceptions of self, or we may focus on a *specific means* of satisfying a function such as transforming perceptions of the opposition through devil or conspiracy appeals. Let us turn now to a discussion and illustration of each of the interrelated, general and specific functions.

Transforming Perceptions of Reality

William Gamson contends that social movements are essentially struggles "over the definition and construction of social reality."[8] Every social movement must make a significant number of people aware that the generally accepted view of reality fostered by political, social, religious, educational, legal, literary, and mass media establishments is false and that something must be done about it. Linkugel, Allen, and Johannesen note, however, that "A problem is not really a problem to an audience until they perceive it as such. A situation may exist, and the audience may know that it does, but in their eyes it remains nothing more than a lifeless fact until they view it as something that threatens or violates their interests and values.''[9] Thus, social movement persuaders must transform how people see the past, the present, and/or the future to convince them that an intolerable situation exists that warrants urgent attention and action.[10]

The Past

Some social movements must transform how people perceive the past if they are to succeed in bringing about or stifling change. *The past may be well-known and ugly.* For instance, the American Nazi party (later known as the National Socialist White People's party) had to address the horrors of World War II and the holocaust in which their German predecessors and hero, Adolf Hitler, killed millions of allied troops, citizens in occupied countries, and Jewish inmates in concentration camps. *The past may be more fiction than reality.* The native American movement has had to overcome the Hollywood-inspired vision of ''injuns'' and ''redskins'' as blood-thirsty savages who killed and mutilated innocent settlers and peace-loving calvary led by John Wayne look-alikes.[11] This version of the past had been fostered not only in film but in classrooms, history books, drama, and hallowed historical sites. Until recently, for example, visitors to the Custer Memorial at the Little Bighorn Battlefield received guided tours complete with a rousing story of how the gallant and brave General Custer made his last stand, outnumbered but defiant until the evil Sioux under Sitting Bull shot him down in cold blood. *The past may be generally unknown.* Revivalistic movements such as the evangelical religious right and pro-life must reveal how wonderful the past was before humanistic and immoral changes led to premarital sex, divorce, homosexuality, a turning from God, and the murder of millions of unborn infants. A resistance movement such as pro-choice must reveal the horrors of back-alley and self-induced abortions that were prevalent prior to safe, legalized abortions after *Roe v. Wade* in 1973.

Social movements use a variety of persuasive tactics and channels to transform perceptions of the past. For example, the American Nazi party has produced ''facts'' to prove that the ''alleged'' holocaust in Europe was a clever creation of the Jews (through untruths, fantastic exaggerations, twisted words, confessions extracted under torture, falsified evidence, a best-seller hoax—the *Diary of Anne Frank*, and fake photographs) to spread the world communist conspiracy.[12] In a leaflet entitled *The Big Lie: Who Told It?* Nazi writers identify who was responsible for spreading lies about Hitler, the German Nazi party, and events during World War II.[13] The native American movement has attempted to change fiction into fact through historical accounts such as Dee Brown's *Bury My Heart at Wounded Knee: An Indian History of the American West*, novels such as the Pulitzer Prize winning *House Made of Dawn* by N. Scott Momaday, and analyses of social interactions such as Vine Deloria's *Custer Died for Your Sins*.[14] Commercially produced movies such as *Little Big Man* starring Dustin Hoffman and *Dances with Wolves* starring Kevin Kostner have given millions of Americans a different view of native American history. Other social movements must reveal a past that is generally unknown. For example, The Reverend Billy James Hargis, founder and leader of the Christian Crusade against communism, often made startling revelations in his radio addresses about President Franklin Roosevelt's deals with Stalin and how the United Nations was a creation by and for the atheistic, communist Soviet Union to further its quest for world domination.[15] The National Abortion Rights Action League has produced statistics to show there have always been abortions (back to ancient times) and that, prior to the Supreme Court decision, a million illegal and self-induced abortions took place each year in the United States. Instead of safe, medical procedures in sterile surroundings, however, abortions took place at back-alley locations or on women's bathroom floors, and these abortions often resulted in mutilations and deaths.[16]

The Present

Nearly all social movements must transform perceptions of the present. Target audiences, particularly when a movement is in its infancy, may (1) be unaware of the problem, (2) refuse to believe that it exists, (3) believe the problem is not severe or does not require drastic action, (4) believe the problem does not affect them, or (5) believe the problem should be and will be handled by appropriate institutions through normal channels and procedures. Nearly all institutions (from schools and political parties to labor unions and the mass media) foster and reinforce these perceptions. After all, a problem that appears on a few evening newscasts and disappears, is on the plains of South Dakota far from us, is apparently sanctioned by the Bible, or is being looked at in congressional committees does not require a mass movement or impolite and inconvenient protests and boycotts. For example, when the anti-slavery movement emerged in the 1830s and 1840s, American institutions did not see slavery as a degradation of the slave but as the slave's birth and salvation as a civilized, Christianized human being.[17] The Bible, according to pro-slavery clergy, supported slavery as God's wonderful and mysterious way to save the black savage-child. When the women's liberation movement emerged during the 1960s, institutions maintained the status of women as housewives and mothers who raised children and supported husbands in their careers.[18] A woman was not to compete in a man's world (not the place for ladies and girls), and a man was not to compete in a woman's world (not a place for a real man). Demands by the gay rights movement in the 1990s to add sexual orientation clauses in human rights ordinances and laws are being countered, on the one hand, with denials that any discrimination exists and, on the other, that discrimination is necessary because homosexuality is a sin condemned by the Bible and homosexuals are responsible for AIDS, child molestation, and the destruction of the American family.[19]

Storytelling is a primary means of altering perceptions of the present. For example, former slaves such as Frederick Douglass, Henry Highland Garnet, and

Sojouner Truth delivered speeches throughout the North prior to the Civil War relating the horrors they had experienced as slaves and their harrowing escapes to freedom in the North.[20] Animal rights pamphlets and leaflets contain gruesome stories of leghold traps as told by trappers. A leaflet entitled *Say No to Torture* includes this bit of testimony: "One day, I saw a large beaver, a front paw caught in a leghold trap. The front paw was no longer covered with skin or flesh, the bone was visible, naked and white. At my approach, the beaver struggled desperately to free itself, the bone broke with a sickening sound."[21] Pro-life persuasion is replete with testimony of nurses and doctors who give heart-rending accounts of aborted fetuses being bashed and smothered to death because they would not die.[22]

When feasible, social movements intensify their stories and claims with gory pictures: animals caught in traps or being subjected to horrible scientific experiments, tiny bodies of aborted fetuses in trashcans or in pieces, a video entitled "The Silent Scream" that purportedly shows a fetus undergoing the agony of abortion, dead women on bathroom floors after "back-alley" or self-induced abortions, and a video produced by the United Farm Workers entitled "The Wrath of Grapes" that shows deformed children and children with cancer allegedly caused by use of pesticides in grape vineyards.[23] Some movements have used the theatre to "tell it like it is." Plays by black authors such as "The Militant Preacher" and "The Job" by Ben Caldwell, "The Bronx Is Next" by Sonia Sanchez, "And We Own the Night" by Jimmy Garrett, and "The Monster" by Ronald Milner portray ministers as Uncle Toms, indict the welfare system, emphasize bad housing, show the detrimental effects of a dominant black mother on her sons and husband, and attack a black college dean who wants to be accepted by whites.[24]

Movement persuaders search for words that communicate the horror and urgency portrayed in stories and pictures. Gary Woodward writes that "We commit ourselves to different realities through the act of naming because words are devices for telling others *how they should see the world.*"[25] Animal rights activists, for instance, use such words as brutality, invasion, ruthless slaughter, oppression, exploitation, and speciesism. A series of pictures in an animal rights leaflet showing a little ermine trying to gnaw its way out of a trap is accompanied by this caption: "Blood-spattered snow provides a nightmare setting for the terror, pain, and despair which the implacable trap elicits from its small victim—a barbaric drama of suffering which has been compared to crucifixion."[26]

Some social movement persuaders emphasize glaring paradoxes or inconsistencies in the rhetoric and practices of established orders or social movements they oppose. John L. Lewis, founder of the United Mine Workers, pointed out in speeches that Illinois had 16 mine inspectors and 147 game wardens while Kentucky, the leading coal mining state, budgeted $220,000 for game wardens and only $37,000 for mine safety. Clearly these states valued wild game over coal miners.[27] Similarly, a recent advertisement placed in college newspapers, by Americans for Medical Progress Educational Foundation, challenged the animal rights movement's preference for animals over people. One headline, How Many

More Will Die Before You Say "No!" To The Animal Rights Movement? introduced an advertisement that read in part:

> The Cure for AIDS will come like every cure before it, through animal research. And yet, there is a growing movement of animal rights activists who oppose any use of animals in biomedical research. As one of their leaders, Ingrid Newkirk, stated: *"Even if animal research resulted in a cure for AIDS . . . we'd be against it."*[28]

Both movements, one innovative and one resistance, emphasize that an establishment's or movement's values are the opposite of what they should be.

The Future

Social movement persuaders also portray a vision of the future that instills a sense of urgency in audiences to organize and to do something *now*. However, audiences tend to be preoccupied with day-to-day needs and desires. If they look ahead at all, they tend to think things will work out (they always have), that institutions will take care of the future, that someone will invent something to resolve the problem, that they cannot do anything about the future so why worry about it, or that society is heading for ruin and there's no way to reverse the trend. As Hans Toch writes:

> For a person to be led to join a social movement, he [or she] must not only sense a problem, but must also (1) feel that something can be done about it and (2) want to do something about it himself [herself]. At the very least, he [she] must feel that the status quo is not inevitable, and that change is conceivable.[29]

Social movement persuaders try to transform perceptions of the future in one of two ways, by showing it as bright and full of hope or dark and full of despair. Which future ultimately comes about will depend upon the "people" and their collective actions.

The rhetoric of hope relies upon one of two appeals or a combination. *Utopian appeals* present a perfect space (often a promised land) while *millennium appeals* present a perfect time (an era when peace, love, and happiness will abound). Eugene V. Debs, a labor and socialist leader and five-time presidential candidate from the 1880s to the 1920s, often spoke of a future when socialism would triumph and life would be wonderful for everyone. In a speech in Girard, Kansas in 1908, Debs described a socialist utopia and millennium:

> Every man and every woman will then be economically free. They can, without let or hindrance, apply their labor, with the best machinery that can be devised, to all the natural resources, do the work of society and produce for all; and then receive in exchange a certificate of value equivalent to that of their production. Then society will improve its institutions in proportion to the progress of invention. Whether in the city or on the farm, all things productive will be carried forward on a gigantic scale. All industry will be completely organized. Society for the first time will have a scientific foundation. Every man, by being economically

> free, will have some time for himself. He can then take a full and perfect breath.
> He can enjoy life with his wife and children, because then he will have a
> home. . . . We will reduce the workday, and give every man a chance. We will
> go to parks, and we will have music, because we will have time to play music
> and desire to hear it. [30]

Notice Debs' careful selection of words and concepts likely to motivate his American, midwestern audience to strive for the future he is portraying: freedom, progress, invention, science, fairness, family, and home. Martin Luther King's "I have a Dream" speech is also a careful blend of utopian and millennium appeals designed to instill hope in the future *if* his audience will continue to support the movement's crusade for change. The rhetoric of religious social movements contain descriptions of paradise, a time and place of eternal happiness.

A rhetoric of dread or despair, particularly prevalent in resistance and revivalistic social movements, warns that the current state of affairs can only get worse unless "the people" act immediately to change the course of events. The *domino theory* predicts that one right, power, possession, place, value, or virtue will fall after another, like dominos, until all is lost. Robert Welch, founder of the John Birch Society, warned in his speech that launched the Society in Indianapolis on December 9, 1958 that:

> Unless we can reverse the forces which now seem inexorable in their movement,
> you have only a few more years before the country in which you live will become
> four separate provinces in a worldwide Communist dominion. . . . We are living,
> in America today, in such a fool's paradise as the people of China lived in twenty
> years ago, as the people of Czechoslovakia lived in a dozen years ago, as the
> people of North Vietnam lived in five years ago, and as the people of Iraq lived
> in only yesterday. [31]

A related appeal is the *slippery slope* that relates how society is sliding inexorably down a slope into oblivion. Randall Lake writes about the "moral landscape" presented in pro-life rhetoric and how it warns of a society sliding into total immorality because it no longer protects its unborn. [32] The environmental movement warns of the greenhouse effect and the end of life as we know it if destruction of the world's rain forests, release of fluorocarbons into the atmosphere, widespread use of fossil fuels, uncontrolled toxic wastes, and water pollution continue at present levels. [33]

Religious social movements or religious elements of movements often use *apocalyptic appeals* when resisting other movements or trying to revive the past. Persuaders are warning state legislatures, city councils, and university senates considering sexual orientation clauses in human rights documents that God destroyed Sodom in ancient Palestine because of its wickedness, particularly homosexuality and other perverse sexual preferences, and will destroy the United States if homosexuality is accepted as normal and therefore advocated. [34] Some cite AIDS as the first installment of God's punishment for our sinful ways. Inherent in many of these messages is the notion that society is in the final battle between good and evil, Armageddon, merely *one step away* from disaster. For example, during the 1980s, the Clamshell Alliance in New England staged mock nuclear disasters on the ocean beaches a short distance from the Seabrook nuclear power plant, then under construction, to show the impossibility of evacuation and massive deaths that would result from an accident if the plant came on line. Nuclear plants, they warned, were always moments away from disasters like the one in the Ukraine: "Chernobyl has made it crystal clear that nuclear power means nuclear death."[35]

Although we can identify many techniques social movements use to transform perceptions of reality, we do not know when movements are most likely to use them and how they might change over time. Studies indicate that revivalistic social movements tend to view the past as a paradise lost that is worth resurrecting at any cost in order to have a possible utopia or millennium in the future.[36] Resistance movements tend to view the present as a paradise achieved and see efforts of social movements and established orders as threatening to return society to a primitive past or transport it to a future devoid of all that is sacred.[37] Innovative movements tend to portray a defective present resulting from or a continuation of an intolerable past and argue that the future can be bright only if the movement is successful.[38]

How do traumatic events affect the amount and nature of persuasion aimed at the past, present, or future? James Darsey has shown, for example, how "catalytic events," particularly the "scourge of AIDS," greatly altered the rhetoric of the gay rights movement from 1977 to 1990.[39] At what point do social movement organizations such as the American Nazi party and the American Indian movement feel they must "correct" versions of the past? How might the rhetorical clearing of Hitler's name and denials of the holocaust help groups resist change? When are dramatic revelations of the past likely to appear in a movement's persuasion? How might social movements revise versions of reality as they age, confront opposition, meet successes and failures, adapt to changing situations, or produce their own heroes, martyrs, and clowns?[40] Do they select new terminology, rely more or less on graphic portrayals, or devote more persuasion to shocking people into consciousness through verbal and nonverbal confrontations and violence? Do aging social movements, like aging soldiers, pay increasing attention to the past, or do they, like prophets, look more toward paradise?

Transforming Perceptions of Society

Social movements transform perceptions of society through a rhetoric of polarization that creates a clear distinction between the *evil opposition* and the *virtuous self*, a clear we-they distinction.[41] The opposition includes all individuals and groups who do not openly support the social movement and thus are responsible for allowing an intolerable situation to come into existence and to worsen day-by-day. "They" includes established institutions, the "silent majority," the mass media, countermovements, competing social movements, competing organizations and factions within the movement, and those for whom the movement is fighting even though they have not yet joined or supported the movement. Bert Klandermans writes that "when two movements are pitted against each other, reality will provide plenty of temptations to see the opposition as evil incarnate."[42] Persuaders hold firmly to the adage, "If you are not with us, you are against us." There is no middle ground, no neutrals, in the struggle between good and evil. "We" includes all the righteous, moral, self-sacrificing individuals and groups—the true believers—who are willing to stand up and say "NO!" to evil conditions, forces, and trends.

The Opposition

Each social movement identifies one or more *devils*. Devils may be *mysterious, somewhat nebulous forces* (the rich, capitalists, men, polluters, secular humanists), *individuals* (Henry Ford during the labor struggles of the 1920s and 1930s, President Johnson during the Vietnam War, Martin Luther King, Jr. for the anti-civil rights organizations during the 1950s and 1960s, and Ralph Nader for far-right and anti-consumerism movements), or *things* (demon rum, nuclear power plants, cruise missiles, commercial developments, acid rain). The ideal devil according to Eric Hoffer is one, omnipotent, omnipresent, foreigner.[43] A single devil provides a clear rhetorical target for the social movement; an omnipotent, all powerful devil requires a mass movement, self-defense, non-institutional tactics, and total commitment; an omnipresent devil is everywhere, involved in all that is evil, and thus requires constant vigilance and confrontation; and a foreign devil (anti-American, anti-Christian, anti-God, anti-free enterprise) creates identification among movement members through antithesis by contrasting them with forces totally alien and without redeeming value.

Movement persuaders heap abuse upon their devils through name-calling, ridicule, negative associations, and metaphors that may dehumanize them into pigs, rats, vermin, parasites, vultures, scum, and feces. Special invective is reserved for persons who refuse to support the movement that is fighting for them. For nearly two centuries, the labor movement has called nonunion workers (particularly strike-breakers) scabs. The black rights movement used the epithets Uncle Tom and handkerchief head for "negroes" who would not fight or allegedly sold out to the white establishment. Native American activists copied the black rights movement with the disparaging epithet Uncle Tomahawk aimed at fellow "Indians" who cooperated with the Bureau of Indian Affairs and federal authorities. A common strategy during confrontations is to provoke the establishment into violent reactions, suppression, and arrests to reveal its true ugliness.[44]

Some social movements perceive their devils to be *conspiring* together in secret agreements to commit "crimes" against the movement and therefore against "the people." The conspiracy may be real or merely imagined, but the process is the same; a chain of apparently unrelated events or actions is linked to reveal concerted actions and intentions to cause all sorts of social, economic, political, religious, and moral problems.[45] The conspiracy appeal can be powerful rhetoric for social movements because it appeals to Americans who have always been fearful of "foreign plots." Catholic immigration in the mid-1800s led to fears of a Papal conspiracy to undermine the republic and claims that Abraham Lincoln was assassinated in a plot directed from the Vatican; the populists of the late 1800s spoke of conspiracies by international bankers and the House of Rothschild in Europe; fear of a communist conspiracy has driven a great deal of American political and religious rhetoric since the 1930s; H. Rapp Brown and other black power leaders of the 1960s condemned a white, genocidal conspiracy; and Christian, evangelical groups fear a secular humanist conspiracy that is plotting to destroy the Christian foundations of the United States.[46]

The conspiracy appeal is effective because it provides a single, simple, and concise explanation for disparate and complex events that leaves nothing unexplained. Radical right groups have used a "principle of reversal" to counter efforts to debunk its conspiracy rhetoric. This principle holds that reality is the exact opposite of what it appears to be, so if you cannot see or identify conspirators or uncover proof of plots, that *proves* conspirators are everywhere, plots exist, and the conspiracy is omnipotent.[47] For instance, Robert Welch of the John Birch Society argued that his knowledge of how communists worked allowed him to see through the facade of Martin Luther King, Jr.:

> The record clearly shows that Martin Luther King was an almost perfect example of the Communist principle of reversal—that is of claiming exactly the opposite of what you are really doing. While always acting under the pretense of advocating non-violent measures, King was actually the leading promoter and instigator of racial violence in America. He was a key figure in the Communist plans to create so much turmoil and anarchy in our country as to enable a Communist-run central government to counter such confusion with the massive use of a national armed force—which is the forerunner of Communist tyranny. Through his own deeds King had been made by his Communist bosses into a deceptive and vicious pro-Communist enemy of his own race, of the American nation.[48]

Welch's statement contains all of the essential ingredients for a successful conspiracy appeal: a powerful, secret alliance with a foreign agency that is scheming, clever, traitorous, deceitful, cruel, and deadly. Any source that questions the conspiracy is automatically suspect, even a highly credible source such as President Eisenhower who had served as the supreme allied commander in Europe during World War II.

Although devil and conspiracy appeals are prominent in the persuasion of social movements, we know relatively little about them and how they are related. Are they more common and vitriolic in certain types of social movements? How do they change as movements encounter Darsey's catalytic events, crises, and violence or as they grow old? Do some movements come into existence to fight dangerous conspiracies while others come to detect conspiracies after confrontations and failures to achieve legitimacy or the support of "the people?" Are conspiracy appeals more or less common in the twentieth century than in preceding centuries?

The Self

Most social movements must alter self-perceptions of members and non-members so they will come to believe in their self-worth and ability to achieve urgent change through collective action. Richard Gregg contends that protest "rhetoric is basically self-directed" and "has to do with *constituting* self-hood through expression."[49] Protestors find themselves in "symbolically defensive positions from which they must extricate themselves before they can realize more positive identities." He argues that protestors identify *against an other*, through contrasts, to create these positive identities and thus elevate themselves in the social hierarchy. Charles Stewart has extrapolated five points of potential contrast from Gregg's theory of protest rhetoric:[50]

1. Innocent victim versus wicked victimizer
2. Powerful and brave versus weak and cowardly
3. United and together versus separate and divided
4. Important and valuable versus unimportant and worthless
5. Virtuous and moral versus sinful and immoral

The dominant contrast in social movement persuasion portrays the oppressed as innocent victims of circumstances and forces beyond their control. As Gregg writes, "If one feels oppressed, he implies that there is an oppressor—someone responsible for the oppression."[51] Persuaders often compare the plight of the oppressed to the most disadvantaged social group.[52] Labor movement leaders identified workers as wage slaves; women's liberation leaders identified women as slaves of the slaves; and movements during the 1960s, 1970s, and 1980s identified students, women, Catholics in Northern Ireland, and French-speaking Canadians as "niggers."[53]

Social movements try to convince the oppressed and members that they need not remain "victims," "slaves," or "niggers." Persuaders emphasize their proud heritage, significant contributions to society, generosity rather than greed, and accomplishments. They preach "you are somebody" and can win this struggle if you believe in yourself, unite, and remain committed to the struggle. Pride, power, and self-worth are instilled through replacing old labels with new ones to make audiences free to discover themselves as substantial human beings and to question traditional social relationships and coalitions. When black Americans rejected the label "negro" and selected black-American or African-American they redefined themselves and began to take symbolic control of their lives and fate. As Karlyn Campbell writes, blacks chose the term "black" to replace "negro" because (1) it was their word, not one placed on them by whites, (2) it traced them to descendants of abused field hands, not "house negroes," (3) it scared whites; (4) it became a badge of pride and strength, (5) it reminded them of their African heritage, and (6) it allowed them to confront whites as equals.[54] Wayne Brockriede and Robert Scott argue that "black power" was more than a new, catchy slogan for the civil rights movement; it was, as Stokely

Carmichael stated, "a black declaration of independence. It is a turn inward, a rallying cry for a people in the sudden labor of self-discovery, self-naming, and self-legitimation."[55] Native Americans reacted similarly to the label "Indian." Lehman Brightman, a South Dakota Sioux and at the time a doctoral student at the University of California at Berkeley, exclaimed in an interview that "Even the name Indian is not ours. It was given to us by some dumb honky who got lost and thought he'd landed in India."[56] And Gerald Wilkinson, a Cherokee, declared, "We weren't meant to be tourist attractions for the master race."[57]

Social movements hope that self-discovery will result in a new "personal identity" and the realization of "a people."[58] The women's liberation movement used "consciousness-raising" groups to enhance self-concepts and each member's awareness of her oppressed state, self-worth, and potential for being more than someone's mother or wife.[59] Chesebro, Cragan, and McCullough discovered four stages in this consciousness-raising process: (1) self-realization of a new identity, (2) group identity through polarization, (3) establishing new values for the group, and (4) relating to other revolutionary groups."[60] The fledgling "men's liberation movement" seems to be going through a similar process with weekend retreats complete with discussion, self-expression, drum beating, yelling, poetry reading, and studying books such as Sam Keen's *Fire in the Belly: On Being a Man* that argues men cannot be themselves without first separating from the world of women.[61] Self-discovery is an important means of creating "we-they" distinctions and a basis of group identification through a sense of shared fate.[62] "We" the "people" comes to represent all that is good while "they" the "oppressors" represent all that is evil.

Although we have many insights into how social movements attempt to transform perceptions of society, interesting questions remain. Which groups have used consciousness-raising sessions? How do social movements opposing things such as alcoholic beverages, nuclear power plants, and destruction of the environment or mistreatment of animals deal with an ego-function when the primary issue is not them or their self-concepts? Do persuaders devote more attention to self-perceptions during the early stages of a movement and increasingly less as the movement progresses? How does degree of change (reform versus revolutionary) affect consciousness-raising rhetoric? How do confrontations with established orders, resistance movements, and other movement organizations affect persuasion aimed at changing, maintaining, or reinforcing self-concept?

Prescribing Courses of Action

Prescribing courses of action constitutes selling the social movement's ideology, what Simons calls its "product."[63] According to John Wilson, ideology "is the generic name given to those beliefs which mobilize people into action in social movements;" an ideology is "a set of beliefs about the social world and how it operates, containing statements about the rightness of certain social arrangements and what action should be taken in the light of these statements."[64]

This set of beliefs addresses what must be done, who must do it, and how it must be done.

The What

In explaining *what* must be done, a social movement presents its demands and solutions that will alleviate a grave condition, prevent catastrophic changes, or bring on the utopia or millennium.[65] Each movement must explain, defend, and sell its program or product. Dolbeare and Dolbeare write that "each ideology is attached to some values, such as equality or justice, in preference to others. The crucial questions are *the way in which such values are understood or defined* by the ideology, and *how they are ranked in priority* when they conflict with each other."[66] For example, when environmentalists strive to protect wetlands from commercial development or the spotted owl from extinction if forests are cut in the northwest, they place values of preservation over "progress," free enterprise, and perhaps freedom to do with one's property whatever one wants to do. Steve Goldzwig notes that "a value or set of values *denied* helps to determine what *is* valued. Thus, a negative reaction to a rhetorical effort is just as clear a mirror of a culture's values as the approval of an act."[67]

Michael McGee argues that "ideographs" link rhetoric and ideology, "one-term sums of an orientation, the species of 'God' or 'Ultimate' term that will be used to symbolize the line of argument" an "individual *would* pursue."[68] Thus, we should be able to detect a social movement's ideology by identifying key words and phrases in its rhetoric because they are "the basic structural elements, the building blocks, of ideology." Words such as freedom, equality, justice, liberty, progress, private property, free enterprise, free speech, right of privacy, right to vote, and right to life have dominated American social movements and distinguished one from another for more than two centuries.

Problems develop not only when institutions say no to demands and solutions but also when organizations within social movements prescribe diverse and perhaps conflicting demands and solutions. In the civil rights movement, for example, Martin Luther King, Jr. saw integration as the way to achieve freedom and equal rights while Malcolm X advocated black nationalism and black capitalism. In the temperance movement, some desired to limit the use of alcoholic beverages and some would settle for nothing less than banning the sale of all alcoholic beverages. In today's pro-life movement, there are those who would allow abortions under a few circumstances such as saving a woman's life and those who will settle for nothing less than the elimination of all abortions, including birth control methods that prevent conception. Charles Stewart writes that intra-movement conflicts seem inevitable because each organization comes into existence because it claims to have created the *perfect* doctrine and set of principles, and there can be no compromise with perfection.[69]

Changing social situations, trends from liberalism to conservatism and back, efforts by established orders to negate or to co-opt a movement's demands and solutions, and the necessity to address a variety of target audiences require alterations in explanations and content of demands and solutions, and perhaps the addition or deletion of ideographs. As John Wilson writes, "When new sensitivities are created by social events and collectives, ideologies, to be accepted, must cater to these new sensitivities."[70] Efforts to adapt to new sensitivities and events, however, always expose social movement leaders and organizations to charges of revisionism by movement purists, the true believers who will brook no changes in sacred doctrine. Bruce Cameron notes that "Sometimes the zeal for 'purity' produces isolation from the general public, or even schisms within the movement."[71] Leaders face charges of going too fast or too slow, of being too rigid or too flexible. If situations seem no better or worse as time passes and crises occur, "Illusions are often offered as solutions, to *solve* problems by predicting a rapid transition to a better world." "The person, faced with an intolerable situation," Hans Toch observes, "searches for and finds a miracle."[72]

The Who

Social movements must prescribe *who* ought to do the job. Their answer, seemingly without exception, is *the people*, a *great grassroots* movement for change or resistance to change. All serious social movement enthusiasts understand, however, that the movement needs organization and leaders of some sort.[73] First, they must convince enough people that only an *uninstitutionalized collectivity* is both willing and able to bring about or resist change; all others are part or cause of the problem. Struggles develop within social movements over how far the movement must distance itself from established institutions. Some elements within the women's liberation movement, for instance, wanted to use the system (congress, courts, state legislators) to achieve changes while others argued the only way women could achieve their true identities and power was to break all ties with men, male-dominated organizations of all types, and male tactics.[74]

Second, social movements must espouse specific types of organization and leadership or specific organizations and leaders best suited to solving urgent problems. This leads inevitably to a striving for perfection that splinters the movement into competing factions and organizations. Fred Powledge, in his book entitled *Free at Last? The Civil Rights Movement and the People Who Made It*, provides extensive documentation of the competition, jealousy, and hostility among the leaders and organizations of the civil rights movement—the National Association for the Advancement of Colored People (NAACP), the Southern Christian Leadership Conference (SCLC), the Student Nonviolent Coordinating Committee (SNCC), and the Congress of Racial Equality (CORE)—that often hampered campaigns and movement progress.[75] One movement faction may declare open warfare against another faction it deems ideologically deviant or inferior in organizational structure and strategies. For instance, in the early labor movement, the American Federation of Labor and the competing Knights of Labor each claimed to be the perfect labor organization based on a perfect set of principles that made it the historical, natural, and moral leader of the movement and cited the other as an unnatural, unscientific, immoral, and obsolete failure that should either be abandoned or absorbed into the one true union.[76] The struggle ended when the Knights ceased to exist. Thus, a rhetoric of polarization may create "we-they" distinctions within a social movement as sharp as those between a social movement and an established order.

And third, social movements may establish membership limitations to create elites capable of dealing with "unsolvable" conditions and the omnipotent forces that produced them. The Ku Klux Klan restricted membership to white, anglo-saxon Protestants; some African-American groups restricted membership to African Americans; some women's groups restricted membership to females; some student rights groups restricted membership to people under thirty; and the American Federation of Labor restricted membership to workers from skilled trades, excluding unskilled laborers and factory workers. Chapter 6 reveals how the John Birch Society used an authoritarian rhetoric that effectively limited its membership to an elite deemed capable of defeating the communist conspiracy in the United States. While some movements limit membership to those who can truly understand the plight of the victims, others do so because they see the excluded as the enemy. The Manifesto for New York Radical Feminists reveals the excluded men as the devils:

> As radical feminists we recognize that we are engaged in a power struggle with men, and that the agent for our oppression is man insofar as he identifies with and carries out the supremacy privileges of the male role. For while we realize that the liberation of women will ultimately mean the liberation of men from their destructive role as oppressor, we have no illusion that men will welcome this liberation without a struggle.[77]

Other social movements (such as pro-life, pro-choice, and the environmental movement) freely admit anyone who will espouse their cause, believing that success can only come from a mass movement able to pressure and scare institutions into change or resistance to change.

The How

Social movements must propose and defend *how* the job must be done. Which strategies, tactics, and communication channels are most appropriate and effective for their causes?[78] A revolutionary, innovative movement organization may have a wide range of tactical choices (boycotts, strikes, symbolic takeovers) because that is what a revolutionary group is expected to do. The range of permissible channels, however, will be narrow, because the group is considered too radical for commercial radio or cable television. A reform-oriented revivalistic organization may have access to many channels (including radio and/or television talk shows and features in news magazines) but a narrow range of moderate, socially acceptable tactics because it does not want to offend its many target audiences. No social movement can rely upon the same means of change for long. Movement followers, the general public, and the mass media become bored with them, and institutions learn how to deal with specific strategies and tactics rather quickly. Saul Alinsky, in his book *Rules for Radicals*, advises would-be social movement persuaders, "*Wherever possible go outside of the experience of the enemy*. Here you want to cause confusion, fear, and retreat."[79] He also advises, "*A tactic that drags on too long becomes a drag*. Man [woman] can sustain militant interest in any issue for only a limited time, after which it becomes a ritualistic commitment like going to church on Sunday mornings."[80] Social movements must search continually for new and different tactics and channels to keep the movement fresh, alive, and moving forward.

Social movements often splinter into factions over differing views on how the job must be done, and some movement members may be more committed to means than to ends. Nearly all movements have "radical" and "moderate" factions, and the differences are often more pronounced in tactics than in ideologies. Roxanne Dunbar, an early women's liberation leader and eventually a staff member of the Southern Female Rights Union, remarked in an interview that her original group, Cell 16, had seriously considered assassinating a man to make their presence known. However, they decided the victim "would become such an important person because we'd chosen him over all these other guys."[81] She remarked that this plan and one in which they would "get shotguns and go to the Boston Common to deal with the men who ogle the secretaries" seemed to "horrify" moderate members. The environmental movement has moderate elements such as the Sierra Club that believe in working through the system and radical groups such as Dave Foreman's Earth First! (eco-guerrillas) that sabotage machinery, equipment, and power lines when they are not conducting blockades and chaining themselves to cranes and trees. Organizations and leaders of the civil rights movement disagreed strongly over tactics. The NAACP advocated working through the courts rather than conducting marches, demonstrations, and sit-ins. The SCLC under Martin Luther King, Jr. advocated any means of non-violent civil disobedience that might further the cause. Malcolm X advocated "black nationalism" and "action." In the "Ballot or the Bullet" speech in Detroit, he attacked the sit-in tactics of SNCC and SCLC:

> As long as you have a sit-down philosophy, you'll have a sit-down thought pattern. And as long as you think that old sit-down thought, you'll be in some kind of sit-down action. They'll have you sittin' in everywhere. It's not so good to refer to what you're going to do as a sit-in. That right there castrates you. Right there it brings you down. . . . Think of the image of someone sitting. An old woman can sit; an old man can sit; a chump can sit; a coward can sit.[82]

Social movements must continually search for new tactics and strategies to keep the movement alive and progressing, but each new selection can lead to conflicts within and between organizations.

Much has been written about the nature of ideology but little about how social movement persuaders try to sell its ingredients (what, who, and how) or about the alteration of these ingredients to an audience of friend, "neutral," or foe. How do social movement ideologies define or obscure, stabilize or upset, strengthen or weaken, relieve or exacerbate situations? How do ideologies rationalize group interests, beliefs, and methods? How do ideologies enhance consciousness-raising? How can ideologies combat routinization and creeping bureaucratization of social movements? How are ideologies stated, developed, and adjusted to attract new members, to sustain members, to forge coalitions, and to appease opposition from inside and outside to meet changing problems and requirements?

Mobilizing for Action

It is not sufficient for a social movement to transform perceptions of reality and society and to prescribe a course of action. Persuaders must also convince large numbers of people to join in the cause, to organize into effective groups, and to unify through coalitions to carry the movement's message to target audiences while confronting institutions and resistance forces. Smith and Windes contend that "The presence of mobilizational exigencies distinguishes, and assists in defining, the rhetorical situation of movements. The rhetorical situation of a movement requires discourse to organize support for united action to reach a shared goal of social change."[83]

Organizing and Uniting the Discontented

Social movements expend great amounts of persuasive effort trying to educate audiences about the "cause" and convincing them of the urgency to *join together* to bring about or to resist change. Mailings, newsletters, newspapers, pamphlets, leaflets, books, videos, interpersonal contacts, and speeches are only a few channels devoted to organizing and uniting the discontented. Audiences are urged not to sit on the sidelines while disaster strikes but to "stand up and be counted." Fund raising appeals, with easy to fill out coupons, are integral parts of most printed persuasive efforts because social movements have few other means to finance full-time leaders, organizational headquarters, publications, phone banks, demonstrations, lobbies in congress and state legislatures, challenges in courts, and mailings.

Getting Americans to join and unite in uninstitutional organizations is no easy task. Traditions of "rugged individualism," belief in the capacity and determination of American institutions to deal with problems effectively once they are identified, and suspicion of "movements" and "agitators" prevent most Americans from protesting—let alone joining and becoming active in "strange" organizations. Social movements must persuade significant numbers of people that only collective action by uninstitutionalized groups using nonconventional (sometimes unlawful) methods can bring about or resist change. They must create a "collective identity" so individuals come to identify themselves as a group through "shared views of the social environment, shared goals, and shared opinions about the possibilities and limits of collective action."[84] Even the largest and most successful social movements, however, manage to organize only a fraction of the "victims" and socially conscious citizens. Very few women, African-Americans, gays, workers, and supporters of the environment ever contribute to or join their respective movements. As we have seen, once people join a social movement, they may splinter into numerous organizations because of differences over tactics, ideology, leaders, personalities, organizational structures, and real or imagined grievances. An established order may aid this splintering by seeming to favor one organization or leader over another—playing the game of divide and conquer.

Pressuring the Opposition

Although all social movements are to a greater or lesser degree self-change oriented (believing that followers must purify themselves before they can change others), they all engage the opposition in symbolic combat. The weapons may be verbal such as mass mailings, name-calling, ridicule, obscenity, and threats or nonverbal such as mass demonstrations, sit-ins, walk-outs, boycotts, strikes, and disruptions. They may attempt to gain control of agencies of influence such as the courts, executive offices, and boards of trustees by voting officials in or out of office, purchasing or creating mass media, or gaining control of corporations through stock proxies.[85] Malcolm X urged audiences to use the ballot effectively to take control of their neighborhoods and lives; the bullet was to be the last resort and only in self-defense. The aim of movements may also be to pressure the opposition to gain recognition, concessions, compromises, or capitulations. A first step may be to make an established order admit there is a serious problem.

Social movements must be aware that tactics designed to pressure the opposition may have adverse effects on other persuasive functions. When native Americans, for instance, put on warpaint and acquired weapons to take over Wounded Knee, South Dakota and Alcatraz Island in San Francisco Bay and held off federal marshalls for weeks, they succeeded in pressuring the establishment and gaining national attention. They also, unfortunately, reinforced the stereotype of the painted savage portrayed by Hollywood—the very image they had been trying to erase.[86] Social movements should confine persuasive efforts to symbols and symbolic actions that are either lawful or protected by the Constitution. As Bowers, Ochs, and Jensen write, violent acts void of symbolism, or that appear to be so, are likely to cost the movement the support of sympathizers and legitimizers and invite outright suppression under the rubrics of law and order, public safety, and national security.[87] Violent acts by movement members (or persons associated with the movement in the public's or institution's eyes) may negate much that has been gained through years of persuasive efforts. For example, radical elements of the pro-life movement who have bombed, burned, and fired bullets into abortion clinics have pressured the opposition but have also compromised their claims of being truly pro-life and frightened away many would-be supporters.

Gaining Sympathy and Support of Legitimizers

Social movement "membership" has a range of commitment and support for the movement and its cause. John Wilson illustrates this commitment as the rings of an onion.[88] At the center are a small number of full-time, paid professionals who are totally committed to the cause and willing to sacrifice anything for it. The first ring around this center consists of full-time, non-paid professionals who can be counted on to populate the front lines in marches and demonstrations and remain committed when the movement is under attack and seems to be going nowhere. The second ring consists of the rank and file where total commitment is rare because the movement is only a small portion of their lives. And the third ring consists of sympathizers who are neither fully inside nor fully outside the movement, and an important part of this membership are "legitimizers."

Legitimizers are social opinion leaders such as judges, politicians, business executives, clergy, sports figures, and entertainers who can help legitimize a movement in the eyes of the public by appearing at rallies, marching in demonstrations, speaking in favor of the cause, donating money, and so on.[89] The environmental, women's liberation, gay-rights, pro-choice, pro-life, and other contemporary movements have capitalized upon support by actors such as Robert Redford and Alan Alda, actresses such as Jane Fonda, Joanne Woodward, and Barbara Streisand, singers such as John Denver and Michael Jackson, Vice Presidents Dan Quayle and Albert Gore, Senators such as Ted Kennedy and Orin Hatch, and clergy such as Jerry Falwell and Jesse Jackson. Some legitimizers can offer more than their names, presence, and money. For example, pro-life sympathizers Ronald Reagan and George Bush supported the movement not only by speaking in its favor and advocating legal and constitutional changes but by outlawing abortion counseling at federally funded clinics, research on fetal tissue, abortions at military hospitals, funding for international population control programs, and the import of the French abortion pill RU-486. Pro-choice sympathizer Bill Clinton overturned the first three actions of the former presidents within two days of his inauguration and announced reconsideration of the fourth. Movements often attempt to provoke institutions or other movements into excessive or repressive acts that reveal the ugliness of the opposition and gain sympathy and legitimizers for the "victims" and their demands. During the day of President Clinton's actions, 75,000 pro-lifers marched in Washington; in the days that followed, thousands of Operation Rescue members were arrested as they blockaded abortion clinics around the country.

A social movement's ability to mobilize forces into action may be hindered by its relationship to established institutions. It may be partially equal to (equal on some grounds and not on others), dependent upon (for communication channels, legitimacy, legal protection, permits to demonstrate), or subjugated (completely dominated and controlled) by the establishment. We know little about how social movements adapt persuasive efforts to various and changing relationships. How, for instance, do pro-life forces adapt to a hostile presidential administration under Clinton after years of friendly administrations under Reagan and Bush? Social movements must attract and employ the mass media, but they have little control over what the media report or how the media report confrontations, speeches, and symbolic acts. We need to learn how social movements employ the media and how the media report social movements. Most movements produce their own newspapers and magazines, but we know little about how these self-produced publications are designed to mobilize members while fulfilling other persuasive functions.

Sustaining the Social Movement

Since social movements usually last for years and experience changing social circumstances, they must use persuasion to sustain their crusades.

Justifying Setbacks and Delays

Every movement attempts to establish we-they distinctions, to instill strong convictions about accomplishing goals, and to preach or imply that its ends justify any means necessary to bring about or to resist change. Inevitably, these convictions, distinctions, and ends lead to impatience with "moderate" leadership, strategies, and slow progress toward goals and to suggestions that "radical" actions are necessary. Malcolm X exclaimed that speeches, sit-ins, singing "We Shall Overcome," the 1963 march on Washington, and integration had failed to bring about real change. It was time for the ballot or the bullet, a time to "stop singing and start swinging."[90] Leaders must use persuasion to maintain order and discipline and to respond to actions that embarrass the movement and threaten its support among sympathizers and legitimizers. They must offer believable and acceptable explanations for apparent setbacks and delays or for few meaningful gains or victories, to explain why agreements with established orders have not been implemented or effective, and to justify why target dates have come and gone without results. The many audiences social movements address may perceive progress, victories, agreements, and priority of goals quite differently. Internal and external opposition may capitalize on delays and setbacks to undermine leadership and organizations, to proclaim superiority over a movement or competing organization.

Whatever its goals, a social movement needs years of untiring efforts from significant numbers of people to gain or to prevent change. It must convince followers that victory is near, or at least inevitable, if all is done correctly, if they remain steadfast in their commitment, if they remain true to sacred principles, and if unity is sustained. Leaders must create and sustain what Eric Hoffer calls an "extravagant hope."[91]

Maintaining Viability of the Movement

Social movements wage continual battles to remain viable. More rhetorical energy may be expended on fund raising, membership drives, acquisition of materials and property, and maintenance of movement communication media than on selling ideologies to target audiences and pressuring the opposition. Reinforcing commitment of members and satisfying membership gratifications limit a movement's ability to perform other functions. Annual meetings may be devoted more to internal squabbles, ferreting out traitors and internal conspiracies, and defending movement administrations than to planning offensive campaigns and attacking external foes.[92] Ironically, a social movement may become too successful or too successful too soon. When African Americans, women, and gays achieved some rights and when environmentalists and animal rights advocates helped to forge some laws, each movement lost both membership and "steam" because the need seemed less urgent. Growth in membership and geographical sphere of influence and creeping institutionalization may seriously reduce the informality of structure and feeling of crisis that initially attracted people to the movement.[93] Thus, a serious decline in membership and commitment may occur when success seems near. To counteract declines in membership and commitment, some movements turn to memories (past campaigns, victories, heroes, martyrs) to keep the struggle alive, while others strive to create new heroes to breathe new life into the aging cause. New, more vibrant organizations may arise to challenge or to replace older, "established" ones. Leaflets, mailings, speeches, and songs often contain personal statements of commitment, sometimes commitment like the persuader's parents had to the movement. Audiences are continually assured, even when an organization or movement is in rapid freefall, that it is growing stronger every day and victory is near or inevitable if unity is sustained.

Maintaining Visibility of the Movement

Social movements must remain visible and are haunted by the old adage, "out of sight, out of mind." Social movement members, the media, and target audiences have insatiable appetites for persuasive happenings, but few movements have adequate leadership, membership, energy, and funds to satisfy these appetites over long periods while fending off the opposition. They try to remain visible through every means imaginable: billboards, bumperstickers, stickerettes, buttons, tee-shirts, jewelry, uniforms and items of clothing, famous women paper dolls, playing cards, Christmas cards, dial-a-message, and coloring books. They resort to rhetorical events and "happenings" such as ceremonies, annual conventions, and anniversary or birthday celebrations to remain visible and to keep the agitational fire going. They may select new symbols; they may create one or more official newspapers or journals to communicate directly with members, because commercial media seem to ignore the movement or treat it "unfairly." Old events, actions, and things receive less and less attention and produce serious drains on movement resources.

We know little about how social movements use persuasion to sustain the zeal created during the early days of the movement when it was highly personal, visible, and active. How do they deal with overconfidence and inflated expectations? How do they recruit new members as the movement ages? How do they use martyrs and heroes, saints and devils, victories and tragedies to sustain the cause? How are persuasive efforts during ceremonies, conventions, and celebrations similar to and different from those in the streets and before mixed or hostile audiences? We need to know more about the internal persuasion of social movements.

Conclusions

Social movements must perform a number of critical persuasive functions if they are to come into existence, grow in size and influence, and effectively bring about or resist change. They must transform perceptions of reality, transform perceptions of society, prescribe courses of action, mobilize the discontented, and sustain the movement until victory is achieved. Unfortunately for social movements, their uninstitutional nature greatly limits their powers, options, and legitimacy and, therefore, their abilities to perform these persuasive functions on a continual basis over long periods.

Endnotes

1 This definition was developed from a discussion of the meaning of the term "function" in Robert K. Merton, *Social Theory and Social Structure*, 2nd ed. (Glencoe, IL: Free Press, 1957), 19–25.

2 Richard B. Gregg, "The Ego-Function of the Rhetoric of Protest," *Philosophy and Rhetoric* 4 (Spring 1971), 71–91; Dale G. Leathers, "The Rhetorical Strategy of the New Right Movement," unpublished paper presented at the annual convention of the Speech Communication Association, 1972.

3 Michael C. McGee, "In Search of the 'People': A Rhetorical Alternative," *Quarterly Journal of Speech* 61 (October 1975), 248.

4 Herbert W. Simons, "Requirements, Problems, and Strategies: A Theory of Persuasion for Social Movements," *Quarterly Journal of Speech* 56 (February 1970), 1–11; Herbert W. Simons, Elizabeth W. Mechling, and Howard N. Schreier, "The Functions of Human Communication in Mobilizing for Action from the Bottom Up: The Rhetoric of Social Movements," *Handbook of Rhetorical and Communication Theory*, Carroll C. Arnold and John W. Bowers, eds. (Boston: Allyn and Bacon, 1984) 807–808.

5 Bruce E. Gronbeck, "The Rhetoric of Social-Institutional Change: Black Action at Michigan," *Explorations in Rhetorical Criticism*, Gerald Mohrmann, Charles Stewart, and Donovan Ochs, eds. (University Park, PA: Pennsylvania State University Press, 1973), 96–113.

6 Charles J. Stewart, "A Functional Approach to the Rhetoric of Social Movements," *Central States Speech Journal* 31 (Winter 1980), 298–305; Charles J. Stewart, "A Functional Perspective on the Study of Social Movements," *Central States Speech Journal* 34 (Spring 1983), 77–80.

7 Michael Lipsky, "Protest as a Political Resource," *The American Political Science Review* 52 (1968), 1144–1148; James Q. Wilson, "The Strategy of Protest: Problems of Negro Civic Action," *Journal of Conflict Resolution* 3 (1961), 291–303.

8 William A. Gamson, "The Social Psychology of Collective Action," *Frontiers in Social Movement*

Theory, Aldon D. Morris and Carol McCLurg Mueller, eds. (New Haven, CT: Yale University Press, 1992), 71.

9 Wil A. Linkugel, R. R. Allen, and Richard L. Johannesen, *Contemporary American Speeches*, 5th ed. (Dubuque, IA: Kendall/Hunt, 1982), 208; Richard L. Johannesen, "The Jeremiad and Jenkin Lloyd Jones," *Communication Monographs* 52 (June 1985), 164.

10 See Ernest G. Bormann, "Fantasy and Rhetorical Vision: The Rhetorical Criticism of Social Reality," *Quarterly Journal of Speech* 58 (December 1972), 396–407; Richard B. Gregg, "A Phenomenologically Oriented Approach to Rhetorical Criticism," *Central States Speech Journal* 17 (May 1966), 83–90.

11 Haig A. Bosmajian, "Defining the 'American Indian': A Case Study in the Language of Oppression," *Speech Teacher* 22 (March 1973), 89–99.

12 *Historical Fact No. 1. Did Six Million Really Die? The Truth at Last* (Chapel Ascote, Ladbroke, Southam, Warks: Historical Review Press, n.d.); Austin J. App, *Holocaust: Sneak Attack on Christianity* (Chicago: National Socialist White People's Party, n.d.).

13 *The Big Lie: Who Really Told It?* (Arlington, VA: National Socialist White People's Party, n.d.).

14 "The Angry American Indian: Starting Down the Protest Trail," *Time*, February 9, 1970, 14–20.

15 From tapes of radio addresses by Billy James Hargis on March 11 and 12, 1963 and others that are undated.

16 *Do You Want to Return to the Butchery of Back-Alley Abortion?* (New York: NARAL, n.d.); *Abortion Fact Sheet* (New York: NARAL, nd.d); *Twelve Abortion Facts* (Washington, D.C.: NARAL, n.d.).

17 Philip C. Wander, "The Savage Child: The Image of the Negro in the Pro-Slavery Movement," *Southern Speech Communication Journal* 37 (Summer 1972), 335–360.

18 Marie J. Rosenwasser, "Rhetoric and the Progress of the Women's Liberation Movement," *Today's Speech* 20 (Summer 1972), 45–56; Karlyn Kohrs Campbell, "The Rhetoric of Women's Liberation: An Oxymoron," *Quarterly Journal of Speech* 59 (February 1973), 74–86.

19 "Local Anti-Gay Seminar to Continue: Varied Viewpoints Clash Over Issue," *The Purdue Exponent* 1 December 1992, 1; "Gays Under Fire," *Newsweek*, September 14, 1992, 35–40.

20 Detine L. Bowers, *A Strange Speech of an Estranged People: Theory and Practice of Antebellum African-American Freedom Day Orations*, unpublished doctoral dissertation, Purdue University, 1992.

21 *Say No to Torture* (Washington, D.C.: Animal Welfare Institute, n.d.).

22 See for example, Aborted Baby Discarded in Hospital Bucket (n.p., n.d.); *This Life Is in Your Hands* (Houston, TX: Houston Right to Life, n.d.); California Doctor on Trial," *The Communicator*, April 1978, 3–4.

23 *Life or Death* (Cincinnati: Hayes Publishing Company, n.d.); *The U.S. Supreme Court Has Ruled It's Legal to Kill a Baby* (Cincinnati: Hayes Publishing Company, n.d.).

24 W. A. D. Riach, "'Telling It Like It Is': An Examination of Black Theatre as Rhetoric," *Quarterly Journal of Speech* 56 (April 1970), 179–186; Kathryn Martin, "The Relation of Theatre of Revolution and Theology of Revolution to the Black Experience," *Today's Speech* 19 (Spring 1971), 35–41; Sam Smiley, "Peace on Earth: Four Anti-War Dramas of the Thirties," *Central States Speech Journal* 21 (Spring 1970), 30–39; George Shafer, "The Dramaturgy of Fact: The Treatment of History in Two Anti-War Plays," *Central States Speech Journal* 29 (Spring 1978), 25–35.

25 Gary C. Woodward, "Mystifications in the Rhetoric of Cultural Dominance and Colonial Control," *Central States Speech Journal* 26 (Winter 1975), 301.

26 *Say No to Torture*.

27 Mary Brigid Gallagher, "John L. Lewis: The Oratory of Pity and Indignation," *Today's Speech* 9 (September 1961), 15–16.

28 *The Purdue Exponent* 31 March 1992, 7.

29 Hans Toch, *The Social Psycology of Social Movements* (New York: Bobbs-Merrill, 1965), 11.

30 Eugene V. Debs, "The Issue," *Debs: His Life, Writings and Speeches* (Chicago: Charles H. Kerr, 1908), 489.

[31] Robert Welch, *The Blue Book of the John Birch Society* (Boston: Western Islands Publishers, 1961), 1.

[32] Randall A. Lake, "Order and Disorder in Anti-Abortion Rhetoric: A Logological View," *Quarterly Journal of Speech* 70 (November 1984), 425–443.

[33] See for example *Greenpeace* 14 (January-February 1989).

[34] Seminar sponsored by local churches, Christian bookstores, and Lafayette Citizens for Decency, December 1, 1992.

[35] *Seabook Alert*, 1981; *Seabrook Clamshell* letter, May 1986; *Seabrook Clamshell* letter, August 1986.

[36] E.J. Hobsbaum, *Primitive Rebels* (New York: Praeger, 1963); Melvin J. Lasky, *Utopia and Revolution* (Chicago: University of Chicago Press, 1976).

[37] Martha Solomon, "The Rhetoric of STOP ERA: Fatalistic Reaffirmation," *Southern Speech Communication Journal* 44 (Fall 1978), 42–59; Philip C. Wander, "The John Birch and Martin Luther King Symbols in the Radical Right," *Western Speech* 35 (Winter 1971), 4–14.

[38] Karlyn Kohrs Campbell, "The Rhetoric of Women's Liberation: An Oxymoron," *Quarterly Journal of Speech* 59 (February 1973), 74–86.

[39] James Darsey, "From 'Gay Is Good' to the Scourge of AIDS: The Evolution of Gay Liberation Rhetoric, 1977–1990," *Communication Studies* 42 (Spring 1991), 43–66.

[40] Parke G. Burgess, "The Rhetoric of Black Power: A Moral Demand?" *Quarterly Journal of Speech* 54 (April 1968), 122–133; Robert L. Heath, "Dialectical Confrontation: A Strategy of Black Radicalism," *Central States Speech Journal* 24 (Fall 1973), 168–177.

[41] John W. Bowers, Donovan J. Ochs, and Richard J. Jensen, *The Rhetoric of Agitation and Control*, 2/E (Prospect Heights, IL: Waveland Press, 1993), 34–36.

[42] Bert Klandermans, "The Social Construction of Protest and Multiorganizational Fields," *Frontiers in Social Movement Theory*, 97.

[43] Eric Hoffer, *The True Believer* (New York: Mentor, 1951), 87.

[44] Robert L. Scott and Donald K. Smith, "The Rhetoric of Confrontation," *Quarterly Journal of Speech* 55 (February 1969), 7–8.

[45] G. Thomas Goodnight and John Poulakos, "Conspiracy Rhetoric: From Pragmatism to Fantasy in Public Discourse," *Western Journal of Speech Communication* 45 (Fall 1981), 299–316.

[46] Justin D. Fultin, *Lincoln's Assassination* (Minneapolis: Osterhus Publishing House, n.d.); Phyllis Schlafly, "Secular Humanism a Real Threat to USA," *USA Today*, April 7, 1986, 8A. "Bernard K. Duffy, "The Anti-Humanist Rhetoric of the New Religious Right," *The Southern Speech Communication Journal* 49 (Summer 1984), 339–360; Howard S. Erlich, "Populist Rhetoric Reassessed: A Paradox," *Quarterly Journal of Speech* 63 (April 1977), 140–151; Leslie G. Rude, "The Rhetoric of Farmer Labor Agitators," *Central States Speech Journal* 20 (Winter 1969), 280–285.

[47] Dale G. Leathers, "Belief-Disbelief Systems: The Communicative Vacuum of the Radical Right," *Explorations in Rhetorical Criticism*, Gerald Mohrmann, Charles Stewart, and Donovan Ochs, eds. (University Park, PA: Pennsylvania State University Press, 1973), 132–133; "Q and A: John Birch Society," Lafayette, Indiana *Journal and Courier*, January 9, 1977, A-11; "Communism's Decline Hasn't Deterred Birch Society," Lafayette, Indiana *Journal and Courier*, October 23, 1991, C-4.

[48] Leathers, 132.

[49] Gregg, 74.

[50] Charles J. Stewart, "The Ego Function of Protest Songs: An Application of Gregg's Theory of Protest Rhetoric," *Communication Studies* 42 (Fall 1991), 240–253.

[51] Gregg, 79.

[52] Stewart (1991), 243–244.

[53] See for example, Jerry Farber, *The Student as Nigger* (North Hollywood: Contact Books, 1969).

[54] Campbell (1971), 156.

[55] Brockriede and Scott, 6.

[56] "The Angry American Indian," 14.

[57] "The Angry American Indian," 14.

58 McGee, 235–249; Campbell (1973), 74–86; Brockriede and Scott, 3–13.

59 Campbell (1973), 74–86; Karlyn Kohrs Campbell, "Feminity and Femism: To Be or Not to Be a Woman," *Communication Quarterly* 31 (Spring 1983), 105.

60 James W. Chesebro, John F. Cragan, and Patricia McCullough, "The Small Group Technique of the Radical Revolutionary: A Synthetic Study of Consciousness Raising," *Speech Monographs* 40 (June 1973), 136–146.

61 "Drums, Sweat, and Tears," *Newsweek*, June 24, 1991, 46–51.

62 Aaron Gresson, III, "Phenomenology and the Rhetoric of Identification—A Neglected Dimension of Coalition Communication Inquiry," *Communication Quarterly* 26 (Fall 1978), 14–23.

63 Simons (1970), 3.

64 John Wilson, *Introduction to Social Movements* (New York: Basic Books, 1973), 91.

65 Wilson, 89–134; Barbara A. Larson, "Samuel E. Davies and the Rhetoric of the New Light," *Speech Monographs* 38 (August 1971), 207–216; Richard J. Ilkka, "Rhetorical Dramatization in the Development of American Communism," *Quarterly Journal of Speech* 63 (December 1977), 413–417.

66 Kenneth M. Dolbeare and Patricia M. Dolbeare, *American Ideologies: The Competing Political Beliefs of the 1970s* (Prospect Heights, IL: Waveland Press, 1971), 3, as cited in Steve Goldzwig, "James Watt's Subversion of Values: An Analysis of Rhetorical Failure," *The Southern Speech Communication Journal* 50 (Summer 1985), 307.

67 Goldzwig, 323.

68 Michael C. McGee, "The 'Ideograph': A Link between Rhetoric and Ideology," *Quarterly Journal of Speech* 66 (February 1980), 7.

69 Charles J. Stewart, "The Knights of Labor vs. the American Federation of Labor: A Rhetoric Rotten with Perfection," unpublished paper presented at annual convention of the Speech Communication Association, 1992.

70 Wilson, 91–97.

71 William B. Cameron, *Modern Social Movements: A Sociological Outline* (New York: Random House, 1966), 15.

72 Toch, 30.

73 Kathleen J. Turner, "Ego Defense and Mass Media: Conflicting Rhetorical Needs of a Contemporary Social Movement," *Central States Speech Journal* 31 (Summer 1980), 106–116; Rosenwasser, 45–56.

74 Campbell (1973), 74–86; Brenda Robinson Hancock, "Affirmation by Negation in the Women's Liberation Movement," *Quarterly Journal of Speech* 58 (October 1972), 264–271.

75 Fred Powledge, *Free at Last? The Civil Rights Movement and the People Who Made It* (Boston, Little, Brown and Company, 1991).

76 Stewart (1992); Samuel Gompers, "Address to the Machinist Convention," *American Federationist* 8 (1901), 251.

77 "Manifesto of the New York Radical Feminists," unpublished paper, n.d.

78 Leland M. Griffin, "The Rhetorical Structure of the 'New Left' Movement: Part I," *Quarterly Journal of Speech* 50 (April 1964), 114–127; Malcolm O. Sillars, "The Rhetoric of Petition in Boots," *Speech Monographs* 39 (June 1972), 92–104.

79 Saul D. Alinsky, *Rules for Radicals: A Pragmatic Primer for Realistic Radicals* (New York: Vinyage Books, 1972), 127.

80 Alinsky, 128.

81 Roxanne Dunbar, "Women's Liberation: Where the Movement Is Today and Where It's Going," *Handbook of Women's Liberation*, Joan Robbins, ed. (Los Angeles: NOW Library Press, 1970) as reprinted in Charles J. Stewart, *On Speech Communication* (New York: Holt, Rinehart and Winston, 1972), 312–313.

82 Malcolm X, "The Ballot Or the Bullet," Detroit 1964, from an audio recording.

83 Ralph R. Smith and Russel R. Windes, "The Rhetoric of Mobilization: Implications for the Study of Movements," *The Southern Speech Communication Journal* 42 (Fall 1976), 1.

84 Klandermans, 81; Verta Taylor and Nancy Whittier, "Collective Identity in Social Movement

Communities,'' *Frontiers in Social Movement Theory*, 105.

85 Alinsky, 165–183.

86 Joyce Frost, ''A Rhetorical Analysis of Wounded Knee II, 1973: A Conflict Perspective,'' unpublished paper presented at the annual convention of the Central States Speech Association, 1974; Randall A. Lake, ''Enacting Red Power: The Consummatory Function in Native American Protest Rhetoric,'' *Quarterly Journal of Speech* 69 (May 1983), 127–142.

87 John W. Bowers, Donovan J. Ochs, and Richard Jensen, *The Rhetoric of Agitation and Control*, 2/E (Prospect Heights, IL: Waveland Press, 1993), 77–78.

88 Wilson, 306.

89 Bowers, Ochs, and Jensen, 22–23.

90 Malcolm X.

91 Hoffer, 18.

92 Stewart (1991); Charles J. Stewart, ''Labor Agitation in America: 1865–1915,'' *American in Controversy: History of American Public Address*, DeWitte Holland, Charles Stewart, and Jess Yoder, eds. (Dubuque, IA: W.C. Brown, 1973), 159–167.

93 Mayer N. Zald and Roberta Ash, ''Social Movement Organizations: Growth, Decay, and Change,'' *Social Forces* 44 (1966), 327–341.

Chapter Four

The Life Cycle of Social Movements

To study a social movement is to study an intricate and ever-changing social drama.[1] Like dramas, social movements involve multiple scenes, acts, agents, agencies, and purposes. Sometimes they are satirical comedies; sometimes they are tragicomedies; and sometimes they are dark tragedies. There are heros and heroines, victims and villains, successes and failures, hope and disillusionment. Always present are movement and change.

William Cameron writes that each "social movement is determined by so many variables that its success or failure, the speed of its growth or decline, the consistency or inconsistency of its operations will not fit any *a priori* formula."[2] Social movements such as women's rights and protection of the environment and social movement organizations such as the Ku Klux Klan and evangelical religious groups disappear and then reappear with altered purposes, ideologies, leaders, structures, and persuasive strategies. Any effort to prescribe a life cycle suitable to all social movements, then, is fraught with dangers. The effort can be productive, however, if the life cycle is constructed with the full realization that social movements differ, change, develop to varying degrees of sophistication, and proceed at varying speeds—rushing forward at times, stalling for long periods at particular stages, retrenching to earlier stages, dying premature deaths before completing all stages, or reappearing after years of absence.[3] Rarely, if ever, do social movements follow a neat, linear pattern.

Various attempts to detect cycles and phases of human interactions are helping us to understand complex communicative events, collectives, and exchanges. A study by Donald Ellis and Aubrey Fisher, for example, reveals three phases of conflict in small group development: interpersonal conflict, confrontation, and substantive conflict.[4] Julia Wood has focused on human relationships and "how communication functions at each stage to contribute to the building or dissolution of a relational culture."[5] Among the stages or states Wood presents are invitational communication, explorational communication, intensifying communication, revising communication, bonding communication, and navigating communication. Mark Knapp has developed a model of interaction stages within relationships.[6] The process of *coming together*, according to Knapp, includes the stages of initiating, experimenting, intensifying, integrating, and bonding; the stage of *coming apart* includes differentiating, circumscribing, stagnating, avoiding, and terminating. Richard Crable and Steven Vibbert theorize that issues pass through five status levels in their life cycles: potential status, imminent status, current status, critical status, and dormant status.[7]

Like the models or phases of relationships, conflict within small groups, and development levels of issues, a portrayal of each stage in the life cycle of "typical" social movements can help us understand the ever-changing persuasive requirements, problems, and functions of social movements and the interaction of social-psychological, political-institutional, philosophical-ideological, and rhetorical forces.[8] The life cycle outlined in this chapter consists of five stages: genesis, social unrest, enthusiastic mobilization, maintenance, and termination.[9]

Stage 1: Genesis

A social movement usually begins during relatively quiet times, quiet at least with respect to the issue that the new movement will address. The "people" and established institutions are unaware of the problem or perceive it as insignificant or of low priority.[10] Other concerns dominate the attention of the people, their leaders and institutions, and the mass media. Individuals, often scattered geographically and unknown to one another at first, perceive an "imperfection" in the existing order.[11] The imperfection may be institutional or individual corruption, abuse of power, inequality (in rights, status, power, income, opportunities, possessions, recognition), an identity crisis, unfilled "legitimate" expectations (all expectations *perceived* to be legitimate), or a threat to the social order, values, or environment. Restless individuals view the imperfection as a serious problem that is likely to grow more severe unless appropriate institutions address it quickly and in earnest.

A social movement's early leaders—sometimes called intellectuals or prophets—strive for salvation, perfection, or the good in society. Although they "see through" an institution or state of affairs and strive to expose the institution's leaders or the status quo, they meet little opposition in the genesis stage because few people take them seriously. As prophets and intellectuals they produce essays, editorials, songs, poems, pamphlets, books, and lectures designed to transform perceptions of reality (past, present, and future) and society (self and others). They define and they visualize. As mentioned in chapter 3, various movements focus on different aspects of our perceptions. Revivalistic movements address a venerable, idealized past in which everything and everyone was pure and in harmony and to which society must return to avoid catastrophe. Innovative movements address an intolerable present with all its evils, dangers, and corruptions and prescribe a means to reach a millennium or utopia. Resistance movements address a terrible future that is certain to befall society or the world if current trends or movements are not stifled. Above all, the social movement's initial leaders believe, often with remarkable naivete, that appropriate institutions will act if the movement can make institutional leaders and followers aware of the urgent problem and its solution. The intellectual or prophet is more of an educator than a rabble rouser, agitator, or fanatic. "Thus," as Eric Hoffer informs us, "imperceptibly the man [woman] of words undermines established institutions, discredits those in power, weakens prevailing beliefs and loyalties, and sets the stage for the rise of the mass movement" by intention or by accident.[12]

In Lloyd Bitzer's words, the prophet not only apprehends an exigence ("an imperfection marked by some degree of urgency. . . a problem or defect, something other than it should be") but attempts to create interest within an audience for perceiving and solving the problem. The prophet, however, often differs little from Bitzer's "man alone in a boat and adrift at sea" who "shouts for help although he knows his words will be unheard." But prophets persist because they believe that "interest will increase insofar as the factual condition" becomes "known directly and sensibly, or through vivid representation."[13] David Snow and Robert Benford call these representations "collective action frames" and contend that they "serve as accenting devices that either underscore and embellish the seriousness and injustice of a social condition or redefine as unjust and immoral what was previously seen as unfortunate but perhaps tolerable."[14]

The genesis stage may last for months, years, or decades. Harold Mixon claims, for instance, that artillery election sermons sowed the seeds of independence in colonial America decades before the Declaration of Independence in 1776.[15] Folk songs by Bob Dylan and others addressed war and peace a year before the Gulf of Tonkin incident thrust the United States into the Vietnam conflict. If comparable social movements are active, a fledgling social movement may take shape rapidly.[16] For example, students involved in the black civil rights movement created the student free speech movement, then the peace movement that opposed the war in Vietnam, and finally the counterculture movement. Female members of these movements who became painfully aware of their second-class status even in organizations fighting for the rights of others were instrumental in establishing the women's liberation movement.

The genesis stage, Leland Griffin's "period of inception," is a "time when the roots of pre-existing sentiment, nourished by interested rhetoricians, begins to flower into public notice."[17] A triggering event, what James Darsey calls a "catalytic event," is usually necessary to move the generally unorganized, ideologically uncertain, and barely visible social movement from the genesis stage to the social unrest stage.[18] The triggering event may be a Supreme Court decision, a nuclear power plant accident, an insensitive reaction or statement by an institutional agent, a new law, an economic recession, a military or police action, or the appearance of a movement-oriented book on the best seller list. For instance, the comment by a North Dakota legislator to a farm delegation in 1915, "Go home and slop your hogs," infuriated farmers and gave rise to the Nonpartisan

League in the midwest.[19] Betty Freidan's *The Feminine Mystique* helped to launch the women's liberation movement and Rachel Carson's *The Silent Spring* served as the impetus for the environmental movement. The initial result of a triggering or catalytic event may be the first real signs of organization with titles that begin "Citizens for . . .," "Concerned Parents Against . . .," "Workers United to . . .," or "Americans Dedicated to . . .".

The "men's movement" of the 1990s appears to be in the genesis stage awaiting some event, person, or organization to propel it into the next stage. The movement began in the 1980s with small groups of men (very similar to the consciousness-raising groups during the early stage of the women's liberation movement) meeting to share their pains, hurts, and frustrations that resulted from experiences with drunken fathers, emasculating bosses, stifling jobs, divorce laws, child custody fights, or advertisements and television programs that portray men as fools.[20] It received national attention in 1990 with a Bill Moyers-narrated PBS special entitled "A Gathering of Men," a documentary on poet Robert Bly and his book *Iron John: A Book About Men.* Since then, hundreds of men's groups have sprung up around the country. Activity consists primarily of weekend retreats during which men can look inward and experience a rebirth through sharing their painful stories and by acting out primitive masculinity through drum beating and sweating around mounds of steaming rocks in teepees. This embryonic movement has created no ideology spotlighting how men are abused and oppressed, but it is rapidly gaining increased attention from American intellectuals. A 1993 issue of the *Chronicle of Higher Education* listed 28 books published since 1990 with titles such as *The Adventurous Male, American Manhood, Running Scared, The First Sexual Revolution,* and *The Inward Gaze.*[21] Most intellectuals seem reluctant, however, to associate with the "mythopoetic" men's movement because they see Bly's *Iron John* and Sam Keen's *Fire in the Belly: On Being a Man* primarily as a backlash against the feminist movement and as an effort to reclaim turf. R. W. Connell, a sociologist at the University of California at Santa Cruz, writes that "In the final analysis, *Iron John* and the 'mythopoetic men's movement' are a massive evasion of reality. Bly is selling simplified fantasy solutions to real problems. In the process, he distorts men's lives and distracts men from practical work on gender inequalities."[22] No organization has yet emerged to bring together a significant number of men for purposes other than consciousness-raising, so the movement continues, at this writing, in the genesis stage. If this movement develops into a full-fledged social movement, it would fit the pattern of trying to capture an idealized past.

The most important contributions of the genesis stage are the apprehension of an exigence, something other than it should be, and the cultivation of interest in the exigence within an audience. Without a genesis stage, there will be no movement. However, if the movement cannot go forward, it will wither and die. Snow and Benford contend that the "failure of mass mobilization" to occur when the time seems ripe "may be accounted for in part by the absence of a resonant master frame"—an altered vision of reality centered on objects, situations, events, experiences, actions, and relationships.[23]

Stage 2: Social Unrest

As growing numbers of people rise up and express their concerns and frustrations over an issue, the social movement passes from the genesis to the social unrest stage. Spokespersons for institutions may openly deny the severity or existence of the problem (exigence) and, often for the first time, take official notice of the fledgling social movement. They may stigmatize the so-called movement as naive, ill-informed, or laughable (women saying they want to be scientists and executives rather than wives and mothers or men sitting around a pile of hot rocks in a teepee sweating profusely and relating their hurts)—clearly outside the mainstream of society. The opposition's strategy is to stall the social movement by ignoring or discrediting it in hopes that it will succumb to ridicule or inattention, that it will simply go away. The mass media may note with interest, amusement, or mild foreboding the infant social movement and its pathetic claims or overtures. When protestors on college campuses constructed shantytowns to make people aware of conditions of blacks in South Africa under apartheid, the *Wall Street Journal* ridiculed these activities as "the latest fad" in an article entitled "Shanty Raids," a play on words referring to panty raids common on college campuses decades earlier. "In spring a young student's fancy turns to political protest," the *Wall Street Journal* remarked. "This year's fashion is shantytowns, and from Yale to North Carolina to Purdue to Michigan to Wisconsin to Berkeley police are confronting student demonstrators. The game works this way."[24]

The prophets and intellectuals turn into, or join, agitators—literally ones who stir things up. It is time to proceed beyond the small study or consciousness-raising groups. Together they begin to organize the disparate elements of the movement and take it beyond the drawing room, talk show, and lecture hall. An initial act is often the calling of a convention or conference of like-minded people for the purpose of framing a manifesto, proclamation, or declaration. For instance, student leaders from a wide variety of organizations (Students for a Democratic Society, National Student Christian Federation, National Student Association, the Young Democrats, Student Peace Union, and SNCC) met in June 1963 at Michigan's AFL-CIO camp at Port Huron, Michigan to work out a manifesto. The product of these deliberations, the *Port Huron Statement*, served as the essential statement of principles for the student movement and later the Anti-Vietnam War and counterculture movements.[25]

A manifesto sets forth the social movement's ideology, an "elaboration of rationalizations and stereotypes into a consistent pattern."[26] It serves three essential functions: (1) to describe the exigence, (2) to identify the devils, scapegoats, and faulty principles that have caused and sustained the exigence, and (3) to prescribe the solution and the gods, principles, and procedures that will bring it about. The ideology identifies the social movement with "the people"—a great grassroots movement—and with established norms and values. For example, both the *Declaration of Sentiments* issued by the First Woman's Rights Convention in 1848 and the *Constitution* drawn up by the National Labor Union in 1868 were modifications of the the the *Declaration of Independence*. The effort is to identify with what is good and holy in America and disassociate from all that is evil. The *Port Huron Statement* begins with these words:

> We are people of this generation, bred in at least modest comfort, housed now in universities, looking uncomfortably to the world we inherit.
>
> When we were kids the United States was the wealthiest and strongest country in the world; the only one with the atom bomb, the least scarred by modern war, an initiator of the United Nations that we thought would distribute Western influence throughout the world. Freedom and equality for each individual, government of, by, and for the people—these American values we found good, principles by which we could live as men. Many of us began maturing in complacency.[27]

The next paragraph begins "As we grew, however, our comfort was penetrated by events too troubling to dismiss," and introduces a litany of problems and disillusionments with society: racial bigotry, the Cold War, the common peril of "the Bomb," politics, the economy, the military-industrial complex, poverty, and communism. Perhaps this sentence sums up the concerns of the students at Port Huron: "Not only did tarnish appear on our image of American virtue, not only did disillusion occur when the hypocrisy of American ideals was discovered, but we began to sense that what we had originally seen as the American Golden Age was actually the decline of an era."[28] Sentences such as these set the tone for each social movement. Theorists note that a social movement's ideology is "considerably more potent" and "strikes a responsive chord" if it identifies successfully with "extant beliefs, myths, folktales, and the like."[29]

An ideology contains a set of common "devil" terms such as liberalism, segregation, wage slavery, commercial development, conformity, and welfare state and a corresponding set of "god" terms such as conservativism, integration, employee-owned cooperatives, natural environment, individualism, and free enterprise.[30] An overarching principle or slogan unifies the movement: "An injury to one is an injury to all" (Knights of Labor), "Never to laugh or love" (pro-life), "Keep abortion legal" (pro-choice), and "All power to the people" (Black Power and new left). For the first time, there is a feeling of "standing together" and "movement" as concerned individuals are now members of the Knights of Labor, Greenpeace, The Clamshell Alliance (against nuclear power plants), or People for the Ethical Treatment of Animals. The act of joining or forming an organization sets members apart from non-members and established institutions and fosters a "we-they" division that becomes more pronounced as the social movement enters succeeding stages. Members increasingly see themselves as an "elite" with a "mission" and a set of strategies for fulfilling the moral crusade. Movement persuaders attempt to instill a new feeling of self-identity, self-respect, and power within members that was absent when they were mere individuals.

Although the social movement pays increasing attention to transforming perceptions of society (creating we-they distinctions) and to prescribing courses of action (citing demands, prescribing solutions, and identifying who must bring about or stifle change and through which strategies), the major persuasive effort is aimed at transforming perceptions of the past, present, and future. Persuaders continue to believe that if they can raise the consciousness of institutional leaders and followers (make them aware of the facts through words, pictures, exposés, symbolic acts, and theatre), institutions will take appropriate actions to resolve the exigence. Faith in progress through the social chain-of-command remains strong. Thus, gay rights advocates portray how they are discriminated against in American society; anti-war advocates portray the horrors of war; animal rights advocates portray the horrors of leghold traps and raising animals for fur, food, and experimentation; and evangelical movements portray the moral decadence of society. Movements expend most of their rhetorical energies during the social unrest stage in "petitioning" courts, city councils, university boards of trustees, corporate boards of directors, state legislatures, Congress, the President of the United States, scientific organizations, and religious synods and hierarchies.[31]

The duration of the social unrest stage depends upon the numbers of people who are attracted to the movement, reactions of institutional agents, and new triggering or catalytic events that may greatly exacerbate the social situation or exigence. The nuclear power plant accidents at Three Mile Island (Pennsylvania) and Chernobyl (Ukraine) and the arrest of Rosa Parks in Montgomery, Alabama because she would not surrender her seat on a city bus to a white male passenger boosted the anti-nuclear and civil rights movements from the social unrest stage to the enthusiastic mobilization stage. The first showed the *real* dangers of nuclear power that words and symbolic actions could not, and the second led to the Montgomery bus boycott that catapulted a local minister, Martin Luther King, Jr., to national prominence and leadership of the movement. Catalytic events cause significant numbers of people to lose faith both in the ability and willingness of institutions to solve exigencies and the effectiveness of normal persuasive means to bring about or to resist change. Members and sympathizers may begin to see the institution as the problem or as part of a conspiracy to sustain power and to defeat all legitimate and reasonable efforts to bring about urgently needed actions. When *frustration* leads to *disaffection* with institutions and their abilities to resolve problems, the social movement enters the stage of enthusiastic mobilization. The growth of social unrest, Bitzer's Stage 1 in the rhetorical situation, culminates in the development of a dominant exigence, an audience, and constraints.[32]

Stage 3: Enthusiastic Mobilization

The social movement in the enthusiastic mobilization stage is populated with true believers who have experienced conversion to the cause. They have grown "tired of being sick and tired."[33] Gone is the old naivete that established institutions will act if they are made aware of the problem through "rational petitions." The converted see the social movement as the *only* way to bring about urgently needed change and believe firmly that the movement's time has come. Optimism is rampant. Important legitimizers—entertainers, senators, clergy, physicians, labor leaders, educators—lend an air of excitement and inevitability to the cause.

Institutions and resistance movements are keenly aware of the movement's growth, change in attitude, altered persuasive strategies, perceived legitimation, and potential for success. For the first time, they see the movement as a clear and present danger to institutional power and authority. They, too, mobilize during the enthusiastic mobilization stage.[34] The greater the threat from a social movement, particularly if it is perceived to seek revolutionary changes, the greater are the counterefforts by institutional agents, agencies, and surrogates. Institutions may encourage the creation of countermovements and provide them with resources, freedom of action, and an aura of legitimacy. The aim is to stifle the social movement through actions of "the people" or "silent majority"—the persons the movement claims it is fighting for—and thus avoid the appearance of institutional involvement. If these actions fail and the establishment comes to see the movement as a radical, revolutionary force, it may unleash police forces to suppress the perceived threat to society.

As social movements expand, evolve, and confront serious opposition from institutional forces and surrogates, they generally abandon judicial and legislative chambers for the streets, marketplaces, hallways, forests, construction sites, vineyards and, in the case of Greenpeace and Save the Whales, the open seas and harbors.[35] They have lost faith in both institutions and institutional means to bring about or resist change. Mass meetings, marches, demonstrations, and symbolic actions replace sedate conventions, conferences, and testimony at hearings.

Coercive persuasion replaces the rhetoric of speeches, leaflets, pamphlets, and newsletters. Protestors burn tractors in front of the Capitol to protest farm prices, bury school buses to protest forced busing to integrate schools, burn flags to protest military actions, and blockade clinics to stop abortions. They boycott table grapes, corporations doing business with South Africa, and hospitals and clinics where abortions might be performed. They set up picket lines, declare strikes, defy laws and court injunctions, and welcome mass arrests that attract television cameras and news coverage and clog the jails. They stage sit-ins, sit-downs, sleep-ins, and die-ins.[36] Protestors harass institutional agents and persons who do not comply with their demands: physicians, contractors, professors, police officers, supermarket managers, fur trappers, hunters, medical researchers, loggers, and women wearing fur coats. Threats work. For example, a woman who fears that wearing a fur coat in public will provoke a protestor to yell at her, throw red paint on her coat, or cut it with a sharp knife, will not buy a fur coat or wear one she purchased earlier. It seems to make little difference whether such acts happen or happen often; the fear that it might happen induces people to stop buying and wearing fur coats. Ultimately, the raising and trapping of animals will cease and fur companies will go out of business.[37]

New organizations such as Martin Luther King's SCLC and Samuel Gompers' AF of L arise and compete with or overshadow earlier organizations such as the NAACP and the Knights of Labor. Charismatic agitators, adept at countering and taking advantage of growing opposition to the movement, replace intellectuals and prophets, though they may pay homage to both. They control the movement by forming strong organizations and coalitions, stir up great excitement within the membership, stage symbolic actions, and confront institutions and resistance movements. Leaders and followers may become martyrs for the cause by suffering physical injury, imprisonment, banishment, or death. They not only accept but may readily seek suffering because the cause has become the true believer's reason for being. The persuasive goal is to raise the consciousness level of "the people" so significant numbers will pressure institutions to adopt the movement's simplified "if-only" images of social processes, problems, and solutions: if women are given the right to vote, women will achieve equal rights; if abortion is outlawed, there will be no abortions; if sexual orientation clauses are added to human rights ordinances, there will be no discrimination against homosexuals; if we stop using animals for medical experiments, we will find cures faster through high technology.

Leaders during the enthusiastic mobilization stage face severe persuasive crises both inside and outside the social movement. Externally, persuaders must employ harsh rhetoric and stage symbolic acts designed to pressure institutions into capitulation or compromise, to polarize the movement and its opposition (all who are not actively supporting the movement), and to provoke repressive acts that reveal the true ugliness of institutions and counterefforts. Persuasion during this stage is replete with name-calling against the devils and conspirators who have perpetrated and prolonged the evil the social movement alone has the will and strength to fight. If leaders are inept at adapting and changing persuasive strategies and judging how far to push for positive results and images, they may provoke institutional and public outrage and suppression of the movement. At the very least, the movement may lose essential support and sympathy from the public, media, and legitimizers. A few violent acts such as the bombing of a University of Wisconsin building in which Army research was conducted, the killing of a doctor at an abortion clinic in Florida, firebombing meat wholesaler trucks, and sabotaging logging equipment may doom years of protest, even if the acts are by fanatical, minuscule, splinter groups such as the Weathermen, Army of God, Earth First! and the U.S. Animal Liberation Front. The public and institutions do not make fine distinctions: an act *in the name of* the social movement and its cause is *an act by the movement*.

Internally, movement persuaders must deal with competing and often antagonistic organizations, each with its own leaders, followers, ideological quirks, and favorite strategies. Even fragile coalitions are essential for the appearance and effect of a united front. Persuasive feats of magic are necessary to sustain coalitions for extended periods. Further splintering of the movement and the rise of fanatical elements that propose violence instead of symbolism or demands unacceptable to either the movement at large or to institutions drain persuasive resources from the cause. Leaders may decide that alterations in ideology or persuasive strategies are necessary to keep the movement fresh, to counter resistance forces, or to meet changing circumstances, and they must sell each change to movement factions or face devastating charges of "revisionism" and selling out. A movement's goals may expand or contract with changes in membership and situation. For example, the pro-life movement came into existence to make abortion illegal but, as it has progressed, it has come to champion the cause of all human life—the aged, infirm, mentally retarded, and minorities as well as the unborn. The National Organization for Women (NOW) organized to fight for a broad range of women's rights but, in the 1990s, has increasingly become centered on the single issue of keeping abortion legal.[38]

When confrontations between the social movement and resistance forces become severe, persuaders stress "we-they" distinctions more sharply and bitterly. Persons who do not join the movement and former members become hated sub-humans and traitors. Leaders may look within and decide that some members (whites, males, non-skilled workers, religious liberals) are incapable of true understanding or involvement in the cause, so they purge memberships to purify movements to prepare for final struggles with the evil forces arrayed against them. The new elites must be explained and justified internally and externally.

Social movements may achieve notable goals and victories during the enthusiastic mobilization stage, but earlier visions of sweeping and meaningful changes usually remain unfulfilled. Instant success is elusive. Leaders are unable to satisfy the insatiable appetites of members and the mass media for new and more spectacular events and achievements. What were once viewed as imaginative and potent persuasive strategies or revolutionary victories, such as the Montgomery bus boycott and civil rights legislation, are ridiculed by new leaders and members. John Wilson notes that "It is easier for the disgruntled to agree on what is wrong with the old than on what is right with the new."[39] Leaders devote increasing amounts of persuasion to explaining and justifying setbacks, delays, lack of meaningful gains, and failures of old successes to fulfill exaggerated expectations.

The extravagant hopes that once energized the movement begin to fade and with them enthusiasm of the movement. Some people join movements with unrealistic expectations that can never be satisfied. Some people join social movements because they are impatient with the gradualism that institutions espouse and have little tolerance for movements that begin to preach a noninstitutional brand of gradualism. Some people join because they believe victory is imminent and become disillusioned or frightened when victory proves elusive. Neither social movement members nor those in the larger society can accept harsh rhetoric and confrontation for long. Fatigue, fears of anarchy, and boredom inevitably set in.[40] The persuasive efforts necessary for mobilizing the social movement may carry the seeds of its own destruction—both within and without—so that when the boiling point is reached, the movement must essentially revert to an earlier posture in order to sustain its existence.

The maturing social movement needs new leadership and a less impassioned and strident rhetoric as it enters the maintenance stage. The loss of a charismatic leader such as Martin Luther King, Jr., Malcolm X, and American Nazi leader George Lincoln Rockwell to assassins may hasten the movement into the next stage because no one else is capable of maintaining mobilization or reenergizing the movement. The remnants of the old enthusiasm may die with the movement's martyr.

Stage 4: Maintenance

The onset of the maintenance stage is a critical turning point for a social movement because one direction is toward ultimate victory of some sort and the other is toward oblivion. Unfortunately, the odds are against victory for, as John Wilson writes, "frustration is the fate of all social movements."[41] The movement undergoes change that is inevitable in all organizations. Lloyd Bitzer notes that "a situation deteriorates when any constituent or relation changes in ways that make modification of the exigence significantly more difficult."[42]

The social movement returns to more quiet times during the maintenance stage as institutions, media, and public turn to other, more pressing concerns. Both movement and society are ready for a respite from exciting but unnerving, disruptive, and often destructive confrontations. Movement persuasion once again emanates from the pen and printer and from legislative, judicial, conference, convention, and lecture halls. It is time to hold onto what has been gained and to consolidate movement organization for the duration. Radical organizations such as WITCH (Women's International Terrorist Conspiracy from Hell), SCUM (Society for Cutting Up Men), and Earth First! disappear and original, more conservative groups such as NOW (National Organization for Women), Planned Parenthood, and the Sierra Club remain to carry the movement forward.

The agitator must change or leave because the social movement during the maintenance stage requires a statesman or administrator, a pragmatist, who can appeal to disparate elements, maintain organizations, and deal more directly and "rationally" with institutional leaders. The agitator is a superb street fighter but a poor bureaucrat whose harsh and uncompromising rhetoric of polarization and confrontation creates too many enemies within and without and is unsuited for diplomatic and administrative roles. As Bruce Cameron observes, "Many a stirring evangelist makes a poor pastor."[43] The pragmatist, a pastor of sorts, must perfect organization, sustain the movement's forward progress as it emerges from its "trial by fire," and work with established institutions. Herbert Simons notes that the militant strategies of the agitator may make the moderate strategies of the pragmatist more acceptable to institutions.[44]

While leaders continue efforts to transform perceptions of reality and society, prescribe courses of action, and mobilize believers and sympathizers, the primary persuasive function is to sustain the social movement. Both membership and commitment decline during the maintenance stage, so leaders must recruit new members and reinforce belief in the movement's ideology and potential for ultimate rather than immediate success. They must sustain or resuscitate hope and optimism. Unfortunately, leaders become more distant from members during the maintenance stage because there are fewer opportunities to see, hear, and talk with them.

Dominant communication channels are newsletters, journals, and movement newspapers rather than interpersonal exchanges and speeches before live audiences.

Incessant fund raising is necessary to support organizations, property, and publications. Any maintenance task—fund raising, recruiting, publications—may become an end in itself, and the leader becomes more of an entrepreneur than a reformer or revolutionary. Routinization of dues, meetings, leadership, decision making, and rituals is essential to maintain a highly structured and disciplined movement organization that will survive to carry the cause forward. These bureaucratic necessities, however, siphon off much of the old spontaneity, excitement, and *esprit de corps* that made the movement vibrant and attractive and set it apart from established organizations. What was improvised during an emergency or passionate moment in an earlier, exciting stage now becomes a "sacred precedent and wisdom of the past."[45] While spontaneous deviation from expected behavior may be glorified as sacred precedent, such spontaneity is unacceptable in the maintenance stage because rigid adherence to organization is the norm.

Lack of visibility is a major preoccupation. The movement is rarely newsworthy during the maintenance stage, and the mass media begin to address the social movement and its leaders in editorials and columns that begin with phrases such as "What ever happened to" and "Where is . . . now?" The adage "out of sight, out of mind" haunts leaders, but their persuasive options are few. Paradoxically, neither members nor the public will support the mass demonstrations of old, and quiet suggests satisfaction with things as they are. There are no charismatic leaders of old to fire up the membership, and there are too few active members to be fired up. The Ku Klux Klan, for instance, continues efforts to arrange mass gatherings and cross burnings, but the fewer than fifty members who usually show up are far outnumbered by police, reporters, the curious, and counterdemonstrators. The Klan is embarrassed more than energized. Institutions may not tolerate or may have learned how to deal quietly with old persuasive tactics such as sit-ins, civil disobedience, or boycotts. Worst of all, institutions may simply ignore outdated symbolic acts and revolutionary rhetoric. Rhetoric is increasingly internal—directed toward maintenance functions—rather than external—directed toward pressuring the opposition and gaining legitimizers. Leaders resort to ceremonies, rituals, annual meetings, and anniversary celebrations during which martyrs, tragedies, events, and victories are recounted and memorialized, but the rhetoric is more melancholy than energizing.

The social movement looks desperately for a triggering or catalytic event to return the cause to the enthusiastic mobilization stage, make the struggle fun and exciting again, and to counteract the gradual hardening of the arteries that aging movement organizations experience. As opposed to a rejuvenative triggering or catalytic event, the movement may just as likely suffer a severe blow from a debilitating or disintegrating event. For instance, the coming on line of the Seabrook nuclear power plant in New Hampshire and Public Service Indiana's economic-based decision to stop construction on its Marble Hill plant in Indiana were devastating events for the anti-nuclear power movement. They failed in their prolonged efforts to stop the first and lost a primary target in the second. The issue no longer seemed urgent. The onset of AIDS significantly affected the gay rights movement. James Darsey writes that:

> AIDS became the obsessive concern of gay rights activists, coloring all activity concerning the welfare of gay men and lesbians in the United States. AIDS presented the gay community with not only a public health crisis, but crises in the social, legal, and psychological spheres as well. AIDS catalyzed a shift in the rhetoric of the gay movement.[46]

The hoped-for rebirth eludes most social movements or arrives too late. For example, when the ideals of women's rights, industrial unionism, and temperance were once again high on the public agenda, original leaders and organizations were history. NOW (National Organization for Women), the CIO (Congress of Industrial Organizations), and MADD (Mothers Against Drunk Driving) arose to champion the causes.

As the movement shrinks or faces a long stalemate, it may focus its rhetorical energies on a single issue or solution. "All will be well once we get": the right to vote, a prohibition amendment, the eight-hour day, equal rights legislation, integration of public schools, or an anti-abortion amendment. The single goal is attractive because it is simple and more attainable than a panacea of hopes and dreams. The shrunken movement can focus its limited persuasive energies on a single less divisive target. Both movement and institutions have grown weary of confrontations, and legitimizers are more likely to support a non-radical goal that is handled through normal means and channels.

The social movement is on the threshold of the final stage, termination, during which it will cease to be a social movement. The only question is whether it will die or become another form of collectivity.

Stage 5: Termination

If a social movement is successful, it may celebrate its victory and disband. The anti-slavery movement did just that in 1865 after passage of the Thirteenth Amendment to the Constitution: "Neither Slavery nor involuntary servitude, except as a punishment for crime whereof the party shall have been duly convicted, shall exist within the United States, or any place subject to their jurisdiction."[47] The movement no longer had a cause for which to fight. Total disbandment is unlikely, however, because elements of every social movement make the cause their reason for being and their livelihood, and they will trust no one else with its principles or their jobs. Also, the social movement's ideology may be so broad or idealistic, such as the end of all prejudice in society, that *all* of its tasks are rarely fulfilled.

If a social movement maintains an effective organization and its principles come to match current mores, it may become the new order—as communist and Nazi movements did in Russia and Germany and the democratic-independence movements did in much of eastern Europe in the 1990s—or a new institution such as Methodist Church and the American Federation of Labor. Leaders of transformed social movements face new and old persuasive challenges. They must strive for obedience among the membership and the people, bring an end to tensions, and establish a "perfecting myth" in which the social movement organization is believed to have reached a state of absolute perfection and morality. Leaders must purge elements who will not accept the transformation of the social movement or who pose threats to the leadership's attempts to achieve peace and harmony among societal elements. Rhetorical confrontations do not end with the transformation of a social movement into an institution. As Elizabeth Nelson points out in her study of Mussolini's rise to power in Italy, former social movements may have to continue their "perpetual struggles" to sustain their new positions and the support of followers.[48] The reformers and revolutionaries of movement days become the priests of the new order or institution and must be able to perform pastoral functions. Inevitably, the movement-turned-institution will face a new generation of reformers and revolutionaries.

Few social movements are totally successful, however. Some shrink into pressure groups (Ralph Nader's consumer-protection organizations), philanthropic associations (the Salvation Army), political parties (the Socialist party), lobbying groups (for milk, rice, or tobacco producers), or social watchdog roles (the Women's Christian Temperance Union). Others are absorbed or co-opted by established institutions such as political parties, religious denominations, and labor unions. Many principles the populists, progressives, and socialists espoused— banking regulations, voting rights and reforms, social security, unemployment insurance—have been adopted into the American system with no recognition of the social movements that championed them for years. Occasionally, an institution will crush a social movement organization such as the Black Panther party, Weathermen, and Communist party because the institution and a significant portion of the public comes to view it as a grave danger to society. Many movements merely fade away.

Social movements shrink and die for many reasons. Leaders and members may despair of ever changing anything or of achieving permanent and meaningful goals equal to the sacrifices made. They may become overwhelmed by the magnitude or multiplicity of the problems they must solve, or they may lose faith in society's capacity for reform. For others, the social movement becomes merely a job, or the new lifestyle becomes boring and meaningless as years pass. Leaders and followers experience fatigue because they cannot continue to endure the dangers, thrills, and privations movements demand.[49] Violent actions by radical groups may frighten movement members, institutions, and the public into seeking "normalcy."

During the termination stage, leaders and followers may become as disaffected with social movements as they once were with established institutions. They may opt for military rather than symbolic warfare and wage a civil war or revolution to achieve change. More likely, however, members and sympathizers drop back into the institutions from which they came.[50] Some leaders such as Eldridge Cleaver, a founder and officer of the Black Panther party, have "conversion" experiences and become born again Christians, capitalists, or government bureaucrats; they may or may not continue to work for change. Sam Riddle, a former Michigan State University rebel, has become an oil company lawyer and remarks, "I can do a lot more with a base of capital than with a pocketful of rhetoric. I'm no longer interested in standing on my soapbox and shouting into the wind. Now I'm more interested in producing the soapboxes."[51] Other movement disciples turn inward, toward "privatism," in an effort to protect or to change themselves or their inner circles of family and friends.[52]

Conclusions

Social movements are intricate and ever-changing social dramas, and each stage requires subtle and blunt changes in acts, scenes, agents, agencies, and purposes. Sometimes they resemble melodramas with ever-present villains lurking about and waiting for the heroes and heroines of the movement, the do-gooders, to make foolish mistakes or fail in gallant efforts to perfect the world. Villains know that time is on their side and that perfection is elusive.

Each stage (genesis, social unrest, enthusiastic mobilization, maintenance, and termination) requires certain persuasive skills and personalities. Genesis, for instance, demands an intellectual or prophet who excels at defining and visualizing, at using words. Enthusiastic mobilization requires a charismatic agitator who confronts and polarizes, excites and insults, unites and fragments. Maintenance requires a pragmatic diplomat who is capable of healing, sustaining, administering, and bargaining.

Each stage poses unique persuasive dilemmas and requires persuasion to serve one or more functions. For example, transforming perceptions of reality dominates the genesis stage. Transforming perceptions of reality and society and prescribing courses of action dominate the social unrest stage. Transforming perceptions of society and mobilization for action dominate the enthusiastic mobilization stage. Sustaining dominates the maintenance stage.

For social movements that reach the final stage, termination, the results are usually disappointing and disillusioning. Early goals, even when partially reached, rarely bring about the perfection envisioned by creators of the movement. Some members condemn society, institutions, and human beings as incapable of reform, unable to attain perfection. Others see the means (social movements, persuasion, coercive persuasion) as impotent tools for achieving meaningful and lasting change. Ultimately, all social movements come to an end and experience a degree of frustration, but this does not mean that social movements have little effect or their causes die with them. As Leland Griffin writes, "And if the wheel forever turns, it is man [woman] who does the turning—forever striving, in an 'imperfect world,' for a world of perfection. And hence man [woman], the rhetorical animal, is saved: for salvation lies in the striving, the struggle itself."[53]

Endnotes

[1] Leland M. Griffin, "A Dramatistic Theory of the Rhetoric of Movements," *Critical Responses to Kenneth Burke*, William Rueckert, ed. (Minneapolis: University of Minnesota Press, 1969), 456–478; Kenneth Burke, *A Grammar of Motives* (Englewood Cliffs, NJ: Prentice-Hall, 1950).

[2] William Bruce Cameron, *Modern Social Movements* (New York: Random House, 1966), 27–29.

[3] Herbert W. Simons, Elizabeth W. Mechling, and Howard N. Schreier, "The Functions of Human Communication in Mobilizing for Action from the Bottom Up: The Rhetoric of Social Movements," *Handbook of Rhetorical and Communication Theory*, Carroll C. Arnold and John Waite Bowers, eds. (Boston: Allyn and Bacon, 1984), 804–809.

[4] Donald G. Ellis and B. Aubrey Fisher, "Phases of Conflict in Small Group Development: A Markov Analysis," *Human Communication Research* 1 (Spring 1975), 195–212.

[5] Julia T. Wood, "Communication and Relational Culture: Bases for the Study of Human Relationships," *Communication Quarterly* 30 (Spring 1982), 75–84.

[6] Mark L. Knapp, *Interpersonal Communication and Human Relationships* (Boston: Allyn and Bacon, 1984), 32–54.

[7] Richard E. Crable and Steven L. Vibbert, "Managing Issues and Influencing Public Policy," *Public Relations Review* 11 (1985), 6–7.

[8] Bruce E. Gronbeck, "The Rhetoric of Social-Institutional Change: Black Action at Michigan," *Explorations in Rhetorical Criticism*, Gerald Mohrmann, Charles Stewart, Donovan Ochs, eds. (University Park, PA: Pennsylvania State University Press, 1973), 98–101.

[9] This life cycle is based on discussions by Carl A. Dawson and Warner E. Gettys, *An Introduction to Sociology* (New York: Ronald, 1935); John Wilson, *An Introduction to Social Movements* (New York: Basic Books, 1973); and Griffin (1969), 462–472.

[10] For a theoretical discussion of the concept of "the people," see Michael C. McGee, "In Search of 'The People': A Rhetorical Alternative," *Quarterly Journal of Speech* 61 (October 1975), 235–249.

[11] Griffin (1969), 457–462; Eric Hoffer, *The True Believer* (New York: Harper and Row, 1951), 120–121.

[12] Hoffer, 20.

[13] Lloyd F. Bitzer, "Functional Communication: A Situational Perspective," *Rhetoric in Transition: Studies in the Nature and Uses of Rhetoric*, Eugene E. White, ed. (University Park, PA: Pennsylvania State University, 1980), 23, 26–29, and 32.

[14] David A. Snow and Robert D. Benford, "Master Frames and Cycles of Protest," *Frontiers in Social Movement Theory* (New Haven, CT: Yale University Press, 1992), 137.

[15] Harold D. Mixon, "Boston's Artillery Election Sermons and the American Revolution," *Speech Monographs* 34 (March 1967), 43–50.

[16] Snow and Benford, 144.

[17] Leland M. Griffin, "The Rhetoric of Historical Movements," *Quarterly Journal of Speech* 38 (April 1952), 186.

[18] James Darsey, "From 'Gay Is Good' to the Scourge of AIDS: The Evolution of Gay Liberation Rhetoric, 1977–1990," *Communication Studies* 42 (Spring 1991), 43–66.

[19] Leslie G. Rude, "The Rhetoric of Farmer-Labor Agitators," *Central States Speech Journal* 20 (Winter 1969), 281.

[20] "Drum, Sweat and Tears," *Newsweek*, June 24, 1991, 46–51.

[21] "Scholars Debunk the Marlboro Man: Examining Stereotypes of Masculinity," *The Chronicle of Higher Education*, February 3, 1993, A6ß

[22] "Scholars Debunk the Marlboro Man," A8.

[23] Snow and Benford, 143–144.

[24] *The Wall Street Journal*, April 9, 1986, 32.

[25] James Miller, *Democracy in the Streets: From Port Huron to the Siege of Chicago* (New York: Simon & Schuster, 1987), 102–125.

[26] S. Judson Crandell, "The Beginnings of a Methodology for Social Control Studies," *Quarterly Journal of Speech* 33 (February 1947), 37; Griffin (1969), 462–463.

[27] Miller, 329.

[28] Miller, 330.

[29] Snow and Benford, 141.

[30] Leland M. Griffin, "The Rhetorical Structure of the 'New Left' Movement: Part I," *Quarterly Journal of Speech* 50 (April 1964), 115.

[31] John W. Bowers, Donovan J. Ochs, and Richard J. Jensen, *The Rhetoric of Agitation and Control*, 2/E (Prospect Heights, IL: Waveland Press, 1993), 20.

[32] Bitzer, 18.

[33] Wilson, 89–90.

[34] Bowers, Ochs, Jensen, 47–64.

[35] Franklyn S. Haiman, "The Rhetoric of the Streets: Some Legal and Ethical Considerations," *Quarterly Journal of Speech* 53 (April 1967), 99–114; Franklyn S. Haiman, "Nonverbal Communication and the First Amendment: The Rhetoric of the Streets Revisited," *Quarterly Journal of Speech* 68 (November 1982), 371–383.

[36] "How Many Gays Are There?" *Newsweek*, February 15, 1993, 46.

[37] "The Fur Flies: The Cold War Over Animal Rights," *New York*, January 15, 1990, 27–33.

[38] "NOW—Join the movement to protect *every* woman's access to abortion," a mailing, fall 1992.

[39] Wilson, 109–110.

[40] Saul D. Alinsky, *Rules for Radicals: A Pragmatic Primer for Realistic Radicals* (New York: Vintage Books, 1972), 159–161.

[41] Wilson, 360.

[42] Bitzer, 35.

[43] Cameron, 93.

[44] Herbert W. Simons, "Requirements, Problems, and Strategies: A Theory of Persuasion for Social Movements," *Quarterly Journal of Speech* 56 (February 1970), 10–11.

[45] Cameron, 87.

[46] Darsey, 55.

[47] Thomas James Norton, *The Constitution of the United States: Its Sources and Its Application* (New York: America's Future, 1949), 232.

[48] Elizabeth Jean Nelson, "'Nothing Ever Goes Well Enough': Mussolini and the Rhetoric of Perpetual Struggle," *Communication Studies* 42 (Spring 1991), 22–42.

[49] Jerry Rubin, "Growing Up Again," *Human Behavior*, March, 1976, 17–23.

[50] Peter Goldman and Gerald Lubenow, "Where the Flowers Have Gone," *Newsweek*, September 5, 1977, 24–30; Margie Casady, "Where Have the Radicals Gone," *Psychology Today*, October, 1975, 63–64, 92; "Yesterday's Activists: Still Marching to a Different Drummer?" *Notre Dame Magazine*, October, 1975, 10–21.

[51] "Yesterday's Radicals Put on Gray Flannel," *U.S. News and World Report*, January 19, 1981, 41.

[52] Jerry LaBlanc, "Unplug the World, We Want to Get off," Indianapolis *Star Magazine*, July 28, 1974, 7–8.

[53] Griffin (1969), 472.

Chapter Five

Leadership in Social Movements

The American public's view of leadership in social movements is heavily influenced by its faith in *individualism*, in the *sanctity* and perfection of American institutions, and the ability of both individuals and institutions to cope with "real" or "serious" problems. Roberta Ash writes that "Only in America is the belief that individualism and collectivism are necessarily in conflict so widely held."[1] After decades of persuasive efforts to organize factory workers, farmers and farm workers, women, African Americans, Hispanic Americans, and gays, only small percentages of each ever became active members of organizations created to resolve their plights.[2] John Wilson discovered that during the farm income decline of the 1950s, "Most farmers had come to feel that the American public was paying too little for its food or else the middle man was taking too large a slice of the cake, and hence believed there was something drastically wrong with the marketing system." Despite this widespread belief, only six percent of farmers actually joined the National Farmers Organization (NFO).[3]

American institutions are able to sustain themselves even in times of massive economic breakdowns and unsettling changes.[4] During the great depression of the 1930s, voters turned to Franklin Roosevelt and the Democratic party to return the nation to economic prosperity and stability rather than to the Socialist or Communist parties. Public opinion polls reveal a persistent confidence in American institutions during periods of disturbing change, uncertainty, and alleged unhappiness with established orders. A Gallup poll conducted in 1990 asked respondents how much confidence they had in several institutions to serve public needs, and the combined percentages of a great deal, quite a lot, and some were as follows:[5]

Military	90%	Supreme Court	78%
Churches	82%	Labor unions	67%
Newspapers	81%	Congress	67%
Public schools	79%	Big business	65%

When asked to look ahead to the year 2000, 82 percent said they were very or somewhat optimistic. Such levels of support for institutions and general optimism about the status quo reveal why it is difficult for social movement leaders to sell their uninstitutionalized collectives and goals for urgent change or resistance to Americans. However, the remainder percentages representing "little" or "no confidence" (ranging from 10 percent to 35 percent) show that the legitimacy of institutions is vulnerable to rhetorical assaults by social movements. Institutions cannot take public support for granted or ignore the challenges social movements pose.

People who choose to *organize* and to operate *outside of* American institutions and to claim an urgent problem is being ignored, hidden, or promoted by the very persons or institutions Americans revere or cherish are likely to be branded as irrational agitators, malcontents, losers, misfits, outcasts, extremists, or rabble-rousers.[6] If these perverse, un-American "troublemakers" persist and organize protests, the public (often with the aid of the mass media and institutional agencies and agents) may attach new labels suitable for social destroyers: demagogues, communists, fascists, terrorists, anarchists, or fanatics.

American institutions such as government agencies and agents, schools and teachers, churches and clergy, labor unions and officers, corporations and executives, and social theorists reinforce the public's attitudes toward social movement leaders. Former Governor of Alabama George C. Wallace was not the first institutional leader, and certainly will not be the last, to characterize social movement leaders as anarchists, social schemers, sex perverts, pinkos, communists, and pointy-headed liberals.[7] Such characterizations are reinforced by strange-looking and acting movement members, many of whom seem to be under the spell of demagogues or revolutionaries, such as the hippies and yippies of the counterculture movement of the 1960s, the Moonies and Symbionese Liberation Army of the 1970s, and the leathermen and drag queens of the gay rights movement of the 1980s and 1990s.[8] Americans are likely, with minimal assistance from institutions, to see Dave Foreman's Earth First! and its self-styled "eco-guerrillas" as both outrageous and dangerous.[9]

Eric Hoffer, the self-made social philosopher, claims in his book *The True Believer* that social movement leaders desire to divest themselves of an "unwanted self." "The revulsion from an unwanted self, and the impulse to forget it, mask it, slough it off, and lose it," Hoffer writes, "produce both a readiness to sacrifice the self and a willingness to dissolve it by losing one's individual distinctness in a compact collective whole."[10] Comments such as these led Herbert Simons to argue that "rhetoricians and other scholars have tended to assume that methods of influence appropriate for drawing room controversies are also effective for social conflicts, including struggles against established authorities."[11] He concludes that scholars "have failed to suggest viable strategies for those engaged in rough-and-tumble conflicts, and some of them have dismissed militant protestors as pathological."

A number of studies by Crane Brinton (the American, French, English, and Russian revolutions), Ming T. Lee (the Communist revolution in China), and Seymour Lipset (the socialist movement in Saskatchewan) provide substantial evidence that *social movement leaders do not come from the marginal areas or "lunatic fringe" of society* but from the higher strata of groups and subcultures: teachers, students, editors, farmers, civil servants, businessmen, clergy, and lawyers.[12] They tend to be more affluent, better educated, and less anxious and disoriented than their nonactivist counterparts.[13] Writing about the leaders of the French and American revolutions, Brinton notes that they "were not in general afflicted with anything the psychiatrist could be called about. They were certainly not riffraff, scoundrels, scum of the earth."[14] Myra Ferree concludes her study of American social movement organizations with the comment, "Social movement participants are as rational as those who study them."[15] "The six who dared" to found the Gray Panthers in 1970 (see page 116) certainly did not fit the stereotypes of bewhiskered, disillusioned, radical revolutionaries. Maggie Kuhn instigated the first meeting, not because she and others wanted to divest themselves of an unwanted self or to fulfill a need for psychological refurbishing, but because they all faced loss of their jobs, income, contacts with associates, and opportunities to continue social commitments and active participation in their communities.[16]

Institutions and the public often dismiss or stigmatize social movement leaders as "demagogues" who lie, oversimplify, exaggerate, and make false accusations; who purposely misuse facts, offer insufficient evidence, and employ logical fallacies; who resort to invective, name-calling, and ridicule; and who rely on emotional appeals.[17] The demagogue will use any means to attain personal power and gain. As Steven Goldzwig points out, "the use of the term 'demagogue' generally denotes a rhetor who employs highly suspect means in the pursuit of equally suspect ends."[18] There is no evidence, however, that the typical social movement leader lies, cheats, misuses facts, and makes false accusations intentionally. Similarly, no evidence exists that leaders join the movement for personal gain and power, even though the FBI and other government agencies tried desperately to prove otherwise during the 1950s, 1960s, and 1970s.[19] Most leaders could attain greater powers and material wealth through institutional means than by operating through noninstitutional organizations. Social movement leaders are guilty of using emotional appeals, invective, oversimplification, exaggeration, and insufficient evidence, but so are political, religious, business, educational, charity, and legal leaders—not to mention advertisers and sales representatives. The negative label "demagogue" accurately describes very few social movement leaders.

The mass media, institutional authorities, and the public too often assume that any person who appears to *act* in behalf of a social movement or cause or *looks like* a movement member (African American, native American, woman, student, elderly person, worker) is a movement *leader*. In his study of the Watts Riot that occurred in Los Angeles in 1965 (not unlike the riot of 1992), Oberschall notes that those who assaulted police, threw rocks, set fire to buildings, and harangued crowds "were neither leaders prior to these incidents nor do they subsequently play a leader role in other incidents."[20] This distinction, however, escaped the media, resistance forces, and many civil rights movement sympathizers and legitimizers. Social movements are often blamed or stigmatized by the words and actions of persons who are at best "bystanders" or true misfits who see opportunities to act under the guise of the movement.

Anthony Oberschall and Herbert Simons recommend that students of social movements look at the rhetorical-social situation leaders face rather than at pathological traits or early childhood experiences. Simons observes that "unless it is understood that the leader is subjected to incompatible demands, a great many of his [her] rhetorical acts must seem counterproductive."[21] The typical leader of a typical social movement has no sanctioned position, no sanctioned authority to implement decisions, no regular salary, no orderly personal or family life, and no job security. At the same time, the leader often encounters threats, harassment, denial of access to the mass media, persecution, arrest, jail terms, exile, the necessity of going into hiding, or death. "Put any ordinary, stable individual into a similar position," Oberschall concludes, "and he [she], too, would probably exhibit what some observers consider confused or arbitrary behavior as a result of the pressures and dilemmas that one is continually faced with as a leader in an uninstitutionalized and emergent organizational setting."[22]

This chapter goes beyond the public and institutional views of social movement leadership and the simplistic typologies many social theorists have developed during the past half-century. It examines the *nature* of leadership in social movements and how it is *attained* and *maintained*.

The Nature of Leadership in Social Movements

Theorists generally agree with John Wilson that "the typical pattern of domination in the typical social movement is subsumed under neither the concept of power nor that of authority."[23] Leadership in social movements, Wilson notes, tends to be more structured than a naked power relationship and less structured than an authority relationship associated with an organizational position. Simons claims the leader, at best, "controls an organized core of the movement (frequently mistaken for the movement itself) but exerts relatively little influence over a relatively larger number of sympathizers on its periphery,"[24] somewhat like the onion ring of membership described by Wilson in chapter 3. Essentially, the leader gains the right (the legitimacy) to exercise specific skills within a specific social movement organization or coalition; these skills are often learned through costly trial and error as the social movement unfolds.[25]

Leaders as Organizers

Leaders must have organizational skills, particularly the ability to attract people to the notion of collectivity and to draw people together into meaningful organizations. For example, Maggie Kuhn was the instigator behind the "six who dared" to form the Gray Panthers, and she was instrumental in attracting people from all ages and many fields of endeavor to join in a movement that would primarily benefit elderly Americans. She and her colleagues began with contacts among friends and former associates, attracted many young people who were also fighting for basic rights and recognition, and then organized all ages to form effective coalitions. Maggie Kuhn became known as the leader of the "gray power movement," a leader who emerged from the bottom up through personal contacts and networking.[26] *The Gray Panther Manual* notes that "The group was built on the network principle, involving individuals and groups: a network of human relationships each of them has stockpiled."[27]

Saul Alinsky, a life-long social activist and creator of a training institute for would-be activists, identified a number of essential attributes for successful organizers in his book *Rules for Radicals: A Pragmatic Primer for Realistic Radicals.*[28] For example, an organizer must have curiosity that becomes contagious. Maggie Kuhn of the Gray Panthers, Frank Kameny of the gay rights movement, and Betty Freidan of the women's liberation movement questioned traditional norms, values, and ways of doing things. They asked "Why?" and "Why not?" questions that agitated both victims and victimizers.

An organizer must be *irreverent*. Malcolm X of the Black Muslims, Stokely Carmichael of SNCC, and Eldridge Cleaver of the Black Panthers detested accepted dogma, defied finite definitions of morality, and challenged and insulted both established orders and established social movement organizations and their tactics.

An organizer must have *imagination* to create new ideas, tactics, and organizational structures. Martin Luther King, Jr. decided that action in the streets, such as the historic Montgomery bus boycott, needed to replace the slow, behind-the-scenes court legal actions of the NAACP. Black student leaders in North Carolina were the first to stage sit-ins; Stokely Carmichael took the movement into a "black power" phase. The imagination of each leader or group of leaders changed the movement forever. Maggie Kuhn's group began as the Consultation of Older and Younger Adults—not a very imaginative title. It took the name Gray Panthers and a unique panther logo at the suggestion of the producer of a television talk show following a very lively and controversial appearance by Kuhn and a group of young people. They adopted it as a "fun name" and more expressive of the group's "quick minds, ready humor, radical and action orientation that characterized the members."[29]

An organizer must have a *sense of humor* to relieve tensions within the movement, to allay fears members may have over imminent nonviolent actions, and to make fun of the opposition through satire and ridicule. For instance, organizers of pro-life's Operation Rescue campaigns joke at training sessions about which religious groups are better at kneeling and crawling when confronting police lines at abortion clinics and laugh at the oddity of their nonviolent tactics.[30]

An organizer must have an *organized personality* to maintain order and structure within the movement organization and to deal with the uncertainties and disorder movements inevitably encounter when confronting institutions. When all else seems irrational, the effective organizer must remain rational and in control. Alinsky writes that "The organizer recognizes that each person or bloc has a hierarchy of values" and is able to work out coalitions in which all blocs or organizations gain something and maintain critical beliefs, attitudes, and values.[31] One of Martin Luther King, Jr.'s most important leadership traits was his ability to bring disparate civil rights organizations together for specific campaigns.[32]

An organizer must also have a *strong ego* but not egotism. Leaders must have a healthy belief in themselves and their abilities to achieve goals if they are to instill confidence and belief in others. At the same time, they must have a realistic notion of the odds against them to be able to accept minimal gains or failures, to make the best of each, and to know when it is time to draw back or retire from the field of battle. In many movements, such as those attempting to protect the unborn, animal rights, and the environment, moderate elements and leaders seem more capable than radical elements of deciding when it is time to "back off" and when a tactic may be getting out of hand.

Leaders as Decision Makers

The social movement leader is also a "decision maker," but rarely has the powers of reward and punishment or the claim to legitimacy of an established authority. Joseph Gusfield notes that although the leader is the head of a decision-making hierarchy within a social movement organization, the leader operates within an environment of clients, enemies, adherents, and potential recruits in which he or she has no authority but merely represents the movement.[33] This environment is fraught with repressive uncertainty, complex conditions, conflicting demands, pressures from inside and outside the movement, power struggles among movement elements and organizations, disagreements over philosophies and strategies, financial crises, and competition among aspiring leaders.[34]

Herbert Simons summarizes perceptively the plight of most social movement leaders:

> Shorn of the controls that characterize formal organizations, yet required to perform the same internal functions, harassed from without, yet obligated to adapt to the external system, the leader of a social movement must constantly balance inherently conflicting demands on his [her] position and on the movement he [she] represents.[35]

A reading of the annual *Proceedings of the General Assembly of the Knights of Labor* supports Simons' observations. Leaders of the Knights spent most of their time fending off charges from members, attacking "traitors" who had left the organization but were continuing efforts to undermine it or to start a competing organization, answering negative reports in the media, explaining strains or ruptures in relationships with other labor movement organizations, reporting on conflicts with institutions such as the Catholic Church, explaining failed actions such as strikes or boycotts, and attacking or negotiating with employers.[36]

The many difficulties social movement leaders encounter and the severe limitations placed upon them are exemplified in the civil rights movement. Our most common images of Martin Luther King, Jr. come from memories and pictures shown on the national holiday honoring him on the third Monday of January. We see him delivering his famous "I Have a Dream" speech on the steps of the Lincoln Memorial, walking arm-in-arm with other civil rights leaders through southern towns, and meeting with the press. These are, however, mere highlights of a social movement leader in action.[37] Most of King's time was spent trying to keep or to make peace among fellow clergymen with giant-sized egos or among competing civil rights organizations such as the NAACP, CORE, SNCC, and his own SCLC. He preferred to be on the front lines of the movement, particularly during major campaigns such as Selma, Montgomery, and Birmingham. More frequently he was in New York or Washington trying to raise the funds necessary to keep campaigns alive. Bail for hundreds of protestors arrested during demonstrations and fines levied for breaking local and state ordinances represented a mere fraction of the expenses incurred in the operations of an enormous organization and movement. Only Martin Luther King could perform these essential fund-raising activities effectively, but friends of the movement often grumbled about his absence at critical moments in the streets of the South. Enemies accused him of cowardice, of running away when things got rough, of accepting bail while others remained in jail. And both smarted over the fame and adulation he achieved.

Leaders as Symbols

Although social movement leaders typically do not have the powers and legitimacy of institutional authorities, *they are able to lead because their skills enable them to function as the symbols of their movements.*[38] Leaders tend to become totally identified with the cause, and often the cause becomes totally identified with them. There would not be a United Farm Workers movement without the persistence and organizing skills of Cesar Chavez, a man's liberation movement without the poetry and writings of Robert Bly, or a native American movement without Russell Means who was willing to demonstrate, picket, shout, lobby, go to jail, and sacrifice his life if necessary. Thus, successful leaders are able to instill absolute devotion, love, trust, and dependence in members.[39] Eugene V. Debs serves as an illustration from the early labor movement. In April 1894, he led his American Railway Union in a victorious strike against the powerful James J. Hill and his Great Northern Railroad, a remarkable victory for a union that was barely two years old. As Debs left by train from St. Paul, Minnesota to return to his home in Terre Haute, Indiana, railroad workers lined both sides of the tracks with their hats in their hands in homage to their leader.[40] Some social movements actually take on their leaders' names: Martin Luther (the Lutheran Church), John Wesley (the Wesleyan movement among British and American protestants), Francis Townsend (the Townsend movement of the 1930s for old age pensions), Joseph McCarthy (the McCarthyite movement of the 1950s that fought alleged communist influences in American government and society), and Karl Marx (the Marxist-communist movement that began in Europe and spread around the world), to name a few.[41]

The leader is the ''face'' of the social movement for members, the public, and the mass media. ''It is with leadership that the public identifies in describing and judging a movement,'' Joseph Gusfield writes, ''the leader personifies the movement in cartoon, picture, story, and legend. For much of the public, the leader becomes synonymous with the movement and its adherents.''[42] For instance, more than one generation of Americans viewed the labor movement among coal miners as synonymous with John L. Lewis. The fiery, bushy eyebrowed founder and leader of the United Mine Workers was seen frequently during newsreels in theaters, on front pages of newspapers and magazines, and in numerous cartoons on editorial pages. As we become an increasingly visual society through television, videotapes, laser discs, and pictorials, pictures of leaders and their activities are likely to dominate our visions of social movements. Appearances on talk shows, as presidential candidates did for the first time in the 1992 campaign, are becoming the primary means for social movement leaders to reach massive, general audiences.

Herbert Simons concludes that ''The primary rhetorical test of the leader— and, indirectly, of the strategies he [she] employs—is his [her] capacity to fulfill the requirements of his [her] movement by resolving or reducing rhetorical problems.''[43] In a very real sense, then, the leader is a *rhetorical* leader of a *social* movement.

How Leadership Is Attained in Social Movements

A leadership position is attained in a social movement when members perceive a person to possess two or more of three attributes: charisma, prophecy, and pragmatism.[44]

Charisma

The charismatic leader's source of legitimacy lies in his or her apparent access to a higher source or divine inspiration.[45] An ''awe-inspiring '' personality, William Cameron writes, leads social movement members to see ''truth'' in the charismatic leader's utterances.[46] The charismatic leader tends to be a showperson with a sense of timing and the rhetorical skills necessary to articulate what ''others can as yet only feel, strive towards, and imagine but cannot put into words or translate explicitly into action.''[47] This person leads followers in direct actions that stir things up.[48] Leaders such as Randall Terry (leader of Operation Rescue for the pro-life movement in the 1980s and 1990s), Phyllis Schlafly (president of the Eagle Forum that resisted the women's liberation movement and alleged secular humanist movement in the 1970s and 1980s), Martin Luther King, Jr. (leader of the civil rights movement of the 1950s and 1960s), Samuel Gompers (a founder and leader of the American Federation of Labor from 1886-1924), Susan B. Anthony (a leader of the women's rights and suffrage movements from 1848 to 1906), or Frederick Douglass (an escaped slave who became an internationally known leader of the anti-slavery movement) supply vigor to social movements and make people believe in the impossible.[49] Susan B. Anthony coined the slogan "failure is impossible" for the women's rights movement.

The charismatic leader feels a duty, not merely an obligation or opportunity, to lead the movement and often exhibits exceptional heroism, bravery, and endurance to the point of martyrdom for the cause.[50] The civil rights movement, for example, included famous martyrs (Medgar Evers, Martin Luther King, Jr., Malcolm X) and little known martyrs, both black and white (James Chaney, Michael Schwerner, and Andrew Goodman murdered in Mississippi, and a Detroit homemaker named Viola Liuzzo who was shot and killed while ferrying Selma-to-Montgomery marchers in Alabama). The intense, unwavering support of followers (even when the charismatic leader blunders in selecting targets, strategies, and times to act) maintains unity within the movement and prevents a shifting of the power structure so common within minimally organized social movement organizations.[51]

Perhaps there is no better example of a charismatic leader than Mahatma Gandhi who, for over thirty years, led India's fight for independence from Great Britain.[52] He developed a philosophy and program called *satyagraha* (literally "truth-force") that embodied a method of persuasion that used moral means to achieve moral ends. Gandhi understood the need for showmanship when leading a mass movement and refined actions that gained international attention, identified himself with the Indian people, and required few resources. He dressed in simple sandals and a loincloth that represented the daily attire of male laborers in India. As a protest against British textile laws, Gandhi learned to weave his own simple clothing and made the spinning wheel a major symbol of independence from British rule and influence. He underwent fifteen fasts, his "fiery weapon," to protest low wages and poor working conditions, to restore peace after riots had erupted during a visit by British royalty, to end violence (particularly among Hindus and Muslims), to protest his own imprisonment, and to pressure several British Prime Ministers into altering actions and decisions.

Gandhi spent nearly a third of his life as a social movement leader conducting propaganda tours that often covered hundreds of miles and lasted for months. Each walk took him among the people most sympathetic with the movement and gained attention and followers. As "sacred pilgrimages," these walks identified Gandhi and the movement with the religious traditions of India. He literally became a "holy man" for millions of Indians. Allen Merriam writes that "The primacy of symbolic behavior in extending Gandhi's influence corresponded to the traditional pattern of Indian gurus, who are identified more by their life-style than by their pronouncements.''[53] Gandhi was assassinated shortly after the movement culminated in an independent but strife-torn India.

Prophecy

The prophet's source of legitimacy lies in his or her apparent proximity to the writings of the social movement, its ideology.[54] The person may have written all or important segments of the movement's doctrine, may be considered the most knowledgeable authority on the doctrine, or may be seen as nearest in spirit to the doctrine. As a spokesperson for the movement's ''god''—capitalism, socialism, freedom, equality, fundamental religious truths, the American way of life—the leader with the gift of prophecy elaborates, justifies, and explains the movement's values, myths, and beliefs.[55] The prophet knows the ''truth'' and sets a moral tone for the social movement.[56] The Reverend Jerry Falwell was just such a leader of the Moral Majority during the 1970s and 1980s as he crusaded against liberals, secular humanism, and those who would compromise the great truths of the Bible and the Constitution and threaten our national security. The prophet alone has the ability to perceive the true nature of the urgent problem, its causes, and its solution. Because the prophet is a person of vision, has a psychological commitment to principles, and perceives the writings of the movement to be sacred, he or she is unlikely to be a reconcilor between movement factions or between movement and the established order.[57] The legitimacy of decisions is judged by reference to ideology, not by ends achieved.

When Robert Welch called eleven men together for a two-day meeting in Indianapolis on December 8 and 9, 1958 to found the John Birch Society, he launched his effort to become the undisputed ''prophet'' for the anti-communist resistance movement in the United States. Welch opened his two-day speech to these eleven like-minded businessmen by establishing his qualifications to lead the movement:

> I personally have been studying the problem increasingly for about nine years, and practically full-time for the past three years. And entirely without pride, but in simple thankfulness, let me point out that a lifetime of business experience should have made it easier for me to see the falsity of the economic theories upon which Communism is supposedly based, more readily, than might some scholar coming into that study from the academic cloisters; while a lifetime of interest in things academic, especially world history, should have given me an advantage over many businessmen, in more readily seeing the sophistries in dialectical materialism.[58]

Welch's two-day speech became *The Blue Book of the John Birch Society*, the organization's bible, and the new anti-communist crusading force was to be named after the first American martyr in the struggle, John Birch, an American army officer apparently killed by communist troops in China shortly before communist forces took over all of mainland China. The *Blue Book* not only exposed the imminent dangers of the world communist conspiracy but outlined in detail how the Society would be led, organized, and proceed in its "battles" in the "war" against communism. Sunday supplements in major conservative newspapers such as *The Chicago Tribune* and *The Arizona Republic* introduced the John Birch Society to millions of Americans in the fall of 1964. An item entitled "He Has Stirred the Slumbering Spirit" presented Robert Welch as a person of vision, wisdom, and commitment in the struggle against the communist menace, a person whose words were gaining scores of converts:

> Mr. Welch's writings have created widespread comment—some critical. Few were ready to believe him when he warned of the impending Communist takeovers by Castro in Cuba, Ben Bella in Algeria, and Sukarno in Indonesia. But with events proving him correct again and again, his writings are now closely scrutinized by all serious students of anti-Communism.[59]

Welch created a monthly periodical for the movement entitled *American Opinion* and remained its editor and frequent contributor until his death in 1986. In an open letter to readers in the October 1978 issue, Welch wrote of the periodical's reason for being:

> You were to read *American Opinion* in order to learn the truth; the plain unmistakable truth about what was really happening. We set out twenty-two [sic] years ago to make this monthly compendium the most accurate, most penetrating, and most widely accepted authority in the world on the nature and the menace of the revolutionary cabal that was steadily undermining our whole civilization.[60]

Welch was never a reconciler in the struggle between good and evil that was a matter of life and death for the American way of life. As a prophet for the anti-communist movement, his Society's purpose was to build a "rededication to God, to family, to country, and to strong moral principles."[61]

Pragmatism

The pragmatist's source of legitimacy lies in his or her apparent organizational expertise, efficiency, and tact.[62] As a person who believes that the social movement must have a secure and stable foundation for growth, the pragmatic leader brings common sense and a healthy skepticism to the movement, seeks to reconcile diverse interests, desires "communication" rather than "excommunication," and replaces unattainable goals with diffuse goals and a broader range of targets.[63] The pragmatist believes that ideals and principles are useless without organization and implementation. This type of leader seeks to make the social movement inclusive rather than exclusive by making it more acceptable to outsiders, including important legitimizers from the established order, and devotes energies to fund raising, recruitment, and organization.[64] The pragmatist is more likely to compromise the "sacredness" of the movement's writings than the "integrity" of the organization and may come to see maintenance of the organization as an end in itself—without the organization, there can be no movement.[65] Leaders such as Maggie Kuhn, Martin Luther King, Jr., and Russel Means see clearly that successful short-term campaigns and long-term social movements require organization, planning, training, discipline, funds, and guidance.

Samuel Gompers, who led (with the exception of one year) the American Federation of Labor from its founding in 1886 to his death in 1924, was primarily a pragmatist. He was keenly aware of the labor movement's history, of labor organizations that had blossomed and wilted, of American opposition to labor "radicals," and of the needs and desires of workers, specifically among the skilled trades. Above all, he understood the need for a strong organization with a central focus (trade unionism) and a sound financial base.[66] Although Gompers was sympathetic with all elements of the labor movement, he refused, for example, to aid the Knights of Labor when it became embroiled in the aftermath of the Haymarket Riot in Chicago and the trial of the accused anarchists. The AFL was too young, could not afford to become identified with the Knights of Labor or the anarchists, and was, after all, in direct competition with the "industrial unionism" espoused by the Knights. Gompers saw the "trade union" as "the historic and natural form of working class organization," one based on scientific principles, and shed no tears when the Knights of Labor declined rapidly after the haymarket affair.[67] Speaking to the Machinists' Convention in 1901, he remarked:

> Those of us who have gone through the movement of the Knights of Labor, which is now happily removed from the path of progress; those who have studied the previous effervescent [bubbly, hissing, show of liveliness] movements of that character, know the danger with which such movements are always confronted.[68]

Gompers understood the American value system and the inherent conservatism of most workers and industrialists in his struggle to make the AFL the accepted umbrella organization for all trade unions. While he tried to avoid unnecessary confrontations within the movement, Gompers was not reluctant to attack elements that posed dangers to his beloved organization. At the AFL convention in 1903, Gompers attacked socialist members head-on:

> And I want to say that I am entirely at variance with your philosophy. I declare it to you. I am not only at variance with your doctrines, but with your philosophy. Economically, you are unsound; socially, you are wrong; industrially, you are an impossibility.[69]

Gompers succeeded in building and maintaining a social movement organization that would withstand the onslaught of industrialists, competing labor organizations, economic depressions, and world wars to become an institutionalized force in American society.

How Leadership Is Maintained in Social Movements

Social movement leaders maintain their positions as long as they hold the confidence of followers, seem to have solutions to problems, meet the exigencies of new and unexpected situations, and perform rhetorical functions necessary for the stage the movement is in at the moment.[70] William Cameron writes that all leaders "do something exceedingly well" and "when they stop doing it well, they often cease to lead."[71]

A Mix of Leadership Attributes

Theorists agree that every successful social movement leader must display two or more of the three essential leadership attributes—charisma, prophecy, and pragmatism—though not necessarily in the same context. Joseph Gusfield, for example, argues that leadership can be conceived as a set of simultaneous roles. As mobilizer, the leader must "breathe the fire and brimstone of enthusiastic mission," and as articulator, the leader "pours the oil of bargaining, compromise, and common culture."[72] John Wilson claims that leaders gain the esteem of fellow movement members because of the peculiar mix of their rhetorical abilities.[73] Anthony Oberschall concludes: "Leaders, in sum, are the architects of organization, ideology, and mobilization for the movement."[74]

Unfortunately, a great many social movement leaders tend to be one-dimensional. Randall Terry, a former car salesman, is effective in organizing and leading Operation Rescue blockades of abortion clinics throughout the United States, partly because he organizes such limited actions well and partly because of his personal bravery and commitment. He has been arrested dozens of times but returns to the action as soon as he is released. It is doubtful, however, that he could lead a large national organization, be content with behind-the-scenes organizing and fund raising, or sit down with other social movement organizations or institutions to reach compromises.

Few spokespersons for black rights during the 1960s were more charismatic—particularly among young black Americans who were becoming disillusioned with the "civil rights" movement—than Stokely Carmichael, Chairman of SNCC (the Student Nonviolent Coordinating Committee), during the famous Meredith March in Mississippi in June 1966. He was attractive, intelligent, articulate, and understood the importance of timing and showmanship. During the Meredith March, Carmichael cooperated with the leaders of the NAACP and SCLC until the march reached Greenwood, SNCC territory, and Martin Luther King, Jr. left for meetings in Chicago. The sheriff arrested Carmichael and others briefly on June 16 for pitching tents in a schoolyard, and Carmichael used the occasion to escalate his confrontational rhetoric at an evening rally: "This is the 27th time I've been arrested, I ain't gonna be arrested no more. . . . Every courthouse in Mississippi should be burnt down tomorrow so we can get rid of the dirt."[75] The next evening Stokely Carmichael delivered more of the same confrontational message and then, on cue, Willie Ricks shouted: "What do you want?" Carmichael responded: "Black power!" and the crowd was soon enthusiastically echoing this new slogan. He had seized the moment beautifully. During the next several months, he traveled throughout the country both explaining and extolling

"Black Power." While Carmichael became a hero among the growing number of young "black nationalists" within the movement, his slogan and confrontational rhetoric shattered the fragile coalition of black rights organizations and polarized white liberal legitimizers and blacks.[76] He lacked the attributes of both the prophet in failing to develop a clear doctrine of "black power" meaningful to all elements of the movement and the pragmatist by attacking other leaders in his speeches to black audiences. In Detroit on July 30, 1966, Carmichael remarked:

> I'm very concerned, because you see we have a lot of Negro leaders, and I want to make it clear I'm no leader. I represent the Student Nonviolent Coordinating Committee. That's the sole source of my power, and that's Black Power. I'm no Negro leader, but I think we have to speak out about the war in Vietnam.[77]

By 1968 Carmichael had left SNCC, reestablished his relationship with Martin Luther King, Jr., and formed a new organization called the Black United Front, an organization that experienced a brief lifespan.[78] He remained an eloquent spokesperson for black power, pride, and independence, but he failed as a leader. William Cameron undoubtedly had one-dimensional movement leaders such as Randall Terry and Stokely Carmichael in mind when he wrote, "many a stirring evangelist makes a poor pastor."[79]

Handling Diverse, Conflicting Roles

Few social movement leaders, even multi-dimensional ones, are capable of handling the diverse and often conflicting roles thrust upon them and the rhetorical dilemmas social movements encounter daily.[80] The leader (1) must adapt to different audiences at once but not appear to be a political chameleon, (2) produce short-run successes but not preclude long-run successes, (3) use militant tactics to gain visibility for the movement but use moderate tactics to gain entry into decision-making centers, (4) foster strong convictions in the movement's principles but control the implication that their attainment justifies any necessary means, (5) strive for organizational efficiency without dampening the enthusiasm and spontaneity generated during the early, less-structured days of the movement, (6) understand that militants are effective with power-vulnerables such as elected and appointed officials and moderates are more effective with power-invulnerables such as judges, business owners, and much of the "silent majority," (7) vilify established orders but be willing and able to work with them when it is to the movement's advantage, and (8) grasp at opportunities to deal with an established order on its own turf without appearing to be "selling out" or "going soft." The difficulty of meeting and adapting to role demands that require different rhetorical skills and tactics typically results in a proliferation of leaders that cause conflict within and among movement organizations and results in fragmentation of structure and persuasive efforts.[81]

The civil rights movement of the 1950s and 1960s produced a variety of leaders who performed *specific* roles skillfully but could not meet all rhetorical demands of the movement.[82] Roy Wilkins of the NAACP, for instance, believed in working through the system (particularly through the courts) to bring about change, and he feared both the tactics and the results of direct actions such as sit-ins, marches, and demonstrations. Andrew Young was highly successful as a conciliator and diplomat within SCLC, particularly among its younger members and elements. However, his soft-spoken style and devotion to Martin Luther King, Jr. prevented him from speaking out on his views and becoming visible beyond the SCLC. Ralph Abernathy was highly visible but usually silent during the movement (seemingly always at King's side in marches, jails, meetings, and press conferences). His loyalty, dedication, and bravery were not sufficient to prepare him to take over the leadership of the SCLC in 1968 following King's assassination. Fred Shuttlesworth founded the Alabama Christian Movement for Human Rights in 1956 and later allied this group with the SCLC. He was highly respected within the movement and feared by the southern establishment for his reckless courage and ability to organize and lead demonstrations, but his efforts to become a major leader were plagued by autocratic, egocentric, and tactless personality traits.

Changing as the Movement Changes

Perhaps the greatest obstacle for leadership tenure in social movements is the necessity for movements to change. As movements change, leaders and followers must change. Wars, economic depressions, the resignation or replacement of institutional leaders, inventions, and political, religious, and social trends may greatly affect the nature and progress of social movements. For example, if the abortion pill RU-486 is made legal in the United States, women could prevent or terminate pregnancies without going to abortion clinics or finding physicians to perform abortions. Both of these are currently primary targets of pro-life pressures and demonstrations, and there would no longer be data or stories available to show the extent and barbarism of abortions. Joseph Gusfield writes that, "The disjuncture between ideology and the adaptive problems of the movement constantly raises the issue of too much or too little accommodation; of renunciation of the mission or overrighteous inflexibility."[83]

Jerry Rubin was an archetypal leader of the student, anti-Vietnam War, and counterculture movements of the 1960s and 1970s.[84] He was intelligent, articulate, imaginative, brave and, above all, outrageous in manner, actions, and dress. He effectively organized civil disobedience at Berkeley, demonstrations against trains carrying troops to fight in Vietnam, the October 1967 march on the Pentagon, and of the "yippies" that created chaos at the Chicago convention of the Democratic party in 1968. He was brilliant at manipulating the media and creating "put-ons" (such as threatening to levitate the Pentagon) that led to both humorous and violent reactions from the establishment, especially police agencies who confronted the Yippies in the trenches. He helped to polarize society along age lines with the slogan, "Don't trust anyone over thirty." As one of the famous

"Chicago Seven," he stood trial for five-and-a-half months charged with "conspiracy" for actions during the Democratic convention.

By the early 1970s, however, Jerry Rubin knew "the movement" was rapidly dwindling in numbers and fervor, society was changing, old methods would no longer be effective, and ironically most leaders (including himself) were nearing or had passed their thirtieth birthdays. Many members of the movement, particularly younger ones, resisted change and both loved and hated Rubin as a symbol of the '60s. They longed for another 1968-style confrontation during the 1972 Republican and Democratic conventions in Miami Beach and called Rubin a "sellout" because he stayed in a hotel instead of a park like the old days. On July 14, Rubin's 34th birthday, a group calling themselves "Zippies" ("put zip back into yip") marched on his hotel in Miami armed with a cake to throw in his face to celebrate his retirement from the movement. Later in the year, a band of Zippies "trashed" Rubin's car in New York to demonstrate their independence from older Yippies. Rubin came to realize that "changes cannot be made on the political level alone, or that society we are changing will be repeated. We must examine our own process."[85] These were not words the movement and its younger members wanted to hear. A number of leaders of the anti-war and counterculture movements committed suicide because they either could not accept or could not adapt to the new social realities.

Adapting to Events

Events may thrust the social movement and its leaders in new directions, and leaders may appear to be mere puppets controlled by events and the whims of some members.[86] Leaders must appear to be in the forefront of necessary change and wise adaptation, while not appearing to abandon major norms, beliefs, attitudes, and values of their movements in order to meet situational exigencies.[87]

Terrence Powderly became General Master Workman (president) of the Order of the Knights of Labor in 1880 and helped make it the largest and most powerful labor union in the history of the United States, reaching some one million members in 1886.[88] But 1886 was to be a fateful year for the Knights. The government, newspapers, churches, and the public identified the Knights of Labor with the anarchists and blamed it for the bloody Haymarket Riot in Chicago that killed several police officers. Membership and influence plummeted year after year in spite of Powderly's charisma, persuasive skills, and considerable organizational abilities. In 1893 with the country in the midst of a terrible depression, Powderly decided that only the most drastic of actions could save the Knights and perhaps all of organized labor, so he approached Samuel Gompers with the notion of merging with the AFL, its major competitor. Other Knights were incensed at his willingness, regardless of his honorable intentions, to compromise the Order's "fundamental and vital" principle of industrial unionism open to the "laboring masses" by merging with a "mere trade union" limited to a few skilled workers and headed by archenemy Samuel Gompers. Powderly and his lieutenants were "retired from office," and new General Master Workman, James R. Sovereign, declared to the assembled Knights at the 1894 convention that "any action by members of this Order inimical to or in contravention to this principle [industrial unionism] and this policy is *treason* to the Order and the best interests of labor."[89] Powderly was expelled from the Order as a traitor and never forgiven for his treachery.

Leading by Not Getting Too Far Ahead or Behind

Bruce Cameron writes that "The leader must seem to lead. In order to lead, he must be a little ahead of his followers, a little wiser, a little more informed. But if he gets too far ahead, contact is broken, and he may be a 'leader' without followers."[90] In a study of Malcolm X's autobiography, Thomas Benson focuses on the final year of Malcolm X's life in which he broke with Elijah Muhammad (founder of the Black Muslims), shifted positions on integration and participation in civil rights demonstrations, and no longer saw "Uncle Toms" and whites as devils.[91] Many of Malcolm X's supporters and enemies viewed these changes as signs of weakness, inconsistency, softening of commitment, or evidence of the "hustler" element resurfacing. Benson argues that a careful reading of *The Autobiography of Malcolm X*, published a few months after his assassination, reveals that Malcolm X "contained a principle of change within himself," that his changes can be "seen as consistent steps forward rather than as random and untrustworthy conversions by faith," and that his growing "sense of brotherhood with all men is not the weakening of militancy or a softening of commitment, but an extension of potency."[92] In the months before his assassination when he was facing growing opposition and harassment, Malcolm X opposed "strait-jacketed thinking, and strait-jacketed societies."[93]

While some leaders streak ahead of their movements and lose contact, others lag behind or are unwilling or incapable of adapting to new circumstances or new stages in their social movements' life cycles. A person with strong attributes of charisma and prophecy, for instance, may be unable to abandon unattainable goals or to reconcile diverse elements for the harmony of the larger movement."[94] On the other hand, events may revitalize a social movement that has settled into a comfortable bureaucratic state with a pragmatist who is task oriented, has administrative skills, and thrives on the routine and mundane. This skilled bureaucrat, unable to instill vigor, set a moral tone, and make followers believe in the impossible, is likely to be thrust aside by a charismatic leader with strong traits of the prophet who can put into words and actions what others can only feel or imagine.[95]

Joseph Gusfield's study of the Women's Christian Temperance Union (WCTU) leadership following repeal of the prohibition of alcoholic beverages amendment in 1933 illustrates a leader who refused to move with the movement.[96] The president of the WCTU was determined to uphold the centrality of total abstinence even though the American public, many Protestant churches, a significant number of members, and other movement organizations such as Alcoholics Anonymous (AA) argued for lesser restrictions on drinking. In her annual report to the WCTU in 1952, Mrs. Z declared:

> In order not to be considered narrow or unable to see both sides some of the Drys have allowed themselves to be maneuvered into accepting the idea that [total abstinence and prohibition] is an old fashioned approach. . . . Between right and wrong there is only one ground and that is a battleground.[97]

Mrs. Z's refusal to modify her stance on principle brought ridicule upon the organization and herself. Movement members and the press described her as being "too rigid," a "one-women drought," a "fire-eating leader," and a "diehard." When Mrs. A assumed the presidency of the WCTU in the 1960s, she emphasized the necessity of finding common ground and common goals within the WCTU and between the WCTU and other temperance organizations. Mrs. A was chosen because she was astride of the movement instead of lagging behind in defense of a principle no longer accepted by much of society and the temperance movement.

Conclusions

Contrary to common American impressions, social movement leaders tend to be much like the rest of us rather than fire-breathing misfits, demagogues, fanatics, or perverts. Like all collectives, however, social movements attract their share of losers, extremists, and the pathological. The public, established orders, and the media too often assume that every person involved in a social movement's activities is a leader, regardless of the person's involvement, commitment, or leadership position.

This chapter has focused on the nature of leadership in social movements and how it is attained and maintained. Typical leaders of typical social movements are decision makers with limited legitimacy and powers to reward and punish while constantly facing conflicting demands on their positions and movements. Leaders are able to lead because they possess one or more of three critical attributes—charisma, prophecy, and pragmatism. They become the symbols and faces of their movements for members, the public, and the media. Attaining leadership positions within social movements is easier than maintaining positions because leaders must sustain an appropriate blend of the three critical attributes, handle diverse and conflicting roles, change as the movement changes, adapt to events, and lead without getting too far ahead or behind their movements.

Endnotes

[1] Roberta Ash, *Social Movements in America* (Chicago: Markham, 1972), 40.

[2] John Wilson, *Introduction to Social Movements* (New York: Basic Books,, 1973), 124.

[3] Wilson, 78.

[4] Ash, 230.

[5] George Gallup, Jr., *The Gallup Poll: Public Opinion 1990* (Wilmington, DL: Scholarly Resources, 1991), 1, 100–103.

[6] Eric Hoffer, *The True Believer* (New York: Mentor, 1951), 119–138.

[7] Richard D. Raum and James S. Measell, "Wallace and His Ways: A Study of the Rhetorical Genre of Polarization," *Central States Speech Journal* 25 (Spring 1974), 28–35.

[8] James Darsey, "From 'Gay Is Good' to the Scourge of AIDS: The Evolution of Gay Liberation Rhetoric, 1977–1990," *Communication Studies* 42 (Spring 1991), 51; Herbert W. Simons, Elizabeth Mechling, and Howard Schreier, "Functions of Communication in Mobilizing for Action from the Bottom Up: The Rhetoric of Social Movements," *Handbook on Rhetorical and Communication Theory*, Carroll C. Arnold and John W. Bowers, eds. (Boston: Allyn and Bacon, 1984), 813.

[9] "Trying to Take Back the Planet," *Newsweek*, February 5, 1990, 24.

[10] Hoffer, 58.

[11] Herbert W. Simons, "Persuasion in Social Conflicts: A Critique of Prevailing Conceptions and a Framework for Future Research," *Speech Monographs* 39 (November 1972), 236.

[12] Crane Brinton, *The Anatomy of Revolution* (New York: Vintage Books, 1952), 107; Ming T. Lee, "The Founders of the Chinese Communist Party," *Civilisations* 18 (1968), 115; Seymour Lipset, "Leadership and New Social Movements," *Studies in Leadership*, Alvin Gouldner, ed. (New York: Harper and Row, 1950), 360.

[13] Simons, Mechling, and Schreier, 816.

[14] Brinton, 127.

[15] Myra Marx Ferree, "The Political Context of Reality: Rational Choice Theory and Resource Mobilization," *Frontiers in Social Movement Theory*, Aldon D. Morris and Carol McClurg Mueller, eds. (New Haven, CT: Yale University Press, 1992), 48.

[16] *The Gray Panther Manual* (Philadelphia: The Gray Panthers, 1978), 3–4; Dieter Hessel, ed. *Maggie Kuhn on Aging* (Philadelphia: Westminster Press, 1977), 9–12.

[17] Steven R. Goldzwig, "A Social Movement Perspective on Demagoguery: Achieving Symbolic Realignment," *Communication Studies* 40 (Fall 1989), 202–228.

[18] Goldzwig, 202.

[19] Fred Powledge, *Free at Last? The Civil Rights Movement and the People Who Made It* (Boston: Little, Brown and Company, 1991), 222, 412–413, 558–559, and 610–612; Kirkpatrick Sale, *SDS* (New York: Vintage Books, 1974), 499–500, 541–544, 551–557, and 643–645; "Congressmen Laugh at Zany CIA Devices," Lafayette, Indiana *Journal and Courier*, September 21, 1977, D-7; "Documents Tell of Army 'Spy' in Peace Group," Lafayette, Indiana *Journal and Courier*, October 4, 1975, C-6; "FBI Documents Show '60s Campus Capers," Lafayette, Indiana *Journal and Courier*, June 25, 1975, B-7.

[20] Anthony Oberschall, "The Los Angeles Riot," *Social Problems* 15 (Winter 1965), 324–326.

[21] Herbert W. Simons, "Requirements, Problems, and Strategies: A Theory of Persuasion for Social Movements," *Quarterly Journal of Speech* 56 (February 1970), 4.

[22] Anthony Oberschall, *Social Conflict and Social Movements* (Englewood Cliffs, NJ: Prentice-Hall, 1973), 148–149. See also William A. Gamson, "The Social Psychology of Collective Action," *Frontiers in Social Movement Theory*, 53–60; Ferree, 38–43.

[23] Wilson, 198.

[24] Simons (1970), 4.

[25] Oberschall (1973), 158.

[26] *The Gray Panther Manual*, 3–21.

[27] *The Gray Panther Manual*, 5.

[28] Saul D. Alinsky, *Rules for Radicals: A Pragmatic Primer for Realistic Radicals* (New York: Vintage Books, 1972), 72–79.

[29] *The Gray Panther Manual*, 6.

[30] "Operation Rescue," on ABC's "20/20."

[31] Alinsky, 76.

[32] Adam Fairclough, *To Redeem the Soul of America: The Southern Christian Leadership Conference and Martin Luther King, Jr.* (Athens, GA: University of Georgia Press, 1987).

[33] Joseph R. Gusfield, "Functional Areas of Leadership in Social Movements," *Sociological Quarterly* 7 (1966), 137.

[34] Oberschall (1973), 158.

[35] Simons (1970), 4.

[36] Charles J. Stewart, "The Internal Rhetoric of the Knights of Labor," *Communication Studies* 42 (Spring 1991), 67–82.

[37] Fairclough.

[38] Yonina Talmon, "Pursuit of the Millennium: The Relation Between Religious and Social Change," *The European Journal of Sociology* 2 (1952), 140–141; Ralph Turner and Lewis M. Killian, *Collective Behavior* (Englewood Cliffs, NJ: Prentice-Hall, 1972), 391.

[39] Hadley Cantril, *The Psychology of Social Movements* (New York: John Wiley and Sons, 1963), 132.

[40] Ray Ginger, *The Bending Cross* (New Brunswick, NJ: Rutgers University Press, 1949), 106.

[41] Joseph R. Gusfield, *Protest, Reform, and Revolt: A Reader in Social Movements* (New York: John Wiley and Sons, 1970), 454.

[42] Gusfield (1966), 141.

[43] Simons (1970), 2–3.

[44] Max Weber, *The Theory of Social and Economic Organizations*, A.M. Henderson and Talcott Parsons, trans. (New York: Free Press, 1964), 328–329; Wilson, 201.

[45] Turner and Killian, 390–392; Neil S. Smelser, *Theory of Collective Behavior* (London: Routledge and Kegan Paul, 1962), 355; Wilson, 203; Kenelm Burridge, *New Heaven New Earth: A Study of Millenarian Activities* (Oxford: Basil Blackwell, 1969), 155–156.

[46] William Bruce Cameron, *Modern Social Movements* (New York: Random House, 1966), 73.

[47] Burridge, 155.

[48] Rex D. Hopper, "The Revolutionary Process: A Frame of Reference for the Study of Revolutionary Movements," *Social Forces* 28 (March 1950), 272; Smelser, 297.

[49] J. P. Roche and S. Sachs, "The Bureaucrat and the Enthusiast: An Exploration of the Leadership of Social Movements," *Western Political Quarterly* 8 (1955), 257.

[50] Theodore Abel, "The Pattern of a Successful Social Movement," *American Sociological Review* 2 (1937), 352.

[51] Turner and Killian, 389–393; Abel, 352.

[52] Allen H. Merriam, "Symbolic Action in India: Gandhi's Nonverbal Persuasion," *Quarterly Journal of Speech* 61 (October 1975), 290–306.

[53] Merriam, 305.

[54] Wilson, 201.

[55] Hooper, 275; Turner and Killian, 394.

[56] Roche and Sachs, 258.

[57] Roche and Sachs, 250–251.

[58] *The Blue Book of the John Birch Society* (Belmont, MA: Western Islands, 1961), xiv–xv.

[59] "The John Birch Society: A Report," *The Arizona Republic*, advertising supplement, October 25, 1964, 6.

[60] *American Opinion*, October, 1978, 56.

[61] "The John Birch Society: A Report," *Chicago Tribune*, advertising supplement, November 15, 1964, 16.

[62] Wilson, 201.

[63] Roche and Sachs, 249 and 259; Mayer Zald and Roberta Ash, "Social Movement Organizations: Growth, Decay, Change," *Social Forces* 44 (1966), 327–340.

[64] Turner and Killian, 394; Roche and Sachs, 250 and 253.

[65] Roche and Sachs, 253.

[66] Walter B. Emery, "Samuel Gompers," *A History and Criticism of American Public Address*, Vol. II, William Norwood Brigance, ed. (New York: Russell and Russell, 1960), 557–559.

[67] Samuel Gompers, "President's Report," December 13, 1887, *Report of the Proceedings: American Federation of Labor*, 1888, 8.

[68] Samuel Gompers, "Address to the Machinists' Convention," *American Federationist* 8 (July 1901), 251.

[69] Samuel Gompers, *American Federation of Labor Proceedings*, 1903, 198.

[70] Cantril, 235; R.L. Hamblin, "Leadership and Crisis," *Sociometry* 21 (1958), 322–335.

[71] Cameron, 164.

[72] Gusfield (1966), 139 and 141.

[73] Wilson, 198 and 201.

[74] Oberschall, 146.

[75] Fairclough, 316.

[76] Robert L. Scott and Wayne Brockriede, *The Rhetoric of Black Power* (New York: Harper and Row, 1969), 1–9.

[77] From an audio recording and Scott and Brockriede, 88–89.

[78] Fairclough, 364–366.

[79] Cameron, 93.

[80] Simons (1970), 1–11.

[81] Smelser, 297.

[82] See Fairclough for discussions of the leadership strengths and weaknesses of civil rights leaders.

[83] Gusfield (1966), 152.

[84] Jerry Rubin, "Growing Up Again," *Human Behavior*, March, 1976, 17–23.

[85] Rubin, 22.

[86] Turner and Killian, 396.

[87] Muzafer Sherif, *An Outline of Social Psychology* (New York: Harper and Row, 1948), 171.

[88] Charles J. Stewart, "Labor Agitation in America: 1865–1915," *America in Controversy: History of American Public Address*, DeWitte T. Holland, ed. (Dubuque, IA: W.C. Brown, 1973), 153–169.

[89] James R. Sovereign, "Annual Address of the General Master Workman," *Proceedings of the General Assembly: Knights of Labor* (1894), 71.

[90] Cameron, 107.

[91] Thomas W. Benson, "Rhetoric and Autobiography: The Case of Malcolm X," *Quarterly Journal of Speech 60* (February 1974), 1–13.

[92] Benson, 7, 9, 10.

[93] Benson, 12.

[94] Zald and Ash (1966), 533–535; Roche and Sachs, 248–261.

[95] Burridge, 155.

[96] Gusfield (1966), 142–145.

[97] *Annual Report of the National Women's Christian Temperance Union* (1952), 85.

Chapter Six

Personal Needs and Social Movements
John Birchers and Gray Panthers

Most students of social movement persuasion agree that recruitment and consolidation are essential functions: Without recruitment there are no members, and without consolidation there is no movement.[1] This chapter considers how two social movement organizations recruited people suited to their organizational efforts and excluded people who would not fit. Chapter 2 presented a social systems approach to persuasion and suggested that personality (or character type) and message are interdependent. This chapter explains how early John Birch Society and Gray Panther rhetoric provided people with gratifications that were primarily psychological rather than political, social, or philosophical. More specifically, John Birch Society materials spoke directly to the needs of a classic authoritarian character structure and Gray Panther materials spoke to the democratic character structure.

Authoritarian and Democratic Personalities

The Hitler phenomenon spurred many psychologists to explore the sources of his appeal, and one of the earliest hypotheses centered around the notion of an authoritarian personality type. Early studies of the authoritarian character structure were based on clinical observation until 1950 when Theodor Adorno and his colleagues presented their California F-Scale for the measurement of Fascist tendencies. These early works were directed at understanding rightist authoritarianism and they concentrated on the study of followers' beliefs about authority and those who exercise it. In the 1960s, Milton Rokeach steered

111

psychological research toward the study of "topic free" open- and closed-mindedness, and interest in ideological authoritarianism waned.[2]

One of the early studies of authoritarian personality remains especially helpful for understanding how messages provide audiences with psychological gratifications. That study is Abraham Maslow's 1943 essay on "The Authoritarian Character Structure."[3] We do not ordinarily recommend framing rhetorical analyses with fifty-year-old studies from other disciplines, but Maslow's is no ordinary essay. It is useful because it synthesizes clinical observations of people's verbal expressions and because it predates psychologists' preoccupation with pencil-and-paper scales. Moreover, it describes two archetypal personality structures that have social, political and rhetorical implications: authoritarian and democratic character structures.

Maslow's Authoritarian Character Structure

For Maslow's authoritarian character structure, everything revolves around authority. The three major premises of the authoritarian worldview are that (a) the world is a jungle that requires both (b) strict hierarchical organization and (c) the glorification of dominance and submission. The fundamental premise of the authoritarian worldview is that life is essentially threatening. Maslow explained that:

> Like other psychologically insecure people, the authoritarian person lives in a world which may be conceived to be pictured by him as a sort of jungle in which every man's [woman's] hand is necessarily against every other man's [woman's], in which the whole world is conceived of as dangerous, threatening, or at least challenging, and in which humans are conceived of as primarily selfish or evil or stupid. . . . This jungle is peopled with animals who either eat or are eaten, who are either feared or despised. One's safety lies in one's own strength and this strength consists primarily in the power to dominate. If one is not strong enough the only alternative is to find a strong protector.[4]

Within this jungle the protector-protected relationship predominates. Because danger is all around, the protector demands total obedience; and because the protected must sustain their relationships with the protector, their submission is willing and even ecstatic.

The authoritarian's worldview makes sense to the extent that the world really is like a jungle. It *is* foolish to wander off from a safari to chat with lions and tigers, but to fear entering a grocery store without an armed guide is paranoid. Most life experiences fall somewhere between these extremes, but the authoritarian character structure treats them all as dangerous. Authoritarians therefore express only contempt for those who fail to recognize that the world is a dangerous place. Because jungle creatures compete relentlessly and unmercifully for the means of survival, every approaching creature must quickly be categorized either as superior and thus to be feared, resented, bootlicked, and admired, or as inferior and therefore to be scorned, humiliated, and dominated. Everyone must be quickly and easily ranked in a hierarchy from strongest to weakest. The authoritarian can therefore tolerate neither diverse goals nor diverse means, because unity is essential for survival. All people, achievements, and events must be measured on one scale, the scale of survival. Different authoritarians may stress different scales—such as strength, speed or cunning—but no authoritarian character can value diversity or tolerance because multiple scales confound superior-inferior ranking and thus compound the danger to all. The person judged superior on that one scale is judged *universally* superior, and inferiors are judged universally inferior.

Because these judgments of superiority must be made quickly, and because superiority is inherently generalizable, the authoritarian character judges by externals. These externals may include titles, physical stature and grooming, wealth, family name, race, gender, age, or behavior. Externals are useful to authoritarians precisely because a superior person is always superior. The authoritarian can note external characteristics and measure them against the single vertical scale to ascertain the person's superior-inferior ranking.

Given the foregoing context for the leader-follower relationship the authoritarian character structure naturally regards any leader's kindness as weakness. Maslow explained that:

> If he [she] is in dominance status, he [she] will tend to be cruel; if he [she] is in subordinate status, he [she] will tend to be masochistic. But because of the tendencies in himself [herself], he [she] will understand, and deep down within himself [herself] will agree with the cruelty of the superior person, even if he himself [she herself] is the object of the cruelty. He [she] will understand the bootlicker and the slave even if he himself [she herself] is not the bootlicker or the slave. The same principles explain both the leader and the follower in an authoritarian group, both the slave-owner and the slave.[5]

Significantly, authoritarian followers glory in subservience to their leader. There can be no negotiation of control because neither party finds such negotiations either valid or productive. Both realize that the worthless inferior is fortunate to have the protector, and both realize that the protector need feel little but contempt for the followers.

Because the authoritarian character structure regards people as fundamentally selfish, evil, stupid, and dependent, inferiors can be used as the superior sees fit. Non-leaders are "tools" or "pawns on a chessboard" and may even be seen as sub-human. This sadomasochistic tendency contributes to an authoritarian value system in which brutality, cruelty, selfishness, and hardness are exalted and in which sympathy, kindness, and generosity are reviled by leaders and followers alike.

Maslow lists several other characteristics of authoritarianism which deserve passing attention. These include an "abyss between men and women" (men being purportedly better able to survive through strength), the soldier ideal, the importance of humiliation as a mechanism for establishing superiority, antagonism toward the education of inferiors, avoidance of responsibility for one's own fate, and the pursuit of security through order, discipline, and a variety of compulsive-obsessive behaviors. Pervading all of these characteristics is the impossibility of satisfaction. The best one can hope for in the jungle is temporary relief from constant danger, but one must be most careful when the jungle seems safest.

Maslow's Democratic Character Structure

Maslow's democratic character sees the world as a basically friendly and supportive place, more greenhouse than jungle. Because there is little danger, there is little need for protection and, therefore, little need for submission, discipline, or orders. Whereas the authoritarian character sees all differences between people in terms of superiority-inferiority, the democratic character tends to view differences between people as unrelated to matters of superiority and inferiority. When superiority-inferiority judgments must be made, the democratic character judges individuals in specific functional terms, appraising specific personal capabilities, functions, and performances. The democratic personality prefers to judge others, when judge it must, on the basis of performance. As Maslow explained, the democratic character:

> customarily gives his [her] permanent respect only to people who are worthy of respect for functional reasons. He [she] doesn't give his [her] respect automatically simply because he [she] is supposed to, or because everybody else respects this person.[6]

The democratic character examines functional characteristics, adjudicates them (as necessary) according to diverse values and creates a leader-follower relationship (when necessary) for the attainment of some specific goal.

The democratic character structure views humans as partners rather than rivals and is reluctant to use or to manipulate them. It exhibits no tendency comparable to the authoritarian's sadomasochistic tendency: there is room for both selfishness and generosity, for hardness and compassion since different people value differently in different circumstances at different times. Democratic character types can be happier for longer since their basic needs have been satisfied and danger is unusual, rather than normal, in everyday life.

Summary

Maslow observes that the authoritarian and democratic character types are constructions of internally consistent beliefs or tendencies, all of which revolve around the premise that the world is (or is not) an extremely threatening and dangerous place. The authoritarian worldview is a psychologically functional framework for interpreting one's environment. Implicit in it is the need for communication. Maslow's description of survival is interpersonal: inferiors are doomed unless they can create and sustain relationships with sufficiently strong protectors. The persuasive process through which this help is enlisted is central to the authoritarian's psychological survival. The democratic character type is a construction of the world that values individual differences as functional or dysfunctional, that grants people the freedom to make their own decisions, and that tends to view the exercise of authority with skepticism.

The psychological makeup of the authoritarian and democratic character structures suggest that they will try to find and create like-minded people. Theoretically, authoritarian leaders should be telling people about dangers and authoritarian followers ought to be listening for good protectors. Democratic leaders ought to be trying to empower people and democratic followers ought to be developing functional relationships to work on problems. We find just such tendencies in the discourse of the John Birch Society and the Gray Panthers.

Two Social Movement Organizations

The John Birch Society and the Gray Panthers are among the most interesting social movement organizations of the last forty years. Both movements were begun by people who had found personal, professional, and financial satisfaction through the established order and both organizations were comprised mostly of people worried about trends they saw in American society.

The John Birch Society

The John Birch Society was founded in 1958 as a secret, activist, anti-communist organization by Robert H. W. Welch, a retired candy executive and former official of the National Association of Manufacturers.[7] Welch wanted a cadre of dedicated and disciplined patriots who would help him *take America back* from the communists. He did not want a large organization because large organizations are difficult to discipline. Welch's central concern was the threat of communism, but while other conservatives watched the Kremlin and opposed communist expansion with foreign aid and military assistance, Welch maintained that most nations (including the United States) were secretly being ruled by communists who had infiltrated and subverted their governments. He opposed expensive military programs as efforts to wreck the American economy and to distract patriotic Americans from the "real" danger of communist subversion. For many years he published an annual rating of the percentage of communist control over every nation in the world.

The Birch Society was active and especially visible during the early 1960s with their efforts to impeach Chief Justice Earl Warren, to prevent fluoridation of water supplies, and to "Get US out of the UN." Conventional wisdom holds that the John Birch Society disintegrated in the mid-1960s as a consequence of two phenomena. The first of these was the Goldwater debacle of 1964—a campaign in which the Birch Society was highly active and visible. The second was the belief dilemma posed for Birchers by the anti-war protests of the 1960s: Birchers opposed both the war (as an effort by American communists to squander our national resources) and protestors of virtually all political stripes (as communist-inspired troublemakers).[8] As the Birch Society's visibility diminished, the public and scholars alike inferred that the Society had become insignificant.

But the John Birch Society did not disband in the mid-1960s, it simply evolved into a new phase. This was evident in the circulation of its two publications: the members' monthly *The John Birch Society Bulletin* and *American Opinion*, Welch's general circulation monthly. The circulation of each periodical was virtually the same in 1979–81 as it had been during the 1963–1965 "peak." Indeed, the mailed circulation of the members only *Bulletin* was 50 percent greater in 1981 than any known estimate of the Society's "peak" membership.[9]

The John Birch Society might better have been called the Robert Welch Society, for Welch was its founder and autocratic leader until his death in the 1980s. The group's ideology was set forth in its manual, *The Blue Book of the John Birch Society*, which consisted of a series of lectures by Welch at the organization's founding in Indianapolis in 1958.[10]

The Gray Panthers

The group that would become known as the Gray Panthers began in March of 1970 at a New York City luncheon of six women approaching forced retirement from careers of public service. The luncheon was called by Margaret Kuhn, Coordinator of Programs in the United Presbyterian Church, Division of Church and Race, and Associate Secretary in the Office of Church and Society. The others included Eleanore French (Director of the Student Division of the YWCA), Helen Smith (Director of the Division of the Laity of the United Church of Christ), Polly Cuthberson (Director of the American Friends Service Committee College Program), Ann Bennett (a religious educator and member of the Student Christian Peace Movement), Helen Baker (a former editor of *Churchwomen* and a United Nations reporter). The women decided that they should not let forced retirement keep them from improving social conditions.[11]

The women continued to meet and each used her large network of personal and professional acquaintances to find new members. Although their primary concern was ageism (discrimination on the basis of chronological age), their goals and priorities expanded to include "justice, freedom, and dignity for and with the oppressed" and "alternative life-styles and opportunities for older and younger people which will eliminate paternalism, discrimination, segregation and oppression."[12] Their specific short-term goals included guaranteed employment for everyone wanting to work, a guaranteed annual income, greater participation in national decision making, a radical tax reform to plug loopholes, and a drastic cut in military spending.

Maggie Kuhn emerged as the Gray Panthers' most visible leader, but unlike Robert Welch she was far from autocratic. The Gray Panthers developed networks of local groups that stressed local autonomy and independent actions. Both their ideology and their organizational style were democratic rather than authoritarian.

The Authoritarian Character of
John Birch Society Persuasion

The central arguments of the John Birch Society provided for all of the psychological needs of the authoritarian character while alienating those of the democratic character. These central arguments are found in *The Blue Book of the John Birch Society*, the transcription of Welch's address at the Society's founding in 1958 that remains the Society's formal ideological statement.[13] By analyzing this core ideology for evidence of authoritarianism and democratic character, we can see how the Society was built around its leader. This enabled Welch, as the protector, to reconcile belief dilemmas for his followers and to increase their dependence on him.

The Birchist World as Jungle

The theme of the *Blue Book* was the danger of subversive communism. If people were not aroused to that danger, said Welch, "in a few short years we shall all be hanging from the same lamp posts while Communist terror reigns all around us (p. x)." He told his readers that:

> the truth I bring you is simple, incontrovertible and deadly. It is that, unless we can reverse forces which now seem inexorable in their movement, you have only a few more years before the country in which you live will become separate provinces in a world-wide Communist dominion ruled by police-state methods from the Kremlin (p. 1).

But unlike most other anti-communists, Welch regarded the danger as neither Soviet aggression nor nuclear war, but subversion. Lenin's strategy, he said:

> is taking us over by a process so gradual and insidious that Soviet rule is slipped over so far on the American people, before they ever realize it is happening, that they can no longer resist the Communist conspiracy as free citizens (p. 19). This subversion comes from a gigantic conspiracy to enslave mankind; an increasingly successful conspiracy controlled by determined, cunning, and utterly ruthless gangsters, willing to go to any means to achieve its end (p. 21).

These conspirators were "like an octopus so large that its tentacles now reach into all of the legislative halls, all of the union labor meetings, a majority of the religious gatherings, and most of the schools of the whole world (p. 60)." Indeed, Welch warned that: "The human race has never before faced any such monster of power which has determined to enslave it. There is certainly no reason for underrating its size, its efficiency, its determination, its power, or its menace (p. 61)." The John Birch Society's world was not a friendly place.

The worldview of the John Birch Society stressed constant, imminent, hidden, ruthless danger. It is difficult to read much of their material without experiencing some sense of duress. But each of us adapts to such duress differently. The prototypical democratic character rejects the argument's central premise, perhaps rejecting valid arguments along with the invalid ones. But the authoritarian character structure is inclined to recognize the fundamental theme and read on. Having accepted the premise that an illusive, dangerous conspiracy is afoot, an authoritarian character must find a protector.

The Birch Tendency Toward Autocracy

The authoritarian character of the John Birch Society's argument becomes more evident when we examine Welch's alternative to communist enslavement. The democratic character type would want to fight communist enslavement with a cooperative effort based upon functional abilities, while the authoritarian would look for leadership and protection. Welch dismissed democracy as "merely a deceptive phrase, a weapon of demagoguery, and a perennial fraud" (p. 147). He observed that a republican form of government had "many attractions and advantages, under certain favorable circumstances . . . but it lends itself too readily to infiltration, distortion and disruption" (p. 146). That left autocracy: "The John Birch Society is to be a monolithic body [which] will operate under completely authoritative control at all levels" (pp. 146–147). This autocratic structure was necessary since "no collection of debating societies is ever going to stop the Communist conspiracy from taking us over" (p. 147).

Welch's autocratic structure did not tolerate negotiations over control. The Society, he said, "cannot stop for parliamentary procedures or a lot of arguments among ourselves" because "we are now being more and more divided and deceived, by accepting within our walls more and more Trojan horses" (p 147). Therefore, "we are not going to have factions developing on the two-sides-to-every-question theme (p. 149)." Thus, Welch offered his readers the prototypical authoritarian solution for danger: a strict autocratic relationship.

But the Society's hierarchy was not simply Welch above the membership. He explained that the Society:

> will function almost entirely through small local chapters, usually of from ten to twenty dedicated patriots. . . . Each will have a Chapter Leader appointed by headquarters . . . or appointed by officers in the field who have themselves been duly appointed by headquarters (p. 51).

Welch's description of the John Birch Society's organizational structure emphasized the danger of the world, a need for a clearly ordered hierarchy in which all authority would flow down from the Belmont, Massachusetts headquarters to the local chapters, and intolerance for dissension and democratic procedures. Even if a person with a democratic character structure wanted to heed Welch's alarm, such a person would be psychologically repelled from the Society by its rigid, monolithic, autocratic structure. But an alarmed authoritarian would seek precisely Welch's sort of autocracy for protection. Welch's organizational plan, therefore, meshed neatly with his alarm to persuade authoritarians and to repel democrats.

A second manifestation of the authoritarian tendency toward hierarchy was the Society's generalization of superiority from external characteristics. The reader of the *Blue Book* is introduced to all 26 members of the Council positionally: a "Boston surgeon," a "worthy son of a famous 'free enterpriser' in the Northwest lumber industry," a "well-known and highly successful Texas businessman" and several corporate, religious, and military figures (p. 172). Not only did Welch fail to indicate the specific, functional relevance of their impressive credentials to an understanding of communism or conspiracies for the benefit of democratic characters, he stated explicitly that the primary purpose of the Council was "to show [potential members] the stature and standing of the leadership of the Society" (p. 172). Stature and standing are important to the authoritarian, but not to the democratic, character structure. Again, the rhetorical depiction of the Council could attract authoritarians but not democrats.

In addition to stature, the John Birch Society tended to generalize superiority based on one's willingness to acknowledge the danger and the solution (in this case, Birchism). Others were judged by their agreement or disagreement with Robert Welch. Historian Oswald Spengler's work "[fit] the known facts of history" while Arnold Toynbee was a "meretricious hack . . . who is one of the worst charlatans that ever lived" (p. 34). Presidents Roosevelt, Truman, and Eisenhower were all judged to have helped communism because Welch disagreed with them.[14] Barry Goldwater and Ronald Reagan were applauded because they understood, while William F. Buckley and Russell Kirk were chastised because they did not.[15] Such pronouncements isolated members from the kind of two-sides-to-every-question controversy that Welch disdained. Metaphorically, anyone who failed to follow the safari leader endangered the whole safari. Yet the democratic character who feared communism might have found something of value in the thoughts of anti-communist conservatives like Buckley or Kirk. Welch was stressing safety through autocracy rather than safety through conservatism. Let us turn our attention, then, to the nature of the autocratic relationship that he prescribed.

Birchist Sadomasochism

The *Blue Book* is replete with references to communists' sadistic treatment of their followers. We are told of the communists' "police state features" that imposed "brutal rule" and "slavery" upon "party members who are wholly subservient" (pp. 20, 17, 28, 60). This was important because communism "has been imposed and must always be imposed, from the top down, by trickery and terror; and then it must be maintained by terror" (p. 61). This terror was directed not only at the slaves but at recalcitrant party members themselves who "are shot in some dark alley or pushed off a subway platform in front of a moving train" (p. 162). Given this alarming picture of sadistic rule by the communists, the democratic character type might reasonably have expected Welch to offer an alternative of kindness rather than brutality, of cooperation rather than slavery, of participation rather than subservience, and of bottom-up rather than top-down organization.

But Welch's alternative to sadistic communist domination was the Birch Society's organizational structure that mirrored the communist monolith. The Society is ordered from the top down with members obeying official directives and subject to removal for noncompliance. Indeed, Welch observed that:

> the biggest of all organizational mistakes is to set up a local group for some continuing purpose, exhort them to do a good job, and then leave them alone to do it. It is the leadership that is most demanding, most exacting of its followers not the one which asks the least and is afraid to ask more that achieves really dedicated support (p. 72).

Contrast conservative-authoritarian Welch's organizational philosophy with that of conservative-democratic Ronald Reagan: "Surround yourself with the best people you can find, delegate authority, and don't interfere as long as the policy you've decided upon is being carried out."[16] The difference between Welch and Reagan stemmed less from differences in their conservatism than from their differing conceptions of authority. In true sadomasochistic fashion, Welch stressed (a) the leader's responsibility to push his selfish, lazy, and stupid followers to their limits, (b) the followers' ecstatic submission to that direction, and (c) his ability to understand and to empathize with the followers pushed to their limits even though "he himself is not the bootlicker." It is important here that Welch argued not only that such leadership was effective, but that it encouraged "really dedicated support" rather than defection or mutiny. These tendencies are unlike anything in the democratic character structure.

Thus, the *Blue Book* suggested supplanting communist domination with Welch's domination until the quantity of government could be drastically reduced and a largely anarchistic polity created in which strength and protection would determine survival.[17] This program functioned psychologically for those of authoritarian character and was dysfunctional for democratic character types, who preferred partnerships. The important point is that Welch's program paralleled the psychological continuum of authoritarianism rather than the political continuum running from freedom to control.

A second manifestation of the Birch Society's sadomasochism was the pattern of gratifications it afforded members for following Welch. Whereas democratic character types look for functional, practical benefits, the authoritarian character type seeks submission to a protector. In this regard, Welch announced that:

> The men [women] who join the John Birch Society during the next few months or few years are going to be doing so primarily because they believe in me and in what I am doing. . . . And we are going to use that [personal loyalty], like every other resource, to the fullest advantage that we can (p. 149).

Even the criterion for continued membership was loyal submission: "those members who cease to feel the necessary degree of loyalty can either resign or will be put out before they can build up any splintering following of their own inside the Society" (p. 149).

But on what basis was the potential Bircher expected to develop this deep personal loyalty to Welch? He explained his credentials as follows:

> With all my shortcomings, there wasn't anybody else on the horizon willing to give their whole lives to the job, with the determination and dedication I would put into it. . . . Whatever I have in me, of faith, dedication, energy, I intend to offer that leadership to all who are willing to help me (pp. 114–115).

Put simply, others might have had better functional credentials for fighting communists, but one should attach oneself to Robert Welch (and only to him) because he alone was obsessed with this safari. The quantity of work and the obsessive-compulsive drive to spend himself thoroughly were regarded as more important than either the kind or quality of work, or the efficiency or prudence of the effort.

Welch's demand for personal loyalty on the basis of his obsession is all the more startling when we recognize that his practical, functional credentials were quite impressive. But the reader of the *Blue Book* learned neither that Welch had studied at the University of North Carolina, the U.S. Naval Academy, and Harvard Law School nor that he had written a primer on salesmanship and served in various official capacities for the National Association of Manufacturers. These seemingly pertinent facts were not divulged until a short postscript to the second printing of the *Blue Book*. The point is that Welch, a master salesman, could have sold his leadership to democratic characters by stressing his functional expertise. Instead, he emphasized (whether intentionally or not) his energy, his commitment, his constant reading of communist materials, and his willingness to exercise authority, dominance, and control—a package highly attractive to authoritarian character types.

Maslow explained that authoritarians revel in superior-inferior relationships. Inferiors know that they deserve to be controlled, while superiors find temporary satisfaction in the exercise of control. This theme pervaded *The Blue Book of the John Birch Society* as Welch condemned communist control and offered only his own control as the alternative. He sold the necessity for "dynamic, personal leadership" and personal loyalty based primarily on his compulsive-obsessive efforts and his readiness to punish those of dubious loyalty rather than on the basis of his notable, and apparently relevant, credentials. Potential members were asked to join the John Birch Society not because it would succeed, not because its tactics were well-conceived, not because they could participate in it or shape its direction, but because they wanted to be personally loyal to Robert Welch.

In summary, *The Blue Book of the John Birch Society* depicted a dangerous, threatening world in which ruthless conspirators were everywhere. It suggested a monolithic, autocratic organization built around members' personal loyalty to one man on the basis of his dedication and energy. But this organization to combat totalitarianism would itself tolerate neither discussion nor parliamentary procedure, and anyone quibbling with its leader would be summarily expelled. Thus, the John Birch Society exemplified all three major characteristics of the authoritarian character structure: a view of the world as a threatening place, a tendency toward hierarchy, and a sadomasochistic tendency.

The Democratic Character of Gray Panther Persuasion

As the ideology of the John Birch Society spoke to the needs of the authoritarian character structure, the ideology of the Gray Panthers spoke to the needs of the democratic character structure. Gray Panthers viewed the world not as a jungle but as an environment that had been created by people who could reshape it if they tried. They advocated not a strict vertical hierarchy but a nearly flat organizational structure that valued local autonomy and independent action. Finally, the Gray Panthers opposed dominance and submission which they regarded as paternalistic and they sought instead to empower persons of all ages.[18]

The Gray Panthers' World as Rational but Misguided

The world described by Gray Panthers was not an especially threatening place, but it was misguided. After all, potential members had lived in the world for six decades or more, and most of them had prospered sufficiently to devote their retirement years to social activism. The group had developed in response to the matter of forced retirement:

> At this magic age of 65, the "golden ager," alias senior citizen, is expected to settle down into a benign twilight of small deeds and trivial sentiments, unhampered by any interests more profound than crocheting, trout fishing, and bingo games. . . . [The Gray Panthers were organized by six professional women, of whom none] was the least bit impressed by crocheting, trout fishing, or bingo. Their lives had been too active for them to willingly fade away. Each devoted the whole of her adult life to social service and social change; concern and commitment was part of them (p. 3).

These women were not people who had lived in fear or under the protective custody of autocratic leaders.

Instead, the women who founded the Gray Panthers had lived professional lives that had accustomed them to altering prevailing social conditions. Had they regarded the world as a jungle, they would have sought ways to lessen the dangers so that citizens could lead their lives without fear or shame. They viewed dangers and problems as challenges to be addressed, not as permanent environmental conditions to be feared.

Nevertheless, the world perceived by the Gray Panthers was far from perfect. Panthers were concerned most by the "societal illness" of ageism: "an arbitrary discrimination on the basis of chronological age, [that] permeates Western culture and our institutions. Such discrimination is harmful to all age groups" (p. 16). Because of ageism older people had been made to feel ashamed of their appearance and the breadth of their experiences, and they were made to feel powerless and socially useless. Gray Panthers identified with other people who perceived themselves as powerless and sought to empower them all.

The world of the Gray Panthers also differed markedly from the world of the John Birchers because they regarded the world as amenable to change. Their 146-page *Manual* devoted nearly 70 pages to methods for effecting social change. Section V of the *Manual* explained how to organize a Gray Panther network with tips on building a constituency, planning the first meeting, holding the first meeting, selecting local officers, developing leadership, fund-raising, and projects and programs. Section VI covered "organizing issues" with suggestions on setting an objective, identifying goals, examples of successes, and even a "social action checklist." Section VII explained organizational strategies, tools for action, and resources. It covered planning for action, legislative advocacy, lobbying, advocacy with respect to administrative agencies, litigation, public hearings, and public relations. All of these suggestions presumed that the legal and administrative system could be made to work more democratically. This was most apparent in the section that explained to local Gray Panthers how to secure funding from foundations, from community development block grants, and from revenue sharing and other federal programs. These suggestions implied a world very different from that of the John Birch Society.

The Gray Panthers' Tendency Toward Egalitarianism

Whereas Robert Welch stressed the need for a vertical organizational hierarchy, the Gray Panthers prescribed an egalitarian network of autonomous local groups. Contrast Welch's monolithic organization of local chapters with no room for debate and leaders appointed by him with the following statement from the Gray Panther *Manual*:

> An organization is shaped and nurtured by knowledgeable and experienced, politically sophisticated, creative and concerned people. . . . We need a powerful and effective national organization. But to build it, we need pieces to put together, local pieces. These local pieces are the Networks, the grass roots Gray Panther groups and individuals around the country (p. 1). . . . All individual Gray Panthers and Gray Panther networks are not created from the same mold, nor are we forced to follow a strict format or role. Variation is the spice of life and we encourage local autonomy. Variations within the movement is an exciting and energizing force which we value (pp. 15–16).

This passage valued many of the things that worried Welch. No authoritarian character type could be attracted to a group that talked about being *forced* to follow a strict format or mold because authoritarians *want* to follow strict formats and roles. A true authoritarian personality would probably not even want to be caught reading a manual that said, "Variation is the spice of life" (because variation is dangerous), "we encourage local autonomy" (because individual autonomy on a safari is reckless and suicidal), or that variation "is an exciting and energizing force'' (because authoritarian character types perceive variation as a dangerous and debilitating force).

Another point of contrast can be found in the Gray Panthers' description of their organization. Did Maggie Kuhn appoint local leaders? Did they have stringent standards for membership? Did they dictate policy from national headquarters? The *Manual* was almost apologetic about the organization's decision to adopt Articles of Agreement in 1975, saying that ''Our hope was to develop minimal structure without violating the spirit of the movement'' (p. 9). The *Manual* had this to say about becoming a member under the Articles:

> Our structure is still fairly loose and flexible. A person or a group may affiliate with the National Gray Panthers by stating in writing their agreement with and willingness to work toward the goals. However, we . . . encourage and support local network autonomy in choosing those issues of importance in their own communities (pp. 15–16).

The Panthers' seriousness about local autonomy was perhaps most evident in their discussion of networks reporting to national headquarters. ''Conveners can keep the national office informed in a number of ways,'' it said, including an Annual Report, press clippings, Task Force reports, local news letters and, for funding proposals, notification of the Project Fund'' (pp. 32–33). Nowhere did the *Manual* suggest that the national office had any power to reject, amend, or even to review these reports. They were simply ways for the autonomous local networks to keep the national office and other local networks informed of their activities.

The Gray Panthers' Desire to Empower

Maslow said that the democratic character structure had no tendency comparable to the authoritarian character's sadomasochism, but he might have been impressed by the Gray Panthers' desire to empower people. Where authoritarians such as the Birchers demanded obedience and rejoiced in submission to their leader, the Gray Panthers tried to advance the frontiers of democracy by fighting against paternalism and by helping people to overcome their feelings of powerlessness.

The theme of empowerment pervaded their 1978 *Manual*. Their movement ''reflects the new mood of outrage and protest against injustices felt by increasing numbers of powerless people'' (p. 15). They fought ageism with an ''intergenerational coalition'' of persons who shared ''our concern for the larger issues of social justice and empowerment'' (p. 17). They saw themselves as a Liberation Movement:

> We identify with these other liberation groups and collectively reflect the widespread nature of the status disadvantaged and call for a massive redistribution of opportunities and privileges as well as major ideological changes (p. 18).

The Gray Panthers' struggle against ageism helped them to see that ''Many of the institutions and organizations that purport to serve people are afflicted with a deep, insidious paternalism, offering little or no voice to the recipients'' (p. 18). Clearly, the Gray Panthers were committed to improving the quality of life for "those who consider themselves powerless" (p. 22).

The democratic character of the Gray Panthers was also evident in the *Manual*'s section on "Developing Leadership." The authoritarian character is unconcerned about developing leaders because real leaders are people high on the survival scale. But democratic leadership entails facilitation rather than command, and its skills can and should be learned by everyone as a means of empowerment. The Gary Panther leader's role was "to inspire the group" and "to point the way" (p. 42). A good leader, the *Manual* said, is interested, personal, encouraging, enthusiastic, sharing, supportive, praising, dependable, willing to assume responsibility, willing to work hard, able to grow, and has a sense of humor (pp. 42–47). The *Manual* failed to mention the qualities of toughness and being demanding that were so important to Welch, just as Welch had put little stock in being encouraging, sharing, supportive, praising, or having a sense of humor. Different personalities require different styles of leadership and followership, and the differences between the democratic Gray Panthers and the autocratic John Birchers are stark.

In summary, the Gray Panther *Manual* exhibited all of the characteristics of the democratic character structure. They saw the world as a misguided but relatively unthreatening place. They were quite egalitarian and they constructed a flat organizational structure that maximized local autonomy. They identified with people who were made to feel powerless and they sought to combat paternalistic practices in society, whether they affected older people or others. Their leaders were taught to be supportive, praising, growing facilitators who empowered their members.

Conclusions

This analysis of the ideological statements of the John Birch Society and the Gray Panthers suggests four conclusions. The first is that the John Birch Society's *Blue Book* depicted a threatening world and stressed the need for ecstatic submission to a dynamic, personal leader within an autocratic hierarchy—a depiction congruent with the archetypal authoritarian character structure and incompatible with the democratic character structure. Through this happy coincidence, Robert Welch in one rhetorical stroke (a) recruited the ardent, dedicated followers he needed and wanted, (b) alienated potentially troublesome democratic character types, and (c) consolidated his recruits into a band of loyalists who (d) became more, not less, reliant on him during times of ideological dissonance. On the other hand, *The Gray Panther Manual* depicted a paternalistic world and stressed the need to empower individuals and groups who perceived themselves as passive and powerless—a depiction congruent with the archetypal democratic character structure and incompatible with the authoritarian character structure. Through this coincidence, the Panthers in one rhetorical stroke

(a) recruited the diverse talented people they needed, (b) alienated potentially troublesome authoritarian character types, (c) consolidated a vast array of autonomous local protests into one national movement, that (d) became less, not more, dependent on particular national leaders who faced all of the risks and dangers of advancing age.

Second, the psychological gratifications provided for authoritarian characters by Welch permitted his ironic and often contradictory arguments: the protection of freedom through dictatorial leadership, the protection of capitalism through noncompetitive organization, and strength through submission. These arguments required the authoritarian character's worldview for proper completion: protectors determine and provide what the protected need. In this case, Welch's alarmist discourse reinforced the authoritarians' conviction that the world is dangerous, thereby increasing their need for a protector. Welch then offered his own form of demanding "dynamic, personal leadership" to fill that need. By creating a strong protector-protected relationship with these protector-hungry authoritarians, Welch reserved for himself the ability to resolve belief dilemmas for his followers. Indeed, belief dilemmas might well have led to ideological defections without a leader like Robert Welch to resolve them.

On the other hand, the psychological gratifications provided to democratic character types by the Gray Panthers enabled them to avoid the passivity that they disliked. By grounding their fight against ageism in the struggle of oppressed peoples against paternalism, they invited the support of democratic personalities of all ages. And by empowering their members with local autonomy they maximized their members' freedom to use their personal skills in the ways that they found most meaningful and rewarding.

These two cases demonstrate that it is possible for social movements to provide psychological, as well as political or philosophical, reasons for membership. Welch's *Blue Book* and *The Gray Panther Manual* were well adapted to the needs of archetypal personality types. Each was likely to appeal to one personality type and to offend or alienate the other character types. Each organization discouraged from membership those persons most likely to disrupt it, while providing gratifications for those most able to advance its work. The arguments worked for members so that the members would work for the organizations. Movements that provide psychological gratifications for their members can cut across political, philosophical, sociological and economic cleavages.

Third, this chapter has demonstrated that persuasive functions do not necessarily bear a linear relationship to social movement messages. It is possible for a movement to recruit, confront, and consolidate, all in one message. Whether Welch the salesman planned it that way or it simply reflected his own character, it seems clear that the John Birch Society's alarmist discourse was more than mere "paranoia"—it was a psychological rhetoric that worked for them, sometimes quite well. The net result was an organization with an authoritarian character structure. Not all members of the John Birch Society fit precisely the description of the authoritarian character structure, but its message spoke to the authoritarian tendencies in each of us. It created for its members an organization which was probably more authoritarian than most of its individual members because they were bound together by their shared mistrust of the world and their need for protection against it. In contrast, the Gray Panthers created a movement that was probably more democratic in character than most of its members because it allowed its individual and collective affiliates to do as they pleased without the review or approval of either the national headquarters or other locals. They were able to combat ageism with an ideology that made membership attractive to democratic personality types of all ages.

Our final observation is that the persuasive discourse of the John Birch Society and the Gray Panthers provided psychological gratifications that were truthful and straightforward. Welch delivered what he promised: an authoritarian, anti-communist organization under his personal control. Never did he claim to offer anything else that might have broadened his appeal. Likewise, the Gray Panthers provided local autonomy and minimal oversight. Some social movement organizations are less straightforward.

During 1992, for example, H. Ross Perot emerged as a political force to be reckoned with. He challenged President George Bush and Bill Clinton for the presidency with a "grassroots" organization called United We Stand. Several polls showed Perot to be the candidate favored by some 30 percent of the electorate, and he won about 15 percent of the popular vote. By June of 1993 several polls showed Perot to be more popular than President Clinton. But Perot's United We Stand organization was less straightforward than either the John Birch Society or the Gray Panthers. Perot's rhetoric used populist democratic themes such as "giving the people what they want," making government responsive, and working together to solve vexing but simple national problems. But despite its democratic rhetoric, Perot's organization was leader-centered, and his organizers acted as his prophets. Although he claimed to be following the will of the people, he expressed his willingness to run for president before there was any showing of public support, he withdrew from the race when he led Bush and Clinton, and then he re-entered the race when barely 10 percent of the electorate supported his reentry. Perot's leadership was not, in other words, the epitome of the responsiveness he promised. The Perot phenomenon differs from the John Birch Society and the Gray Panther cases because it addresses the authoritarian character type's need for a strong leader in the rhetoric of democratic empowerment.

Endnotes

[1] In addition to the chapter on functions see Bruce E. Gronbeck, "The Rhetoric of Social-Institutional Change: Black Action at Michigan," *Explorations in Rhetorical Criticism*, G. P. Mohrmann, C. J. Stewart, and D. J. Ochs, eds. (University Park: Pennsylvania State University Press, 1973), 96–123; Herbert W. Simons, "Requirements, Problems, and Strategies: A Theory of Persuasion for Social Movements," *Quarterly Journal of Speech* 56 (February 1970), 1–11; and Charles J. Stewart, "A Functional Approach to the Rhetoric of Social Movements," *Central States Speech Journal* 31 (Winter 1980), 298–305.

[2] For further information on authoritarianism and dogmatism, see T. W. Adorno, Else Frenkel-

Brunswik, Daniel J. Levinson, and R. Nevitt Sanford, *The Authoritarian Personality* (New York: Harper, 1950); Erich Fromm, *Escape from Freedom*, (New York: Avon Library, 1965); and Milton Rokeach, *The Open- and Closed-Mind* (New York: Basic Books, 1960), 39–51.

[3] Abraham Maslow, "The Authoritarian Character Structure," *Journal of Social Psychology* 18 (1943), 401–411.

[4] Maslow, 402–403.

[5] Maslow, 408.

[6] Maslow, 406.

[7] Several sources (including *Who's Who*) have reported that Robert Welch served in important capacities with the National Association of Manufacturers during the 1950s. The N.A.M. disputes this contention, insisting that Mr. Welch was only one of some two hundred honorary officials and that he never held a position of responsibility in their organization. Personal correspondence with Dr. Jane Work, Department of Legislative Planning, National Association of Manufacturers, April 15, 1983.

[8] Stephen Earl Bennett, "Modes of Resolution of a 'Belief Dilemma' in the Ideology of the John Birch Society," *Journal of Politics* 33 (1971), 735–772.

[9] Circulation data are published in accordance with federal statute in the December issues of these publications. Circulation is the best index of Society membership since their rolls remain secret and their primary activities are educative. The dearth of published materials about the Society since 1971 reassures us that the data are not inflated by subscriptions from researchers.

[10] For background on the John Birch Society, see J. Allen Broyles, *The John Birch Society: Anatomy of a Protest* (Boston: Beacon Press, 1966); Gerald Schomp, *Birchism Was My Business* (New York: Macmillan, 1970); and two reports by the Anti-Defamation League of B'nai B'rith: Benjamin R. Epstein and Arnold Forster, *Report on the John Birch Society, 1966* (New York: Random House, 1966), and *The Radical Right: Report on the John Birch Society and Its Allies* (New York: Random House, 1967). Welch's account of Birch's life is presented in *The Life of John Birch* (Chicago: Henry Regnery, 1954). A more dispassionate and informative treatment is James Hefley and Marti Hefley, *The Secret File on John Birch* (Wheaton, IL: Tyndale House, 1980). By either account, Birch was a fundamentalist Baptist missionary in China who became involved in American intelligence operations during World War II. Despite his compatriots' efforts to restrain him, Birch seems to have displayed too much bravado in an encounter with a Chinese officer. Welch regards Birch as the first casualty in the final struggle against communism. A survey of 1965 members indicates that 62 percent joined for "ideological" reasons (only 21 percent found such satisfaction), 18 percent "to associate with like-minded people" (19 percent found it), 11 percent to become informed (16 percent found it), and 8 percent for political commitment (36 percent found this); see Fred W. Grupp, "Personal Satisfaction Derived from membership in the John Birch Society," *Western Political Quarterly* 24 (1971), 79–83; and "The Political Perspectives of Birch Society Members," *The American Right Wing*, Robert A. Schoenberger, ed. (Atlanta: Holt, Rinehart, and Winston, 1969), 83–118.

[11] *The Gray Panther Manual*, Harriet L. Perretz, (compiler), (Philadelphia: The Gray Panthers, 1978), 3–4.

[12] Perretz, 22.

[13] Unless otherwise noted all references to Welch or the John Birch Society's persuasion refer to Robert H. W. Welch, Jr., *The Blue Book of the John Birch Society*, (Belmont, MA: Western Islands, 1961).

[14] Robert Welch, *The Politician*, (Belmont, MA: Belmont Publishing, 1963), see esp. 279.

[15] Welch strongly supported the Goldwater candidacy as early as the 1958 organizational session (see 109). But Welch believed that the conspiracy had the political process rigged so as to prevent Goldwater's election. For his part, Goldwater was not a Welch supporter. After reading *The Politician*, Goldwater "urged him not to print it. I said I couldn't accept his theory that Ike was either a dunce and a dupe or a conscious sympathizer. Most of the John Birchers are patriotic, concerned, law-abiding, hardworking and productive. There are a few whom I call Robert Welchers, and these are the fanatics who regard everyone who doesn't totally agree with them as communist

sympathizers." Barry Goldwater, *With No Apologies*, (New York: William Morrow, 1979), 119.

[16] Ann Reilly Dowd, "What Managers Can Learn from Manager Reagan," Fortune, (September 15, 1986), 33–41. The same management philosophy was expressed during the first debate between Reagan and Mondale published in *The Weekly Compilation of Presidential Documents* 20 (October 7, 1984), 1446.

[17] Welch's utopia is a highly individualistic society epitomized by his slogan, "Less Government and More Responsibility" (117). The problem with government, he says, is neither its form nor its quality, but its quantity: "the increasing quantity of government in all nations has constituted the greatest tragedy of the twentieth century" (123). If the authoritarian conceives of life as taking place in a jungle, then government represents civilization—which distorts the natural order of survival.

[18] Unless otherwise indicated all references to the ideology of the Gray Panthers or their manual refer to *The Gray Panther Manual*.

Chapter Seven

Legitimizing the
Social Movement

The word "legitimacy" or "legitimation" appears with nagging persistence in writings on the rhetoric and sociology of social movements. Theorists have presented it as the principal goal or demand of social movements, the primal challenge of movements to established institutions, and the most critical obstacle leaders of movements must overcome.[1] Gaston Rimlinger and Joseph Gusfield, for example, argue that for a social movement to be successful, its demands and methods must somehow become legitimate in the eyes of institutions, government, the public, and potential members.[2] The struggle to gain legitimacy, Klandermans writes, "is the challenge a movement organization faces in mobilizing consensus in the context of action mobilization."[3]

The uninstitutionalized nature of social movements relegates them to near-zero legitimacy when they come into existence. They have in their favor only the somewhat mythical American tradition of tolerance for dissent, a tolerance most evident when dissent is nonthreatening or ineffective. Moreover, social movements may lose even this grudging level of legitimacy as they challenge social institutions, norms, and values. As Robert Cathcart writes, "The leadership of the movement is not recognized, for it has no legitimacy, and to confer with it would be tantamount to doing business with the devil."[4]

The Notion of Legitimacy

The notion of "legitimacy" contains two inherently rhetorical elements. The first element is the act of conferring, by one person or group to another person or group, the "right to exercise authoritative influence in a given area or to issue binding directives."[5] Tradition, laws, rules, charisma, assumed power, performance of mythic feats, and the dictates of a "higher authority" (perhaps a divine source) are the bases upon which legitimacy is conferred most often.[6] The second element is the act of retaining legitimacy once it is conferred. Robert Francesconi, for example, sees legitimation as "an ongoing process of reason-giving, actual and potential, which forms the basis of the right to exercise authority as well as the willingness to defer to authority."[7] "Rhetoric," Francesconi writes, "bridges the gap between legitimacy as claimed and legitimacy as believed."[8] Herbert Simons characterizes legitimacy "as the perception by receivers that the source has a right to exact obedience from" them.[9] It is not surprising then that legitimacy almost always accrues to established institutions that in turn strive to "engender and maintain the belief that the existing . . . institutions are the most appropriate ones for the society."[10]

Although the elements of legitimacy are well-known and the importance of legitimacy to the rise and success of social movements is widely recognized, Herbert Simons' assessment in 1972 that "The legitimacy variable is among the most neglected and most important variables in credibility research" remains accurate today.[11] This chapter discusses why social movements must employ both coactive and confrontational strategies to attain the legitimacy essential for bringing about or resisting change. A rhetoric of legitimacy for protestors and reformers can be understood, however, only if first we review the elements of the rhetorical situation that make the attainment of legitimacy a major obstacle for social movements.

The Social Movement's Rhetorical Situation

As noted earlier, social movements usually emerge during relatively quiet times when the people and established institutions are going about business as usual. If either people or institutions are aware of a problem (whether it be social, political, religious, economic, educational, or environmental) they typically view it as insignificant, of low priority, or unresolvable—"the poor will always be with us." If a serious problem is recognized, the usual stance is that it can and will be resolved in due time, after thorough and exhaustive study by appropriate committees or task forces, by legitimate institutions through legitimate channels and means.

Societies and their institutions have prevalent ideologies (symbolic systems of norms and values) that explicitly and implicitly support and are supported by the prevailing social structure.[12] Educational systems, for instance, help to legitimize and preserve the social order by disseminating approved norms and values, identifying established heroes and villains, and telling authorized versions of history and historical events.[13] All such institutions aid in defining and constructing the generally accepted version of social reality.[14] Thomas Farrell claims that the fundamental function of political communication is to legitimize the political system, and Herbert Simons has argued on several occasions that persuasion theorists have identified with the maintenance of existing social systems and have deemed social movements to be unnecessary, irrational, dysfunctional, and potentially dangerous.[15] William Gamson observes that social movement persuaders

> face a field of combat that is already occupied by a competing legitimating frame that is established and quiescent rather than emergent and action-oriented. When truly hegemonic, the legitimating frame is taken for granted. Would-be challengers face the problem of overcoming a definition of the situation that they themselves may take as a part of the natural order.[16]

When a people or social order confers legitimacy upon a person or institution, it also confers powers of retention. This bestowal of power has led Robert Cathcart to identify the struggle between institutional and noninstitutional forces as "a true moral battle for power and the legitimate right to define the true order."[17] "It is a formidable task," Gameson observes, "to cut what Freire calls the 'umbilical cord' of magic and myth which binds the [oppressed] to the world of oppression."[18] Specifically, legitimacy confers five powers which, in combination, perpetuate the original grant.

The *power to reward* is perhaps the most important retentive power because it allows legitimate institutions to reward those who conform and obey and to coerce or to punish those who strive to be different or challenge approved norms, values, or institutional arrangements.[19] Institutional leaders urge protestors and reformers to consider the positive and negative consequences of their actions, typically the granting or denial of tangible benefits and rewards such as diplomas, jobs, official positions, advancements, incomes, recognition, land, research and development grants, and tax exemptions. If the disaffected refuse to take the carrot, an institution may resort to the stick to gain compliance and to justify its use of coercive persuasion (perhaps even violence) in the name of God, the founding fathers, the people, the Constitution, the law, social harmony, progress, the common good, or national security.[20] Philip Zimbardo and Herbert Simons note that people who modify their behaviors as a result of coercive persuasion by legitimate authorities "are more likely to make the attribution error of overestimating the extent to which they have had choice in the matter."[21] This attribution error is understandable because institutions define rewards and reward systems and thus are able to meet or to withhold expectations, to distribute finite resources, and to alienate groups and individuals when it is to an institution's advantage.

The *power of control* allows legitimate institutions and leaders to regulate the flow of information and persuasion to members of organizations and the populace. Thus, they are able to determine if, how, when, where, under what circumstances, and with whom communication will occur. Piven and Cloward contend that "The ideology of democratic political rights, by emphasizing the availability of legitimate avenues for the redress of grievances, delegitimizes protest; and the dense relationships generated by electoral politics also divert people from protest."[22] Not infrequently, institutional leaders brand reformers or agitators as well-meaning but "ignorant of the facts" that are well-known only to established authorities: the military, the President, the FBI, religious hierarchy, or corporate leaders.

In the "information age" of the 1990s, control of information and information flow may be more important than military and police forces. Control power also helps institutions to maintain perceptions that the established order is in compliance with accepted values and standards, is meeting the legitimate expectations of persons and groups (particularly those of protestors), is employing appropriate avenues in dealing with alleged problems, and is on the side of good in its struggle with evil.[23] In a sense, then, institutions act interdependently with audiences in rewarding those who hear, agree, and acquiesce.

The *power of identification* accrues to established orders because they are the keepers, protectors, and proselytizers of the sacred symbols, emblems, places, offices, documents, codes, values, and myths of the institution or order.[24] They are typically seen as the legitimate heirs or successors of the order's founding fathers, patriots, revered leaders, prophets, martyrs, or high priests. Identification with the sacred (flags, memorials, holidays, hymns, heroes, myths) is easy and frequent. As Anthony Oberschall writes, their positions allow institutional leaders to provide "elaborate systems of beliefs and moral ideas upon which legitimacy rests."[25] Thus, while social movements must struggle endlessly to attain a collective identity, institutions bask in long-established national, corporate, religious, social, and political identities that enhance their legitimacy.[26]

The *power of terministic control* allows social orders to control language and thereby to define the "legitimated meanings for such politically sensitive terms as order, violence, repression, deviance, protest, persuasion, coercion, and symbolic speech."[27] Thus, violence by established orders is the legitimate maintenance of law and order, never "terrorism."[28] Over-zealous supporters of the order are patriots, never fanatics. As pundits have long noted, winners in power struggles are called "founders" while losers are called "traitors." "National security" justifies withholding or distortion of information pertaining to everything from infiltration of protest groups and spying on citizens to results of studies by presidential commissions and secret files on social movement leaders, members, and sympathizers.

The *power of moral suasion* allows institutions to exert control by operating in the realms of attitudes and emotional attachments.[29] R. R. McGuire claims that people often come to see obedience or deference to legitimate authority as a moral obligation.[30] Thus, institutions are able to persuade people that they have a duty to honor institutional decisions even when these decisions have "unpleasant consequences."[31] Herbert Simons writes that "one important means by which influence agents may persuade us to want to do what we would not otherwise choose to do is first convince us that they have legitimate authority over us and hence that we are duty bound to obey them."[32] The potential emotional consequences of disobeying legitimate authority keeps many people under control. Louis Kriesberg, for example, contends that "people learn rules and if they accept them they may become so internalized that violation would be shunned in order to avoid the feelings of guilt or shame which would follow violation."[33]

Thus, when uninstitutional forces collide with institutional forces, the rhetorical deck is heavily stacked in favor of "legitimate" institutions and leaders. People tend to "maintain the faith" even in the face of massive economic and social breakdowns in society.[34] How, then, can social movements use persuasion to meet situational exigencies and counter the powers granted to legitimate authorities? A rhetoric of legitimation must be a combination of coactive and confrontational strategies.[35] Coactive or common ground strategies emphasize similarities, shared experiences, and a common cause with target audiences. The social movement is projected as respectful of societal norms, values, and institutions and hence deserving, by worth and right, of legitimate status.[36] Confrontational or conflict strategies emphasize dissimilarities, diverse experiences, and conflict with target audiences. Such strategies are essential to deprive institutions and leaders of all or part of the legitimacy they enjoy and thus to elevate the social movement to a transcendent position in the societal hierarchy.[37]

Legitimacy Through Coactive Strategies

If, as Robert Francesconi claims, "an implicit requirement" of legitimacy is a "rationality of good reasons," then social movements must identify with fundamental societal norms and values if they are to transport themselves from the margins of society to the centers where legitimacy resides.[38] They must access the very sources that institutions claim as their rightful domains.

First, social movements may identify with what Max Weber refers to as the "sanctity of immemorial traditions."[39] Molefi Asante (Arthur Smith) and John Wilson note that social movements usually link themselves with the traditional rights and values of equality, justice, and dignity, while Irving Zaretsky and Mark Leone claim that nonlegitimacy of religious social movements is a function of appearing to threaten deeply held secular values.[40] While most Americans saw Malcolm X as a dangerous radical, even a cursory review of his speeches reveals that he appealed continually to the fundamental American values of a virtuous life dedicated to family, community, religious beliefs, hard work, ingenuity, and the free enterprise system, hardly radical or revolutionary beliefs. Movements are wise to identify with the moral symbols, sacred emblems, heroes, founding fathers, and revered documents of society rather than to attack them as many movements are prone to do.[41] Klandermans argues that "attempts to persuade will be more or less successful depending on the degree to which movements can anchor their views to existing beliefs or identities."[42] The "Women's Declaration of Independence" adopted by the Seneca Falls convention in 1848 was modeled closely after the Declaration of Independence with such modifications as "We hold these truths to be self-evident, that all men *and women* are created equal." The National Labor Union used the same strategy when it adopted its "Platform of Principles" in 1868: "We hold these truths to be self-evident, that all *people* are created equal." Social movements may rework the pieces of tradition into new stories that befit their ideologies.[43] Thus, to avoid being stigmatized as a mere fad, "people going crazy together," or an evil force in society, movements may emphasize the hallowed tradition of protest in American history, for instance showing what our founding fathers really were, *revolutionaries*.[44] Carl Oglesby, president of the SDS (Students for a Democratic Society), asked an audience during the antiwar march in Washington on October 27, 1965 what would happen if Thomas Jefferson and Thomas Paine would sit down with President Johnson to discuss the Vietnam War:

> Our dead revolutionaries would soon wonder why their country was fighting against what appeared to be a revolution. The living liberal would hotly deny that it is one: there are troops coming in from outside, the rebels get arms from other countries, most of the people are not on their side, and they practice terror against their own. Therefore, *not* a revolution.
>
> What would our dead revolutionaries answer? They might say: "What fools and bandits, sirs, you make then of us. Outside help? Do you remember Lafayette? Or the 3,000 British freighters the French navy sunk for our side? Or the arms and men we got from France and Spain? And what's this about terror? Did you never hear what we did to our own loyalists? Or about the thousands of rich American Tories who fled for their lives to Canada? And as for popular support, do you not know that we had less than one-third of our people with us? That, in fact, the colony of New York recruited more troops for the British than for the revolution? Should we give it all back?"[45]

"Reconstructing" history can alter perceptions of social reality and show the social movement as more legitimate than institutions because it alone is telling it like it *really* is.

Second, social movements may strive to establish their actions as those of legitimate organizations.[46] They can achieve this in part by incorporating into legal organizations and operating openly to avoid American fears of secretive societies. They may identify with the legal status of protest in America by conforming to rules and accepted procedures perceived to be formally correct by the populace and social orders and by avoiding direct attacks on basic institutions and authorities.[47] Most movements emphasize the importance of the ballot box rather than violence or coercion in bringing about or resisting change. Endorsements of a social movement by organizations and individuals with legitimacy may produce a "rub-off" effect because social movements, like individuals in society, are judged by their associations. They work hard to attract "legitimizers"—organizations, speakers, writers, senators, clergy, entertainers, scientists, military leaders, war veterans, ex-presidents, and medical professionals—who are respectable, safe, and beyond reproach.[48] Movements may link themselves with other social movements that are active at the time and have gained a degree of respect.[49] Thus, the civil rights movement helped to legitimize the native American, women's liberation, and gay rights movements in the United States and the Catholic civil rights movement in Northern Ireland.

Third, social movements may employ a strategy of transcendence by identifying themselves with what is large, good, important, and of the highest order in society. Movements typically claim to speak in the name of the people, for the will of the people, and in the "soul and spirit" of the people.[50] They are the true heirs of societal norms, values, and traditions. Size itself often becomes a sign of acceptance and thus of legitimacy. A movement may portray itself as a "majority movement," a "great people's movement," or the "largest grassroots citizens' movement in recent history."[51] *The Gray Panther Manual* relates how the Panthers grew rapidly into a powerful, national organization:

> Throughout 1973 the Gray Panthers grew tenfold again. . . .The ABC-TV network did a documentary entitled: "Gray Panthers," with nationwide viewing. Local Gray Panther Networks were convening in Philadelphia, Tucson, Dayton, D.C., Chicago, Los Angeles, San Francisco, Charlotte, New York, Denver, Decatur, Kansas City, Portland, and Baltimore. Panthers were on the prowl all over.[52]

Anthony Oberschall notes that visible signs of large-scale disaffection may shake confidence in established orders and thus undermine the legitimacy of institutional leaders.[53] Social movements, particularly religious ones, stress a sense of mission and claim to operate in accordance with a predetermined divine plan.[54] They identify with the American belief that divine plans transcend the temporal ones of social orders, argue that "expressive" values (symbols, reflections, meanings) rather than "instrumental" values (means, instruments, tools) are the truly universal ones, and try to locate the movement within what Irving Zaretsky and Mark Leone call a "sacred cosmos."[55] Moral obligations to the state, protestors claim, are limited by moral obligations to humanity and a higher authority.[56] Thus, the "Articles of Agreement of the National Gray Panthers" lists purposes and goals (such as to eliminate ageism, "to advocate justice, freedom, and dignity," and "to foster the concept of aging as growth during the total life-span") "To affirm the ethical, moral, and social foundation upon which the Gray Panther movement is built."[57]

A coactive rhetoric is essential, then, for a social movement in its struggle for legitimacy because it chips away at three powers enjoyed by the social order: identification, terministic control, and moral suasion. Coactive rhetoric obviously serves more than the "managerial" or "reinforcement" functions often ascribed to it, for it demonstrates that a social movement deserves legitimacy by both *worth and right*.[58] With worth and right established, institutions can no longer call into question the fundamental legitimacy of a social movement but, as Rhodri Jeffreys-Jones explains, must attack its tactics instead.[59] Bowers, Ochs, and Jensen address the importance of a coactive rhetorical approach in establishing legitimacy when they argue that the early employment of a strategy of "petition" (asking authorities to address an urgent concern) is crucial because:

> If the establishment can show that the petition stage was not attempted by the dissenters, it can discredit the agitators as irresponsible firebrands who reject normal decision-making processes in favor of disturbances and disruption. Unless they first attempt petition, activists are unlikely to win support through more drastic strategies.[60]

Thus, coactive strategies tend to dominate the rhetoric of social movements during the early stages of protest when persuaders are attempting to make the people and institutions aware of an urgent, unaddressed problem and to gain entree to the "playing field" where such problems are debated and resolved.

A coactive rhetoric by itself, however, cannot attain legitimacy for a social movement because it merely establishes the movement as "similar" to the social order in important ways—legal, law-abiding, supporter of traditions, moral—and therefore worthy of a degree of legitimacy.[61] There is always the danger that some people may see the social movement as so similar to the social order that there is no need to join while others may become estranged from the movement because it fails to differentiate itself significantly from evil or impotent institutions. Thus, a coactive rhetoric is likely to produce, at best, a rhetorical stalemate between institutional and uninstitutional forces that leaves institutions with their powers possibly diminished or shared but intact. A confrontational rhetoric is required to break the rhetorical stalemate by bringing institutional legitimacy into question and allowing the social movement to transcend the social order in perceived legitimacy.

Legitimacy Through Confrontational Strategies

If a confrontational rhetoric is to raise the social movement to a transcendent position in society, it must make a significant number of people see the social order as illegitimate or at least less legitimate than the social movement.[62] Carol Jablonski argues that a "rhetoric of discontinuity" is necessary to "establish the legitimacy of the collective's grievances as well as the need to induce changes from the outside."[63] Clearly, social movements gain legitimacy through confrontations with institutions, countermovements, and competing social movement organizations.[64]

Movements employ a variety of confrontational strategies to show that establishment leaders, organizations, rules, and norms systematically distort communication, create barriers to will formation, and constrain and distort an alleged "reciprocal accountability." Thus, as R. R. McGuire writes, social movements hope to demonstrate that the order is "irrational and hence illegitimate—involving no moral obligation."[65] Institutions must "maintain a perceived consistency between values and actions" and appear to follow approved patterns of operation.[66] Movements try to exploit this societal restriction on institutional actions. The civil rights, Hispanic, gay rights, animal rights, and pro-life movements, for example, employ strategies of nonviolent resistance and civil disobedience—strikes, boycotts, sit-ins, demonstrations, symbolic acts, and violations of ordinances and laws—to reveal the inconsistency, and therefore the illegitimacy, of values and establishment procedures, customs, and laws.[67] Social movements may take advantage of outdated laws or quasi-legal practices of authorities by demanding that authorities stick to the letter of the law, actions that might make authorities look ridiculous, unfair, or heavyhanded.[68] Saul Alinsky, in his book *Rules for Radicals*, urges would-be-radicals to "*Make the enemy live up to their own book of rules.* You can kill them with this, for they can no more obey their own rules than the Christian church can live up to Christianity.''[69] If an institution represses peaceful, nonviolent dissent or refuses to enforce or to obey the laws, it may seriously undermine its legitimacy in the eyes of the people and other institutions.[70] Competing organizations or countermovements, like institutions, must also live up to their ideologies or face loss of legitimacy to the challenging organization or movement.

Militant confrontational strategies (such as disruptions, verbal violence, and assaults on property, symbols, and police) may provoke the establishment into overreactions and violent suppression, for, as Robert Cathcart claims, ''The establishment, when confronted, must respond not to the particular enactment but to the challenge to its legitimacy.''[71] If the establishment ''responds with full fury and might to crush the confronters, it violates the mystery and reveals the secret that it maintains power, not through moral righteousness but through its power to kill.''[72] Protestors have learned the value of mass arrests and real or apparent police brutality, particularly when television news cameras are present. Televised images of police dragging men and women, some of them members of the clergy, to police vans may outrage significant numbers of an institution's constituency and be counterproductive to control efforts.[73] The use of police dogs, billy clubs, and fire hoses against unresisting civil rights protestors in the south during the 1960s cut deeply into the legitimacy of southern institutions and brought widespread sympathy to the movement. Police have shown remarkable restraint in recent years in handling pro-life's Operation Rescue sit-ins and efforts to penetrate police lines; they obviously learned valuable lessons in ''protest-management'' from the failed efforts of the 1960s and 1970s.

Protestors charge that the ''civility and decorum'' of authorities ''serve as masks for the preservation of injustice'' and constitute a thin veneer that hides a vicious, repressive—and thus illegitimate—social order.[74] Robert Scott and Donald Smith write that social movements prod the established order to ''show us how ugly you really are.''[75] And Robert Cathcart claims that ''Confrontational rhetoric shouts 'Stop!' at the system, saying, 'You cannot go on assuming you are the true and correct order; you must see yourself as the evil thing you are.' ''[76] Authorities discredit and humiliate themselves when they lose control and thereby become collaborators with protestors bent on stripping them of legitimacy. Violent acts on behalf of established institutions against civil rights protestors in Selma and Birmingham, anti-Vietnam War protestors at Kent State University and Chicago, and innocent women and children in My Lai, South Vietnam were seen on television in millions of American homes and aided the efforts of the civil rights and anti-Vietnam War movements by revealing ugly sides of institutions rarely witnessed by the American populace.[77]

There may be two significant by-products of ugly and sometimes violent confrontations between protestors and social orders. First, violent suppression by an institution allows the social movement to claim that it acted in self-defense—a noble and legal act—to institutional force and violence.[78] Second, verbal and nonverbal violence by institutions and militant elements of movements may confer legitimacy upon moderate movement leaders and organizations because they stand out as rational and safe in comparison.[79]

A confrontational rhetoric is essential, then, for a movement to gain legitimacy because it chips away at four powers enjoyed by the establishment: reward, control, identification, and moral suasion. A confrontational rhetoric breaks the rhetorical stalemate between institutional and noninstitutional forces by demonstrating that the institution deserves neither its claim of legitimacy nor its high place in the social hierarchy. A confrontational rhetoric clearly distinguishes the social movement from institutions by polarizing the competing forces. A confrontational rhetoric reveals the ugliness of a situation and a social order that needs urgent remedy. Relying on principles of rhetorical theorist Kenneth Burke, Cathcart argues that:

> Hierarchy includes what is not proper, not useful, not valuable; thus, 'the negative.'
> Man, the seeker after perfection, recognizes the negative and becomes aware of
> his own guilt. And to remove guilt he must seek redemption either through striving
> to perfect the hierarchy (i.e., established order) or by recognizing the evil of
> the erroneous system, confession to his own victimage (mortification) and
> confronting the evil system with a new, more perfect order (redemption).[80]

Although a confrontational rhetoric is essential for a social movement in its struggle for legitimacy, it alone cannot attain legitimacy for the movement. Destruction or reduction of Order A's legitimacy does not automatically bestow legitimacy on Order B, even when Order B was instrumental in revealing the evil and unworthiness of Order A. The Yippies, for example, artfully unveiled the ugliness of Chicago police and officials during the 1968 Democratic convention, but the Yippies and other movements involved gained little if any legitimacy for having done so. Frank Sullivan, the press officer for the Chicago police, charged that the demonstrations were perpetrated by a "pitiful handful" of "communist revolutionaries," and polls indicated that a great many Americans agreed with this assessment.[81] Social movements must effectively present themselves as the "innocent victims" of established orders out of control. This is why nonviolent civil disobedience, as taught by Gandhi and Martin Luther King, Jr., can be effective if established orders cooperate by resorting to violence and lawlessness. A social movement, then, can assume its rightful place in society by establishing its worth and right to assume the mantle of legitimacy stripped from the established order through confrontational strategies.

Conclusions

Theorists agree that perhaps the greatest challenge social movements encounter is the necessity of being perceived as legitimate in the eyes of the people, institutions, and other social movements. Legitimacy, and the powers that accompany it, traditionally and legally accrues to societal institutions, so the rhetorical deck is heavily stacked against uninstitutional forces. In this chapter, we have described the rhetorical situation social movements face in their efforts to achieve legitimacy necessary to bring about or to stifle change, and we have discussed two rhetorical strategies essential for meeting situational exigencies and achieving legitimacy: coactive and confrontational.

Societies create institutions that legitimize and preserve the social order and its attendant systems of norms and values and confer at least five powers to aid institutions in carrying out these tasks. The power to reward allows institutions to compensate those who conform and obey and to punish those who do not. The power of control enables institutions to regulate the flow of information and persuasion. The power of identification makes institutions the protectors of society's sacred symbols, places, documents, stories, codes, and values. The power of terministic control permits institutions to control language and thus to define good and evil. And the power of moral suasion allows institutions to exert control in the realms of attitudes and emotional attachments to establish a moral obligation to obey legitimate authority.

The rhetorical situation requires social movements to develop a rhetoric of legitimation that is a blend of coactive and confrontational strategies. A coactive or common ground approach allows the social movement to establish itself as respectful of societal norms, values, and institutions—deserving of legitimacy by worth and right. A confrontational or conflict approach allows the movement to provoke the institution into actions that reveal the institution as a violator of societal norms and values and thus undeserving of all or part of the legitimacy it enjoys. Neither approach by itself is sufficient. A coactive approach may produce a rhetorical stalemate in which both movement and institution enjoy degrees of legitimacy but in which the institution remains in control. Or the social movement may appear to become so similar to the institutions it opposes that it disappears as a noninstitutional force for change or resistance. This was the fate, for instance, of the National Labor Union when it became best known as the National Labor party and the socialist movement when it became little more than the Socialist party. A confrontational rhetoric may strip legitimacy from an institution, but this success contains no guarantee that the lost legitimacy will be transferred to the movement. Indeed, a confrontational rhetoric may boomerang as the public comes to see the movement as an outrageous violator of norms and values—if not a grave threat to the whole social order—and urge institutions to repress the irrational, dangerous threat to all that is sacred. Militant groups such as the Industrial Workers of the World, the Black Panthers, and the Weathermen suffered this fate.[82] Only a rhetoric of legitimation that includes both coactive and confrontational strategies permits social movements to establish their worthiness and institutions' unworthiness of legitimacy and to neutralize, or transfer, those powers that attend legitimacy.

Endnotes

[1] Joseph R. Gusfield, *Protest, Reform, and Revolt: A Reader in Social Movements* (New York: John Wiley & Sons, 1970), 310; Arthur L. Smith (Molefi Asante), *Rhetoric of Black Revolution*

(Boston: Allyn and Bacon, 1969), 1; John W. Bowers, Donovan J. Ochs, and Richard J. Jensen, *The Rhetoric of Agitation and Control*, 2/E (Prospect Heights, IL: Waveland Press, 1993), 13.

2 Gaston V. Rimlinger, "The Legitimation of Protest: A Comparative Study in Labor History," in Gusfield, 363.

3 Bert Klandermans, "The Social Construction of Protest and Multiorganizational Fields," *Frontiers in Social Movement Theory*, Aldon D. Morris and Carol McClurg Mueller, eds. (New Haven, CT: Yale University Press, 1992), 91.

4 Robert S. Cathcart, "Movements: Confrontation as Rhetorical Form," *Southern Speech Communication Journal* 43 (Spring 1978), 246.

5 Herbert W. Simons, *Persuasion: Understanding, Practice and Analysis* (Reading, MA: Addison-Wesley, 1976), 234.

6 Max Weber, *The Theory of Social and Economic Organization*, A. M. Henderson and Talcott Parsons, trans. (New York: The Free Press, 1964), 130–132; Simons (1976), 234–236; Gerald S. Mathisen, "Evangelical Social Concern: A Case Study in the Rhetoric of Legitimization," unpublished doctoral dissertation, Purdue University, 1982, 3–6; Anthony Oberschall, *Social Conflict and Social Movements* (Englewood Cliffs, NJ: Prentice-Hall, 1973), 120.

7 Robert A. Francesconi, "James Hunt, The Wilmington 10, and Institutional Legitimacy," *Quarterly Journal of Speech* 68 (February 1982), 49.

8 Francesconi, 50.

9 Herbert W. Simons, "Persuasion in Social Conflicts: A Critique of Prevailing Conceptions and a Framework for Future Research," *Speech Monographs* 39 (November 1972), 244.

10 Oberschall, 188.

11 Simons (1972), 244.

12 Roberta Ash, *Social Movements in America* (Chicago: Markham, 1972), 3; William B. Cameron, *Modern Social Movements* (New York: Random House, 1966), 72; Weber, 130.

13 Simons (1972), 241.

14 William A. Gamson, "The Social Psychology of Collective Action," *Frontiers in Social Movement Theory*, 71.

15 Thomas B. Farrell, "Political Communication: Its Investigation and Praxis," *Western Speech Communication* 50 (Spring 1976), 96; Herbert W. Simons, Elizabeth W. Mechling, and Howard N. Schreier, "The Functions of Human Communication in Mobilizing for Action from the Bottom Up: The Rhetoric of Social Movements," *Handbook of Rhetorical and Communication Theory*, Carroll C. Arnold and John W. Bowers, eds. (Boston: Allyn and Bacon, 1984), 800.

16 Gamson, 68.

17 Cathcart (1978), 246.

18 Gamson, 65.

19 Herbert W. Simons, "The Carrot and the Stick as Handmaidens of Persuasion in Conflict Situations," *Perspectives on Communication in Social Conflict*, Gerald R. Miller and Herbert W. Simons, eds., (Englewood Cliffs, NJ: Prentice-Hall, 1974), 196; Simons, Mechling, and Schreier, 820).

20 Simons (1974), 193; Francesconi, 56; Weber, 131 and 328; Simons (1976), 235.

21 Simons (1974), 192.

22 Frances Fox Piven and Richard A. Cloward, "Normalizing Collective Protest," *Frontiers in Social Movement Theory*, 303.

23 Mathisen, 6; James L. Wood and Maurice Jackson, *Social Movements: Development, Participation, and Dynamics* (Belmont, CA: Wadsworth, 1982), 126; Cameron, 72; Robert L. Scott and Donald K. Smith, "The Rhetoric of Confrontation," *Quarterly Journal of Speech* 55 (February 1969), 3; John Wilson, *Introduction to Social Movements* (New York: Basic Books, 1973), 69; Oberschall, 61.

24 Cameron, 72.

25 Oberschall, 188.

26 Verta Taylor and Nancy A. Whittier, "Collective Identity in Social Movement Communities," *Frontiers in Social Movement Theory*, 105.

[27] Simons, Mechling, and Schreier, 810.
[28] Michael Stohl, "Demystifying Terrorism: The Myths and Realities of Contemporary Political Terrorism," *Politics of Terrorism*, Michael Stohl, ed. (New York: Marcel-Dekker, 1988), 1–28; R. D. Duvall and Michael Stohl, "Government by Terror," in Stohl (1988), 231–271.
[29] *The Oxford Universal Dictionary* (Oxford: Clarendon Press, 1955), 2054; Weber, 130.
[30] R. R. McGuire, "Speech Acts, Communicative Competence and the Paradox of Authority," *Philosophy and Rhetoric* 10 (Winter 1977), 31 and 33.
[31] William A. Gamson, *Power and Discontent* (Homewood, IL: Dorsey Press, 1968), 127.
[32] Simons (1974), 191.
[33] Louis Kriesberg, *The Sociology of Social Conflicts* (Englewood Cliffs, NJ: Prentice-Hall, 1973), 111.
[34] Ash, 230.
[35] Simons (1972), 239–247.
[36] Herbert Simons coined the term "co-active" persuasion to refer to all persuasive efforts that reach "out to persuadees both physically and psychologically" and emphasize "similarities between persuader and persuadee." See Simons (1972), 236; and Simons (1976), 121–122.
[37] Robert Cathcart describes rhetorical confrontation as a "ritual enactment that dramatizes the symbolic separation of the individual from the existing order (1978), 236; Robert Scott and Donald Smith emphasize the "sense of division" in confrontational strategies, Scott and Smith (1969), 2.
[38] Francesconi, 50; Simons, Mechling, and Schreier, 792.
[39] Weber, 328.
[40] Smith, 1; Irving I. Zaretsky and Mark P. Leone, *Religious Movements in Contemporary America* (Princeton, NJ: University of Princeton, 1974), 10 and 26.
[41] Cameron, 72.
[42] Klandermans, 93.
[43] See, for example, David Carr, *Time, Narrative, and History* (Bloomington, IN: Indiana University Press, 1986); and Walter R. Fisher, *Human Communication as Narration: Toward a Philosophy of Reason, Value, and Action* (Columbia: University of South Carolina Press, 1987.)
[44] Gusfield, 310; Zaretsky and Leone, 500; Wilson, 125; Richard L. Johannesen, "The Jeremiad and Jenkin Lloyd Jones," *Communication Monographs* 52 (June 1985), 156–172; Gamson (1992), 54.
[45] Contained in the collection of SDS papers compiled by James F. Walsh.
[46] Rhodri Jeffreys-Jones, *Violence and Reform in American History* (New York: New Viewpoints, 1978), 12, 16, 38; Ash, 2–3, 9.
[47] Weber, 125; Gusfield, 310.
[48] Simons (1976), 235; Simons, Mechling, and Schreier, 810; Cameron, 55; Bowers, Ochs, Jensen, 22–23.
[49] Gusfield, 366.
[50] Michael C. McGee, "In Search of 'The People': A Rhetorical Alternative," *Quarterly Journal of Speech* 61 (October 1975), 235–249; Cameron, 72; Wilson, 125.
[51] Wilson, 171–172.
[52] *The Gray Panther Manual* (Philadelphia: The Gray Panthers, 1978), 8.
[53] Oberschall, 308.
[54] Wilson, 126; Zaretsky and Leone, 509.
[55] Zaretsky and Leone, 500 and 510.
[56] McGuire, 33.
[57] *The Gray Panther Manual*, 105.
[58] Cathcart, 237; Simons (1972), 236.
[59] Jeffreys-Jones, 16, 30, and 38.
[60] Bowers, Ochs, Jensen, 20.
[61] Cathcart, 238; Robert S. Cathcart, "New Approaches to the Study of Movements: Defining Movements Rhetorically," *Western Speech* 36 (Spring 1972), 87.
[62] Wood and Jackson, 126.

[63] Carol J. Jablonski, "Promoting Radical Change In the Roman Catholic Church: Rhetorical Requirements, Problems, and Strategies of the American Bishops," *Central States Speech Journal* 31 (Winter 1980), 289.

[64] Klandermans, 91.

[65] McGuire, 44.

[66] Francesconi, 51; Farrell, 96.

[67] Bowers, Ochs, and Jensen, 36–43; Gusfield, 310.

[68] Ash, 2.

[69] Saul Alinsky, *Rules for Radicals: A Pragmatic Primer for Realistic Radicals* (New York: Vintage Books, 1971), 128.

[70] Simons, Mechling, and Schreier, 835.

[71] Cathcart (1978), 246.

[72] Cathcart (1978), 246.

[73] Kriesberg, 176.

[74] Simons (1972), 243; Scott and Smith, 8.

[75] Scott and Smith, 8.

[76] Cathcart (1978), 243.

[77] See for example, Daniel Walker, *Rights in Conflict: The Violent Confrontation of Demonstrators and Police in the Streets of Chicago During the Week of the Democratic National Convention* (New York: Bantam Books, 1968); and Fred Powledge, *Free at Last? The Civil Rights Movement and the People Who Made It* (Boston: Little Brown and Company, 1991).

[78] Wilson, 244; Simons, Mechling, and Schreier, 829.

[79] Simons, Mechling, and Schreier, 829; Theodore Otto Windt, "The Diatribe: Last Resort for Protest," *Quarterly Journal of Speech* 58 (February 1972), 14.

[80] Cathcart (1978), 242–243.

[81] Walker, 327.

[82] The Industrial Workers of the World (IWW) were active in the labor movement during the early 1900s; the Black Panthers were active in the black power movement of the late 1960s; and the Weathermen were active in the anti-Vietnam War and counterculture movements of the late 1960s and early 1970s.

Chapter Eight

Resisting Social Movements

As noted in previous chapters, efforts to initiate (or stifle) change threaten established institutions (governments, religious denominations, corporations, industries, educational systems) and generate resistance. The specific sources, forms, and types of response to social movements are varied and complex. Rather than identifying particular agents, agencies, or beneficiaries of resistance, this chapter investigates the nature of resistance to social movements by focusing on the philosophical bases of response as well as strategies and tactics institutions and their surrogates utilize.

Institutions and Social Order

Every organization has a set of explicit or implicit purposes that include self-preservation, perpetuation, value-maintenance, policy making, and enforcement.[1] All societies are protective of territorial boundaries and cultural norms and values. Enemies exist from within as well as from without. Leaders and rulers must concern themselves with authority, legitimacy, and power. Emblems of authority and rituals such as civic holidays, religious holy days, days of thanksgiving, days of honoring founders and military heroes, inaugurations, college commencements, insignia, uniforms, and limousines readily reinforce the status quo—and the current allocation of influence.

Power is a concept relevant to individuals and groups. In chapter 7, we noted that when society confers legitimacy upon institutions, it confers powers to perpetuate this grant. Bowers, Ochs, and Jensen discuss how French and Raven's five "social powers" (legitimate, coercive, reward, referent, and expert) are distributed between institutions and social movements.[2] They maintain that an institution always controls legitimate power (is perceived to have a charter, social contract, or assigned position through which it can exert influence) and normally is capable of exerting coercive power (is perceived as able to influence by threat of punishment). Institutions and social movements, according to Bowers, Ochs, and Jensen, share reward power because each is capable of conferring some rewards. While both share referent power (ability to identify with groups and individuals) and expert power (the image of having superior knowledge or skill in a particular area), social movements "depend almost completely on referent power and expert power."[3]

Andrew King argues, from a group perspective, that power is derived from three bases: material resource base, psychosocial base, and organizational/syntactic base.[4] In feudal times, the material resource base was primarily land; the material resource today tends to be money. The psycho-social base provides a sense of identity for group members who are bound together by common interests, habits, culture, and values. Organizational/syntactic bases of power are legislative rules, regulations, and norms of behavior. Power, then, is a multidimensional offensive and defensive weapon of institutions and social movements. We will discuss later how established orders and their surrogates use the forms of power.

According to Hugh Duncan, social order is always expressed in some kind of hierarchy.[5] Hierarchy differentiates people into ranks based on variables such as age, sex, race, skills, knowledge, and wealth, and these ranks function as societal structures that allow institutions to maintain control. Forms of social drama help to create national symbols that unify and transcend local, isolated concerns. Drama, as enacted within situations that provide legitimacy and continuation of regimes, ultimately results in social order and control.

Legitimacy offers the most promising point of attack for social movements. Regimes must actively demonstrate that they are competent, fair, just, and reasonable in order to maintain public support. Social control is usually viewed as the result of institutional influences such as laws or the police, but social order is not totally dependent upon agencies of control. No institution can long survive solely on the threat of force. Public communication is a vital tool; through it, institutions create and control images that legitimize their authority.

Situations are never neutral. They are experienced by people through language, and throughout society a variety of people describe similar situations in a variety of ways. Events do not simply exist. They are interpreted by those affected by them. Consequently, the "definitions of situations" are a valuable commodity that both leaders of institutions and social movements compete to control and "own." Public perceptions and impressions are influenced by "significant symbols" that are emotional, intense, and cultural in nature —such as freedom, justice, and equality. Society, therefore, is a dynamic, interacting entity consisting of many levels acting and competing simultaneously. The fight for legitimacy is a fight for public perceptions; symbols are important weapons in that struggle.

Institutions are accustomed to defining situations in their terms. How should they respond to challenging definitions of situations ("the corporation provoked the confrontation"), symbols ("our legal system is prejudiced and unjust"), or acts of violence ("the police attacked us because of our appearance")? The philosophy of democracy and free speech makes institutional response to social movement challenges and activities troublesome.

Democracy and Resistance to Social Movements

There is probably no concept more important to the theory of democratic government than free speech. Freedom of expression is a First Amendment right guaranteed in our Constitution. Historically, however, institutions have made many attempts to limit, to control, or to suppress freedom of expression by the press and individuals. For instance, the Sedition Law of 1798 attempted to suppress newspapers that attacked the American government for remaining neutral when the Republic of France declared war upon England. This law forbade the publication of matter intended to defame the government or to bring its officers into disrepute. The Sherman Antitrust Act of 1890 was used to stifle the organizing activities of labor unions. The Espionage Acts of 1917 forbade anyone to cause or to attempt to cause insubordination, disloyalty, mutiny, or refusal of duty in the armed forces. These acts made it unlawful to write or speak against American involvement in World War I. Eugene V. Debs, longtime leader of the socialist movement, was arrested in Canton, Ohio in 1918 shortly after he gave a speech opposing America's involvement in a "European war." He was tried under the Sedition Acts and received a ten-year sentence, entering a federal prison four months after the war had ended. During World War II, Congress established the U.S. Office of Censorship to monitor all actions and written materials that challenged the wisdom of America's presence in Europe and Asia. Colleges and universities routinely restricted the speaking activities of politicians, activists, and unapproved student groups on their campuses.

During the mid-1960s, demonstrators brought numerous challenges to laws restricting free expression. The civil rights, students' rights, and anti-Vietnam War movements stimulated the consideration of free speech issues such as limits of expression, limits of criticism of public officials, citizen surveillance, the right to privacy, and the right to wear emblems such as peace symbols, flags, and black armbands.[6] In response to the broadening of civil rights and rights of expression, institutions have sought to control access and dissemination of information as the principal means of shaping and guiding public understanding of social policy. The "war" over the freedom of expression has become the war over the freedom of information.[7] Beginning with President Lyndon Johnson, the press has had less access to government leaders and information. Official information from many government agencies has become "secret," "classified," and "selective," so it is increasingly difficult to distinguish fact from fiction, truth from propaganda. "Good" reporters get interviews and important news leaks while others get little of either. Presidents have tended to view the press as an enemy rather than a partner in the democratic process and attacked the "liberal," "eastern establishment," and "biased" press. The University of Wisconsin and other educational institutions have recently created policies to guarantee "politically correct'' speech and to eliminate ''hate speech'' such as racial, ethnic, and gender name-calling from their campuses. The courts have ruled against many of these policies as infringements on freedom of expression.

In resisting social movements, how much free expression should be tolerated? Are all opinions equal? Is there a difference between the form and content of expression sufficient to limit some expressions rather than others? These are difficult and important questions, especially for a democracy, and a balance is difficult to maintain. For example, communication scholars generally agree that speakers who appeal only to the emotions of audiences impede logical and critical thinking. Thus, many scholars have concluded that such appeals are unethical and undemocratic because they undermine the free, full, and rational discussion of issues. Wayne Flynt argues that during the 1963 civil rights disturbances in Birmingham, Alabama, prominent leaders took undemocratic stances, employed faulty logic, and appealed to white fear, frustration, and anger.[8] A former mayor of Birmingham publicly charged that he was ''Kicked out of the city hall by niggers'' and that the new mayor would probably make the African violet the city's official flower.[9] Is such rhetoric more unethical, however, than protestors shouting insults and obscenities at clergy, public officials, and police officers?

Another troublesome area for established orders is the level of response. The national government may be most concerned with issues, policy, and movement leaders, while the local government may focus primarily on property, events, maintenance of order, and citizens' rights. Local police, for example, believe they are charged with maintaining law and order. A ''good'' officer is one who strictly enforces the law. A ''bad'' officer is one who uses discretion and overlooks certain offenses. Police have often viewed protestors as disruptors of peace and users of tactics that would lead ultimately to anarchy. And, of course, protestors have viewed police as brutish ''pigs'' and mindless enforcers of suppression.[10] Law enforcement officers have often been more reactors to rather than initiators of either protest or institutional counteractions. Police, for example, have responded to individual demonstrators and their actions rather than to or from an ideological view of gay rights, pro-life, or the environment. Protestors' actions tend to be contrary to the basic values and upbringing of police officers. While local responses to social movements have often been more ''in-the-flesh'' direct, and sometimes counter to national policy, they were often symbolic of national attitudes and responses.

This discussion suggests problems inherent in institutional bureaucracies. First, there is little agreement on whether negotiations with social movements should rest with the executive, legislative, or judicial branch of government. Second, institutions are comprised of individuals with their own beliefs, attitudes, and values. Third, consensus and policy implementation are not merely matters of issuing directives because there are differences between theory and practice, issues and policy implementation. And fourth, democracy is not an entity but a process of regulating human behavior. This process is often slow and insensitive with contradictory principles. How does an established order balance the rights of society against individuals, the majority against the minority, or the popular against the unpopular? For most social movements, the *cause* is supreme, the resources are *few*, and the time to act is *now*. The urgency expressed by social movements encounters the rhetoric of democratic government, based on the premise that politics enacted are the will of the *majority* and politics rejected are favored by only a *small* minority.

Thus, the philosophical principles as well as the operational structure of a democracy dictate not only the strategies and tactics of social movements but also the forms and types of institutional responses. Democracy makes resistance to social movements varied and complex. According to Theodore Windt, "administrative" rhetoric is characterized by a defensive posture that views all questions of policy as attacks on the authority and credibility of the institution.[11] In the same vein, Bowers, Ochs, and Jensen write that the principle that governs the rhetorical stance of decision makers is the assumption that the worst will happen in any instance of outside agitation.[12] Institutional leaders, to maintain their power and credibility within the hierarchy, must continually provide evidence of superiority, control, and the willingness to respond quickly and decisively to all threats or attacks upon the institution. It is mandatory, then, for institutional leaders to confront the opposition to maintain support among establishment members and sympathizers.

In summary, institutions seem to maintain a universal perspective toward outside threats and attacks. All challenges are viewed as questioning established authority. For most protestors, however, their challenges are questions of legitimacy, such as "How good are certain policies or actions?" Obviously, these divergent views toward challenges influence the nature and types of establishment responses to social movements. The remainder of this chapter focuses on six strategies institutions employ in response to outside challenges: evasion, counter-persuasion, coercive persuasion, coercion, adjustment, and capitulation.[13]

The Strategy of Evasion

The strategy of evasion is usually the first strategy employed. Institutions attempt to ignore a social movement—to pretend that it does not exist or that it is too insignificant to recognize. The media devote little time or space to coverage of the new or continuing social movement, so most Americans are unaware, for example, that a fledgling men's movement exists or that a temperance or native American movement is continuing its struggle. "Invisible" social movements are not consulted or represented on task forces dealing with their concerns, do not appear on election ballots, and are denied meeting places or parade permits because they are not recognized as legitimate student, religious, political, or civic groups. For example, during the Democratic Convention in Chicago in 1968, Chicago Mayor Richard Daly denied permits for the Yippies to use Soldier's Field and members of the National Mobilization Committee to use Lincoln Park after curfew hours.[14] Organizers of the annual Saint Patrick's Day parade in New York have attempted to deny permission for gay Irish men and women to take part.

Institutional leaders avoid meeting with representatives of social movements. Such a meeting could be interpreted as symbolizing that the movement is worthy of serious consideration or encounter. Bureaucratic procedures allow institutions to delay official response to a social movement. Institutional bureaucracies are adept at "passing-the-buck," being "unavailable for comment," and giving "the run-around." Institutions maintain the appearance of addressing issues by referring them to committees, special commissions, or task forces. Postponement tactics slow or delay the decision-making process regarding a social movement's charges and demands. Some issues—such as civil rights and women's rights—are tied up in the courts or congress for years while little or no change takes place. When laws or decisions are made, some are so ambiguous or full of loopholes that offenders can easily circumvent them; some lack enforcement mechanisms or teeth to make them effective; and some are simply not enforced by institutions that are unsympathetic to social movement demands. The hope is that protestors will become discouraged and go away or that the issue will disappear. During the civil rights movement's efforts to integrate public schools, a common strategy for white citizens was to close public schools or to create their own schools to avoid integration. In 1963 Reverend George Fisher, pastor of the Edgewater Baptist Church in Birmingham, Alabama, obtained 75,000 signatures on petitions endorsing the closing of schools rather than enforce integration.[15]

The Strategy of Counter-Persuasion

Institutions employ a strategy of counter-persuasion when they can no longer avoid problems or encounters with social movements. They use this strategy to challenge a social movement's version of reality and to discredit leaders, members, and demands. The secret to success is not to overreact but to characterize the social movement, its leaders, and its ideas as ill-advised and lacking merit.

By manipulating the social context, an institution can expand, narrow, or selectively alter arguments and definitions of the situation.[16] It may appeal to fundamental motives and fears. Thus, institutional agents and agencies argue that environmentalists are endangering the American economy and threatening factory workers, loggers, and fish workers with the loss of their livelihoods; that anti-war or anti-military groups are unpatriotic and a threat to national security; and that gay rights advocates are immoral and grievous threats to the American family and way of life. During the early part of this century, the media warned Americans that terrible things would happen if women gained the right to vote. Cartoonists portrayed female army officers reviewing all-female military units, women at political rallies while husbands were at home taking care of the children, and women smoking and drinking in saloons while husbands were doing the laundry. In 1983 when ABC-TV was about to air its famous nuclear holocaust video entitled *The Day After*, Phyllis Schlafly (President of the Eagle Forum) sent leaflets to schools throughout the nation denouncing the video in advance as "virulently anti-American," "dishonest," and a "vicious smear of America" because it suggested that the United States might have started the war. To Schlafly *The Day After* was a thinly veiled "political" video created to support the pro-pacifist and anti-nuclear movements and "offensive to President Reagan and to religious people."[17]

Cries of anarchy help to unite the "silent majority" by identifying protestors as dangerous criminals and degenerates. Institutions throughout American history have found it easy to generate feelings of suspicion toward those who are "different" or "foreign" and to create fears about social movement motives and objectives. Local officials during the racial confrontation in Birmingham in 1963 identified integration with despised external movements and threats such as communism.[18] Thus, integration became a tool of the communist conspiracy that was a grave threat to Christian and democratic principles and values. Movement leaders must spend a great amount of rhetoric and time explaining and justifying actions and ideology to sympathizers as well as the public.

Moral outrage and righteous indignation justify counterattacks that nearly always employ labelling and name-calling. Lawrence Rosenfeld defines coercive semantics as attempts "to discourage real discussion of alternatives, and to render counterarguments meaningless by labelling the opponents as evil."[19] Henry Gonzalez, elected to Congress in 1961 from Texas, led an aggressive counterattack against militant Chicanos. His charges followed three themes: (1) militants practiced reverse racism and preached hate based upon race; (2) militants displayed bad qualities and harmed the Mexican-American community; and (3) militant attacks on him were personal and unfair. Gonzalez's perspective was that the militants "have adopted the same positions, the same attitudes, the same tactics as those who have so long offended them."[20] Nearly identical charges have been made in the 1980s and 1990s against the Nation of Islam leader Louis Farrakhan for allegedly making anti-Semitic statements and the Black Panthers in Indianapolis for urging African Americans to boycott Korean American-owned stores in their neighborhoods. S. I. Hayakawa, President of San Francisco State University in 1968, claimed that rebellious students were attempting to overthrow the government and were all drug addicts. He referred to students as "cowards who resort to violence, lies, and deceit."[21] Martha Solomon, in examining the rhetorical strategies of the Stop ERA Movement, found that opponents of the women's movement ridiculed members as unattractive and lesbian. She concluded that "with sharp satire the group paints an unappealing picture of the feminists' physical appearance and nature, emphasizing their disregard for traditional standards of feminine attractiveness and sexuality."[22] Men were not alone in stereotyping pro-ERA (Equal Rights Amendment) women. Phyllis Schlafly proclaimed, "if man is targeted as the enemy, and the ultimate goal of women's liberation is independence from men and the avoidance of pregnancy and its consequences, then lesbianism is the highest form in the ritual of women's liberation."[23] Ridicule may weaken the self-confidence and self-esteem of protestors and challenge their efforts to attain legitimacy among potential sympathizers and members.

Counter-persuasion deals primarily with social movement leaders and members rather than the movement's issues and demands. Name-calling, labelling, and ridicule attack individuals directly. Perhaps the easiest way to discredit a movement is to discredit its leaders and most fervent followers. If the leaders and "true believers" are evil, then the motives, goals, and objectives of the movement must be evil.

The Strategy of Coercive Persuasion

The strategy of coercive persuasion involves tactics ranging from threats to general harassment. These tactics tend to evolve when avoidance and counter-persuasion fail to stifle a social movement and an institution commits itself to direct action and sustained conflict.

Institutions have a war chest of potentially lethal threats at their disposal and have exhibited little reluctance to use them. They may threaten to fire workers, expel students, deport the "foreign born," excommunicate the true believer, deny sacraments to the faithful, or discharge the members of the military who "come out of the closet." Employers fought the labor movement for years with threats to "blacklist" union members by sending their names throughout the country so no one would hire them. The Roman Catholic Church has threatened to expel pro-choice nuns from their religious orders and to deny the sacraments to elected officials who espoused pro-choice views.[24] University administrators and police photographed student demonstrators in the 1960s and 1970s to identify students they threatened to expel and report to their parents and draft boards. Anti-environmental groups such as the Wise Use Movement and the Sahara Club have not only telephoned threats and warnings to environmental activists but have recorded license plate numbers and videotaped activists as a signal of future retaliation—activists have been identified and can be found.[25]

Some institutions have threatened to "replace" social movement organizations with more "cooperative" ones. Corporations played the CIO and AFL against one another during the 1930s and 1940s. Grape growers in California signed contracts with the Teamsters union to counteract the United Farm Workers' efforts to unionize grape workers. Nine growers and right wing organizations actually created, financed, and hand-picked the leaders for a counter-organization called the AWFWA (Agricultural Workers Freedom to Work Association)—allegedly a farm workers' organization. The courts eventually outlawed the AWFWA organization as a flagrant violation of fair employment laws.

Harassment tactics may be covert. During the Nixon Administration, agencies of the federal government such as the FBI, the CIA, Army Intelligence, and the Treasury Department investigated anti-war demonstrators and student leaders for communist connections or sympathies upon which the government might base administrative actions. Students were secretly photographed, files and lists of "suspected communist sympathizers" were created, letters (many allegedly from parents and concerned citizens) were sent to boards of trustees and school boards suggesting that certain teachers be fired, and some college officials reported activities of students to parents. President Clinton's secret file created while he was a college student and anti-Vietnam War protestor was used against him as he campaigned for the presidency in 1992. The file included details of a visit he made to the Soviet Union while a Rhodes Scholar at Oxford University. Government agents and sympathizers routinely infiltrate "radical" groups in the United States with the primary purpose of gathering information to inhibit their activities. It was discovered years after Malcolm X's assassination that his chief bodyguard was an undercover New York police officer. Another purpose of infiltration is to instigate militant and violent acts that will discredit the movement. Michael Stohl reports that "regimes and their agent provocateurs (both official and self-identified) have both encouraged insurgent groups to plan and execute terrorist actions not only to provide grounds for arrest but also to alienate potential supporters within the population."[26]

The Strategy of Coercion

Institutions often rely on surrogates to suppress social movements. Jerome Skolnick claims that counterdemonstrators have attacked many protestors with the knowledge and tacit approval of administrative and civil authorities. For example, the Ku Klux Klan and White Citizens' Councils served as surrogates for southern state and community authorities during the civil rights struggles. Skolnick writes that "by far the greater portion of physical harm has been done to demonstrators and movement workers, in the form of bombings of homes and offices, crowd-control measures used by police, physical attacks on demonstrators by American Nazi party members, Hell's Angels and others, and random harassment such as the Port Chicago Vigil has endured."[27]

In an overt form of harassment, the head of the Selective Service System ordered the reclassification of leading student protestors.[28] For example, Peter Wolff and Richard Shortt had II-S student classifications as full-time students at the University of Michigan. When they participated in a demonstration protesting American involvement in Vietnam, the local Selective Service Board reclassified both as I-A, eligible for the draft. The Board argued that by participating in the anti-war demonstration, Wolff and Shortt became "delinquents" and thus were in violation of Section 12(a) of the Universal Military Training and Service Act. They further argued that a student deferment was not a "right" but a "legislative grace."[29] Direct forms of harassment are often used to intimidate. National Guardsmen were called out to "protect students" in a two-day march on the Pentagon in 1967. The large number of heavily armed troops restricted the movement of and access to the student marchers. It soon became clear that the troops were present to control rather than to protect the protestors; this establishment show of force cost the taxpayers more than one million dollars.[30] In addition to videotaping environmental activists and taking down their license plate numbers, Wise Use and Sahara Club members have picked fights with demonstrators, assaulted movement leaders, and set fire to homes.[31]

The easiest method of coercion is the passage and implementation of restrictive legislation and policies. For example, the University of California at Berkeley in 1964 established a policy prohibiting individuals from the solicitation of funds and advocacy of political causes on campus. The administration had several students arrested for violating this policy.[32] This undemocratic and unconstitutional policy suppressed student actions until protest organizations challenged it in court. Some cities used zoning laws during the 1960s and 1970s to eliminate underground presses in private homes, contending that such presses were businesses and could not be operated in homes zoned as family dwellings. Legal challenges of restrictive policies and legislation takes time and money, assets that favor institutions rather than social movements.

Some coercion is indirect and opportunistic. For instance, a student at the University of California at Berkeley was arrested for public obscenity because he carried a sign that read "Freedom Under Clark Kerr" (Kerr was president of the University). The first letter of each word was highlighted.[33] This arrest was obviously aimed more at the protestor than the "offending" obscenity. The establishment's arsenal of laws, rules, and regulations is a vast and powerful tool of suppression. Arrest is perhaps the most common form of coercion and has been used in recent years against anti-nuclear power, environmentalist, anti-apartheid policies of South Africa, pro-choice, pro-life, and gay rights activists. Multiple charges can tie up movement leaders for years with court appearances, bad publicity, and drains on a movement's precarious financial state. Bowers, Ochs, and Jensen write that the Black Panthers were involved in more than sixty criminal prosecutions requiring $300,000 in bail money in the first six months of 1967.[34]

While the courts have made many rulings in favor of protestors during the past quarter-century, perhaps most notably the expansion of freedom of "speech" (meanings words) to "symbolic speech" (including symbols and symbolic actions), rulings still place severe limits on social movements. For instance, protestors may speak against the government but they cannot advocate its overthrow, cannot put the American flag to "an ignoble use," cannot exceed the bounds of "rational" discourse, cannot invade the privacy of others, cannot place "undue strain" on a community's resources, and cannot "inconvenience" people not in the target audience. Institutions, of course, will determine when protest is advocating overthrow of the government and what is ignoble, rational, invasion of privacy, undue strain, and inconvenience.[35]

The most severe forms of coercion are expulsion and assassination; threats become reality. Governments exile or deport social movement leaders. Schools suspend or expel students. The military discharges gay members who dare to testify for gay rights and female members who make claims of sexual harassment. Religious organizations excommunicate members or deny them important rites or sacraments. The Roman Catholic Church, for example, barred an eleven-year-old child from a Catholic school because she would not renounce her mother's pro-choice activism and denied sacraments to members of NOW in California because the organization is pro-choice.[36] Assassinations are often acts of individuals rather than institutions and institutional policies. Nevertheless, many movement leaders and followers have been killed in the United States. Students at Jackson State and Kent State, members of the Black Panthers, Medgar Evers, Malcolm X, and Martin Luther King, Jr. are merely the best known. Very few people have ever come to trial or been convicted for killing movement activists. Michael Stohl writes that "disappearance" of leaders and followers "is one of the quiet terrors employed by many governments in the modern world."[37]

Coercion has several advantages for institutions. First, coercive tactics generate fear among a social movement's leaders, followers, and sympathizers. Michael Stohl notes that "The violence of the terrorist act is not intended simply to destroy but also to be heard." "For regimes," he continues, "the terror is a message of strength, a warning designed to intimidate, to ensure compliance without the need to physically touch each citizen."[38] Thus, social movement leaders may become hesitant to act; members may become hesitant to take part in demonstrations; and sympathizers may withdraw moral and financial support. Second, coercion isolates leaders from followers. And third, coercion enables institutions to portray social movement leaders as common criminals and dangerous social deviants.

The Strategy of Adjustment

The strategy of adjustment involves making some concessions to a social movement while not accepting the movement's demands or goals. Adjustment tactics give the appearance of being responsive to movement concerns.[39] Accommodation, according to Andrew King, is usually a short-term solution that, for the establishment, buys time, saves face, and appears gracious.[40] This strategy, by design, addresses only superficial elements of conflict and seldom results in permanent solutions to social unrest and movement demands. Adjustment tactics range from symbolic gestures to concrete acts of concession.

Symbolic tactics include issuing press releases that promise investigation of problems or the naming of special committees and commissions to study the issues raised by the social movement. Such gestures provide a visible response and show of concern while reducing the sense of urgency of social movement demands— which buys time for the establishment. Presidents, governors, and political candidates address concerns such as equal rights, the environment, animal rights, and the needs of senior citizens and then go about business as usual. Although this tactic is somewhat similar to bureaucratic delays, it does involve a public acknowledgement of the movement's demands.

Sacrificing personnel is a common tactic of institutional leaders. University deans and presidents, police chiefs and officers, and mid-level executives often are dismissed from their positions when they become targets of social movements, are portrayed as unresponsive to citizen or group needs, or become convenient and expendable symbols of establishment "responsiveness." This tactic may be particularly effective when a social movement focuses its agitation and hatred upon a single individual or unit. Elimination of the individual or unit leaves the movement without a target. Public sympathy for an institution may increase when sacrificed individuals are seen as tragic victims of radical protestors.

A subtle adjustment tactic is cooperation with protestors and movement organizations by providing protection, access to facilities, or material support. Open and publicized cooperation frustrates social movements by making institutions less of an obvious enemy and target of outrage. Cooperation may defuse a movement's energy, momentum, and recruiting efforts, buy time for counterefforts, encourage attitudes of neutrality among citizens, and generate favorable press. Cooperation may lead to outright *co-optation* of the cause in which institutions seemingly take on the cause. Congress, for example, seemed to take on the civil rights cause in the years following the assassination of John F. Kennedy by passing civil rights and voting laws and creating an equal employment opportunity commission. Many establishment groups, including corporations and the Advertising Council, literally took over the "ecology" movement in the 1970s.

Incorporation of movement leaders and sympathizers within institutional bodies is another common adjustment tactic. During the 1960s and 1970s, students, blacks, and women became appointees, often as "tokens," to committees, boards, and study commissions. Governmental agencies, schools, religious groups, and corporations began to hire a few minorities and to appoint them to serve in a variety of nonthreatening positions. For example, American colleges and universities appointed students to serve on boards of trustees, grievance committees, grade appeal committees, and curriculum committees. "Representation," however, did not mean power to influence policy decisions. In the 1990s, the phrase "glass ceiling" still has significance for women and minorities who lag far behind white males in salaries and leadership positions.

The strategy of adjustment can be tricky for institutions because they must not appear to be deceptive, cynical, weak, or tyrannical. Nearly any concession may rejuvenate a social movement by renewing hope of immediate or ultimate victory. Adjustments are most often mere tokens to appease public questioning and social movement demands.

The Strategy of Capitulation

Capitulation is the total acceptance of a social movement's ideology: beliefs, goals, objectives, and solutions.[41] This has rarely happened in American history because (1) institutions control rewards, channels of communication, and regulatory agencies, and (2) as noted in previous chapters, Americans cherish the institutions they have created, adapted, and borrowed from other societies and are not inclined toward social-political instability or revolutionary change. Indeed, as Raymond Duvall and Michael Stohl write, Americans can hardly imagine their governments being evil:

> Particularly in the American political culture, the concept of the state as neutral
> conflict manager or arbiter of social conflict within society is so ingrained that

many have difficulty emotionally accepting the idea of state terrorism. Terrorism is felt to be something done by revolutionaries against the state. How could a government—at least a legitimate government like that in the United States—be thought to engage in terrorism? Surely such talk must be revolutionary rhetoric![42]

Conclusions

Institutions must confront challenges and threats to their beings even though complete annihilation of existing institutions seldom occurs in today's world. For an institution, any concession to dissenters may be costly. Even negotiations create strains within an order by creating an atmosphere of tension and risk in a win-lose situation. Thus, established orders and their surrogates tend to employ a combination of six strategies in meeting the threats posed by social movements: evasion, counter-persuasion, coercive persuasion, coercion, adjustment, and capitulation.

Over time, bits and pieces of social movement ideologies find their way into institutional policies. Social security, farm supports, unemployment benefits, the eight-hour day, civil rights, equal opportunity, voting rights, collective bargaining, and fair housing were social movement demands long before established political parties enacted them into law. The task for institutions is to allow, perhaps even to encourage, dissent without threatening social, political, economic, or religious orders. Institutions and their surrogates have many more resources than social movements, and responses may emanate from individuals, organized resistance groups, local leaders, statewide organizations, and national authorities that may include the whole federal government. The trick for an institution is to use the best strategy for the situation and to avoid the appearance of overreacting or abusing the powers granted to it by "the people."

Endnotes

[1] See John W. Bowers, Donovan J. Ochs, and Richard J. Jensen, *The Rhetoric of Agitation and Control*, 2/E (Prospect Heights, IL: Waveland Press, 1993), 11–12.

[2] Bowers, Ochs, and Jensen, 13–14.

[3] Bowers, Ochs, and Jensen, 14–15.

[4] Andrew King, *Power and Communication* (Prospect Heights, IL: Waveland Press, 1987), 48–53.

[5] Hugh Duncan, *Symbols in Reality* (New York: Oxford University Press, 1968), 78–92.

[6] For specifics of such issues, see Robert O'Neil, *Free Speech* (Indianapolis: Bobbs-Merrill, 1972).

[7] Dale Minor, *The Information War* (New York: Hawthorn Books, 1970).

[8] Wayne Flynt, "The Ethics of Democratic Persuasion and the Birmingham Crisis," *Southern Speech Communication Journal* 35 (Fall 1969), 44.

[9] Flynt, 44–45.

[10] For a discussion of police response to protestors, see Irving Horowitz, *The Struggle Is the Message* (Berkeley, CA: The Glendessary Press, 1970), 48–58.

[11] Theodore Windt, "Administrative Rhetoric: An Undemocratic Response to Protest," *Communication Quarterly* 30 (Summer, 1982), 247.

[12] Bowers, Ochs, and Jensen, 47.

[13] See the discussion of the four strategies of avoidance, suppression, adjustment, and capitulation in Bowers, Ochs, and Jensen, 48–64.

[14] Bowers, Ochs, and Jensen, 68–69.

[15] Flynt, 45–46.

[16] King, 27.

[17] ABC Film *The Day After*, Eagle Forum, November 1983.

[18] Flynt, 49.

[19] Lawrence Rosenfeld, "The Confrontation Policies of S. I. Hayakawa: A Case Study in Coercive Semantics," *Today's Speech* 18 (Spring 1970), 18.

[20] John Hammerback, Richard Jensen, and Jose Gutierrer, *A War of Words* (Westport, CT: Greenwood Press, 1985), 104.

[21] Rosenfeld, 20.

[22] Martha Solomon, "The Rhetoric of Stop ERA: Fatalistic Reaffirmation," *Southern Speech Communication Journal* 44 (Fall 1978), 47.

[23] Solomon, 47.

[24] Lafayette, Indiana *Journal and Courier*, December 19, 1984, A13; Lafayette, Indiana *Journal and Courier*, September 21, 1986, A13; *Newsweek*, January 14, 1985, 29.

[25] CBS, "60 Minutes," June 6, 1993.

[26] Michael Stohl, ed., *The Politics of Terrorism* (New York: Dekker, 1983), 5.

[27] Jerome Skolnick, "The Politics of Protest," *Dissent: Symbolic Behavior and Rhetorical Strategies*, Haig Bosmajian, ed. (Boston: Allyn and Bacon, 1972), 156.

[28] Horowitz, 56.

[29] Harold Medina, "Students Have Rights Too," *Free Speech and Political Protest*, Marvin Summers, ed. (Lexington, MA: D.C. Heath, 1967), 102.

[30] Horowitz, 58.

[31] CBS, "60 Minutes," June 6, 1993.

[32] Windt, 245.

[33] Windt, 246.

[34] Bowers, Ochs, and Jensen, 55.

[35] Bosmajian, *Dissent*.

[36] Lafayette, Indiana *Journal and Courier*, August 16, 1986, C1; Lafayette, Indiana *Journal and Courier*, April 28, 1975, A10.

[37] Stohl, 3.

[38] Stohl, 3.

[39] Bowers, Ochs, and Jensen, 60–63.

[40] King, 27–38.

[41] Bowers, Ochs, Jensen, 63–64.

[42] Raymond Duvall and Michael Stohl, "Governance by Terror," in Stohl, *The Politics of Terrorism*, 181.

Chapter Nine

Symbolism in Social Movements
The Theories of Kenneth Burke

The study of social movements is an interdisciplinary endeavor. It requires familiarity with theories and concepts from the disciplines of sociology, psychology, history, and communication. A social movement, as we have noted in previous chapters, is a complex, dynamic, evolving, and synergistic entity with communication as its life blood. Human communication, in all of its forms, gives life to ideas and, consequently, to behavior. How we communicate determines how we relate to each other as social beings. This notion is true whether we are discussing our one-to-one relationships or our relationships within the larger society.

It is difficult, therefore, to find a comprehensive theory of human communication that accounts for the various forms and levels of human interaction. The writings of Kenneth Burke, however, provide a synthesis of the views of symbolic action. He offers a philosophy of human communication, a theory of social behavior, and a method for analyzing symbolic acts so that we can recognize the important relationship between symbolic acts and the environment in which they occur. As a theorist, Kenneth Burke demonstrates how motives and behavior arise and exist in communication. As an analyst, he provides tools for studying the effects of symbols on human motivation. In this chapter we will discuss Kenneth Burke's philosophy of human communication, his theory of dramatism, his methodological considerations, and the implications of his notions for the study of persuasion and social movements.

Kenneth Burke's Philosophy of Human Communication

Burke's philosophy of human communication provides the basis for a general conception of human beings and human relations. Burke defines the human being

as the "symbol-making," "symbol-using," and "symbol-misusing" animal.[1]
It is our symbol-using capacity that distinguishes us from other animals. Language,
as the medium of communication, is the defining characteristic and essence of
human life. We use symbols to define, accept, or reject situations.

Burke makes an important distinction between the realms of "motion" and
"action." The realm of "motion" is the physical animal world that is deterministic
and in which nature continues its endless process of life (i.e., "the splashing of
waves against the beach"). In contrast, the realm of "action" consists of acts
that occur because of the symbolic nature of "man." Burke writes that " 'Action'
is a term for the kind of behavior possible to a typically symbol-using animal
(such as man) in contrast with the extra symbolic or nonsymbolic operations of
nature."[2] Action allows humans to overcome the deterministic nature of the world
and to mold, shape, or create "reality" for themselves. Action involves free choice
and occurs only when we "will" it or if there is a "purpose" to the action. In
short, "the difference between a thing and a person is that one merely moves
whereas the other acts."[3]

The implication of the distinction between the realms of action and motion are
twofold. First, our "reality" is a product of our symbol-making," "symbol-
using," and "symbol-misusing" behavior. "However important to us is the tiny
sliver of reality each of us has experienced first hand," Burke writes, "the whole
overall 'picture' is but a construct of our symbol systems."[4] Second, our symbolic
behavior is grounded in the nonsymbolic. As Burke states, "If man is the symbol-
using animal, some motives must derive from his animality, some from his
symbolicity, and some from mixtures of the two."[5]

Language is the human vehicle for action. Language is action because it involves
individual selection, choice, and judgment. Rachel Holloway argues that language,
as symbolic action, reflects, selects, and deflects reality. "The words people
choose to express their perceptions betray and display their particular world views.
They state what for them is reality and act on the basis of that reality."[6] Language
is essentially persuasive in that, according to Burke, "the use of language is a
symbolic means of inducing cooperation in beings that by nature respond to
symbols."[7]

Through group interaction, common terms evolve to represent events,
experiences, and judgments. Leaders of social movements are continually
competing with other political leaders in defining and redefining our world. The
"reality" of American life for civil rights activists was one of discrimination,
oppression, and social inequality. The Vietnam War had been characterized as
an international act of aggression threatening world peace and democracy.
Protestors, however, viewed the Vietnam conflict as a limited civil war—a divided
country's struggle for "self- determination." Over time and after much debate
and confrontation, the "realities" of civil rights and the Vietnam War were altered
for many Americans. Through language, resulting from human symbol-making
capacity, human action occurs and society—or at least our perceptions of
it—changes.

"Motive" for Burke is a key term that is not used as causal explanation of human behavior, but rather as "short hand terms for situations."[8] Almost any behavior, because of the ambiguity of language, can be rationalized or justified by appealing to a motive that is simply a linguistic label for a situation. From Burke's perspective, motive is an explanation of action. The labels attached to an act or a linguistic interpretation of an act implies a motive for the act. Abortion can be labeled as an act of murder or as a medical procedure. Consequently, the agent of the act becomes a murderer or a healer. The motives attributed to the agent of the act differ greatly between the two descriptions of the act. The names we give to people, places, events, and things determine our behavior toward them. Thus, Kenneth Burke is primarily interested in the attribution of motives to action through communicative behavior. This is important because if we can determine the motive of a speaker, writer, or singer, then we should be able to determine with an acceptable degree of accuracy the persuader's view of reality.

Terms, and hence motives, may change as they are linked with other terms to form clusters. Holloway argues that the term "law and order," for example, changes meaning through clustering. Traditionally, the term "law and order" means social calm and the proper functioning of the justice system. However, specific circumstances may modify the term's meaning. "For example, for many southerners during the 1960s, law and order meant keeping blacks in their places, with illegal force, if necessary. In the 1970s, frightened city dwellers used the term to justify vigilantism. And in the 1990s, the term 'law and order' often is described as a code word for sanctioned discriminatory police practices."[9] In each case, the term represents different motives and a group's specific position on an issue. Terms play a role in determining sides of a conflict, specific views of reality, notions of right and wrong, and needed corrective actions.

Burke is concerned about order in society, hence the relevance of his philosophy of human communication and action to the study of social movements. For Burke, society is a process of symbolic interaction. Social life is a product of establishing and re-establishing mutual relations with others. Because the human condition is one of imperfect communication, we solve our problems in society through "recalcitrant and mystifying" symbols.[10] Ironically, symbols cause many problems among people. "But, however remote and strange the mystery of another may become," Burke writes, "there must be some way of transcending this separateness if social order is to be achieved."[11]

Finally, it is important to appreciate Burke's view of the persuasive nature of human symbolic behavior. His orientation emphasizes subtle, psychological, and subconscious attempts at persuasion. As noted, persuasion is inherent in the nature of symbolism and language. For Burke, "there is no chance of our keeping apart the meanings of persuasion . . . and commuication."[12]

Kenneth Burke's Theory of Dramatism

Dramatism, created and developed by Kenneth Burke, is grounded in the symbolic nature of humans. Burke argues that as symbol-using animals, we must stress symbolism as a motive in any discussion of social behavior. By 1968, he had promoted dramatism to an equal status with "symbolic interaction" and "social exchange" as being one of three areas of "interaction" discussed in the *International Encyclopedia of the Social Sciences*.[13] In his article, Burke summarizes dramatism as:

> A method of analysis and a corresponding critique of terminology designed to show that the most direct route to the study of human relations and human motives is via a methodical inquiry into cycles or clusters of terms and their functions.[14]

He calls his method dramatism "since it invites one to consider the matter of motives in a perspective that, being developed from the analysis of drama, treats language and thought primarily as modes of action."[15]

Thus, action is at the heart of dramatism, for dramatism is a means for analyzing human action.[16] An "act" is a "terministic center" from which many related influences and considerations derive.[17] Daily "actions" constitute dramas with created and attached significance. Drama, for Burke, serves as an analytic model of the social world. He explains:

> Though a drama is a mode of "symbolic action" so designed that an audience might be induced to "act symbolically" in sympathy with it, insofar as the drama serves this function it may be studied as a "perfect mechanism" composed of parts moving in perfect adjustment to one another like clock-work.[18]

As already noted, the human being is a symbolic creature. Thus, distinctively human behavior and interaction are carried on through the medium of symbols and their attached meanings. We alone can create, manipulate, and use symbols to control our behavior and the behavior of others.

Nearly all human action is symbolic. Human action usually represents something more than what is immediately perceived. Symbols form the basis of our overt behavior, so human action is the by-product or the stimulus of symbols. Before we can formulate a response to any situation, we must define and interpret the situation to ensure an appropriate response to the specific situation. Without exaggerating, therefore, symbols are the foundation of social life and human civilization. We derive meanings for symbols from interactions in specific social contexts. Reality, therefore, is a social product arising from interaction or communication and is limited, specific, and circumscribed.

According to Kenneth Burke, "if action is to be our key term, then drama is the culminative form of action. But if drama, then conflict. And if conflict, then victimage. Dramatism is always on the edge of this vexing problem, that comes to a culmination in tragedy."[19] This process is readily apparent when we consider social movements. Social movements are created and sustained through action: people articulating problems, defining issues, offering solutions, identifying enemies, stating courses of action, and both recruiting and activating followers. Such actions lead to confrontation and often to conflict and, in society, conflict must be explained, justified, or rationalized. Usually there are identifiable victims and corresponding human tragedy. This evolution is true both for individual and society-wide events.

Classical rhetoric stressed the explicit design of persuasion. Humans, as rational animals, responded to arguments supported by reasons, information, and evidence. Today, we view rhetoric as more complex and subtle because we believe that our beliefs, attitudes, and values are often impacted without conscious direction by a particular agent. Elements of the drama seem to impact all of our senses.

The mass media and news industries have heightened the nature of political drama and, in many ways, have become the nervous system of our society. The media are the major sources of information about politics and the state of the polity. Americans receive political information from the media through political advertising, news stories, and feature stories; the media are now perceived as more truthful and accurate than our families and friends.

Broadcast media attract, focus, and direct attention to specific social problems (while ignoring others) quickly and efficiently while serving as channels for public persuasion and mobilization. In mobilizing groups or "kinds of public," the media help to sustain these groups and their causes and confer status and legitimacy to the groups, issues, and ideas.

The result of this transformation of the role of the media in American society, according to Dan Nimmo and James Combs, is that few people learn about politics or social issues from direct experience.[20] Nimmo and Combs argue that political realities are "mediated" through group and mass communication. A result is the "creation, transmission, and adoption of political fantasies as realistic views of what takes place."[21] Fantasy is defined as:

> A credible picture of the world that is created when one interprets mediated experiences as the way things are and takes for granted the authenticity of the mediated reality without checking against alternative, perhaps contradictory, realities so long as the fantasy offers dramatic proof for one's expectations.[22]

Thus, from Nimmo's and Combs' perspective, television news is storytelling and employs elements of the dramatic narrative, utilizing verbal and nonverbal symbols, sound, and visual imagery.

News must be entertaining and highly visual because of the demands of television. News crews trim stories to support film and visual elements, so film footage is no longer used to illustrate stories but to tell the story.[23] Footage often stands alone with little or no perspective or analysis. Peter Jennings, anchor of ABC's "World News Tonight" states that "television is afraid of being dull . . . in television you're obligated to write to the pictures."[24] Lane Vernardos, executive producer of "The CBS News with Dan Rather," builds news stories around exciting video rather than the strongest hard news stories.[25] The news industry looks for and shares "news that wiggles," and the more in-depth the coverage, the less "wiggle" attained. Thus, the elements of action and movement are stressed over cognitive elements. Emotional responses are the ones the public remembers. Such responses help define future reactions to people and events. The important point is that for both participants and spectators, the elements of drama, social movements, and events consume the public.

Dramatism is clearly illustrated in the 1970s anti-war demonstrations at Kent State University that resulted in the killing of four students and the wounding of nine others by Ohio National Guardsmen.[26] The decade of the 1960s experienced much discussion, debate, and protest over the issues of civil rights and the Vietnam War. By 1970, student opposition to the war was strong, but the intensity of protest appeared to be declining. There was a drop in draft calls and, on April 20, 1970, President Nixon announced withdrawal of an additional 150,000 troops from Vietnam over the next twelve-month period. Ten days later, Nixon appeared to back away from his promises when he announced that American troops had invaded Cambodia to eliminate enemy strongholds and that American troops would penetrate farther in Indochina. Students felt betrayed by Nixon's announcement and viewed the Cambodia action as an escalation of what seemed to be an "endless" war.

Symbolic actions began to occur on the campus of Kent State University. On Friday night, students met at the center of campus, built a large bonfire, chanted anti-war slogans, and delivered speeches. The students soon marched downtown, broke windows, and had minor skirmishes with police. The drama had begun. The symbolic activities of speeches, slogans, obscene gestures, and stone throwing articulated the issues, grievances, hopes, desires, and frustrations of the protestors. Conflict followed. On Saturday, Mayor LeRoy Satrom of Kent closed the bars, issued an emergency proclamation, placed a curfew on the campus, and requested help from the Ohio National Guard. Rioting developed that evening. Students started fires, threw rocks and bottles at Guardsmen, shouted obscenities and threats at the Guardsmen, and attempted to burn down the R.O.T.C. building. By Monday morning, the National Guardsmen (some of them with minor injuries) had little patience or sympathy for the demonstrators, and the students were angry over the harassment, curfew, and National Guard tear gas. At 12:18 P.M., May 4, 1970, while attempting to disperse demonstrators at an illegal rally, several Guardsmen turned their rifles on a crowd of students and killed four of them.

After conflict comes victimage. The tragedy at Kent State University shocked the nation. It seemed to be the time for reflection, understanding, and justification. Scapegoats and victims of the event were identified, discussed, and by some, condemned. Official and unofficial sources questioned the National Guardsmen: Were they sufficiently provoked? Were they in serious danger? Were they murderers? Were they properly trained? Was the force justified or excessive? Was the shooting planned ahead of time? Other questions were aimed at the demonstrators: Were they lawless? Were they communists? Were they "hippies"? Were they attempting to attack the National Guardsmen? Did they get what was coming to them? And other questions were directed to Ohio Governor James Rhodes: Was the National Guard needed at Kent State? Were loaded weapons necessary? Were his instructions to "keep the university open at all costs" and "to restore civility" necessary?

The initial statement from the White House included the observation that "when dissent turns to violence it invites tragedy." Thus, Kenneth Burke's final component of drama—tragedy—is recognized. The event at Kent State University was a series of symbolic actions in the form of a human drama. The era of people in masses taking their grievances to the streets, to demand equal rights and an end to the war in Vietnam, ended with the tragedy at Kent State. The demonstrations and tragedies of the 1960s and 1970s had finally created a consensus in America that our involvement in Vietnam had been a tragic mistake and that laws were needed to end racial discrimination in American society. As Kenneth Burke proclaims, "politics above all is drama."[27]

As a method of analysis, then, dramatism provides a framework for investigating human communication behavior. It is primarily descriptive in nature, but dramatism can provide guidelines for enhancing and understanding communication between people. Hence, dramatism is a "communication theory of human behavior." The value of the method, according to Burke, is that it makes us "sensitive to the 'ideas' lurking in 'things' which might even as social motives seem reducible to their sheerly material nature, unless we can perfect techniques for disclosing their 'enigmatic' or 'emblematic' dimension."[28]

Key Concepts in Burkean Theory

As is true of all methodologies, key concepts function as fundamental tools of analysis. We need to understand several important concepts in Burke's theories of persuasion in order to understand clearly the perspective of dramatism and its application to the persuasive efforts of social movements.

Identification

There is a great deal of division—separateness—in our society, but communication can help us to articulate our differences and to relate to one another. Through communication we "transcend" to higher plains of meaning that enable us to overcome differences. Thus, in communicating with one another, we seek similarity or common references—Burke calls this process "identification."[29] All people are different, but we have common factors in which we are "consubstantially" or substantially the same. The process of identification reduces ambiguity and, hopefully, encourages cooperation.

There is a very close relationship between "identification" and "persuasion." Burke argues that "we might well keep in mind that a speaker persuades an audience by the use of stylistic identifications; his [her] act of persuasion may be for the purpose of causing the audience to identify itself with the speaker's interests; and the speaker draws on identification of interests to establish rapport between himself [herself] and his [her] audience."[30]

For Burke, identification is more than merely relating to others; it is an instrument of transformation. At some level, reality, an event, or a group makes sense (is rational) even though one person's rationalization is another's factuality. Our responses and conclusions, however, are the results of the process of transformation, which originates from our awareness of division. In the *Rhetoric of Motives*, Burke argues that "the statement of the thing's nature before and after the change is an identifying of it."[31]

Division is the counterpart of identification. In response to division, which is constant and certain, we seek transformation resulting in identification—a level of understanding if not harmony. Transformation occurs at various levels from the most obvious to the most subtle. Thus, when you "put identification and division ambiguously together, so that you cannot know for certain just where one ends and the other begins, you have the characteristic invitation to rhetoric."[21]

There are several levels of identification. Perhaps the most obvious is a persuader's attempt to establish "common ground" with an audience. This happens, for instance, when a United Farm Worker organizer wears work clothes while speaking to farm laborers, proclaims a farm worker (and perhaps Mexican and Roman Catholic) background, and advocates programs that will benefit farm workers. But for Burke, identification is a more encompassing notion than the simple expressions of common ground. Through interaction and identification, we can become involved in many groups, causes, or movements; formulate or change allegiances; and vicariously share in the role of leader or spokesperson. There are at least seven ways that we can enhance or create a sense of identification with audiences.[33] First, when we become involved in groups or participate in group actions, we may become more tolerant, if not sympathetic, to the views of persuaders or groups.

Second, we may share aspects of appearance with the group. Dorothy Mansfield studied the 1960s ministry of the Reverend Arthur Blessitt to the so-called "hippies." In appearance "his hair was trimmed well below his ears; his vestments were a brightly printed, full-sleeved shirt, leather vest, bell-bottom hip-hugger trousers, and boots.[34]

A third form of identification is adapting language to audiences. Two speeches of Stokely Carmichael, leader of SNCC (Student Nonviolent Coordinating Committee), on "Black Power" illustrate this method of identification.[35] He gave one of the speeches to a predominantly black audience in Detroit on July 30, 1966 and the other to a predominantly white audience in Whitewater, Wisconsin on February 6, 1967. The addresses were surprisingly similar in content and examples, but they differed greatly in style and persuasive appeals. For the black audience, Carmichael personified the ideology he was advancing—in delivery, style, and attitude, while for the white audience, he dwelt mainly on an explanation of ideology. For the black audience, he interpreted the notion of "black power" in terms of pride, self-identity, and political mobilization, while he interpreted this slogan for the white audience in terms of mainstream American ideals, using such phrases as "social and political integration" and "pluralistic society." He advocated violent resistance in the Detroit speech, but in the Whitewater address he used milder references to violence and used them in a context of self-defense. Carmichael's delivery to the black audience was "cool and very hip," while his delivery to the white audience was that of an intellectual or "politically enlightened leader." The Detroit address contained more slang than the Whitewater address.

Clearly, Carmichael "identified" with each audience.

A fourth form of identification is content adaptation. Content adaptation refers to attempts by persuaders to use examples easily understood by listeners or readers in order to emphasize similarity between persuader and audience. Frederick Douglass, a free slave speaking before a white audience commemorating the Fourth of July in 1852, illustrated the similarity between "slaves" and "masters" in terms of abilities, jobs, and domestic roles:

> Is it not astonishing that, while we are plowing, planting, and reaping, using all kinds of mechanical tools, erecting houses, constructing bridges, building ships, working in metals of brass, iron, copper, silver, and gold; that, while we are reading, writing, and ciphering, acting as clerks, merchants, and secretaries, having among us lawyers, doctors, ministers, poets, authors, editors, orators, and teachers; that while we are engaged in all manner of enterprises common to other men, digging gold in California, capturing the whale in the Pacific, feeding sheep and cattle on the hillside, living, moving, acting, thinking, planning, living in families as husbands, wives, and children, and above all, confessing and worshipping the Christian's God, and looking hopefully for life and immortality beyond the grave, we are called upon to prove that we are men![36]

A fifth means of identification is the attempt to reflect a group's values. The day after the Kent State University shootings, President Nixon expressed full agreement with the goals of the demonstrators: "They are trying to say they want peace. They are trying to say they want to stop the killing. They are trying to say that we ought to get out of Vietnam. I agree with everything that they are trying to accomplish."[37]

A sixth method of identification is the use of visual symbols. It is not unusual for a leader or "outsider" to wear a symbol such as a cross, a button, an article of clothing, or an armband common to an audience, or to make symbolic gesture that communicates a similarity of feelings or experiences. For instance, one United States Congressman often wears a red ribbon to indicate his concern for the AIDS epidemic. This symbolic gesture communicates sympathy and agreement with the gay rights movement.

Seventh, a persuader may create identification by referring to individuals or organizations that an audience approves, honors, or respects. Then Vice President Hubert Humphrey, a well-known advocate of black rights, used this tactic several times in an address before the annual convention of the National Association for the Advancement of Colored People on July 6, 1966. He declared:

> I am proud to be back among my friends of the NAACP who have led this march for 57 years . . . the road to freedom is stained with tears and the blood of many Americans—including men such as Medgar Evers—men already counted among authentic American heroes. . . . And through the years the NAACP has played a role second to none in terms of dedication and determination of sacrifice and courage.[38]

At the heart of the notion of identification, then, is the belief that symbols unite people. Language, as symbols, reveals the persuader's attitude about an issue or group, and the persuader can induce cooperation, or at least insure a fair hearing under most circumstances, by demonstrating similarities with the audience. But there is competition. To unite with one group, cause, or movement is to separate ourselves from some other group, cause, or social movement. If there were no divisions, there would be no need for rhetoric. Perfect identification would require no further communication. Burke relates that, "Since identification implies division, we found rhetoric involving us in matters of socialization and faction."[39]

By analyzing a persuader's language, the rhetorical analyst may be able to reveal the substance of the persuader's attempts at identification and thereby to structure the persuader's strategies. The result should be a better understanding of the failures and successes of social movement leaders in their efforts to communicate with a wide variety of audiences: movement members, movement sympathizers, legitimizers, the mass media, and the agents and agencies of established institutions.

The Pentad

Kenneth Burke developed the "dramatistic pentad" in order to discover the motives behind action. The pentad consists of five elements—act, scene, agent, agency, and purpose—and provides a way to view or to reconstruct action/motive. Burke explains the five elements of dramatism as follows:

> For there to be an act, there must be an agent. Similarly, there must be a scene in which the agent acts. To act in a scene, the agent must employ some means, or agency. And there cannot be an act, in the full sense of the term, unless there is a purpose.[40]

The pentad forces us to become aware of the many elements and influences in each persuasive situation and how key individuals, groups, and/or institutions attempt to "construct reality." It serves as an "elegant" organizing function by providing dynamic interlocking elements that limit courses of action. As Michael Overington notes, this orientation is valuable when assessing political definitions of situations:

> As a method, dramatism addresses the empirical questions of how persons explain their actions to themselves and others, what the cultural and social structural influences of these explanations might be, and what effect connotational limits among the explanatory (motivational) terms might have on these explanations, and hence, on action itself.[41]

Thus, the pentad provides "a kind of simplicity that can be developed into considerable complexity."[42] A systematic application enables an observer to reconstruct various perspectives of "reality."

Individuals may define a specific problem and advocate a solution based on their perceptions of motive centered on one of the five elements. Favoring one term over another creates different definitions of the situation. For example, to argue that a person is dying from cancer because it is God's will is defining the situation from the perspective of purpose. If the cause is from the deteriorating environment and increased pollution, then the definition is from the perspective of scene. And if the cancer is from poor diet, then the definition is from the perspective of act.

According to Burke, the disposition to define most things in life from one term tends to serve as the core ideology for an individual. Barry Brummett provides an insightful pentadic analysis of ideologies of the gay rights movement.[43] Essentially, the pro-gay rights advocates' ideology is dominated by the "agent" term of the pentad. People are gay as a state of being just as people may be black or Asian. "People are what they are and must be dealt with on their own grounds."[44] Thus, gays have a right to be protected and free from discrimination. Conversely, anti-gay rights advocates' ideology is dominated by the "act" term of the pentad. People are gay by their actions ("behavior" or "lifestyle") and are thus "immoral." Gay acts are sinful and should be subject to legal standards of conduct. Anti-gay advocates separate agents from their acts by arguing that they can "love the sinner but hate the sin." Politically, gay actions are therefore criminal. For anti-gay rights advocates, sexual orientation is a matter of choice, not a matter of "being." In the case of gay rights rhetoric, Brummett argues that "one's ascription of causative, defining power in the world will be different depending on the agent or act ideology. That ideology will determine one's position on what it means to be human, political, and sexual."[45]

Three levels of application of the pentad can aid us in sorting out motivational elements. First, any specific event, episode, or sociodrama may be analyzed by investigating its elements. For example, suppose there was a mass demonstration on a college campus against the expansion of nuclear weapons in Europe. In pentadic terms, the act was the mass student demonstration; the scene was the college campus where the demonstration occurred; the agents were the students participating in the demonstration; the agency of the act might have been speeches and marches by the students; and the purposes of the act were to create awareness of the problem and to protest further deployment of nuclear weapons in Europe by the United States. This brief scenario seems simple and obvious. Each element, however, could be investigated further. Suppose the students shouted obscenities (agency) that resulted in a violent confrontation with police (act). What elements of the scene encouraged the conflict? Were all of the agents students or were some professional agitators? The point is that, as an organizing device, the pentad can provide categorical headings under which further analytical and evaluative observations can be rendered.[46]

A second level of application may be a specific social movement. We could use the pentad to isolate movement stages, strategies, tactics, goals, ideology, and organization. For example, in terms of the pro-life movement, the agent might be a national organization, a local affiliate of a national organization, or a splinter group. Analysis of the scene might reveal a reaction to the growth of a secular society with its threat to the family and religion, the women's liberation movement, or the predominate concern over individual rights regardless of age, sex, or race. Acts may include lawsuits, demonstrations, media events, or disruptions of abortion clinics. Agency considerations include posters, newspapers, television reports, buttons, pamphlets, and bumperstickers. Such analyses not only emphasize the interrelatedness of the various elements but can reveal which were most important at a given time.

A third level for applying the pentad to society might prove beneficial in isolating societal factors that encourage the formation, organization, decline or rejection of a specific social movement. The goal is to account for as many motivational influences upon symbolic behavior as possible. The pentad provides the framework for analyzing the element or elements that persuaders dwell upon in a specific message or situation: act, scene, agent, agency, or purpose. Such analyses may reveal the perceptions (of self, others, situation, the world), motives, and character or personality of persuaders or their audiences.

For Kenneth Burke, therefore, all discussions of human motivation arise out of investigations of the five elements of the pentad. We may discover upon analysis that one element is the key and all others seem to grow out of this single term. The featuring of a single term in a drama may lead to different conclusions about human motivation. For illustrative purposes, let us return to the drama at Kent State University. The act was the shooting of the four students. The scene was the culmination of three days of demonstrations and rioting. The agents were the Ohio National Guardsmen. The agency was the rifles. The purpose of the act remains debatable, but it would seem to have been either planned retaliation or spontaneous self-defense. In analyzing this drama, we might stress the act of shooting the students as the organizing element. Those who believe that the National Guard should not have been called to the campus might argue that the act-agent ratio is the key to understanding the drama. The Guardsmen, in defending their actions, might focus on a scene-act ratio, arguing that the three days of demonstrations and provocations best explains the other elements. The victims of the drama might argue from a purpose-act ratio in explaining the event. For them, the purposes or motives of the shooting were prejudice, intolerance, and retaliation. For some governmental investigators, the cause of the tragedy is revealed in an agent-agency consideration. The Guardsmen should not have been allowed to carry weapons; alternatively, empty rifles or blanks rather than live ammunition could have been employed.

This example shows the utility and versatility of the pentad. The various ratios reveal attitudes and motivations of participants in dramas. This enables the analyst of the persuasive efforts of social movements to develop a more complete understanding of the perspectives and arguments in a drama. The pentad allows for division and unity and, as individual elements, provides singular focus and organization. Taken together, the elements work in unison to provide understanding of dramatic symbolic behavior.

Burkean Analysis of Social Movements

Nature of Society

Historically there have been two dominant approaches to understanding society. From a dramatistic perspective, each approach is too deterministic. The sociological approach emphasizes structure: behavior results from factors such as status, position, cultural prescriptions, norms, values, social sanctions, role demands, and general system requirements. These factors are viewed as causes of behavior while ignoring the social interactions that influence each of them. Similarly, the psychological approach emphasizes motives, attitudes, hidden complexes, and general psychological processes as ways to account for behavior, but it ignores social interaction. Rather than focusing on causative factors, the psychological approach focuses on the behavior such factors produce.

From a dramatistic perspective, social interaction is of vital importance. Herbert Blumer, a founder of this perspective, views symbolic interaction as "a process that forms human conduct instead of being merely a means or a setting for the expression or release of human conduct."[47] Thus, dramatism emphasizes the dramatic, changing nature of society. Society arises, matures, and continues to exist through communication. Individuals are constantly interacting, developing, and shaping society. People exist in action and consequently must be viewed in terms of action. To analyze human society, then, the student of persuasion and social movements must begin with an analysis of the human engagement in action. Society may be defined as individuals in interaction, individuals acting in relation to each other, individuals engaging in cooperative acting in relation to each other, individuals engaging in cooperative action, and individuals communicating with self and others. From this definition we may argue that people "make society" and society "makes people." As Blumer argues:

> The activity of human beings consists of meeting a flow of situations in which they have to act and their action is built on the basis of what they note, how they access and interpret what they note, and what kind of projected lines of action they map out."[48]

Social Control

Social control is usually viewed as a result of institutional influences such as laws, the police, or Congress. But social order is not entirely dependent upon "agencies of control." No regime can long survive on a threat of force alone. Communication is the most important means of social order, for within the communication lies the power to create and to control the images that legitimize authority. Communication joins all people. Hugh Duncan, a student of Kenneth Burke, observes that:

> Images, visions, and all imaginings of the future are symbolic forms, for when
> the future becomes the present, and thus becomes "real" new futures are created
> to guide our search for solutions to problems in the present which emerge as
> we try to create order in our relationships.[49]

Social order, according to Duncan, is always expressed in some kind of hierarchy. Hierarchy differentiates people into ranks based on many variables—age, sex, race, skill, wealth, education, etc. "All hierarchies," Duncan argues, "function through a 'perfection' of their principles in final moments of social mystification which are reached by mountings from lower to higher principles of social order."[50] Thus, the task for authorities is to invest local symbols with universal symbols that "transcend" local, isolated concerns.

The community "lives" because of frequent and intense reenactment by its members of key roles believed to be necessary to social order. "We learn to act, not simply by preparing to act, or by thinking 'about' action, but by playing various kinds of dramas."[51] For Hugh Duncan, there are seven basic forms of social drama: games, play, parties, festivals, ceremonies, drama, and rites. In terms of government, ceremonies, rites, and ritual are the most formalized types of social dramas. Success is dependent upon the elements of glory and efficiency:

> Glory is a dignification achieved through style (a way of life) which inferiors
> use to identify themselves with superiors. Superiors, in turn, use styles of
> performance (their "presence") to move the hearts and minds of inferiors to loyalty
> and reverence.[52]

Social order, therefore, is legitimized through symbols grounded in nature, man, society, language, or God. When followers, through socialization, have been taught "significant symbols" which uphold social order, they require their leaders to "play" their roles within the principles established.

Conversely, disorder originates in society through disorder in communication. Duncan argues that "when people cannot communicate they cannot relate. Disrelationships are not reflected in communication; they originate in communication."[53] According to Burke, the division of labor and the handing down of property gave rise to classes.[54] Order among the classes involves the distribution of authority. This distribution, in turn, establishes a hierarchical form. "Thus," Burke observes, "the purely operational motives binding a society become inspirited by a corresponding condition of mystery."[55] For Burke, mystery arises resulting from our division and separateness and ultimately serves to maintain and preserve hierarchy. According to Foss, Foss, and Trapp, mystery preserves the existing hierarchy by performing two very important functions.[56] First, it encourages "willing" obedience to authority. Government works best when laws are followed without contest or question. Second, mystery enhances communication among members of the hierarchy. It hides the differences and allows members to identify, interact, and persuade one another. Leland Griffin—interpreting Burke—concludes:

Wherever there is mystery there is corresponding communication that results in understanding—the understanding that makes piety possible. But the maintenance of piety involves the need for obedience—which is to say, the painful need for self-control (self-restraint, self-moderation) and out of this obligation comes the possibility of disobedience. . .[57]

Social Movements

As we have noted, social movements do not instantaneously occur and develop or "just happen." When the seeds of discontent are planted, much nurturing and microscopic growth occurs long before the first stem breaks the soil for all to see. A social movement is a process of transformation from societal order (the prevailing hierarchy, beliefs, attitudes, values, goals, and cessation of identification with the prevailing hierarchy), action (symbolic behavior of articulating grievances, altering perceptions of society, providing courses of action), drama (symbolic acts, events, episodes), conflict (separation, confrontation, violence, tragedy), victimage (identification of the causes of societal evil, conflict, and violence that must be destroyed), transcendence (the purging and removal of social ills while establishing new levels of social identification, cooperation, and unity), redemption (forgiveness of social sins), and order (hierarchy and societal values accepted, sanctioned, and legitimized). When one phase ends and another begins is often difficult, and sometimes impossible, to isolate.

Leaders and superiors must create and use symbols that unite and transcend individual and collective differences. "The legitimation of authority," argues Duncan, "is based on persuasion."[58] Leaders, in their struggles for power and attempts to stay in power, must provide integrative symbols for the masses to transcend the ambiguities and conflicts of heroes and villains, of loyalty and disloyalty, of concern and indifference, of confidence and fear, of obedience and disobedience, of hierarchy and anarchy, of peace and violence. The notions of faith and reason are on the side of order. Faith is expressed by accepting the authority of others as legitimate. Reason is expressed by the acceptance of authority based upon the quality of performance and positive impact upon the quality of life. The temptations of emotions and prevalence of imagination are on the side of disorder. Emotions are articulated through dramatic actions, issues, and statements.[59] Imagination creates a new order, governmental system, or social utopia. In simple terms, therefore, when division in society is so great that symbols no longer possess common meanings, people will turn to leaders who will create new symbols. When symbols can no longer transcend differences among people, conflict can only be resolved through violence.

Michael Osborn identifies five functions of depiction that directly relate to the drama of social movements.[60] The first function of depiction is presentation of the world. Rhetoric is not reflective but constructive. Our world, as noted before, is symbolic, mediated, and purposeful. The second function is intensification of feeling. Depiction adds color, shading, and emphasis to people, places, and events. War, for instance, can be presented as heroic or tragic with each extreme generating emotional responses. The third function is a resource for identification. Commonality in all forms contributes to a sense of community and oneness. The fourth function, implementation, refers to "time of action." Implementation articulates the future, provides plans of action, and sustains group activity. The fifth function is reaffirmation of reality. In a ceremony, for example, a group's heroes and martyrs are praised, and rituals are developed to maintain the symbols and memories of the group.

Thus, within depiction, one can note the "strings of consciousness" or the view of the world as seen by others. Depiction is a process composed of many "snapshots" of the world. From this perspective, the creation of a social movement lies in the failure of communication among groups, and the results are rejection of the symbols of those in power, cessation of identification with the prevailing hierarchy, and the spreading of disloyalty. The civil rights movement of the 1960s was successful in rejecting the symbols of American society. The movement redefined the heritage of "negro" into "Afro-American;" reinforced a positive self-concept of "Black is beautiful"; and declared a new political activism in "Black Power." Once separated from the existing order, although with a sense of guilt, the disaffected are moved to articulate grievances and to dream of salvation—a state of redemption. Blacks defined American society as one of discrimination, oppression, and inequality. The Reverend Martin Luther King, Jr. articulated their dream beautifully from the steps of the Lincoln Memorial in Washington, D.C.:

> I have a dream . . . that this nation will rise up and live out the true meaning of its creed . . . that all men are created equal; . . . that one day on the red hills of Georgia the sons of former slaves and the sons of former slaveowners will be able to sit down together at the table of brotherhood; . . . that one day even the state of Mississippi . . . will be transformed into an oasis of freedom and justice; . . . that my four little children will one day live in a nation where they will not be judged by the color of their skin but by the content of their character; . . . one day right there in Alabama little black boys and black girls will be able to join hands with little white boys and white girls as sisters and brothers; . . . and the glory of the Lord shall be revealed, and all flesh shall see it together.

Now, with a sense of duty and purpose, the followers of the social movement act, shout "No" to the existing order and proclaim a new beginning. In the words of Martin Luther King:

> This is no time to engage in the luxury of cooling off or to take the tranquilizing drug of gradualism. Now is the time to make real the promises of Democracy. Now is the time to rise from the dark and desolate valley of segregation to the sunlit path of racial justice. Now is the time to lift our nation from the quicksands of racial injustice to the solid rock of brotherhood. Now is the time to make justice a reality for all of God's children . . . . Go back to Mississippi, go back to Alabama, go back to South Carolina, go back to Georgia, go back to Louisiana, go back

to the slums and ghettos of our northern cities, knowing that somehow this situation can and will be changed.

Burke states that four basic motives arise in human communication: hierarchy, guilt, victimage, and redemption.[61] For him, these motives are revealed in observing human relationships, and they encompass all human motivation. These motives describe the process of birth, maturation, and death of social movements. "Hierarchy" stems from human desire for order, and rejection of an established hierarchy produces a sense of "guilt." From Burke's perspective, "Language produces hierarchies, hierarchies produce categorical guilt as well as provide man with a means of purging and redeeming himself through the dialectic of transcendence made possible by symbolic action and the verbal hierarchy."[62] Guilt is relieved through "victimage" or the sacrifice of a scapegoat that epitomizes the evils of society: Jews, capitalists, communists, landlords, agitators. Victimage, then, is a mode of purification. The extreme forms of victimage are homicide (of others) and suicide (of selves). In homicidal victimage, there is the polluted and the pure. The former is the scapegoat; the latter is the sacrifice. The act of making others suffer for our sins is at the heart of victimage. Thus, one person's or group's guilt demands some other person's or group's death or injury.[63] In primitive societies, purification came from sacrificing animals to a god. In the sophisticated and complex societies of today, however, purification comes from endowing a person, government, idea, or practice with social evils that dictate removal. Removal can range from redefinition to murder. Burke identifies three ways a person is made "worthy" of sacrifices.[64] First, a person may be made worthy of sacrifice legalistically, as an offender against legal or moral principles of justice. Second, a person may be worthy because of a subtle kind of poetic justice. Third, a person may be worthy of sacrifice because of "fate," perhaps the least rational of the three. Scapegoats become the "sacrificial animal" upon whose back is ritualistically placed all of a social movement's real or perceived evils.

"Redemption" follows victimage. Order is restored; evil is defeated; and sins are forgiven. Mystification returns and promotes social cohesion. Symbol users transcend the mysteries of class, and the world is redefined. New attitudes and values are tested and legitimized primarily in the symbolic realm.

Sociodramas

Because aspects of the transformation and development of entire social movements are difficult to isolate and to manage, individual episodes or sociodramas are easier to investigate. Wherever there is action there is drama, and, as Hugh Duncan writes, "failure to understand the power of dramatic form in communication means failure in seizing and controlling power over men."[65] Sociodramas are not merely symbolic screens or metaphors; they are social reality because they are forms of social interaction and integration.

We need to identify some act or action in order to analyze a social drama. If we focus on dramas of authority, we might ask: Under what conditions is the act being presented? What kind of act is it? What roles are the actors assuming? What forms of authority are being communicated? What means of communication are used? What symbols of authority are evoked? How are social functions staged? How are social functions communicated? How are the messages received? What are responses to authority messages?

The scope of a social drama is prescribed by the investigator. The drama may involve one person or many, a symbolic (rhetorical) event or a physical event; one moment or a specified period in time. Sociodramas are the acts and scenes that comprise our lives. Individual photographs capture moments and evoke reflection, memories, analysis, and emotions of joy or sadness. Taken together and shown sequentially, the snapshots produce movement, action, and behavior. Although a drama can be analyzed frame by frame, it is essentially a composite of individual acts.

In Burkean terms, then, a social movement is a study of drama composed of many acts. They are acts of hierarchy, transformation, transcendence, guilt, victimage, redemption, and salvation. Burke suggests that we investigate the scenes that encompass and surround the acts as they provide the context for an act. We must consider the agents involved in the act—the actors who mold, shape, create, and sustain movements. Likewise, consideration of the agency or the channels of communication in an act reveal the impact of persuasive activities. And consideration of the purpose of an act aids in discovering the ultimate motives or meaning of an act.

Conclusions

Kenneth Burke offers a philosophy of human communication, a theory of social behavior, and a method for analyzing the symbolic act. At the heart of his perspective is the discovery of how motives and behavior arise and exist through communication. Our daily interactions are mere episodes in the drama of social life. Order is created, manipulated, sustained, and altered through symbols.

A social movement is a process of transformation from order, division, drama, conflict, victimage, transcendence, redemption, and reestablished order. As symbol-using animals, we transcend the motion of our animal nature and engage in action. Property, rights, duty, loyalty, and obligation are concepts resulting from actions and must be guarded, defended, and negotiated. Division is a natural state which breeds conflict, and conflict results in associated guilt and the corresponding cancellation of the guilt—the process of victimage and redemption. Our task in a democratic society is to participate actively in sociodramas that enhance the quality of our lives. "For better or worse," Burke writes, "the mystery of the hierarchy is forever with us, let us, as students of rhetoric, scrutinize its range of entrancements both with dismay and in delight."[66]

Kenneth Burke's perspective of human action and his method of analysis are useful to students of social movements because they allow us to investigate all phases and aspects of social movement phenomena. We may analyze any level of symbolic behavior and any action: a single message; an individual persuader over time; a large event with many participants; a group, organization, or collectivity; social cultures or societies; and historical timeframes.

When investigating individual persuaders and messages, each Burkean concept may help us to discover stylistic characteristics; beliefs, attitudes, and motivations; or persuasive strategies. In terms of symbolic event, episode, or sociodrama, Burkean concepts can help us to identify the correlations and strategies of participants; to reveal basic or recurring rhetorical patterns and strategies; or to investigate the stages or phases in the dramatistic process. The methodology, in short, is applicable to many "symbol-making, symbol-using, and symbol-misusing" behaviors.

Endnotes

[1] Kenneth Burke, *Language as Symbolic Action* (Berkeley: University of California Press, 1966), 6.

[2] Kenneth Burke, "Interaction-Dramatism," *International Encyclopedia of Social Sciences* (New York, 1967), 447.

[3] Burke, *Language as Symbolic Action*, 53.

[4] Burke, *Language as Symbolic Action*, 5.

[5] Burke, *Language as Symbolic Action*, 63.

[6] Rachel Holloway, *In the Matter of J. Robert Oppenheimer* (Westport, CT: Praeger, 1993), 31.

[7] Kenneth Burke, *A Rhetoric of Motives* (Berkeley: University of California Press, 1969), 43.

[8] Kenneth Burke, *Permanence and Change* (New York: Bobbs-Merrill, 1965), 29–30.

[9] Holloway, 33.

[10] Burke, *Permanence and Change*, xvii.

[11] Burke, *Permanence and Change*, xxxiii.

[12] Burke, *A Rhetoric of Motives*, 46.

[13] Burke, *IESS*, 445–452.

[14] Burke, *IESS*, 445.

[15] Kenneth Burke, *A Grammar of Motives* (Berkeley: University of California Press, 1969), xxii.

[16] Michael Overington, "Kenneth Burke and the Method of Dramatism," *Theory and Society* 4 (Spring 1977), 129–156.

[17] Kenneth Burke, "Dramatism," *Communication Concepts and Perspectives*, Lee Thayer, ed. (Washington, DC: Spartan Books, 1967), 332.

[18] Burke, *IESS*, 449.

[19] Burke, *Language as Symbolic Action*, 55.

[20] Dan Nimmo and James Combs, *Mediated Political Realities* (New York: Longman, 1983).

[21] Nimmo and Combs, xv.

[22] Nimmo and Combs, 8.

[23] David Altheide and Robert Snow, *Media Logic* (Beverly Hills: Sage, 1979), 109–110.

[24] As quoted in Martin Schram, *The Great American Video Game* (New York: William Morrow, 1987), 58.

[25] Schram, 51.

[26] For an excellent account of the Kent State shootings, see Milton Viorst, *Fire in the Streets* (New York: Simon and Schuster, 1979), 508–543.

[27] Kenneth Burke, *The Philosophy of Literary Form*, 3rd ed. (Berkeley: University of California Press, 1973), 310.

[28] Burke, *Language as Symbolic Action*, 429.

[29] Burke, *A Rhetoric of Motives*, 21-45.

[30] Burke, *A Rhetoric of Motives*, 46.

[31] Burke, *A Rhetoric of Motives*, 20.

[32] Burke, *A Rhetoric of Motives*, 25.

[33] These seven ways of identification are discussed by Wayne Thompson, *The Process of Persuasion* (New York: Harper and Row, 1975), 430-431.

[34] Dorothy Mansfield, "A Blessitt Event: Reverend Arthur Blessitt Invites Youth to "Tune In, Turn On, Drop Out," *Southern Speech Communication Journal* 37 (Winter 1971), 165.

[35] For speeches and excellent analysis, see "Stokely Carmichael: Two Speeches on Black Power," Wayne Brockriede and Robert Scott, *The Rhetoric of Black Power* (New York: Harper and Row, 1969), 84-131.

[36] Frederick Douglass, "An Ex-Slave Discusses Slavery, July 4, 1852," *A Treasury of the World's Great Speeches*, Houston Peterson, ed. (New York: Simon and Schuster, 1965), 481.

[37] As reported in Viorst, 540.

[38] Hubert Humphrey, "Address at the NAACP Convention, July 6, 1966," in Scott and Brockriede, 66.

[39] Burke, *A Rhetoric of Motives*, 45.

[40] Burke, "Dramatism," 332.

[41] Overington, pp. 129-156.

[42] Burke, *A Grammar of Motives*, xvi.

[43] Barry Brummett, "A Pentadic Analysis of Ideologies in Two Gay Rights Controversies," *Central States Speech Journal* 30 (Fall 1979), 250-261.

[44] Brummett, 252.

[45] Brummett, 261.

[46] Richard Crable and John Makay. "Kenneth Burke's Concept of Motives in Rhetorical Theory," *Today's Speech* 20 (Winter 1972), 13.

[47] Herbert Blumer, *Symbolic Interactionism* (Englewood Cliffs, NJ: Prentice-Hall, 1969), 8.

[48] Blumer, 16.

[49] Hugh Duncan, *Symbols in Society* (New York: Oxford University Press, 1968), 48.

[50] Duncan, 73.

[51] Duncan, 61.

[52] Duncan, 205.

[53] Duncan, 130.

[54] Burke, *Permanence and Change*, 276.

[55] Burke, *Permanence and Change*, 276.

[56] Sonja Foss, Karen Foss, and Robert Trapp, *Contemporary Perspectives on Rhetoric*, 2/E (Prospect Heights, IL: Waveland Press, 1991), 193-194.

[57] Leland Griffin, "A Dramatistic Theory of the Rhetoric of Movements," *Critical Responses to Kenneth Burke*, William Rueckert, ed., (Minneapolis: University of Minnesota Press, 1969), 457.

[58] Duncan, 200.

[59] Michael Osborn, "Rhetorical Depiction," in Herbert Simons and Aram Aghazarian, eds., *Form, Genre, and the Study of Political Discourse* (Columbia, SC: University of South Carolina Press, 1986), 79.

[60] Osborn, 81.

[61] Burke, *Permanence and Change*, 274.

[62] William Rueckert, *Kenneth Burke and the Drama of Human Relations* (Berkeley: University of California Press, 1982), 145.

[63] Rueckert, 146.

[64] Burke, *Philosophy and Literary Form*, 40.

[65] Duncan, 25.

[66] Burke, *A Rhetoric of Motives*, 333.

Chapter Ten

Language Strategies of Social Movements

Symbols provide shared meanings, perceptions, and security among groups. For Richard Weaver, language is a "Social and cultural creation functioning somehow within the psychic constitution of those who use it. . . . The question of stability in language cannot be considered apart from the psychic stability of the culture group."[1] Language usage or styles can signal conformity or rebellion in a society. Although subtle in some cases and overt in others, symbols help to create, sustain, and define role behavior.

Every desire and emotion is a valid reason to initiate symbolic exchange. Emotional responses may be bad reasons for acting, but they are valid when grounded in one's reality. "The real art," Wayne Booth asserts, "lies always in the proper weighing—and what is proper is a matter finally of shared norms, discovered and applied in the experience of individuals whose very individuality is forged from other selves." Thus, "every protest implies an affirmative ground for protest; every affirmation implies many negations."[2] Emotional expressions may contribute to social movement cohesiveness. Humans have a basic need to identify with others in similar circumstances, and language creates this sense of interpersonal identification. Robert Cathcart contends that "movements are carried forward through language, both verbal and nonverbal, in strategic ways that bring about identification of the individual with the movement."[3]

Thus, language operates in society as "social symbols." The intended and perceived meanings of these symbols may be difficult to grasp and their impact or stimulation may differ among individuals and groups. Hugh Duncan emphasizes that "it is the ambiguity of symbols which makes them so useful in human society. Ambiguity is a kind of bridge that allows us to run back and forth from one kind of meaning to another until we take firm resolve to cross the bridge into new and fixed meanings."[4] From "new and fixed meanings," we think, we feel, and ultimately we act.

Robert Brooks demonstrated the phenomenon of symbolic bridge crossing in his investigation of how three groups (black college students, white college students, and white police officers) interpreted the meaning of the phrase "black power."[5] He discovered three dominant dimensions. The first was aggression. Whites perceived aggression, violence, confrontation, and racial domination inherent in the concept of black power. The second was goals. Blacks associated various political goals such as equal rights and equal opportunity with the phrase. The third dimension was mystique. Blacks endowed "black power" with nonmaterial attributes such as self-identity, pride, and awareness. Words serve as the symbolic justifications for feelings and actions and provide a bridge or link to social action. Hugh Duncan concludes, "Symbols, then, create and sustain beliefs in ways of acting because they function as names which signify proper, dubious, or improper ways of expressing relationships."[6]

Because language operates as significant symbols or key words that have a standard meaning in a group, they serve both expressive and persuasive functions. Harold Lasswell recognizes that influencing collective attitudes is possible by the manipulation of significant symbols such as slogans.[7] He believes that a verbal symbol might evoke a desired reaction or organize collective attitudes toward a symbol. Murray Edelman writes that "to the political scientist patterning or consistency in the contexts in which specific groups of individuals use symbols is crucial, for only through such patterning do common political meanings and claims arise."[8] Thus, language evokes specific responses, and these words provide us with an index of group beliefs, attitudes, values, and conceptual rationales for claims.

It is a truism among social movement theorists and practitioners that the *agent that controls language controls the world*. And the language that sanctifies actions and feelings, establishes social symbols, crosses the bridge into new and fixed meanings, sustains beliefs, and signifies proper, dubious, and improper means of expression is selected, reinforced, and maintained by social institutions such as schools, churches, courts, and legislative chambers. J. Vernon Jensen writes about how the British used the family metaphor when referring to and attempting to control colonists on the eve of the American Revolution. Colonists were called "offspring," "children," and "sons" of the "mother country," and "homeland;" were urged to return to the "breast" or "bosom" of their mother; and were chastised as "recalcitrant children" for their "misconduct," "waywardness," and "mischief."[9] Philip Wander reveals how the pro-slavery movement in the South used the image of the "savage child" to argue that freeing adult slaves was dangerous both to society (to turn inferior, uneducated, and uncivilized "savages" loose in the states) and to the slaves themselves (to turn "children" loose who could not fend for themselves in any way without white, adult supervision and discipline).[10]

All social movements struggle to free themselves from words that degrade and consign them to lower rungs on the hierarchy—to gain control of their worlds. When protestors insist on being called blacks or African Americans instead of negroes or niggers, native Americans instead of Indians or redskins, black men instead of boys, and women instead of girls, they are demanding far more than "political correctness." They are seeking equality, dignity, legitimacy, and the right to name themselves rather than live under names or labels placed upon them by slaveowners, European colonists, and a male-dominated society. When black nationalists such as Malcolm X substituted "colony" for "ghetto," they communicated the notion of exploitation associated with colonialism and changed black Americans from a national minority to an international majority.[11] The gay rights movement of the 1990s is struggling to replace sexual "preference" with sexual "orientation," "special rights" with "civil rights," and "agenda" with "goals." Each change is designed to alter perceptions of gay and lesbian individuals, organizations, and demands. As Will Perkins, founder of an anti-gay rights organization in Colorado, declares, "Language doesn't shape the campaign—it *is* the campaign."[12]

Social movements also attempt to label events to cast them in a light to engage supporters—that is, to control or to alter perceptions of reality. Black leaders after the Watts riot in 1965 and the Los Angeles riot in 1992 (in response to the first Rodney King verdict) characterized the events as "insurrections" and "rebellions"—not random violence and looting by out-of-control citizens but uprisings of exploited victims who had grown sick and tired of their exploitation. Kurt Ritter reveals the genius of the colonists, particularly Samuel Adams, in labeling a minor riot by a handful of rowdies in Boston in 1770 as "the Boston Massacre." This label conjured up visions of a "horrid massacre" of many victims, soon to be martyrs for the cause of liberty, whose "innocent blood" cried "to God from the streets of Boston."[13] The animal rights movement today refers to trapped and ranched animals as "martyred victims" of "torture," of the "slaughter of the innocent" subjected to "sadistic" and "barbaric methods of capture and killing."[14]

James Andrews addresses the essential roles of language in the persuasive efforts of social movements to alter perceptions, prescribe courses of action, and mobilize followers:

> The exciting, and frustrating, characteristic of a social movement is that it moves and what makes it move, in large measure, is the way language is manipulated to control or interpret events. In this sense, rhetoric makes moving possible—moving in all directions, pushing, shoving, lurching forward and falling backward as the movement encounters its environment. Growing out of the environment, intruding into the environment, reacting to the environment, and becoming a part of the environment, the social movement is simultaneously a rhetorical response and a rhetorical stimulus.[15]

In the remainder of this chapter, we will focus on three language strategies common in social movements' efforts to gain control of the words that define their world, their relationships, their dreams, their demands, and their actions: slogans, obscenity, and ridicule.

Slogans

George Shankel defines a slogan as "some pointed term, phrase, or expression, fittingly worded, which suggests action, loyalty, or which causes people to decide upon and to fight for the realization of some principle or decisive issue."[16] Protestors have for centuries chanted, shouted, and sung slogans; printed them in leaflets, pamphlets, and social movement newsletters and newspapers; worn them on buttons, tee-shirts, jackets, and the seats of their pants; and have written, painted, or pasted them on billboards, posters, banners, automobile bumpers, buses, subways, sidewalks, and walls.

Slogans are so pervasive in today's society that it is easy to underestimate their persuasive power. They have grown in significance because of the medium of television and the advertising industry which have made a science of sloganeering. Advertisers have discovered that it is easier to link product attributes to existing beliefs, ideas, goals, and desires of the consumer rather than to try to change them. Thus, to say that a cookie tastes "homemade" does not tell us if the cookie is good or bad, hard or soft, but simply evokes fond memories of Mother's baking. Slogans do this well by crystallizing in a few words the key idea or theme one wants to associate with an issue, group, product, or event.

Slogans have a number of attributes that enhance their persuasive potential for social movements. They are unique and readily identifiable with a specific social movement or social movement organization. They are easy to say and to remember. Slogans are often fun because they contain active verbs and adjectives, are witty, and rhyme. Slogans are often repetitious or are designed to be repeated or chanted. They may serve as a way to release pent-up emotions and frustrations and act as a verbal surrogate for physical aggression. Finally, slogans may create a "blindering" effect by preventing audiences from considering alternative ways of thinking, feeling, and/or acting.[17] They tend to be definitive statements of the social movement's "truths" and rely on audience dispositions to achieve expected responses. By recognizing the symbols to which audiences have been conditioned to respond, social movement persuaders may formulate slogans that will have profound, persuasive, organizing effects.

Social movements use three types of slogans. *Spontaneous slogans* are original, impromptu creations of individual protestors improvised during demonstrations or gatherings. They are often short, rhythmical chants such as "Shut it down" (counterculture movement), "Freedom, freedom, freedom" (civil rights movement), and "ROTC has to go" (anti-war movement). Other spontaneous slogans are longer and more issue-oriented, such as "Housewives are unpaid slaves" (women's liberation movement) and "We have our Bible, we don't need your dirty books" (censorship movement). *Sanctioned slogans* are "official" slogans of social movement organizations and are often placed on movement-produced materials. Examples are pro-life's "Give to the unborn their first civil right—Life," "Never to laugh or love," and "We are Protestants, protesting abortion." Sanctioned slogans often appear on mastheads of publications. For instance, the masthead of *The Call*, published by the Marxist-Leninist October

League, contains the slogan "People of the world unite to defeat imperialism;" and the native American newspaper *Wassaji* uses the slogan "Let my people know." *Advertising slogans* are found most often on buttons, bumperstickers, and tee-shirts. They tend to be short statements that emphasize a single demand or keep the social movement visible. "Issue" examples are "Recall Ralph Nader" (radical right groups) and "Solar employs, nuclear destroys" (anti-nuclear power movement). "Organizational" examples are "Gray Panthers" (gray power movement) and "The Wobblies are coming" (labor movement). Whether spontaneous, sanctioned, or advertising in nature, slogans perform a variety of persuasive functions for social movements.

Transforming Perceptions of Reality

Many slogans encapsulate an intolerable situation in a few striking, memorable words such as "No playing today kids—smog by General Motors" (environmental movement), "Abortion: the American holocaust" (pro-life movement), and "War is not healthy for children and other living things" (anti-war). The Save the Whales slogan "Our look can kill" attempts to make people aware that whales are slaughtered to make cosmetics. And the NORML (National Organization for Reform of Marijuana Laws) slogan "This little plant can turn your life upside down" warns audiences that violation of unfair marijuana laws might cost them their money and their freedom.

Protestors may include graphic pictures with slogans to enhance persuasiveness. For instance, the environmental movement's slogan "Ecology is for the birds" is accompanied by a picture of an oil-soaked duck. And a picture of a starving child in filthy surroundings accompanies the United Farm Worker slogan "Every grape you buy keeps this child hungry." Some slogans attempt to redefine reality, such as "Fetus is Latin for child" (pro-life), "Peace is more than the absence of war" (anti-nuclear weapons), and "porn is violence disguised" (women's liberation).

Slogans may attempt to create negative expectancies in the minds of audiences by visualizing what will happen if change is initiated or stifled. The anti-nuclear weapons movement warns that "Nuclear war is nuclear suicide," anti-nuclear power warns parents "In case of nuclear accident kiss your children goodbye," and the environmental movement pleads "Save our grandchildren now, not when it's too late." Movements may play verbal ping-pong with adversaries. For example, pro-life warns that "Abortion today justifies euthanasia tomorrow," while pro-choice asks "Do you want to return to the butchery of back-alley abortion?" Anti-nuclear power groups advise "Better active today than radioactive tomorrow," while pro-nuclear power warns "No nukes, no heat, no lights."

Transforming Perceptions of Society

When social movements are engaged in frequent conflicts with institutions and countermovements, they use slogans to identify their devils. Anti-Vietnam

War protestors chanted, "Hey, hey, LBJ, how many kids have you killed today?" Gay rights advocates used the slogans "Anita Bryant sucks oranges" and "Anita Bryant—Empress of the bigots" to attack the former actress and spokesperson for the Florida citrus industry who led a countermovement against gay rights in Florida. And the United Farm Workers used the slogan "Boycott Campbell's cream of exploitation soup." Most slogans, however, identify nebulous, unnamed evil forces or things such as men, communism, the rich, and capitalists. Typical slogans are "Don't trust anyone over 30" (counterculture), "Bless those who declare war, they're usually too old to fight" (anti-war), and "Pill-em or kill-em groups make $'s from abortion" (pro-life).

Slogans address the self in a variety of ways. The most common appeal is to self-worth, proclaiming "I am somebody," "I am important," or "I should be in a position of power." Typical are "Women are not chicks" and "A woman's place is in the house—and in the senate" (women's movement), "Discover America with real Americans" (native American movement), and "God loves gays" (gay rights). Less direct but clever attempts to enhance self-concept are the women's liberation slogan "Trust in God, She will provide" and the gay rights slogan "I am your worst fear, I am your best fantasy." Other slogans appeal to feelings of power and strength, such as the Gray Panther slogan "Panthers on the prowl." The simple but powerful slogan "Black power" generated a host of imitations: "Brown power," "Red power," "White power," "Gray power," "Woman power," "Senior power," "Poor power," "Gay power," and "All power to the people." Some slogans express the social movement's ability and will to act. A women's liberation slogan declares "The hand that rocks the cradle should rock the boat," a Hispanic slogan states "We are not a minority," and a NORML slogan proclaims "You can change the world." Other slogans appeal to pride in self and the social movement and allow protestors to declare who they are: "Say it loud, I'm black and I'm proud," "I am an Indian and I am pretty damn proud of it," and "I am lesbian and I am beautiful."

Prescribing Courses of Action

Demands and solutions make up a large portion of slogans, particularly those of contemporary social movements.[18] Slogans contain key ideographs of movements such as equality, happiness, free speech, freedom, justice, rights, and peace.[19] Some are quite specific. For example, a radical right slogan demands "Freedom for Rudolf Hess" (former German Nazi leader), an anti-apartheid slogan urges institutions to "Ban the Krugerrand" (a South African gold piece sold in America), and a native American slogan demands that authorities "Free the Wounded Knee 300." Nearly all slogans that address demands and solutions are what Bowers, Ochs, and Jensen refer to as imperative statements: commands, edicts, or fiats.[20]

One of the most important persuasive functions of slogans is their simplification of complex issues, problems, solutions, and relationships. Thus, slogans polarize:

"America—love it or leave it" (pro-Vietnam War), "Make love not war (anti-Vietnam War), and "Abortion kills babies—choose life" (pro-life). Other slogans propose simple solutions without recognizing the complicated steps involved or the difficulties of implementation: "No more nukes" (anti-nuclear power), "Dump Israel" (American Nazi party), and "Humanize America" (radical left). Slogans may reveal the growing impatience and frustration of movement members and leaders. In John Wilson's words, protestors have grown "tired of being sick and tired."[21] This feeling is apparent in slogans such as "Enough! Out Now" (anti-Vietnam War), "End the arms race now" (anti-nuclear weapons), and "Equal rights now" (women's liberation). And slogans espouse vague dreams, hopes, and visions such as "Every child a wanted child, every mother a willing mother (pro-choice), "For a bicentennial without colonies" (native American), and "What if they gave a war and nobody came?" (anti-war).

Thus, slogans allow social movements to simplify and package their perceptions of the world that produce impressions of action, direction, analysis, and thoroughness.[22] If, as Joseph Lelyveld claims, television has reduced the "attention span of the ordinary viewer" to "fractions of minutes" and "has made political communication a matter of fleeting impressions," then slogans are essential persuasive vehicles for social movements.[23]

Mobilizing for Action

Since many slogans are created during enthusiastic mobilization periods, they often call upon members and sympathizers to take some sort of action. Slogans simply urge the faithful to repent, fight, picket, support, wake up, vote, help, or "do it." Others urge specific actions such as "Boycott Chiquita bananas" (United Farm Workers), "Sign up here to keep Taiwan free" (radical right), and "Occupy Seabrook" (anti-nuclear power).

A few slogans, such as the native American slogan "All for one, and one for all," appeal explicitly for unity. Very few call upon audiences to join a specific social movement organization, but slogans do urge action on behalf of a cause or campaign. One radical right slogan proclaims, "I think it's time for us to stand up and be counted," and another challenges the masculinity of the potential joiner, "Don't be half a man, join the Klan." A radical left slogan challenges audiences, "Dare to struggle, dare to win."

Unlike protest songs and other largely in-group persuasive efforts, slogans are often aimed implicitly or explicitly at nonmembers whose support is essential for social movement success. When the United Farm Workers demonstrate in front of supermarkets or liquor stores, for example, they carry signs and chant slogans such as "Don't buy Red Coach Iceberg lettuce," "Help the grape workers win their strike," and "Don't swallow Gallo's wine." These appeals are primarily to the public, retail customers, and the media. The same is true when Save the Whales protestors use the slogan "Wake up! to the alarming facts" and when environmental activists urge people to "Breathe deeply, then revolt."

The majority of slogans apply direct or indirect pressure on other social movements, institutions, or institutional agents. Nearly every demand is phrased as an imperative statement and shouted or displayed at rallies attended by hundreds or thousands of protestors in and around state legislatures, capitols, corporations, churches, courthouses, colleges, stores, beauty pageants, logging operations, and nuclear power plants. Slogans such as "Ratify ERA now" (women's liberation), "No bus for us" (radical right), and "Convert Rocky Flats" (anti-nuclear power) pressure oppositions. The same is true for expressions of power such as "Gray power," "White power," and "We are everywhere" (gay rights).

Nearly all social movements employ slogans as signs of defiance that embolden members and sympathizers and threaten institutional legitimacy. Slogans are fun and relatively safe ways to agitate and threaten the powers that be. Protestors shout threatening slogans such as "Tell him what to do with the broom" (women's liberation), "Hell no, we won't go" (anti-Vietnam War), and "We will remember in November" (women's liberation). Some social movements go beyond defiance and mild threats with slogans such as "Kill the pigs" (counterculture), "Shut it down" (radical left), and "Buy more guns" (black rights).

Social movement slogans act as social symbols and symbolic justifications to create impressions, alter perceptions of reality, self, and other, elicit emotional responses, make demands, and pressure oppositions. The ambiguity of slogans enables them to serve as verbal bridges from one meaning to another and allow individuals and groups to interpret them according to their own perceptions and needs. They simplify complex problems, solutions, relationships, and situations while demanding instant corrective actions. And many slogans readily identify specific social movements and social movement organizations.

Obscenity

The act of swearing has always been a part of human social interaction. Sigmund Freud suggests that "the first human being who hurled a curse instead of a weapon against his adversary was the founder of civilization."[24] Obscenity is a form of swearing that makes use of indecent words or phrases and plays many roles within the realm of politics, what political scientist Harold Laswell calls "the process by which the irrational bases of society are brought out into the open."[25] As Wendell Phillips, an anti-slavery agitator before the Civil War, observed:

> The scholar may sit in his [her] study and take care that his [her] language is not exaggerated, but the rude mass of men [women] is not to be caught by balanced periods—they are caught by men [women] whose words are half battles. From Luther down, the charge against every reformer has been that his [her] language is too rough. Be it so. Rough instruments are used for rough work.[26]

Obscenity is indeed a rough instrument because it is the ultimate form of symbolic conflict.

Obscenity may be verbal, nonverbal, or a combination of both, and usually appears as adjectives that constitute indecent words, phrases, and actions. It is a potentially powerful tool for social protestors. "Dissent," argue Fabrizio, Karas, and Menmuir, "has its own rhetoric, one that can be studied in its full range of tones—resentful or resigned, angry or agonized, irate or ironic, furious or downright funny."[27] Ashley Montagu observes that "swearing constitutes a species of human behavior so little understood, even by its most devoted practitioners, that an examination of its meaning and significance is long overdue."[28]

Rhetorical Characteristics of Obscenity

Verbal and nonverbal obscenity became a public issue during the protests of the 1960s and 1970s. Protestors against the war in Vietnam and American culture used obscenities to express rage, frustrations, and perceptions of American society. They argued that obscene rhetoric was appropriate for describing and attacking an obscene society. Early protestors of the civil rights and anti-war movements utilized traditional languaging strategies and forms of prose, but when these failed to change established policies and practices, they turned to less traditional methods, including obscenity. Denied the instruments of power and access to the mass media, protestors created a new language of protest to attract attention and publicity. Saul Alinsky observes that "The passions of mankind have boiled over into all areas of political life, including its vocabulary.[29] Haig Bosmajian writes that "The dissenter wants to be heard, to be listened to and if shouting obscenities is the only way he [she] can get people to listen to him [her], so be it."[30] A student who took part in the 1967 march on the Pentagon and the 1968 demonstrations at Columbia University commented, "I and the others had reached the point where we could no longer tolerate being disregarded. I and the others had to own our lives."[31] An obscene word, phrase, or gesture can provide a summation of the group situation that lends emotion to the group's political and social interests and reifies and magnifies issues at hand. Thus, the use of obscenity reflects a political reality of frustration with and separateness from institutions.

No symbol is intrinsically or literally "dirty." Obscenity, like beauty, is in the eye and mind of the beholder. Words become dirty or taboo because of social conventions, not logical bases of argument, and specific words, phrases, and gestures may be viewed as more or less obscene over time. The contextual elements of who and where are vital to the use of obscenity. For instance, sex, position, age, and status influence our perceptions of taboo symbols. Obscenities by women, children, teenagers, and high-status individuals are more shocking than when used by middle-aged men or dock workers. Police officers have reacted most angrily to obscenities by young protestors, particularly females. Murray Edelman argues that "the politically relevant setting is not merely physical but also social in character" and "is fundamental to symbol formation."[32] The outrageousness of obscenity, particularly when used in public or "sacred" places and by young people, women, and professionals jolts people into awareness that a significant number of people are disaffected enough with society to violate its fundamental rules of conduct.

Obscenity is metaphorical because it implies meanings and disengages the word from the thing signified. Verbal obscenity implies a link between a person, group, or object to some religious, sexual, or excretory reality. For instance, calling someone a ''son of a bitch'' implies more than birth heritage because it attacks an individual by linking the person to a socially negative construct. The strength of obscenity, then, lies in the linking or comparative process. Michael Hazen observes that:

> By making comparisons with those things which are at the heart of a culture's values, a verbal obscenity draws on the strength and vitalness of a society. The values that are being drawn on are those which are important to society. Sex, body functions, and religion are at the heart of how we perceive ourselves and our relationship to the world. Thus, the verbal obscenity, as a metaphor, draws its strength from the culture's definition of what is proper in several inherent realms of human values.[33]

Verbal obscenities violate societal norms and expectations. And the more obscene the language, the greater are the violations against social norms and the potential impact upon an audience. Within the realm of social protest, obscenity is emotional and intense because it expresses inner feelings and reflects the extent of a persuader's pessimism, futility, and anger.

The Persuasive Functions of Obscenity

Perceptions of Reality. During the Vietnam War, anti-war protestors used obscenity to alter the way Americans viewed the military conflict and society. Jerry Rubin argued that a new language of protest was critical because institutions controlled the old language and thus perceptions of the war and its opposition:

> When they control the words, they control everything, and they got the words controlled. They got ''war'' meaning ''peace;'' they got ''fuck'' being a ''bad word;'' they got ''napalm'' being a good word—they got decency that to me is indecent. The whole thing is like backwards, and we gotta turn it around.[34]

To turn it around, Theodore Windt writes, anti-war protestors resorted to verbal obscenities and public sexual acts to communicate their belief that ''while sex is natural and creative'' and exhibits love, ''war is unnatural and destructive'' and exhibits hatred.[35] Jerry Farber wrote a popular and highly controversial essay entitled ''The Student as Nigger'' to influence the way readers viewed the American educational system, particularly universities. He wrote that ''In California state colleges the faculties are screwed regularly and vigorously by the Governor and the Legislature.'' For students ''There is a kind of castration that goes on in schools.''[36]

Perception of the Opposition. Persuaders use obscenity to polarize social movements from their oppositions. Dan Rothwell argues that:

> The principle effect of verbal obscenity is polarization, which emanates from the social disapproval of this type of language. . . . The results of this polarization are sometimes profound and diverse. Few people are capable of remaining apathetic to the use of verbal obscenity by anyone, much less agitators. Consequently, the agitator wins at least a superficial, if not a consequential victory by forcing the majority into separate and opposing camps preparing for battle. . . . It is important that the agitator know his [her] allies and his [her] foes.[37]

Agitators employ obscenity in a variety of ways to establish a we-they distinction between movement and establishment.

Social movement persuaders heap obscenities upon their perceived devils to discredit and humiliate them. Students at Kent State University called National Guard members "fascist bastards;" students at Jackson State College called police "motherfuckers."[38] Eldridge Cleaver, a leader of the Black Panthers, exclaimed in a speech on the UCLA campus that his hatred and hostility was for a "fucked up system, that has fucked up our lives, and fucked up the world we live in, that we have to deal with for ourselves and for posterity."[39] These obscenities are not purposeless, gutter profanities. They enable social movements to define and stereotype the opposition as vile, hypocritical, impotent, and stupid—as obscene. They exhibit a profound contempt for and revolt from established institutions, norms, and values that are responsible for an obscene situation.

Social movements attempt to goad institutions into exhibiting their "true" natures for all to see. Scott and Smith write that the confronter communicates to opponents, "We know you for what you are. And you know that we know."[40] And "the confronter who prompts violence in the language or behavior of another has found his collaborator. 'Show us how ugly you really are,' he [she] says, and the enemy with dogs and cattle prods, or police billies and mace, complies." Protestors in Chicago in 1968 bombarded the police with nonstop obscenities— both verbal and nonverbal: "motherfuckers," "pigfuckers," "brainless assholes," and "fuck the nazis."[41] These continual taunts eventually resulted in what *The Walker Report to the National Commission on the Causes and Prevention of Violence* called "unrestrained and indiscriminate police violence," "a police riot." Police gassed, clubbed, kicked, and used motorcycles to run over innocent onlookers, pedestrians, residents, delegates to the Democratic Convention, photographers, and reporters as well as hated protestors. And they resorted to the ugly rhetoric of the demonstrators by charging into crowds with cries of "Get their fucking cameras," "Let's get these fucking bastards," "Fuck your press credentials," and "Get out of the park you motherfuckers."[42] The demonstrators in Chicago had indeed found their collaborators. Members of the establishment discredited and humiliated themselves because they lost control, a major sin for institutions and their agents.

Perceptions of Self. Obscenities that discredit and humiliate the opposition enhance the self-concept of protestors. Richard Gregg writes that "By painting the enemy in dark hued imagery of vice, corruption, evil, and weakness, one may more easily convince himself [herself] of his [her] own superior virtue and thereby gain a symbolic victory of ego-enhancement.''[43] When members of the labor movement sang a song entitled ''You Low Life Son of a Bitch,'' they were undoubtedly ''establishing, defining, and affirming'' their selfhood by ''engaging in a rhetorical act'' against employers.[44] The sexual mocking of authority figures relieves the protestor of personal feelings of inadequacy and reduces authority figures below the protestor's own perceived social worth. Each obscenity gives the user the power to mock and challenge the most powerful of foes in relative safety. Rarely is the boss, president, draft board, or institutional agent, aside from police officers, present to answer the charges hurled.

Obscenity may also demonstrate the user's ''sexual, social, and political liberation'' from a repressive, ''parental establishment.''[45] Steven Spender writes that obscenity ''is based on speaking the unspeakable. It is a style of protest, the basic protest being against censorship: not just official censorship which inhibits you from saying anything you like to anyone anytime.''[46] Radical gay rights groups such as Act-Up and Queer Nation appear half-naked and exhibit erotic lovemaking during demonstrations and marches. Thus, obscenity demonstrates social and political independence, exhibits freedom over one's mouth and body, and is a tactic the established order cannot easily co-opt.

Prescribing Courses of Action.   Social movements that rely upon obscenities divorce themselves from societies they believe have no values or norms worth redeeming. They often have no solutions or courses of action to prescribe, so obscenity is a means of putting down the system and escaping the responsibility of finding a replacement. Protestors after the 1968 Democratic Convention carried signs reading ''Bullshit!''—no demands or solutions, merely a condemnation of everything.[47] Before the convention, Abbie Hoffman advocated ''Revolution for the hell of it,'' and remarked, ''They know something's up, something's going on down there, something's happening, some change coming on in this country. . . . We won't tell 'em what it is. What do you want to tell them for? Don't tell 'em shit. Never. . . . That's the problem you have when you focus in on an issue, when you make a demand. They can deal with a demand. We put a finger up their ass and tell them, ''I ain't telling you what I want,'' then they got a problem.''[48] H. Rapp Brown, leader of the Student Nonviolent Coordinating Committee, outlined a somewhat different strategy for confusing enemies of black power: ''If white folks say gray suits are fashionable, you go buy a pink one. If they say america [sic] is great, you say america [sic] ain't shit. Chairman Mao says, 'Whatever the enemy supports, we oppose. Whatever the enemy opposes, we support'.''[49] Obscenity-laden strategies preclude meaningful courses of action or dialogue with the enemy, but it does express an extreme contempt for society's standards and a burning desire for revolutionary change. ''Civility,'' Dan Rothwell observes, ''is an instrument of the status quo; verbal obscenity is a symbol of rebellion against the power structure. Agitators seek profound change, and profanity offers a profound change from the accepted style of dissent."[50]

Mobilizing for Action. When orthodox means of persuasion fail to gain attention, social movements may resort to what Windt calls the "diatribe," moral dramaturgy intended to assault sensibilities, to turn thought upside-down, to turn social mores inside-out, to commit in language the same barbarisms one condemns in society."[51]

Obscene words and acts gain and control media attention. Jerry Rubin, a founder of the Yippies, wrote about efforts to manipulate the mass media: "We're living TV commercials for the revolution. We're walking picket signs. Every response to longhairs creates a moral crisis for the straights. We force adults to bring all their repressions to the surface, to expose their raw feelings."[52] Rubin, Abbie Hoffman, and other agitators of the 1960s and 1970s learned quickly that obscenity not only attracted media attention but gave protestors a degree of control. Radio, television, and the press could not broadcast or print obscenities or pictures of obscene acts, but all three could report the sights and sounds of police reactions to obscenities. Speaking in Lincoln Park in Chicago during the Democratic convention, Abbie Hoffman instructed demonstrators on media control and coverage:

> If you don't want it on TV, write the word "Fuck" on your head, see, and that won't get on TV, right? But that's where the theater is at, it's TV. I mean our thing's for TV. We don't want to get on Meet the Press. What's that shit? We want Ed Sullivan, Johnny Carson Show, we want the shit where the people are lookin' at it and diggin' it. . . . The media distorts. But it always works to our advantage.[53]

Ugly, symbolic, and sometimes violent confrontations make moderate social movement elements and critics within the system more respectable. Windt writes that, "Just as Stokely Carmichael legitimized the moderate, nonviolent posture of Martin Luther King, Jr., so too, the violent acts of the Weatherpeople and the absurd acts of the Yippies contributed to acceptance of traditional criticism of the war and enhanced the ethos of those critics who held positions of power."[54]

Obscenities may enhance the credibility of movement leaders because they have the nerve to shout what others only feel. For instance, Rothwell notes that "the Black Panthers' obscene vilification of police apparently expresses the private feelings of many black Americans. Although they may not approve of the Panther terminology, they may admire those who have the courage and audacity to insult policemen."[55]

Obscenity may contribute to social movement cohesiveness. Humans have a basic need to identify with others in similar circumstances, and obscenity can create a sense of interpersonal identification among protestors and potential sympathizers and legitimizers.[56] Social action organizer Saul Alinsky explains why he uses the obscene:

> Every now and then I have been accused of being crude and vulgar because I have used analogies of sex or the toilet. I do not do this because I want to shock,

particularly, but because there are certain experiences common to all, and sex and toilet are two of them. Furthermore, everyone is interested in those two—which can't be said of every common experience.[57]

Group chanting of obscenities makes everyone equal, involves everyone in the protest, and both shares and reduces the risk involved. Peter Farb maintains that "the common denominator of all slang whether it be the speech of adolescents or the jive talk of musicians, is that it tests who belongs to the group and who is an intruder."[58]

Obscenity allows movement members to release pent-up hostility and fear. Psychologist Chaytor Mason asserts that obscenity serves as a safety valve that helps society function without excessive frustration.[59] Verbal aggression is often a surrogate for physical aggression and, consequently, may have a therapeutic value for society and spare it from bloodshed. Verbal aggression permits protestors to challenge society verbally to ascertain the boundaries of expression.

Adverse Effects of Obscenity on Social Protest

While obscenity is an effective means of performing persuasive functions for social movements, it may have serious adverse effects. First, although obscenity may capture the attention of the public and the media, it may draw attention to itself and away from the social movement's demands. The issue becomes not *what* is being said but *how* it is being said and by *whom*. David Dellinger, the defender of the Chicago Seven on trial following the Democratic National Convention, warned the movement:

> We become intoxicated by the slogan "By any means necessary," and forget the interrelationship of means and ends. Like the hot-rod who was caught in traffic and bottomed out racing across a field, we rush into shortcuts that take us for an exciting ride but don't get us where we want to go. The movement falls into its own brand of tokenism, preferring the showy symbolism of insulting a "pig" or trashing a window to the reality of winning over the people to resist the authority of the state and the corporation.[60]

Saul Alinsky berates those who forget the cause, the end for which the social movement is fighting: "These rules make the difference between being a realistic radical and being a rhetorical one who uses the tired old words and slogans . . . and has so stereotyped himself that others react by saying, 'Oh, he's one of those,' and then promptly turn off."[61]

Second, attention gained through obscenity tends to be short-lived. As Windt writes, "Once attention has been gained and criticism voiced, the diatribe diminishes in usefulness. People demand serious remedies, seriously treated. Moral dramaturgy must give way to conventional rhetorical forms."[62] When the shock of seeing and hearing obscenities wears off, there is nothing left. The Yippie movement is an excellent illustration of this hollowness. We recall their vulgar and often weird language, actions, and dress but little or nothing of what they stood for, demanded, or attained.

Third, since obscenity is the most extreme form of verbal aggression, the social movement cannot become more radical without resorting to actual violence. People soon grow tired of the same old words. As Alinsky warns, "A tactic that drags on too long becomes a drag."[63]

Fourth, the social unacceptablity of verbal and nonverbal obscenity relegates its use to minorities in both society and social movements. "Most people castigate those who dare to speak obscenities in the public forum," Rothwell writes, "despite the fact that a substantial portion of the 'Silent Majority' seems to have little aversion to private cursing."[64] The repugnance for the public use of profanity denies to social movements the support of important legitimizers outside of and moderates within movements. Neither group can condone or be associated with elements that resort to obscenity. Tom Hayden chastised his fellow SDS (Students for a Democratic Society) members, "There's no reason to continue to verbally put down white liberals for only contributing money or legal defense and going no further. There's no reason to verbally antagonize anyone unnecessarily—that is a form of pseudo politics, a substitute for action."[65] Verbal obscenity tends to become both contagious and noxious to growing numbers of people as protest escalates in intensity and time.

And fifth, obscenity may produce violent reactions that members do not anticipate. Shortly after noon on May 4, 1970, a group of approximately fifty protestors approached a line of Ohio National Guardsmen on the Kent State University campus. The protestors were shouting obscenities, and a photograph clearly shows several students making obscene gestures. The Guard moved forward to dispel the students from the Commons; confrontations occurred; and at 12:25 the Guardsmen lowered their rifles and fired into the crowd. Seconds later four students lay dead and nine were wounded.[66] Some of the victims were hundreds of yards away from the confrontation and were either watching the activities or going to class. On May 14, 1970, a group of between seventy-five and two hundred students at Jackson State College in Mississippi confronted state and local police after two days of rock- and bottle-throwing and incessant obscenities. Shortly before midnight police fired into a crowd and into nearby dormitory windows. Two students were killed and twelve were wounded.[67] During the five days of the Democratic National Convention, 192 police officers and approximately 1,000 demonstrators and non-demonstrators were treated for injuries and 668 people were arrested.[68]

Whether the advantages of capturing attention, polarizing friends from enemies, enhancing self-image, and liberating the social movement from a repressive establishment outweigh the disadvantages—and for how long—depends upon the particular movement and the context in which it operates.

Ridicule

Social activist Saul Alinsky claims that "ridicule is man's [woman's] most potent weapon" because "it is almost impossible to counterattack ridicule. Also

it infuriates the opposition, who then react to your advantage.''[69] Ron Roberts
and Robert Kloss write that ridicule is a form of humor usually employed by
social movements and countermovements ''to demean the status of another
individual or group,'' and claim that ''Ridicule has been used with some success
in keeping people 'in their place'.''[70] What, then, is this potent rhetorical tool?

Dictionaries tell us that to ridicule is to make a person, group, place, thing,
action, or idea an object of laughter and even of scorn.[71] There is a notion of
process in definitions of and synonyms for ridicule. Thus, to ridicule is to mock
or make fun of; to make fun of is to exaggerate every real or alleged fault or
weakness; to exaggerate every fault and weakness is to distort, deform, and uglify;
to distort is to make someone or something appear absurd, laughable, or
outrageous; and to make outrageous is to dehumanize. It is obvious from this
notion of ridicule as a language strategy and process why Alinsky claims it is
a potent weapon for social agitators who desire change or the stifling of change.
Ridicule attacks the basic worth and credibility of persons and ideas and thus
endangers the legitimacy assigned or claimed. A target of verbal assaults, even
those laced with obscenity and invective, can take some comfort in being of such
importance or threat as to provoke attack or counterattack by enemies well-
deserved. There can be little comfort in being the object of laughter—of ridicule—
because few people take forces seriously that appear laughable or absurd.

The Levels of Ridicule

Social movements and countermovements employ ridicule in speeches,
essays, songs, poetry, slogans, and cartoons. Legitimate political cartoonists,
satirists, and singing groups use their pens and skills to make fun of institutions
and social movements. The use of ridicule may be placed along a continuum of
severity or virulence ranging from making fun of a person, group, place, thing,
action, or idea for being (1) inconsistent, to (2) illogical, (3) inept, (4) silly,
(5) monstrous, and (6) inhuman.

Cartoonists are particularly adept at portraying *inconsistencies and self-
contradictions* in institutional or movement beliefs, claims, and actions. For
instance, a cartoon during the Vietnam War portrays a heavily armed and bomb-
laden President Johnson telling a young black protestor, ''You're setting a bad
example with your violence.''[72] A cartoon during the anti-apartheid movement
of the 1980s depicts a South African police officer beating a black citizen while
the South African prime minister lectures, ''How many times do I have to tell
you? We won't talk to any black leader who doesn't renounce violence.''[73]
Numerous cartoons note contradictions between pro-life's beliefs and the murder
of Dr. David Gunn in Pensacola, Florida in March of 1993. One portrays a man
holding a Bible in one hand and a gun in the other near a clinic; the caption reads
''The right-to-lifers have spoken.''[74] And a second depicts the words ''RESPECT
LIFE'' written with bullet holes on a blood-stained wall and an outstretched hand
in a pool of blood near a stethoscope.[75] Ridicule at this level attacks beliefs, claims,

and actions directly and persons or groups indirectly. The assault is more ideological than personal but reveals glaring inconsistencies and self-contradictions does challenge a movement's or institution's trustworthiness by mocking or making fun of its alleged sincerity, honesty, and fairness, important traits of credibility in American society.

At the second level of ridicule, persuaders get more personal while mocking a group's ideas, actions, and statements as *illogical, irrational, or unreasonable.* An anti-Vietnam War poster and bumpersticker reads, "Join the army; travel to exotic, distant lands; meet exciting, unusual people and kill them."[76] A native American cartoon printed at Thanksgiving portrays a colonist walking away from three Indian braves, one of whom is saying, "They've shot twenty-nine of our braves, polluted all the rivers, killed most of the game, and raped the chief's sister. Now he wants us to drop over next Thursday for turkey dinner will all the fixin's."[77] And a cartoon that ridicules the far right's agenda shows a large mushroom-shaped cloud in the background as an angry figure shaking a fist while holding his Bible in the other hand shouts, "Blast! I suppose this pre-empts our giant anti-abortion, support James Watt, and put prayer back in the schools, book burning rally tomorrow!"[78] These exaggerated irrationalities of the Army, colonists, and far right members attack the opposition's competence by ridiculing its powers of reasoning, judgment, and fairness. Fundamental competence is questioned.

Not all ridicule is aimed at the opposition. Persuaders may taunt their own supporters and sympathizers. At a "Free Huey" rally (demanding the release of Huey Newton, a leader of the Black Panther party), Bobby Seale provoked his audience to cheers rather than jeers:

> For over four hundred years, he taught you white nationalism, and you lapped it up. You taught it to your children. You had your children thinking that everything black was bad. Black cows don't give good milk. Black hens don't lay eggs. Black for funerals, white for weddings. That's white nationalism. Santy Claus, a white honky who slides down a black chimney and comes out white.[79]

Malcolm X employed this tactic frequently in speeches to predominantly black audiences. In one of his "The Ballot or the Bullet" speeches in Detroit, he addresses the need for black capitalism and the foolishness of many black would-be entrepreneurs:

> You can't open up a black store in a white community. The white man won't even patronize you. He's not wrong. He's got sense enough to watch out for himself. It's you who don't have sense enough to look out for yourself. The white man is too intelligent to let someone else come and gain control of the economy of his community. But you will let anybody come in and control the economy of your community, control the housing, control the education, control the jobs, control the businesses under the pretext you want to integrate. No, you're out of your mind.[80]

The intent of assaults on an audience's abilities to reason and make good judgments is not to demean but to activate, to alter audiences' perceptions of reality, and to shake them into doing something about it. It is the proverbial "wake-up call." Rebecca Leonard writes that "black liberation" agitators of the 1960s "actually insulted their audiences in an apparent attempt to motivate them to act in defiance of the agitator's insult."[81]

At the third level of ridicule, persuaders get increasingly personal as they make fun of the opposition as *inept, stupid, or senseless*. One native American cartoon depicts Columbus landing in the New World being met by a male and a female native; the male comments to the female, "That's a laugh . . . This guy thinks we're Indians."[82] Another native American cartoon depicts an overweight and well-dressed white couple standing before the Washington Monument telling three native Americans: "If you don't like it here in America, why don't you go back where you came from?"[83] In a speech at the University of Kansas, George Lincoln Rockwell, founder of the American Nazi party, ridicules "queer, Jew, communists" for corrupting art forms and praising paintings by two Baltimore apes. At one showing of these paintings, Rockwell claims, a Jewish critic who was unaware that the artists were apes described one as a "beautiful, sensitive painting; it shows tremendous feeling."[84] Anti-civil rights recordings played on jukeboxes in the South during the 1960s are clones of the old Amos and Andy radio show. The recordings play on a whole repertoire of black stereotypical features: lazy, ignorant, stupid, cowardly, drunken, and corrupt.[85] This level of ridicule brings into question a wide range of credibility traits: intelligent, knowledgeable, mentally alert, honest, rational, dynamic, and industrious. Charges of ineptness and stupidity not only demean the opposition, but imply obvious superiority of the attacker.

The fourth level of ridicule attacks the opposition as *silly, trivial, or comical*. A cartoon during the student protests of the 1960s portrays a placard-carrying group of students marching down a street while a well-dressed, older couple looks on. The caption has the woman saying to her husband, "I don't think it's anything intellectual, dear—they're from the university."[86] Anti-United Nations cartoons show members blowing halloween whistles, wearing buckets and lampshades on their heads, and having a water faucet coming out of an ear. One of the most famous songs of the 1960s student and anti-war movements, Arlo Guthrie's "Alice's Restaurant Massacre," makes police officer "Opie," a blind judge, and military recruiters look silly and ridiculous. This level of ridicule attacks persons and their actions more than ideas and claims and depicts oppositions as unworthy of serious consideration because they are so trivial and comical. Institutional and uninstitutional collectives must sustain perceptions that they are forces to be contended with, otherwise they will be neither feared nor respected, only ignored. And to be ignored is to cease being an agent of change or resistance.

The fifth level of ridicule attacks the opposition as *monstrous, bizarre, and grotesque*. Opponents are not silly buffoons but ugly monsters. An anti-capitalist cartoon depicts an incredibly gross and bloated male in a suit saying, "Starvation's God's way of punishing those who have little or no faith in capitalism."[87] An anti-pro-life cartoon portrays two ugly, dirty-old-men carrying protest signs reading "Outlaw Abortion" and "Keep Em Barefoot and Pregnant," with the caption, "If we can't outsmart them Commies, we gotta outnumber 'em."[88] The anti-Vietnam War song "Masters of War," sung by Bob Dylan, attacks those who build the big guns, best planes, and bombs to destroy and kill while hiding in their mansions as "the young people's blood flows out of their bodies and is buried in the mud."[89] This level of ridicule shows oppositions not merely as inconsistent, illogical, inept, or silly but as vicious, evil human monsters who will do anything to fulfill their desires and beliefs. They are not merely incompetent but dangerous to humanity, particularly because they are industrious and vigorous in their efforts to exploit and harm others under their control.

And the sixth level of ridicule attacks oppositions as *inhuman and brutish*. Males are "chauvinist pigs" and "rats;" liquor dealers are "rummies;" American nazis are "cancers;" women's rights activists are "bra-burners" and "libbers;" and black males are "bucks." A cartoon depicts the American Nazi Party as helmeted, hideous varmints emerging from under a rock.[90] And those who should support the movement but do not are strike-breaking "scabs," "oreos" ("negroes" who are black on the outside and white on the inside), and "apples" ("Indians" who are red on the outside but white on the inside). This level of ridicule dehumanizes oppositions by portraying them as animalistic or inanimate objects. They are the epitome of evil without the abilities to reason, know, make judgments, or act fairly or sympathetically.

The Functions of Ridicule

Ridicule can be an effective means of polarizing the social movement and its opposition. On the one hand is a villain that represents all that is evil and unwholesome: inconsistent, irrational, stupid, silly, monstrous, and inhuman. On the other hand is the movement's true believer that represents all that is good and wholesome: consistent, rational, intelligent, wise, beautiful, and humane. And this polarization by vilification, Marsha Vanderford notes, "formulates a specific adversarial force" by providing a "clear target for movement action."[91] Vilification through ridicule casts this target "in an exclusively negative light," "attributes diabolical motives to foes," and "magnifies the opponents' powers."[92] In short, ridicule can depict an ideal devil for the movement or countermovement to confront, for it is the epitome of evil that creates a need for urgent action and long-term commitment to the cause.

The six levels of ridicule also support Richard Gregg's claim that "the primary appeal of the rhetoric of protest is to the protestors themselves, who feel the need for psychological refurbishing and affirmation."[93] An implied comparison is present in all instances of ridicule. If the opposition is irrational, the movement is rational; if the opposition is stupid, the movement is intelligent; and if the opposition is monstrous, the movement is natural and attractive. Gregg writes that "Throughout all these interactions a person constructs an order; he weighs, evaluates, and orients toward goals so that a symbolic hierarchy is established in which he locates himself."[94] The more the villain is demeaned and reduced from an intelligent, rational force to an irrational, monstrous animal or thing, the more the movement member is transported up the social hierarchy, and the greater is one's self concept. Indeed, depicting the opposition as inhuman places it below the scale of a social and symbolic hierarchy. Denise Bostdorff identifies a number of tropes, figures of speech, that make the cartoon an effective rhetorical agent in enhancing selfhood:

> metaphor identifies the cartoon villain as a threat; irony furthers this identification by dialectically enjoining the villain with cultural icons; synecdoche represents the villain as a whole by substituting a part; and metonymy attacks the villain by converting actions downward through reduction.[95]

But the power of ridicule lies not merely in reducing the worth of the opposition but in the act itself. Gregg claims that:

> The rhetoric of attack becomes . . . a rhetoric of ego-building, and the very act of assuming such a rhetorical stance becomes self-persuasive and confirmatory.[96]

The act of ridicule gives persuaders feelings of power, control over their environment and lives, and superiority. As a language strategy often tied to music, drawings, or photographs and to phrasing that give it a mean-spiritedness on many occasions, ridicule is both a coactive and confrontative strategy.

Ridicule is an important weapon in the struggle over legitimacy. It challenges the five powers of legitimacy by characterizing adversaries "as ungenuine and malevolent advocates." Marsha Vanderford writes that "Rather than differentiating opponents as good people with a difference of opinion, vilification [such as ridicule and name-calling] delegitimizes them through characterizations of intentions, actions, purposes, and identities."[97] How can an institution or social movement claim the *power to reward* those who conform to norms and values and to punish those who do not when it appears to violate the very norms and values it claims to espouse? Is it not guilty of hypocrisy and sanctimoniousness? How can an institution or social movement claim the *power of control* over information and persuasion when it appears to be self-contradictory, illogical, and stupid in its actions and rhetoric? How can an institution or social movement maintain the *power of identification* with sacred symbols, codes, and myths when it is identified with what is trivial, grotesque, and brutish? Are they the successors of a society's founding fathers, prophets, and high priests, or its demons? How can an institution or social movement sustain or attain the *power of terministic control* when depictions of its rhetoric and actions are the opposite of sensitive terms such as order, nonviolence, reason, restraint, sensitivity, and justice? How can an institution or social movement claim the *power of moral suasion* when it appears to be irrational, monstrous, and inhuman, the very epitome of immorality and evil?

Conclusions

Language strategies such as slogans, obscenity, and ridicule have been with us for centuries. They act as social symbols and symbolic justifications that enable collectives to control their worlds. Social movements and countermovements employ a variety of language strategies to create impressions, alter perceptions of reality, self, and other, elicit emotional responses, make demands, attain and sustain commitments to causes, and pressure oppositions. The ambiguity of words and phrases allow them to serve as verbal bridges from one meaning to another and allow individuals and groups to interpret them according to their own perceptions. They simplify complex problems, solutions, situations, and peoples while demanding instant corrective actions. And they help to determine the legitimacy granted to and stripped from institutions and social movements. Perhaps it is fitting to end a chapter dealing with such powerful language strategies as slogans, obscenity, and ridicule to alter the old addage about swords to read "the agent that lives by the word may die by the word."

Endnotes

[1] Richard Weaver, *Language as Sermonic* (Baton Rouge: Louisiana State University Press, 1970), 120–121.

[2] Wayne Booth, *Modern Dogma and the Rhetoric of Assent* (Chicago: University of Chicago Press, 1974), 164 and 193.

[3] Robert Cathcart, "New Approaches to the Study of Movements: Defining Movements Rhetorically," *Western Speech* 36 (Spring 1972), 86.

[4] Hugh Duncan, *Symbols in Society* (New York: Oxford University Press, 1968), 8.

[5] Robert D. Brooks, "Black Power: The Dimensions of a Slogan," *Western Speech* 34 (Spring 1970), 108–114.

[6] Duncan, 22.

[7] Harold D. Laswell, "The Theory of Propaganda," *American Political Science Review* 21 (1927), 627.

[8] Murray Edelman, *The Symbolic Uses of Politics* (Urbana, IL: University of Illinois Press, 1967), 115.

[9] J. Vernon Jensen, "British Voices on the Eve of the American Revolution: Trapped by the Family Metaphor," *Quarterly Journal of Speech* 63 (February 1977), 43–50.

[10] Philip C. Wander, "The Savage Child: The Image of the Negro in the Pro–Slavery Movement," *Southern Speech Communication Journal* 37 (Summer 1972), 335–360.

[11] Karlyn Kohrs Campbell, "The Rhetoric of Radical Black Nationalism: A Case Study in Self-Conscious Criticism," *Central States Speech Journal* 22 (Fall 1971), 151–160; Robert L. Scott, "Justifying Violence—The Rhetoric of Black Power," *Central States Speech Journal* 19 (Summer 1968), 96–104.

[12] Lawrence Ingrassia, "Fighting Words," *The Wall Street Journal*, May 3, 1993, A1.

[13] Kurt W. Ritter, "Confrontation as Moral Drama: The Boston Massacre in Rhetorical Perspective," *Southern Speech Communication Journal* 42 (Winter 1977), 114–136.

[14] *Say No to Torture* (Washington, D.C.: Animal Welfare Institute, n.d.); *Vivisection . . .* (New York: CIVIS, n.d.); *A Time to Choose* (Neptune, NJ: Friends of Animals, n.d.).

[15] James R. Andrews, "History and Theory in the Study of the Rhetoric of Social Movements," *Central States Speech Journal* 31 (Winter 1980), 274.

[16] George E. Shankel, *American Mottoes and Slogans* (New York: Wilson, 1941), 7.

[17] Ashley Montagu, *The Anatomy of Swearing* (New York: Macmillan, 1967), 2.

[18] In a study by the authors of 585 slogans, 43% appear to be demands or solutions.

[19] Michael C. McGee, "The 'Ideograph': A Link between Rhetoric and Ideology," *Quarterly Journal of Speech* 66 (February 1980), 1–16.

[20] John W. Bowers, Donovan J. Ochs, and Richard J. Jensen, *The Rhetoric of Agitation and Control*, 2/E (Prospect Heights, IL: Waveland Press, 1993), 28.

[21] John Wilson, *Introduction to Social Movements* (New York: Basic Books, 1973), 89-90.

[22] Nelson Polsby and Aaron Wildavsky, *Presidential Elections* (New York: Scribners, 1971), 178.

[23] Joseph Lelyveld, "The Selling of a Candidate," *New York Times Magazine*, March 18, 1976, 16.

[24] As reported in "A Good Word for Bad Words," *Time*, December 14, 1981, 77.

[25] Harold Lasswell, *Psychology and Politics* (Englewood Cliffs, NJ: Prentice-Hall, 1960), 184.

[26] As reported in Mary G. McEdwards, "Agitative Rhetoric: Its Nature and Effects," *Western Speech* 32 (Winter 1968), 38.

[27] Ray Fabrizio, Edith Karas, and Ruth Menmuir, *The Rhetoric of No* (New York: Holt, Rinehart and Winston, 1970), vi.

[28] Montagu, 5.

[29] Saul Alinsky, *Rules for Radicals: A Practical Primer for Realistic Radicals* (New York: Vintage, 1971), 48.

[30] Haig A. Bosmajian, "Obscenity and Protest," *Dissent: Symbolic Behavior and Rhetorical Strategies* (Boston: Allyn and Bacon, 1972), 299.

[31] As reported in Bosmajian, 299.

[32] Edelman, 103.

[33] Michael Hazen, "The Rhetorical Functions of Verbal Obscenity in Social Protest: The Limits of Cultural Values," unpublished paper presented at the annual convention of the Speech Communication Association, San Antonio, Texas, November 1979.

[34] As reported in Theodore Windt, Jr., "The Diatribe: Last Resort for Protest," *Quarterly Journal of Speech* 58 (February 1972), 10.

[35] Windt, 11-12.

[36] Jerry Farber, "The Student as Nigger," in Fabrizio, Karas, and Menmuir, 414, 416, 417.

[37] J. Dan Rothwell, "Verbal Obscenity: Time for Second Thoughts," *Western Speech* 35 (Fall 1971), 240-241.

[38] *The Report of the President's Commission on Campus Unrest* (Washington, D.C.: U.S. Government Printing Office, 1970), 266 and 439; Daniel Walker, *Rights in Conflict: The Violent Confrontation of Demonstrators and Police in the Streets of Chicago During the Week of the Democratic National Convention* (New York: Bantam Books, 1968), 135, 146, 154.

[39] Eldridge Cleaver, Speech at UCLA, October 4, 1968, from a tape recording.

[40] Robert L. Scott and Donald K. Smith, "The Rhetoric of Confrontation," *Quarterly Journal of Speech* 55 (February 1969), 7 and 8.

[41] Walker, 248.

[42] See for example, Walker, 1, 5, 8, 139, 154, 158, and 181.

[43] Richard B. Gregg, "The Ego-Function of the Rhetoric of Protest," *Philosophy and Rhetoric* 4 (Spring 1971), 82.

[44] Gregg, 74.

[45] Bosmajian, 298.

[46] Stephen Spender, *The Year of the Young Rebels* (New York: Random House, 1969), 7-8.

[47] Mitchell Goodman, *The Movement Toward a New America: The Beginnings of a Long Revolution* (Philadelphia: Pilgrim Press, 1970), 95; Walker, 41, 43.

[48] Walker, 46.

[49] As reported in Rothwell, "Verbal Obscenity," 234.

[50] Rothwell, "Verbal Obscenity," 234.

[51] Windt, 7-8.

[52] As reported in Windt, 13.

53 Goodman, 361-362.

54 Windt, 14.

55 Rothwell, "Verbal Obscenity," 236.

56 Robert S. Cathcart, "New Approaches to the Study of Movements: Defining Movements Rhetorically," *Western Speech* 36 (Spring 1972), 86.

57 Alinsky, 83-84.

58 Peter Farb, *Word Play: What Happens When People Talk* (New York: Bantam Books, 1975), 86.

59 Rothwell, *Telling It Like It Isn't*, 106.

60 As reported in Bosmajian, 296.

61 Alinsky, xviii.

62 Windt, 8-9.

63 Alinsky, 128.

64 Rothwell, "Verbal Obscenity," 232-233.

65 As reported in Bosmajian, 296. "McCarthy kids" refers to the young followers of Senator Eugene McCarthy a Democratic candidate for President in 1968.

66 *Report of the President's Commission*, 265-410.

67 *Report of the President's Commission*, 421-444.

68 Walker, 351-358.

69 Alinsky, 128.

70 Ron E. Roberts and Robert Marsh Kloss, *Social Movements: Between the Balcony and the Barricade* (St. Louis: C.V. Mosby, 1974), 154.

71 *Webster's New Collegiate Dictionary* (Springfield, MA: G. & C. Merriam, 1977), 996; *The Oxford Universal Dictionary on Historical Principles* (Oxford: Clarendon Press, 1955), 1736; *Roget's International Thesaurus* (New York: Thomas V. Crowell, 1958), 584-585, 632, and 636-637.

72 Cartoon by Ben Roth, *London Tribune*.

73 Cartoon from *Newsday*, Los Angeles Times Syndicate.

74 Cartoon by Olpihant, *The Denver Post*, Los Angeles Times Syndicate.

75 Cartoon by SAOC, *Star Tribune*.

76 Poster by Rosner.

77 Cartoon from *Playboy Magazine*, 1969.

78 Cartoon by Oliphant.

79 Bobby Seale speech from a tape recording of the rally.

80 Malcolm X speech from a tape recording.

81 Rebecca Leonard, "The Rhetoric of Agitation in the Abolition and Black Liberation Movements," unpublished master's thesis, Purdue University, 1970, 93.

82 Cartoon by Werk.

83 Cartoon by Wright, *Palm Beach Post*.

84 George Lincoln Rockwell from a tape recording, February 20, 1964.

85 From tape recordings.

86 Cartoon from *Punch*, London.

87 Cartoon from *Sawyer Press*.

88 Cartoon by Bill Mauldin, *Chicago Sun Times*.

89 From a tape recording.

90 Cartoon by Oliphant.

91 Marsha L. Vanderford, "Vilification and Social Movements: A Case Study of Pro-Life and Pro-Choice Rhetoric," *Quarterly Journal of Speech* 75 (May 1989), 166.

92 Vanderford, 166-167.

93 Gregg, 74.

94 Gregg, 75-76.

95 Denise M. Bostdorff, "Making Light of James Watt: A Burkean Approach to the Form and Attitude of Political Cartoons," *Quarterly Journal of Speech* (February 1987), 48.

96 Gregg, 82.

97 Vanderford, 166.

Chapter Eleven

The Persuasive Functions of Music in Social Movements

The persuasive potential of music has attracted attention for centuries, particularly when social agitators have composed and performed protest songs. Plato warned in *The Republic*, written in the fourth century B.C., that "any musical innovation is full of danger to the whole state, and ought to be prohibited."[1] Jeremy Collier, famous for his controversial pamphlets and moral essays that demanded social reforms in seventeenth-century England, remarked that music is "as dangerous as gunpowder."[2] Slaves on southern plantations before the Civil War used songs disguised as religious hymns ("Steal Away," "Run to Jesus," "Follow the Drinking Gourd," and "Many Thousand Gone") to urge slaves to run away from plantations and to explain how to locate the underground railroad to Canada. The songs "We Shall Overcome" and "We Shall Not Be Moved" helped thousands of Americans confront institutional violence and hatred while carrying the civil rights struggle forward during the 1950s and 1960s.

Although reformers and agitators have used music for centuries to aid their efforts to bring about or to resist change, researchers did not begin to study the persuasive nature and effects of protest music until the 1960s and 1970s. Songs of this period demanded civil rights for African-Americans, criticized American society, condemned the war in Vietnam, and raised the consciousness of women. For the first time in American history, protest music became popular and commercially lucrative. Records by the Kingston Trio; the Chad Mitchell Trio; Peter, Paul, and Mary; Simon and Garfunkel; and Bob Dylan sold in the millions. Establishment elements became frightened when leftist singers of the 1930s such as Pete Seeger, Woody Guthrie, and The Weavers (blacklisted during the Senator Joseph McCarthy era) were "rediscovered" and "whitewashed" into union or labor singers so they could become popular folk singers. College and high school students loved them, while David Noebel of the Christian Crusade warned in his book, *The Marxist Minstrels: A Handbook on Communist Subversion of Music*, that "The communist infiltration into the subversion of American music has been nothing short of phenomenal and in some areas, e.g., folk music, their control is fast approaching the saturation point under the able leadership of Pete Seeger."[3]

Near panic set in when "The Eve of Destruction," sung by Barry McGuire, reached the number-one position on popular music charts and remained there for weeks in 1965. Through a combination of lyrics, voice, and instrumentation, it painted in dark-hued colors a world filled with hatred, prejudice, destruction, and hopelessness and institutions that were incapable of reform. Resistance began immediately as established groups feared that millions of young people would "drop out" of schools and society because, they reasoned, if young people bought the record, they must have bought the message. The future of America was at stake. Decca Records countered with "The Dawn of Correction" and "Better Days Are Yet to Come," sung by the Spokesmen, that portrayed the good in society and how things could get better if we all tried. Atomic bombs, for instance, assured the peace and would not destroy the world because no one was crazy enough to use them, and the Peace Corps was helping to make the world a better place. The American Broadcasting Company warned affiliates they might lose affiliation if they insisted on playing music that was dangerous to society. The Federal Communication Commission reminded radio and televisions stations of their responsibility and accountability to the American public, a veiled threat to revoke or not renew broadcasting licenses if they played the wrong music. David Noebel declared that "The Eve of Destruction" was "obviously aimed at instilling fear in our teenagers as well as a sense of hopelessness. Thermonuclear holocaust, the button, the end of the world, and similar expressions are constantly being used to induce the American public to surrender to atheistic, international communism."[4] The impact and danger of popular protest songs were greatly exaggerated, however. Sociologist R. Serge Denisoff discovered in a study of the "The Eve of Destruction" that only 36 percent of young listeners interpreted the song in the composer's terms while 23 percent totally misconstrued the lyrics. Of the 73 percent that assimilated all or part of the message, only 44 percent approved of the message while 39 percent disapproved.[5]

While protest music does not produce the cataclysmic results often feared by established institutions, it does serve a variety of persuasive functions for social movements and has a number of advantages over speeches, leaflets, editorials, and essays. Charles Stewart writes that "Songs are created and designed for repetition, and they are often sung (perhaps with the addition of timely lyrics) throughout the life cycles of social movements."[6] They have powerful nonverbal (voice and instruments) as well as verbal (lyrics) components. Songs give persuaders a "poetic license" to challenge, exaggerate, and pretend in ways that would be unacceptable or unbelievable if spoken or written in prose.[7] Since protestors often sing songs *together* or *along with* a leader, they are active participants in the persuasive process, not passive listeners to speeches or readers of printed materials.

This chapter focuses on how protest music, through both verbal and nonverbal elements, has performed a variety of persuasive functions for American social movements from the Revolution to the 1990s: transforming perceptions of reality, transforming perceptions of society, prescribing courses of action, mobilizing for action, and sustaining the movement. A study of the lyrics of 714 songs, created for or adopted by social movements throughout American history, and a review of literature on the nonverbal aspects of protest music (voice, instrumentation, melody, rhythm) will also reveal which persuasive functions dominate protest music, how functions have changed over the past two centuries, and how they vary from stage to stage of long-lived social movements and between moderate and radical elements of movements.[8] The 714 protest songs come from the following social movements: American independence movement, anti-American aristocracy movement, anti-slavery/abolition movement, labor movement, migrant worker movement, socialism, populism, farm movement from 1926–1980, black rights movement from 1865–1954, civil rights movement, anti-civil rights movement, temperance movement, women's rights/suffrage movement, women's liberation movement, anti-war movement during the Civil War, anti-war movement from 1865–1940, anti-Vietnam War movement, counterculture movement of the 1960s and 1970s, gray power movement, gay liberation movement, and anti-nuclear power movement.[9]

Transforming Perceptions of Reality

The Past

Few protest songs refer to the past, and only one song in this study deals solely with the past, a ballad of the black rights movement entitled "Gray Goose" that deals metaphorically with the plight and invincibility of the black man.[10] Most references are brief portions of songs and portray the past as a time of misery, suffering, privation, anguish, and despair. For instance, the civil rights song "Freedom Is A Constant Struggle" exclaims that "we've struggled so long," "cried so long," "sorrowed so long," and "died so long." The socialist song "The Long-Haired Kings" describes the brutal life under the "warrior kings of old" "who polished off the natives." Even songs of social movements with pasts for which members might justifiably long do not dwell on them. For example, only occasionally does a labor song look to the pre-industrial era prior to "wage slavery," an anti-war song refer to times of peace and tranquility, or a counterculture song relate how America was pristine before its corruption. A few exceptions are found in anti-civil rights songs. For instance, the song "Johnny Reb" tells of Johnny's heroic exploits against union soldiers in the Civil War; and "We're Not for Integration" declares that "Our southland got along just fine until those integrators came down here stirring up the mess with outside agitators." Another anti-civil rights song asks, however, "when we whites gonna have our day" in spite of more than two centuries of subjugating African-Americans with slave and Jim Crow laws and customs. The women's rights song

"Don't I Wish I Was a Single Girl Again" contrasts an innocent past with the brutal present of the late nineteenth century; here are a few verses:

> When I was single, I went dress'd fine,
> Now I am married, go ragged all the time.
> Lord, don't I wish I was a single girl again.
> When I was single, my shoes they did screak,
> Now I am married, my shoes they do leak.
> Lord, don't I wish I was a single girl again.

There are no apparent differences in references to the past between songs of moderate and radical elements or songs popular during different life cycles of movements. Twentieth-century songs are a bit more concerned with the past than nineteenth-century songs, perhaps because more history is available for reference. In general, protest songs tend not to look back at either a glorious or a miserable past.

The Present

The majority of protest songs focus on the present, and most of these paint the scene in the darkest hues of suffering and misery.[11] Titles suggest the stark reality contained within: "Hard Is the Fortune of All Woman Kind" (women's rights), "Cotton Farmer Blues" (farm), "What It Is to Be a Slave" (anti-slavery), "If There's Hell Below," (civil rights), "Cold Iron Shackles" (black rights), "Father's a Drunkard, and Mother Is Dead" (temperance), and "Only a Pawn in Their Game" (counterculture). The anti-slavery song "Sometimes I Feel Like a Motherless Child" describes the plight of the slave. The anti-civil rights song entitled "The Great Society" describes the terrible state of the country under Lyndon Johnson. And the satirical anti-Vietnam War song "Kill for Peace" exclaims that when Americans do not like the way people walk, talk, or threaten their status, they "kill, kill, kill, burn, burn, burn." The counterculture song "Pollution" describes life in the city:

> Just go out for a breath of air,
> And you'll be ready for Medicare.
> The city streets are really quite a thrill,
> If the hood don't get you, monoxide will.
> Pollution, pollution,
> Wear a gasmask and a veil,
> Then you can breathe long as you don't inhale.

The life cycle of social movements seems to determine how much songs emphasize the present. For instance, eight out of ten songs of movements such as the black rights and farm movements that rarely went beyond the stage of social unrest focus on the present compared to only about three in ten songs of the civil rights and populist movements that had lengthy periods of enthusiastic mobilization.[12] Social movements seem to devote more attention to transforming perceptions of reality when they are attempting to create awareness of an urgent problem and less attention to such perceptions once they become dynamic forces clashing with institutions.

The Future

While more songs address the future than the past, the numbers are far smaller than ones focusing on the present. Unlike treatments of either the past or the present that tend to be dreary, most portrayals of the future are positive.[13] For example, the eight-hour movement song "Divide the Day" envisions a day when there will be work for all, plenty of food, and joy in the homes of the workers. In "When the Revolution Comes," socialists sing of a future when robbers, editors, policemen, landlords, and capitalists will no longer frighten workers and will have to "live by honest labor!" And "Dawn of Correction" counters the "Eve of Destruction" with a future full of peace, inventions, medical breakthroughs, and a better life for all.

Not all portrayals of the future are positive, however. Anti-civil rights and counterculture movements portray gloomy visions of the future in songs such as "Darling I'm Growing Old," "Black Power Never," "Trouble Comin' Everyday," and "Child of Our Times." The anti-nuclear power movement alludes often to the future because, except for a few plant accidents, it has only the future to warn about. "No Seabrook Over Me" is sung to the tune of the civil rights song "Oh, Freedom" and contains such verses as:

> No radiation gettin' me . . .
> No fail-safe systems failin' me . . .
> No human errors wastin' me . . .
> No radioactive garbage dumped on me . . .
> No thermal pollution cookin' me . . .

The majority of both negative and positive portrayals of the future are brief. For example, the anti-slavery song "My Father, How Long" alludes to a time when "The Lord will call us home . . . where pleasure never dies" and "We'll walk the golden streets of the New Jerusalem." No song is devoted solely or predominantly to transforming perceptions of the future.

If, as Elizabeth Kizer theorizes, "Protest lyrics and their music line have a synergistic effect" by complementing "each other to produce a sum greater than their parts," then verbal and nonverbal elements of protest music can be effective combinations to help social movements transform perceptions of reality.[14] Instruments such as drums, trumpets, guitars, and harmonicas can create a somber, forbidding, haunting, and even apocalyptic mood.[15] Rhythm may reduce inhibitions and defense mechanizations and make audiences more susceptible to rhetorical elements that portray an intolerable situation that warrants urgent attention and action.[16] Cheryl Thomas argues that "rhythm can have a subliminal effect to push the message more strongly.[17] Repetition, sometimes referred to as the heart of persuasion, is a traditional characteristic of music that allows the persuader to reinforce again and again the miserable plight of the slave, laborer, woman, student, white citizen, or gay person. Irvine and Kirkpatrick discovered that "repeated patterns in the melodic structure tend to produce an almost instant light hypnosis" and, "when combined with the physiological responses," may "create a situation in which the listener [singer] has almost no control over the potential persuasion inherent in the lyrical structure of the musical message."[18]

Transforming Perceptions of Society

The Opposition

The majority of protest songs identify the social movement's devil, its major antagonist.[19] Not surprisingly, movements engaged in frequent conflicts with institutions and other social movements and generally regarded as radical and revolutionary contain the most devil appeals, while songs of moderate, less confrontative social movements contain the fewest devil appeals.[20] Most devils are nebulous, unnamed evil forces, groups, or things such as capitalists, men, bankers, bosses, landlords, integrators, war machines, generals, nuclear power plants, and demon rum.[21] Lack of specificity is not surprising. First, few protest songs, unlike speeches or editorials, are created for specific situations or events. Songs are sung in a variety of situations over a period of years or decades and do not become dated when an antagonist dies or resigns or an event fades from memory. Indeed many songs are passed from one social movement to another. "We Shall Overcome," for instance," began as "We Will Overcome," a southern labor song in the 1920s and 1930s, was revised slightly for the civil rights movement, became an important song for black nationalist movements in Africa, and was eventually the anthem for the Catholic rights movement in Northern Ireland.[22] Second, The citation of specific devils (persons or groups) can be dangerous for members of social movements such as anti-slavery and labor who can be easily harmed legally, socially, and economically. Third, social movements tend to be more concerned with large problems such as suffrage, civil rights, and working conditions rather than with individuals or specific organizations.

When a social movement or organization is in direct conflict with a specific person or group, songs identify this devil such as Henry Ford (labor movement of the 1920s and 1930s), Lyndon Johnson (anti-Vietnam War movement), Martin Luther King, Jr. (anti-civil rights movement), the Pullman Palace Car Company and its owner (labor movement of the 1890s), the Nuclear Regulatory Commission (anti-nuclear power movement), and Governor George Wallace of Alabama, Governor Ross Barnet of Mississippi, and Police Chief "Bull" Connor of Birmingham (civil rights movement). A few songs are devoted entirely to devils. For example, anti-nuclear power groups sang "The Meldrim Thompson Song" (Governor of New Hampshire) and "The Lemon Tree" (attacking the Public Service Company) during their efforts to stop construction of the nuclear power plant at Seabrook, New Hampshire. The Labor song "Ballad of the Chicago-Memorial Day Massacre of 1937," composed after a bloody confrontation at Republic Steel, attacked its owner Tom Gilder.

Very few songs contain conspiracy appeals, claims that two or more groups were making secret and concerted efforts (literally conspiring) to harm the movement. The populist movement and the 1900–1940 period of the labor movement use conspiracy appeals most frequently. Populists sing about "the cursed snare—the Money Ring," spying and plotting by landlords, banks, and merchants, and the banding together of monopolies. Labor songs refer to members being "framed up by the law," mine owners "framing men to jail," and "The bosses' justice" ordering "cops and thugs to give them lead." Even social movements that clash frequently with a variety of institutions and resistance movements, encounter organized opposition, and have a paranoid flavor in their persuasive efforts, do not sing of conspiracies. These movements and movement organizations include the I.W.W. (Industrial Workers of the world), anti-civil rights, anti-Vietnam War, counterculture (moderate and radical), socialist, temperance, women's rights, women's liberation, gay liberation, anti-slavery, and the pre-Civil War labor movement. Perhaps conspiracy appeals are too complex for brief songs; it is simpler to list a devil or two. Another possibility is that we have overestimated the role of conspiracy appeals in social movement rhetoric.

Songs employ surprisingly mild language toward the opposition. Only about one in four songs contains invective, and this is almost always aimed at the social movement's devil: tyrants, usurpers, thugs, agitators, oppressors, masters, and lords.[23] A few sing about "race hate fascists," "ghouls of gain," "mule-hearted screwers," "fornicating preachers," and "mean . . . wicked . . . heartless . . . cruel deceivers." Very few approach the level of verbal venom exhibited in the labor movement's "You Low Life Son of a Bitch" with its profanity and references to the boss as thief, snitch, skunk, pimp, swine, snake, cheat, and "baby-starving . . . organizer of death." Movements that perceive themselves locked in a "no-holds-barred" mortal conflict with vicious institutions or other social movements resort to invective far more often than reform-oriented movements noted for moderate persuasive tactics.[24]

Although many practitioners and students of social protest agree with Saul Alinsky that "Ridicule is man's most potent weapon,"[25] few songs employ ridicule. As we might expect, radical-revolutionary movements or organizations use ridicule most often, and moderate reform movements that try to minimize confrontations use no ridicule, including black rights, civil rights, farm, temperance, and anti-nuclear power movements. When ridicule occurs in social movement music, it tends to be a heavy-handed effort to degrade the opposition. Thus, civil rights advocates are niggers, apes, and jigaboos; police are pigs; factory owners are cowardly fobs; and workers and blacks who do not join or support the movement are scabs, Uncle Toms, stools, cruel knaves, or slackers. Anti-civil rights songs such as "Banjo Lip," "Who Likes a Nigger," and "That's the Way a Nigger Goes" contain vicious caricatures of black Americans. Labor songs such as "The Scabs Crawl In," "Casey Jones the Union Scab," and "Scissor Bill" attack nonunion workers, especially ones that helped owners to break strikes.

A few songs employ satire or parody, and most of these appear in two twentieth-century movements: anti-Vietnam War and moderate counterculture.[26] Anti-war protestors, for instance, sing "The Draft Dodger Rag," "With God on Our Side," "Feel Like I'm Fixin' to Die Rag," and "Kill for Peace." Counterculture protestors sing "The Merry Minuet," "The Lament of a Minor Dean," "Mine Eyes Have Seen the Horror of the Coming of the Reds," and "Hex on Sex." Interestingly, most music of these two movements, unlike social movement music of earlier periods, is composed and sung by professional commercial artists. The labor movement 1865–1900 did have its parody of "America"; the I.W.W. satirized "Christians at War"; and the abolitionists had a special version of "My Country." The majority of social movement songs, however, are either devoid of humor or employ a meat cleaver approach to ridicule that appeals to the guttural instincts of movement members rather than a scalpel approach of satire and parody that would appeal to a variety of audiences.

The Self

The majority of social movement songs identify workers, blacks, whites, women, wives, gays, or farmers as innocent victims of circumstances and forces beyond their control.[27] The guilty forces range from humans (white folks, husbands, bosses, preachers, landlords, rumsellers, and bankers) to things (idol gold, rum, and mushroom clouds), to an all encompassing "they." Songs identify the innocent victims for which the movement is struggling as slaves, wage slaves, factory slaves, white slaves (prostitutes), and even slaves of the slaves (women). Some songs try to enhance self-concept by claiming victims were duped, deceived, lied to, embezzled, or framed. For every innocent victim, there was an evil and overpowering victimizer taking advantage of their naivete, trust, weak condition, or ignorance.

Social movements that feel a critical need to establish or to defend self-identity or self-worth delve often into the self through music. Songs dealing with self-concept cry out: we are somebody; we are important; we make contributions; or, we are strong! These declarations dominate songs such as "I Am Woman," "Don't Put Her Down," and "The Liberated Woman's Husband's Talking Blues" of the women's liberation movement; "The Farmer Is the Man," "A Hayseed Like Me," and "The Hand that Holds the Bread" of the populist movement; and "Okie from Muskogee," "Segregation Wagon," and "Nigger Hatin' Me" of the anti-civil rights movement. Some songs describe the achievements or contributions of the social movement's primary audience. For example, the socialist "Hymn of the Proletariat" asks:

Who hammers brass and stone?
Who raiseth from the mine?

Who weaveth cloth and silk?
Who tilleth wheat and vine?
Who worketh for the rich to feed,
Yet lives himself in sorest need?
It is the men who toil, the Proletariat.

Some songs attempt to counteract commonly held negative stereotypes about black, gay, female, or elderly Americans. The Gray Panther song "Over 65" paints a different picture of senior citizens in these sample verses:

Over sixty-five and I'm not only alive,
I'm up and at it,
Where some have had it.
Not only out and doing,
Indeed the blood's renewing.
There's no glimmer of a rocker,
Next week I'm starting soccer.
And the fastest Knickerbocker beware!
Though I'm retired,
I'm more inspired and more admired than ever before.
I've taken up Karate,
So I'll take on anybody, foul or fair!

More than half of the songs that treat self-concept overtly attempt to activate audiences rather than to enhance feelings of self-identity or self-worth. One tactic is to challenge singers and listeners to "show the world you're a man" (anti-civil rights); "Be brave, be human, not a slave" (socialist); "Come forth and prove your manliness . . . come forth, ye women, be true mothers" (labor 1865–1900); and "Dare to be a union man: Dare to stand alone" (labor 1865–1900). A second tactic is to pose challenging rhetorical questions. The labor song of the 1930s entitled "Which Side Are You On?" asks, "Will you be a lousy scab, Or will you be a man;" the civil rights version of this labor song asks, "Will you be an Uncle Tom, Or will you be a man?" A labor song of the 1865–1900 period asks, "Shall we yield our manhood, and to oppression bow?" The song "Freedom," sung by the eight-hour workday movement, asks, "Has nature's thrift given thee naught but honey's gift? See! the drones are on the wing, have you lost your will to sting?" A third tactic is to relate personal conversion experiences. The populist song "A Hayseed Like Me" begins the first verse with "I was once a tool of oppression" and the last verse with "But now I've roused up a little." The gay liberation song "Second Chance" contains the following verse:

You know once I was something like you,
I was scared to try anything new.
Well then love it conquered,
Let's see what it can do for you.

The 1930s labor song "Boom Went the Boom" tells how "I thought the boss was my best friend" but "I wish I had been wise, next time I'll organize." A fourth tactic is to arouse guilt feelings. For example, the anti-Vietnam War song "Better Days" admits that "I remember I was smiling as they sent you off—to where? I don't remember." The civil rights song "The Ballad of Bill Moore" relates the bravery of an assassinated civil rights protestor and notes, "he dared to walk there [Alabama] by himself, none of us here were walking with him." "Radiation Blues," an anti-nuclear power song, has a child of the future asking:

> Tell me Papa why you didn't say no,
> To nuclear power years ago.
> Tell me Papa why you didn't say no,
> You let it slip away.

Labor movement songs of the nineteenth century allude to the bravery of the American revolutionaries and the cowardliness of their children. "The Working Men" song declares, "To break, we should be ashamed, the bond our fathers framed." And the song "Swell Our Ranks" laments:

> Oh, ye old and peerless heroes!
> Who did battle for us all,
> In the days of freedom's life-throes,
> Look not earthward on our fall!
> Look not on your servile offspring,
> Who to brothers bend the knee,
> Afraid to utter thoughts within them,
> Or do battle with the free.

A fifth tactic is to portray the terrible status of the oppressed. "Woman Is Nigger of the World" relates how society forces women to behave, dress, and think while turning them into "the slave of the slaves." The black rights song "Ain't It Hard to Be a Nigger" describes how blacks are treated in society and at work. One verse reads:

> Nigger and white man,
> Playin' seven-up;
> Nigger win de money,
> Skeered to pick it up.

The importance for social movements to polarize society by creating we-they distinctions is undisputed. However, social movement music seems to be more effective in creating and attacking devils than in enhancing the virtuous selves. After studying the ego function of protest songs, Charles Stewart notes that the often repeated image of an innocent, duped victim, while satisfactory for the early consciousness-raising stages of a movement, must be replaced with an image of bravery, power, unity, importance, and virtue as the movement progresses. "A rhetoric that emphasizes these points," he claims, "is essential for locating protestors positively in the social hierarchy, for extricating them from symbolically defensive positions in a hostile environment, and for achieving a new unity, identity, and condition.''[28] Escaping from victimage might allow music to enhance self-concepts more effectively because of its unique characteristics. For example, Ralph Knupp writes that "Protest songs provide a forum in which a movement can talk about itself at its best and its opponents at their worst, without accountability to provide reasons.[29] Irvine and Kirkpatrick note that "A steady line in the progression of chords induces in the listener a sense of confidence and/or well-being."[30]

Prescribing Courses of Action

The What

Demands and solutions appear in the majority of social movement songs, but most are ambiguous references.[31] The references are to what Michael McGee terms classic "ideographs" such as freedom, liberty, justice, equality, reform, fair share, human rights, and dignity.[32] Some demands or solutions are vague allusions to ending the war, gaining civil rights, killing Jim Crow (southern segregation laws), achieving integration, attaining fair compensation (rewards for toil, higher wages, just pay), working shorter hours, obtaining leisure time, and having peaceful homes with quiet firesides. A few songs contain specific demands such as equal pay for equal work, a limit to the workday (ranging from four to twelve hours), the right to vote, collective bargaining, greenbacks and bonds, and an end to nuclear tests and nuclear power plants. Highly specific demands appear in songs from single-issue oriented social movements (an eight-hour workday from the eight-hour movement and universal suffrage from the suffrage phase of the women's rights movement) or in songs written for specific social movement campaigns ("No Seabrook" in the anti-nuclear power effort to end construction of the Seabrook power plant and "60 Cents a Ton" during a coal miner's strike in the 1900–1940 period of the labor movement).[33]

Very few songs include "solutions," and most solutions are simple and nondetailed.[34] For example, the I.W.W. proposes "One Grand Union"; an anti-Vietnam War song proposes to "Stop the War, right now"; an anti-nuclear power song recommends that America "look toward the sun and the wind" for power; socialists propose a "worker's commonwealth"; and two versions of the same song ("Talking Union" and "Talking Lesbian") urge listeners and singers to "build you a union." An occasional song provides some detail. For instance, "Arise Ye Garvey Nation," a song popular during Marcus Garvey's "back to Africa movement" of the 1920s, mentions getting ships and materials strong enough to withstand the storms of the seven seas, training Black Cross nurses, and creating a "motor corps" to "take up the wounded dead" from the battlefields to come. Detailed demands and solutions are few undoubtedly because they are inappropriate and almost impossible for brief, poetic songs.[35]

The Who

Some songs mention the movement, organization, leader, or elite (true believers) who must bring about or stifle change.[36] Most refer to unnamed organizations or movements, but a few name specifics such as the Knights of Labor, the I.W.W., and the Weathermen. Highly organized social movements and ones espousing organization as a means to an end refer to organization most often.

Very few songs mention specific leaders, but a few name Martin Luther King, Jr., Marcus Garvey, and James Sylvis (founder of the first national labor union in America). Some songs name leader-heroes in their songs such as Coxey and his army of unemployed workers, Eugene Debs and the Pullman Strike, and Joe Hill and his miners. The typical social movement song contains no references to leaders, perhaps because songs are "timeless" and not anchored to the here-and-now like speeches, newspapers, and leaflets.

Heroic elites of true believers who are carrying out the social movement's cause appear in some songs. For example, civil rights songs mention freedom riders and freedom fighters; radical counterculture songs praise the Weathermen; and the I.W.W. lauds the "wobblies," as they called fellow I.W.W. members. Few songs praise the elite more profusely than the "Noble Knights of Labor" in the post-Civil War labor movement. One verse reads:

> Oh, the great Knights, the noble Knights of Labor,
> The true Knights, the honest Knights of Labor,
> Like the good old Knights of old, they cannot be bought or sold,
> The great Knights, the noble Knights of Labor.

Highly organized movements and ones confronting established institutions refer to elites most frequently.

The How

Some protest songs prescribe strategies, tactics, and communication channels movements should employ to accomplish their ends.[37] Recommendations include picket lines, marches, demonstrations, strikes, boycotts, votes, sit-ins, stand-ins, agitation, singing, nonviolent protest, disruptions, freedom rides, talk, thoughts, organization, and running away. Some suggestions are original. The song "Over 65" by the gray power movement explains, "And when a nose needs tweaking, I'm right at it and critiquing everywhere." The anti-civil rights song "Black Power Never" urges audiences to "wear your never buttons, and wave your rebel flags." The labor song "Stick 'Em Up" recommends placement of black and red stickerettes "on every slave-pen in the land, on every fence and tree" so "No matter where you look you'll see a little red stickerette."

Contrary to stereotypes of social movement actions, very few songs advocate violence. One anti-civil rights song recommends running civil rights leaders out of town on a rail, and another proposes shipping "twenty million jigaboos" back to Africa on leaking boats so they will drown on the way. One women's liberation song, "Don't Say Sister (Until You Mean It)," urges violence in self-defense: "When they stab you in the back, Give me a knife and watch me use it." Only one movement, radical counterculture, advocates violence over persuasion. For example, this movement advocates assassination in "Stop Your Imperialist Plunder," gasoline bombs in "We Are the Trashmen," armed struggle and riots in "White Riot," and attacks on police in "Fa La La La La." The most frequently recommended strategy in songs, however, is the ballot box. Even socialists who advocated "revolution" and the I.W.W. with its radical image propose the ballot as the primary means of bringing about change. All phases of the labor movement advocate change through peaceful, constitutional means. A Knights of Labor song entitled "The Grand Labor Cause" declares that "the ballot's our only salvation." Another song declares, "Not by cannon nor by saber . . ., Thought is stronger far than weapons." Although society often perceives social movements as collectives of bomb-throwing radicals, most social movement songs advocate moderate and legitimate means of change.

Highly organized social movements in the stage of enthusiastic mobilization and preoccupied with means refer most frequently to strategies, tactics, and channels. For example, two out of ten civil rights songs and no black rights contain references to strategies, tactics, and channels. Sociologist R. Serge Denisoff claims that as social movements have become less ideological during this century, their songs have grown less ideological.[38] If what, who, and how are the primary elements of ideology,[39] twentieth-century protest songs are neither more nor less ideological than their nineteenth-century counterparts. Songs do present highly simplified versions of movement ideology, and they appear not to have changed much since the nineteenth century.[40] Degree of organization, movement life cycle, and cause appear to be more influential in whether or not ideology is present than historical period.

Mobilizing the Movement

Calls to Action

The majority of songs call upon audiences to act in some way: sing, march, demonstrate, picket, vote, organize, strike, talk, disrupt, agitate, and run away. A few challenge listeners to "stand up and be counted," "go tell it on the mountain," "give your hands to the struggle," or "dump the bosses off your back." Actions are often dangerous because of possible institutional reactions and sometimes embarrassing for conservative religious groups and others that have always had a reverence for the law and avoided calling attention to themselves in public. Rhythm of music may "reduce the inhibitions and defense mechanisms" of singers and listeners and make them more willing to lie down in front of an abortion clinic, sit-in a dean's office, be dragged to a police van, or face the taunting jeers and threats of those unsympathetic to the movement.[41] Singing can also give protestors the courage to demonstrate and continue the fight in the face of violence or arrest.[42] A Georgia NAACP organizer comments that "the people were cold with fear until music [broke] the ice."[43] Martin Luther King, Jr. commented in a television interview:

> These freedom songs serve to give unity to a movement, and there have been those moments when disunity could have occurred if it had not been for the unifying force of freedom songs. . . . The movement has also been carried on by these songs because they have a tendency to give courage and vigor to carry on.[44]

Most movements have songs that create this courage and vigor in the face of resistance. Civil rights has "We Shall Overcome" and "We Shall Not Be Moved"; the abolition movement has "Many Thousand Gone" and "I'm on My way"; and women's liberation has "I Am Woman" and "I've Got a Fury."

The most common pleas are to join and unite in the struggle against evil. "The Liberty Tree" of the American Revolution proclaims, "Let the far and the near, All unite with a cheer, In defense of our Liberty Tree." The refrain of the black rights song "Arise Ye Garvey Nation" contains these lines: "On and on swell the chorus, On and on, Marcus Garvey, on before us, On and on swell the chorus." The civil rights song "Keep Your Eyes on the Prize" exclaims, "The only chain that a man can stand, Is that chain of hand in hand." A number of theorists have pointed to the unifying factor of music that comes from singing as a group rather than as individuals. Cheryl Thomas writes that the "sing along" nature of social movement music creates and reinforces feelings of unity, togetherness, and camaraderie.[45] Elizabeth Kizer notes that protest music reinforces and promotes "a sense of community among followers."[46] And David Bloodworth claims that music is effective in uniting a group behind a certain cause.[47] Singing allows the individual to become an active part of the whole that is the social movement.

Because songs are usually sung either by highly credible sources or by audiences themselves, they present excellent opportunities for self-persuasion through statements of personal intent. As Irvine and Kirkpatrick write, The "new amplificative meaning generated includes identification and commitment from the auditor. The new meaning is personalized and, therefore, self-persuasive."[48] For example, a black rights song declares, "Well now I shall not be moved"; a civil rights song exclaims, "I gotta fight for my freedom"; a labor song proclaims, "I'm too old to be a scab"; an anti-nuclear power song declares, "I'm gonna stand here and protest"; a gray power song warns, "so I'll take on anybody, foul or fair"; and a migrant worker's song intones, "The picket sign, the picket sign, I carry it all day long." Twentieth-century songs contain more personal intents more frequently than do nineteenth-century songs, perhaps because social movements of this century have faced less brutal repression and have moved into later stages of their life cycles. In fact, many of them are essentially continuations of social movements started last century, particularly black rights, women's rights, and labor.

Appeals Beyond the Movement

Following a comparison of samples of labor songs with anti-Vietnam War songs, Ralph Knupp concludes that "The rhetorical patterns in protest songs suggest that they are largely in-group activities."[49] The present study supports this conclusion because only a handful of the 714 selected songs appeal overtly to outsiders or to potential legitimizers for sympathy or assistance. Occasionally a song appeals to the feelings and consciences of outsiders. For example, the labor song "Thirty Cents a Day" tells of a young maiden dying from long hours, brutal work, and starvation. The last verse begins, "Too late, Christian ladies! You cannot save her now; She breathes out her life, See the death damp on her brow." The anti-slavery song "A Pilgrim of God" describes the condition of slaves and their pleas for help. It ends:

> But while your kindest sympathies
> To foreign lands do roam,
> I would ask you to remember
> Your own oppressed at home.

"Links on a Chain" by Phil Ochs appeals to labor unions to help blacks in their struggle for equal rights and jobs.

While most protest songs do not appeal directly for outside support, many appeal for help and legitimacy indirectly. For instance, many protest songs are modeled after or sung to the tune of traditional religious hymns or patriotic songs. Denisoff writes that this practice ties the social movement to religion, traditions, and the national heritage.[50] Thus, songs use the patterns or melody of "Casey Jones," "Battle Hymn of the Republic," "Marching Through Georgia," "America," "Dixie," "Swanee," "The Old Rugged Cross," and "Oh Freedom." Thomas, Irvine, and Kirkpatrick claim that legitimacy can be transferred to the social movement from religious, common, and traditional songs or verses.[51] Some movements use the originals. For instance, Roman Catholic protestors have marched to pro-life Operation Rescue sites singing "Ave Maria," one of the best known and loved of Catholic hymns.[52]

About one in ten songs make overt threats to established institutions or their agents. The anti-slavery song "Nat Turner," written shortly after Nat Turner's bloody slave uprising, warns slave owners:

> You might be as rich as cream,
> And ride you a coach and four-horse team;
> But you can't keep the world from moving around,
> And Nat Turner from gaining ground.

The I.W.W. tune "Harvest War Song" warns, "We are coming home, John Farmer, We are coming home to stay." The civil rights song "Oh Wallace" warns the Alabama governor: "Oh Wallace, you never can jail us all, Oh Wallace, segregation's bound to fail." And the gay rights song "Leaping" contains these verses:

Here come the lesbians,
Here come the leaping lesbians.
We're going to please you, tease you,
Hypnotize you, try to squeeze you.
We're going to get you if we can,
Here come the lesbians.
You can't escape, you're in our hands,
Here come the lesbians.

Although threats appear in some songs, social movement music seems to talk a great deal more about the opposition than to the opposition. As Knupp claims, songs tend to be for in-house consumption.

Victory is Near

Some songs predict that victory is at hand for the social movement.[53] For instance, the black rights song "One Day Old and No Damn Good" portrays a hard present and then reassures, "This nightmare, babe, can't last the night; We'll end it soon, both black and white." Other songs proclaim that "Freedom's comin' and it won't be long;" "Oppression's expiring, and soon will be past;" "The joyful hour is coming, 'tis the dawn before the day;" and "It's coming fast—our turn, at last—the social revolution." The majority of social movement songs tend to be dreary and pessimistic, particularly twentieth-century songs. All songs with the fewest references to immediate victory are in the twentieth century, perhaps because many struggles have gone on too long to believe success is imminent.

Sustaining the Movement

Justifying Setbacks and Delays

None of the 714 selected songs attempt to explain setbacks and delays either in the past or the present. This was the only function not apparent in protest songs.

Commitment to the Movement

Some songs attempt to reinforce commitment to the social movement.[54] They assure listeners that "perseverance conquers all," that "the union makes us strong," and that "our hearts and hands in union strong, not fear or threats can swerve." Other songs urge listeners to "stick together," to "hang in there a little bit longer," to "hold the fort," to "fight on undaunted," and to "be firm and valiant-hearted." Others involve audiences in singing pledges of commitment. A Revolutionary War-era song proclaims, "We are the troop that will never stoop to wretched slavery." A Ku Klux Klan song promises, "we always can be counted on, when there's a job to do." A civil rights song pledges, "We're gonna keep on fighting for freedom, in the end we will be free." A few songs include personal pledges or intentions to remain committed to the cause. A women's rights song pledges not to be silenced: "No, I will speak my mind if I die for it." A labor song of the 1930s declares, "I'm a miner's son, and I'll stick with the union, 'til every battle's won." A civil rights version of this labor song exclaims, "I'm a freedom son, I'll stick right with this struggle until the battle's won." Interestingly, the black rights song "I Shall Not Be Moved" was changed to "We Shall Not Be Moved" during the civil rights movement, perhaps an effort to stress the need for collective action and unity rather than individualism. Social movement songs tend to urge people to remain committed or to include collective pledges rather than resort to potentially more persuasive personal pledges. These preferences may reduce opportunities for the influence of highly credible sources or self-persuasion, but they emphasize *collective* action and commitment.

Ultimate Victory

Some songs assure movement supporters that victory will come ultimately if they sustain their efforts.[55] For example, perhaps the most famous of all social movement songs, "We Shall Overcome," proclaims "We shall overcome someday" and "we'll walk hand in hand someday." The temperance song "Victory" predicts that "In the sweet by and by, we'll conquer the demon of rum." The song "Better Days Are Yet to Come," designed to lessen the influence of "Eve of Destruction," pleads "Listen to me everyone, better days are yet to come." The Knights of Labor song "The Good Time Coming" begins with this verse:

> There's a good time coming, boys,
> A good time coming;
> We may not live to see the day,
> But earth shall glisten in the nay,
> Of the good time coming.

Optimism is higher in nineteenth-century songs than in twentieth century-songs and more frequent in songs of highly organized and less confrontational movements. The overall level of optimism, however, is lower than one would expect of protest songs, perhaps because many struggles have faced too many setbacks and gone on too long for expressions of optimism.

The Movement's Heritage

A number of writers have claimed that social movement songs rely heavily upon references to past heroes, martyrs, victories, and tragedies to sustain commitment of supporters and the movement's forward progress. This study does not substantiate these claims. Only about one in ten songs mention heroes or martyrs. The majority refer to assassinated leaders or followers such as Medgar Evers, Bill Moore, Malcolm X, and Martin Luther King, Jr. of the civil rights movement; to persons unfairly arrested and convicted or executed such as Joe Hill, Sacco and Vanzetti of the labor movement, and the Scottsboro boys and Ferguson brothers of the black rights movement; or to victims such as peasants in Vietnam, coal miners, "labor's sons and daughters," child factory workers, and mythical workers such as John Henry. A small number refer to heroes such as the Founding Fathers, Abraham Lincoln, Mother Jones (an early labor leader), Momma Rosa Parks (a black seamstress who refused to give up her seat to a white male passenger and thus sparked the Montgomery bus boycott led by the young Reverend Martin Luther King, Jr.), James Meredith (the first black student at the University of Mississippi), and Harriet Tubman (a black anti-slavery leader).

Very few songs refer to tragedies or victories. For instance, a handful of labor songs relate the details of disasters such as "The Ludlow Massacre," "1913 Massacre at Calumet, Michigan," "The Marion, North Carolina, Massacre," and "The Ballad of the Chicago-Memorial Day Massacre of 1937." About the same number recall victories such as successful strikes, passage of important legislation such as an eight-hour law in Illinois, or the bringing down of Chicago during the 1968 Democratic National Convention.

Few songs are designed to sustain social movements. Most are composed during the social unrest and enthusiastic mobilization stages, before most tragedies and victories take place and before most heroes and martyrs are enshrined. When movements sing during the maintenance stage, they apparently select from among the movement's traditional songs such as "We Shall Overcome," "Solidarity Forever," and "We Shall Not Be Moved" rather than compose new ones.

Conclusions

All of the general and specific persuasive functions except justifying setbacks and delays appear in the 714 social movement songs analyzed for this chapter. Most songs perform two or more major persuasive functions; more songs perform all five major functions than perform a single function. Thus, although they are simplistic, brief, and poetic in nature, they are more complex persuasive channels than suggested by some theorists.[56]

The majority of song lyrics describe the present, identify one or more devils, list demands or solutions, and urge movement members to act and remain committed to the cause. They tend to be negative rather than positive, pessimistic rather than optimistic, general rather than specific, and mild rather than abrasive in language. While most songs address the in-group rather than potential legitimizers or the opposition, they are rarely "organization centered." Songs attempt to enhance self-concept (identity or self-worth) and praise the movement, movement options, leaders, and the elite. They are more concerned with transforming perceptions of the present rather than the past or the future. They dwell upon large problems rather than individuals and tend to identify abstract demands (freedom, equality, liberty, justice) rather than specific problems or solutions. Songs contain few threats and prescribe few violent actions. They plead, instead, for fair treatment and urge followers to use lawful means, primarily the ballot box, to bring about or resist change. Few songs seem designed to sustain social movements overtly. A few urge audiences to remain committed to the cause and assure them of ultimate victory. Very few mention movement heroes, martyrs, tragedies, or victories.

The persuasive content of songs varies considerably from song to song within the same movement, between movements, and over time. Although many differences are not explainable, there are some apparent patterns. For instance, twentieth-century songs refer to the past and to movement heritage more often than do nineteenth-century songs, perhaps because there is more of each to talk about. Twentieth-century songs include tasteful satire more often (perhaps because of involvement of commercial composers in the 1960s and 1970s), more statements of personal intent, and a greater degree of pessimism. The songs of highly organized social movements exude more optimism, are more movement centered, and address more often the strategies, tactics, and communication channels movements should employ to achieve their ends. Songs of single-issue movements or composed during social movement campaigns are more specific, especially when treating demands and solutions. Songs of radical social movements and ones in desperate struggles with established institutions deal more with the opposition and employ more ridicule and invective. Attempts to transform perceptions of reality appear more often in and tend to dominate songs composed during the social unrest stage of social movements.

The nonverbal elements of music complement the verbal. For example, instruments help to create the somber, forbidding, and haunting views of reality presented in lyrics. Rhythm may reduce inhibitions and defense mechanisms to aid movement members in viewing reality and social relationships in prescribed ways and make them willing to act in spite of dangers, social pressures, and social inhibitions. Repetition ''drums in'' versions of reality, the evil of devils, the plight of victims, demands, the necessity of unity, and commitment. The steady line in the progression of chords may induce a sense of confidence and well-being. And since singing is often a group activity, it not only promotes feelings of togetherness but may enhance self-persuasion.

Endnotes

[1] Plato, *The Republic*, B. Jowett, trans. (New York: Modem Library, n.d.), Book IV, 424, 135.

[2] R. Serge Denisoff, *Sing a Song of Social Significance* (Bowling Green, OH: Bowling Green University Popular Press, 1972), 19. Cited from Jerome Rodnitzky, ''The New Revivalism: American Protest Songs, 1945–1968,'' paper delivered at American Studies Association convention, 1969.

3 David Noebel, *The Marxist Minstrels: A Handbook on Communist Subversion of Music* (Tulsa: American Christian College Press, 1974), 1.

4 Denisoff (1972), 137.

5 Denisoff (1972), 137–145.

6 Charles J. Stewart, "The Ego Function of Protest Songs: An Application of Gregg's Theory of Protest Rhetoric," *Communication Studies* 42 (Fall 1991), 241. See also David M. Rosen, *Protest Songs in America* (West Lake Village, CA: Aware Press, 1972), 21–23; and R. Serge Denisoff, *Great Day Coming: Folk Music and the American Left* (Urbana, IL: University of Illinois Press, 1971), 18–39. Stephen Kosokoff and Carl W. Carmichael, "The Rhetoric of Protest: Song, Speech, and Attitude Change," *Southern Speech Communication Journal* 35 (Summer 1970), 295–302.

7 John David Bloodworth, "Communication in the Youth Counter Culture: Music as Expression," *Central States Speech Journal* 26 (Winter 1975), 304–309.

8 Texts for the songs came from records, tape recordings, and printed sources such as Philip S. Foner, ed. *American Labor Songs of the Nineteenth Century* (Urbana: University of Illinois Press, 1975); Tom Glazer, ed. *Songs of Peace, Freedom, and Protest* (New York: David McKay, 1970); John Greenway, ed. *American Folk Songs of Protest* (Philadelphia: University of Pennsylvania Press, 1953); David M. Rosen, ed. *Protest Songs in America* (Westlake Village, CA: Aware Press, 1972); *Songs of the Workers: To Fan the Flames of Discontent* (Chicago: Industrial Workers of the World, 1974).

Each song was coded according to how it appeared to perform the general and specific functions presented in chapter 3. Each song was coded twice and students in a persuasion course at Purdue University coded a sample of songs both to refine the coding scheme and to reduce the problem of identifying persuasive functions that were not apparent in the content of the songs. Because songs are brief messages, no count was made of each occurrence of the same function in each song. The procedure was to note if and how each function was performed in a given song. Frequency counts were limited to social movements for which a minimum of ten songs was available for analysis.

9 The anti-American aristocracy movement developed after the Revolutionary War in opposition to placing political power in the hands of wealthy landholders. The populist movement was strong in the late 19th century and demanded more control for the "common people," laws to protect farmers and enhance their economic status, the free coinage of silver, and government control of monopolies. The counterculture movement of the 1960s and 1970s demanded fundamental changes in American society and values and all power in the hands of "the people." The antiwar movement from 1865 to 1940 opposed all involvement of America in military conflicts, including the Spanish-American War, World War I, and World War II. The Farm movement from 1925–1980 demanded better prices and economic security for farm owners.

10 Only 13% of the songs studied contain references to the past.

11 Sixty-one percent of the songs studied portray the present, and 96% of these portrayals are negative.

12 Eighty-one percent of black rights and 83% of farm movement songs deal with the present compared to 39% for the civil rights movement and 29% for the populist movement.

13 Eighteen percent of selected songs portray the future, and 73% of these are positive.

14 Elizabeth J. Kizer, "Protest Song Lyrics as Rhetoric," Popular Music & Society 9 (1983), 6.

15 Cheryl Irwin Thomas, "'Look What They've Done to My Song, Ma': The Persuasiveness of Song," *Southern Speech Communication Journal* 39 (Spring 1974), 260–268.

16 James R. Irvine and Walter G. Kirkpatrick, "The Musical Form in Rhetorical Exchange: Theoretical Considerations." *Quarterly Journal of Speech* 58 (October 1971), 272–284.

17 Thomas, 261.

18 Irvine and Kirkpatrick, 275–276.

19 Sixty percent of the selected songs identify a social movement's devil.

20 Social movement songs with most references to devils are: radical counterculture 83%, Populist 82%, I.W.W. 81%, and Labor 1900–1940 79%. Songs with fewest references to devils are: moderate counterculture 42%, anti-slavery/abolition 42%, civil rights 41%, and anti-nuclear power 36%.

21 Eighty percent of devils are nebulous, vague persons or forces.

22 Rosen, 80.

23 Twenty-seven percent of selected songs contained invective or name-calling.

24 Social movement songs with most invective are: I.W.W. 57%, eight-hour 54%, anti-civil rights 50%, radical counterculture 50%, and labor 1865–1900 48%. Social movement songs with the least invective are: moderate counterculture 9%, civil rights 5%, women's liberation 4%, gay liberation 4%, and anti-Vietnam war 3%.

25 Saul D. Alinsky, *Rules for Radicals: A Practical Primer for Realistic Radicals* (New York: Vintage Books, 1972), 128.

26 Only 3% of selected songs use parody or satire.

27 Stewart, 242–243.

28 Stewart, 251.

29 Ralph E. Knupp, "A Time for Every Purpose Under Heaven: Rhetorical Dimensions of Protest Music," *Southern Speech Communication Journal* 46 (Summer 1981), 377–389.

30 Irvine and Kirkpatrick, 276.

31 Fifty-four percent of selected songs contain demands or solutions.

32 Michael C. McGee, "The 'Ideograph': A Link Between Rhetoric and Ideology," *Quarterly Journal of Speech* 66 (February 1980), 1–16.

33 Social movement songs with most demands and solutions include eight-hour 96%, socialist 82%, labor 1865–1900 77%, and civil rights 75%. Social movements songs with fewest demands and solutions include moderate counterculture 21 %, radical counterculture 17%, farm 17%, and black rights 14%.

34 Five percent of selected songs contain solutions.

35 Gerald P. Mohrmann and F. Eugene Scott, "Popular Music and World War II: The Rhetoric of Continuation," *Quarterly Journal of Speech* 62 (April 1976), 145–156.

36 Twenty-seven percent of selected songs mention who ought to do the job.

37 Nineteen percent prescribe how movements should attain their ends.

38 Denisoff, 78–79.

39 John Wilson, *Introduction to Social Movements* (New York: Basic Books, 1973), 89–150.

40 Social movement songs with most references to demands and solutions are socialist 82%, labor 1800–1900 78%, civil rights 75%, anti-nuclear power 68%, and gay liberation 65%.

41 Irvine and Kirkpatrick, 277.

42 David A. Carter, "The Industrial Workers of the World and the Rhetoric of Song," *Quarterly Journal of Speech* 66 (December 1980), 373–374.

43 Denisoff 1972), 57.

44 Denisoff (1972), 75–76.

45 Thomas, 262–263, 265.

46 Kizer, 7.

47 Bloodworth, 309.

48 Irvine and Kirkpatrick, 278, 274.

49 Knupp, 388.

50 Denisoff (1972), 57.

51 Thomas, 263; Irvine and Kirkpatrick, 279.

52 ABC's "20/20," "Operation Rescue."

53 Eleven percent of selected songs proclaimed that victory is near.

54 Twenty-one percent of selected songs urged commitment.

55 Twenty-four percent of selected songs predicted ultimate victory.

56 Mohrmann and Scott, 156.

Chapter Twelve

Political Argument in Social Movements

This chapter explores social movement persuasion by developing a typology of political argument that we can use to compare the persuasive efforts of different movements over time. A typology of political argument enables us to study the types of argument that recur in various movements and in ordinary systemic political rhetoric. Much as the chemist looks for the combination of known elements, the rhetorical analyst can study the ways different social movements use and combine basic kinds of argument. Traditional analysts have relied on the writings of Aristotle and his successors to describe recurrent rhetorical techniques. But, as Herbert Simons suggested many years ago, social movements and the people who carry their arguments can rarely afford to use the logic of polite discussion or university seminars.[1] If we want to taste the distinctive flavor of a social movement's persuasion, we need to approach it on its own terms by studying how the flavor derives from its unique blend of the arguments available to it. A typology of political arguments can help us to understand the kinds of ingredients from which the movement's persuasion is blended.

Rossiter's Political Spectrum

Clinton Rossiter needed a typology of political philosophies within which to discuss *Conservatism in America*.[2] He created a circle marked by seven roughly equidistant points shown in Figure 1. The first of the seven philosophical positions, *Revolutionary Radicalism*, sees societal institutions as "diseased and oppressive, traditional values dissembling and dishonest; and it therefore proposes to supplant them with an infinitely more benign way of life." *Radicalism* is "dissatisfied with the existing order, committed to a blueprint for thoroughgoing change, and thus willing to initiate reform, but its patience and peacefulness set it off sharply

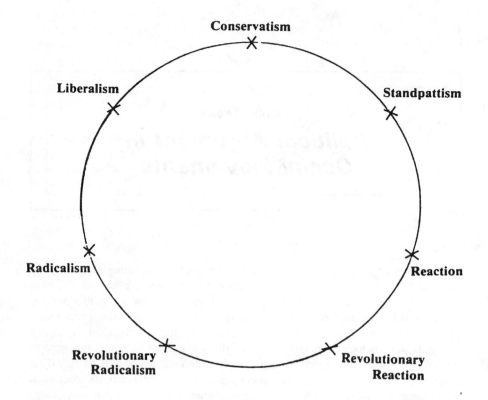

Figure 1

Rossiter's Political Spectrum

from the revolutionary brand." *Liberalism* is generally satisfied with the existing order and believes that this way of life can be improved "substantially without betraying its ideals or wrecking its institutions." *Conservatism*, like Liberalism, is satisfied with the existing order and sees change as necessary and inevitable. But unlike Liberalism, Conservatism is suspicious of change. "The Conservative," says Rossiter, "knows that change is the rule of life . . . but insists that it be sure-footed and respectful of the past . . . . [The Conservative's] natural preferences are for stability over change, continuity over experiment, the past over the future." *Standpattism*, however prefers today over either past or future. Rossiter's Standpattism opposes any change, no matter how respectful of the past. "Despite all evidence to the contrary," Standpattism believes that "society can be made static." If Standpattism prefers today over yesterday and tomorrow, and Conservatism prefers tomorrow over yesterday, *Reaction* "sighs for the past and feels that a retreat back into it, piecemeal or large scale, is worth trying." Reaction is unlike Standpattism in two ways: it is unwilling to accept the present, and it is amenable to changing the present state of society. Reaction, like Radicalism, limits the means it will employ to effect that change. But *Revolutionary Reaction* is willing and anxious to use subversion and violence to overthrow established values and institutions and to restore the era it views as the "Golden Age."

Rossiter's typology contains several rhetorical implications which merit scrutiny. First, it reveals that "revolutionaries" have much in common, whether they seek a New Age or a Golden Age. They are willing to subvert and to kill, and they disdain discussion and compromise.

A second rhetorical implication is that philosophies adjacent to one another share enough fundamental assumptions that their disagreements can be argued in roughly compatible worldviews. The believers in adjacent philosophies appear reasonable to one another in that each regards the other as a potential, if misguided, ally. They concur enough to converse but differ enough to argue.

The third rhetorical implication is that philosophies opposite one another on the circle share no common assumptions. Thus, believers in opposite philosophies make little sense to one another. These partisans have great difficulty persuading one another because their fundamental differences preclude compromise and constrain their ability to adjust to the other's assumptions. Indeed, they are more likely to talk about one another than with one another.

The fourth rhetorical implication of Rossiter's spectrum is consistent with the social judgment approach to attitude change: we distort our comparative judgments when we are ego-involved.[3] This is particularly important to the study of social movements where we are likely to find an abundance of ego-involved persons. When we are ego-involved in a topic, we distance ourselves from all those with whom we disagree and lump them into one perceptual category—even if they disagree with one another. We presume that they must agree with one another if they disagree with us. People also exaggerate their agreement with people whose positions are close to their own.

But despite its usefulness, Rossiter's spectrum has several shortcomings. The points on his circular model are too narrow to capture most political arguments. Moreover, he ignores apathy, ambivalence, and indecision in political theory and argument, thus omitting from his model the intensity and fervor that are so important to social movement rhetoric. Finally, Rossiter overlooked the fact that each of the philosophies he described was an argument with some other philosophy. This is so because, as British social psychologist Michael Billig writes, the process of thinking is argumentative:

> All too often, psychologists have ignored the essentially rhetorical and argumentative dimensions of thinking. Human thinking is not merely a matter of processing information or following cognitive rules. Thinking is to be observed in action in discussions, in the rhetorical cut-and-thrust of argumentation. To deliberate upon an issue is to argue with oneself, even to persuade oneself. It is no linguistic accident that to propose a reasoned justification is rightly called "offering an argument."[4]

Thus do people create, rediscover, and rehearse arguments in anticipation of a chance to voice them. Every argument faces in some direction and implies disagreement with at least one other position. This is not to say that all arguments will be well chosen or supported; indeed they may not be voiced at all. But the set of arguments heard from a social movement provides evidence of their individual and collective thinking.

The Types of Political Argument

We can retain the advantages of Rossiter's spectrum while overcoming its disadvantages by (a) considering the area of the circle as well as its perimeter and (b) regarding the center of the circle as apathy, ambivalence, and/or indecision. The alterations allow us to conceive of Rossiter's seven philosophical types as spokes on a wheel rather than points on a circle, with the pure philosophical stances located on the rim and apathy at the hub. We can imagine various arguments (a) located along some spoke and (b) facing some other philosophical position. The arguments of radical speeches and pamphlets would cluster toward the rim, while dispassionate academic discussions of social injustice might cluster toward the center.

Arguments along the seven spokes (Revolutionary Radical, Radical, Liberal, Conservative, Standpat, Reaction, and Revolutionary Reaction) attempt to reinforce, sustain, intensify, or energize that stance. It is through ''in-group'' argument that, for example, radicals decide just how radical they wish to be. The arguers agree about the nature of change, but disagree about the intensity of their beliefs or about the need for action. The spokes of the wheel delineate seven types of political argument. Arguments found among the spokes—between Radical and Liberal positions, for example, or between the Revolutionary Radical and Revolutionary Reaction positions—are arguments that reflect the arguer's philosophical assumptions rather than their degree of conviction. The seven types of argument delineated by Rossiter's philosophical stances are: Insurgent, Innovative, Progressive, Retentive, Reversive, Restorative, and Revolutionary (see Figure 2). Let us examine each in turn.

Insurgent Argument. Insurgent Argument falls between the Revolutionary Radical and Radical spokes of the model. It is typified by agreement on the corrupt, mendacious, and exploitative nature of societal norms, values and institutions. The established order is vilified and particular individuals, institutions, and groups are held directly accountable for problems. Seldom is heard an encouraging word.

The Industrial Workers of the World (I.W.W.) blamed employers, as a group, for social conditions in America. The preamble to their Constitution of 1908 declared that:

> The working class and the employing class have nothing in common. There can be no peace so long as hunger and want are found among the millions of working people and the few, who make up the employing class, have all the good things in life. Between these two classes a struggle must go on until the workers of the world organize as a class, take possession of the earth and the machinery of production, and abolish the wage system.[5]

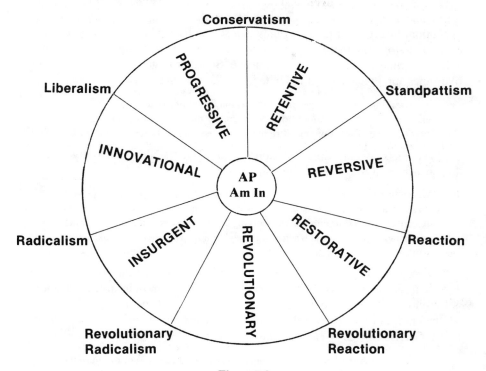

Figure 2
Typology of Political Argument

Labor leader John Swinton was more specific in his denunciation of President Grover Cleveland for breaking the Pullman Strike of 1894:

> [President Cleveland] has this year stood out as a servile, mercenary and pusillanimous politician, the ally of money against manhood, fully ready to exercise his power, real and assumed, for the enslavement of the laborious masses who elected him to office.[6]

Roughly fifty years later, Black Muslim leader Malcolm X blamed the American government in its totality for the condition of Black America. In "The Ballot or the Bullet" he argued that:

> You and I in America are faced not with a segregationist conspiracy, we're faced with a government conspiracy. Everyone who's filibustering is a senator—that's the government. Everyone who's finagling in Washington, D.C. is a congressman—that's the government. You don't have anyone putting blocks in your path but people who are part of the government. The same government that you go abroad to fight and die for is the government that is in a conspiracy to deprive you of your voting rights, deprive you of your economic opportunities, deprive you of decent education.[7]

The I.W.W., John Swinton, and Malcolm X all attributed blame for undesirable social conditions to a group or class of people, an important individual, or institution. Insurgent arguments imply that social ills can be cured by destroying the perpetrator. The more revolutionary strains of insurgent argument condone, at least implicitly, subversion and violence. Socialist Eugene V. Debs, who ran five times for President of the United States, proclaimed that:

> The working class must get rid of the whole brood of masters and exploiters, and put themselves in possession and control of the means of production. . . . It is therefore a question not of reform, the mask of fraud, but of revolution.[9]

Clifford Odets concluded his 1934 proletariat play, "Waiting for Lefty," with this speech by a tough insurgent cab driver:

> AGATE: Christ, we're dyin' by inches! For what? For the debutantees to have their comin' out parties at the Ritz! . . . It's slow death or fight. It's war! . . . Hello America! We're stormbirds of the working class. Workers of the world . . . our bones and our blood! And when we die they'll know what we did to make a new world![9]

Because violent revolution is one boundary of the insurgent category, insurgent arguments do not always call for violent change. Indeed, most insurgent argument is anti-violent. These advocates are not willing to let the new order evolve slowly and naturally, but neither are they prepared to shed blood. Abolitionist William Lloyd Garrison in 1844 exhorted his followers:

> Up, then, with the banner of revolution! Not to shed blood—not to injure the person or estate of an oppressor—not by force of arms to resist any law—not to countenance a servile insurrection—not to wield any carnal weapons! No, ours must be a bloodless strife, excepting our blood be shed . . . to overcome evil with good. . . . Secede, then, from the government. Submit to its exactions, but pay it no allegiance, and give it no voluntary aid."[10]

Even in "Waiting for Lefty," Odets has a disillusioned wife tell her cabdriver husband how to fight the "bosses:"

> JOE: One man can't . . .
>
> EDNA: I don't say one man! I say a hundred, a thousand, a whole million, I say. But start in your own union. Get those hack boys together! Sweep out those racketeers like a pile of dirt! Stand up like men and fight for the crying kids and wives. . . . Get brass toes on your shoes and know where to kick![11]

Insurgent argument, then, is confrontational. It focuses upon one or more social ills, and blames them on persons, institutions, or values which are integral parts of the established order. Strategically, insurgent argument calls for strong action which may or may not be violent.

Innovative Argument.   Innovative argument falls between the Radical and Liberal spokes of the Rossiter model. It is characterized by a nagging dissatisfaction with the existing order and a preference for experimental change. There is an almost equal aversion to violence and the status quo. Fundamental questions include: Is the political system part of the problem or part of the solution? Can the normal channels produce sufficient change? Can actual practice be made to conform with traditional values?

Smith and Windes suggest that it is advisable for social movement persuaders to identify discrepancies between traditional values and current practice and to argue that their innovation is, in fact, more traditional than the status quo.[12] This is a recurrent feature of innovative arguments. American Federation of Labor founder Samuel Gompers tied the goals and tactics of his movement to "Americanism." In a 1908 article, he explained that:

> We American trade unionists want to work out our problems in the spirit of true Americanism—a spirit that embodies our broadest and highest ideals. If we do not succeed, it will be due to no fault of ours. We have been building the A. F. of L. in conformity with what we believe to be the original intent and purpose of America.[13]

Similarly, Martin Luther King's "I Have a Dream" speech grounded his call for integration in both Americanism and Christianity:

> I still have a dream. It is a dream deeply rooted in the American dream. It is a dream that one day this nation will rise up and live out the true meaning of its creed: "We hold these truths to be self-evident; that all men are created equal."
> . . . I have a dream that one day every valley shall be exalted, every hill and mountain shall be made low, the rough places will be made plane and crooked places will be made straight, and the glory of the Lord shall be revealed, and all flesh shall see it together.[14]

A 1993 mailing from the Native American Rights Fund (NARF) begins with an observation by Twila Martin-Kekanhbah, former Chairperson of the Turtle Mountain Band of Chippewa, that voices America's professed values:

> Every Chippewa is taught from birth that these seven basic qualities must guide us as individuals and tribal members: honesty, respect, generosity, kindness, fairness, sharing and spirituality. Only by keeping this path can we meet our responsibilities to ourselves and to one another.[15]

The letter from NARF's Executive Director, John Echowak, proceeds quickly to argue that his people often stand alone with these values:

> Because my people are abused by a system of government that is *not* honest with us, is *not* respectful of our culture or our fundamental rights; a government that continues to degrade and abuse the land on which we all depend.[16]

The problem is that the practices of institutions are unfaithful to the fundamental values that are being upheld by the social movement. "I ask you," writes Echowak, "can America continue to stand proud as a nation revered for its freedoms when its government allows religious freedom—the *first* freedom enunciated in the *First* Amendment—to be just a hollow promise to the *first* Americans?"[17]

Of course, innovative arguments are frequently met by the response that their innovation is unwise or impractical. Many innovative arguments anticipate this response by differentiating the situation in question from similar situations in the past. In a familiar but often misquoted passage, industrialist Henry Ford dismissed history as a standard by which to assess proposed innovation:

> What do we care what they did 500 or 1000 years ago? It means nothing to me.
> History is more or less bunk. It's tradition. We don't want tradition. We want
> to live in the present and the only history that is worth a tinker's damn is the
> history we make today.[18]

Innovative argument, then, seeks substantial changes in the norms, values, or institutions of society without violent action. It grounds its proposals in the society's dominant creeds or values and rejects as irrelevant the suggestion that the innovation cannot or will not work. It is easy to see that innovative argument is safer than insurgent argument. Innovators embrace rather than scorn the principles upon which the society is founded, and they can claim a moral advantage over both their insurgent and institutional adversaries. This enables innovators to confront the immediate but transient manifestations of the social order such as a corrupt official, a discriminatory law, or an unfair labor practice without confronting the social order itself.

The danger of innovative argument is that the more moderate elements of society often mistake innovative argument for insurgency because it seeks major change through the use of "unpleasant" tactics. Just as Gompers' message contrasts with that of Debs, and as King's dream contrasts with Malcolm X's indictment; so any innovative argument should be advanced as a reasonable alternative to insurgency. It argues that major changes are necessary in order for the established order to fulfill its own destiny. But when innovative arguments fail to present such a clear contrast, they are vulnerable to characterization as "subversive" or "revolutionary."

Progressive Argument.   Progressive argument is a clearly "systemic" approach to political argument. By this we mean that unlike insurgent arguments that seek to replace the established means for reconciling differences or innovative arguments that believe in the underlying creed but object to the ways that the society practices that creed, progressive argument takes established procedures as givens.

The philosophies of Liberalism and Conservatism agree that change of some sort is inevitable and that the established system for resolving disagreements should be used. Neither Liberalism nor Conservatism pursues change through "extra-systemic" or proscribed means such as subversion, violence, or illegal strikes. Progressive argument is therefore conducted within the "rules of the game." Cathcart has described this as "managerial" rather than "confrontational" rhetoric.[19]

Lyndon Johnson's answer to critics who charged that "The System" was responsible for poverty, discrimination, and other social ills was a "War on

Poverty.'' In his first State of the Union address, Johnson told Congress and the nation that:

> We have in 1964 a unique opportunity and obligation—to prove the success of our system; to disprove those cynics at home and abroad who question our purpose and our competence. If we fail, if we fritter and fumble away our opportunity in needless, senseless quarrels between Democrats and Republicans, or between the House and the Senate, or between the South and North, or between the Congress and the administration, then history will rightfully judge us harshly.[20]

Johnson offered his audience an implicit choice: keep pride in your established system by making serious efforts to change socioeconomic conditions or keep socioeconomic conditions roughly as they are at the expense of proving the insurgents and innovators correct.

Of course, the logical extension of the latter choice is insurgency or revolution. Thus, progressive argument often attempts to stress the feasibility of patience and compromise with ''The System,'' as Johnson did in his 1968 State of the Union address:

> A moment ago I spoke of despair and frustrated hopes in the cities where the fires of disorder burned last summer. We can—and in time we will—change that despair into confidence, and change those frustrations into achievements. But violence will never bring progress.[21]

In her stirring keynote address to the 1976 Democratic National Convention, African-American Congresswoman Barbara Jordan made it clear that she believed in the political system and the Democratic party. She also distanced herself from the insurgent argument of Malcolm X and, more subtly, from the innovative argument of Martin Luther King: ''We cannot improve on the system of government handed down to us by the founders of the Republic, there is no way to improve upon that. But what we can do is to find new ways to implement that system and realize our destiny.''[22] But the rules of the game supported by Johnson and Jordan are illusive: the system praised by Jordan in 1976 was not the same system faced by Dr. King in 1963 or Malcolm X in 1965. Labor unions today are often able to resolve grievances through collective bargaining—the system for which they struggled prior to the New Deal. Thus, yesterday's insurgency and innovation can become today's Standpattism.

The rules of the game supported by progressive argument pose a serious dilemma for insurgent and revolutionary persuaders: refusal to follow the rules or procedures leaves them vulnerable to both prosecution and vilification. Yet following the established rules renders them subservient to the guardians of the established order and minimizes their own demands for change. A general consensus in support of the system is necessary at all times, and progressive argument often refers to the insurgent threat in order to press for moderate change.

Retentive Argument.   Retentive argument revolves around Conservative and Standpat efforts to preserve important elements of the status quo. The Standpatter would retain it in its entirety, while the Conservative regards this as impossible, infeasible, and hopeless. But the Conservative prefers the present to the proposed future, and attempts to insure that only necessary and practical changes are instituted. Retentive argument concerns cautious, minimal change, and it will therefore often seem trivial or stubborn to Radicals and Reactionaries, both of whom want substantial changes.

Since retentive argument seeks to retain important procedures or qualities that are under attack, it often exhibits an ominous tone. In his memoirs, Senator Barry Goldwater reveals his hope that, ''If what I have to say strikes a response in the hearts and minds of other Americans, perhaps they will enlist in the cause to keep our country strong and to restrain those who seek to diminish the importance and significance of the individual.''[23] Segregationists argued for retention of the old ways by wearing buttons that said simply, ''NEVER!'' and (as we will see in chapter 13) the New Right Movement coalesced around arguments to retain control over the Panama Canal.

Retentive argument is heard in presidential campaigns when we are warned about opponents. Gary Allen, who frequently wrote for the John Birch Society, warned in 1976 that:

> If even half of the Carter program is adopted, the average worker in America will face crippling new taxes, horrendous new regulations, and a spiraling rate of inflation that could wipe out any savings he hopes to have. It is a program for Big Government and ''efficient Socialism.'' It is enough to make any sensible person wring his hands in horror.[24]

Jimmy Carter Democrats in 1980 and Walter Mondale Democrats in 1984 said comparable things about the anticipated effects of the Reagan programs on the poor, the elderly, and delicate foreign relations, and many Bush supporters in 1992 echoed Allen's critique of Carter. All four campaigns lost, a sign that threatening apocalyptic visions often reflect more fear than they generate.

Not all retentive argument is threatening. While Governor of California, Ronald Reagan ridiculed criticism of socioeconomic conditions in America by dwarfing social ills with material accomplishments:

> I think if you put your minds to it you could match the Soviet Union's achievements. You would only have to cut all the paychecks 75 percent, send 69 million people back to the farm, tear down almost three-fourths of the houses in America, destroy 69 percent of the steel-making capacity, rip up fourteen of every fifteen miles of road, two-thirds of the railroad track, junk 85 percent of the autos, and tear out nine out of ten telephones.[25]

In short, retentive argument seeks to save or to preserve as much of the present as possible. It may range from Allen's alarm to Reagan's ridicule. In either case, retentive argument usually presents an unattractive picture of its adversaries, impugns their motives, and reduces progressive, innovative, and insurgent argument into one pattern which it characterizes as insane, ill-conceived, evil, and/or dangerous.

Reversive Argument. Reversive argument concerns efforts to return to a previous societal or political condition. Rather than urge retention of ''today,'' it uses the proposed "tomorrow" to argue that society has gone too far and that the tide must be reversed. In reversive argument, Standpatters struggle against the Reactionary's call for reversive change just as they struggle against the Conservative's call for careful, respectful change.

One Right to Life pamphlet urges its audience to reverse the *Roe v. Wade* decision's legalization of abortion because of the precedent it set:

> The U.S. Supreme Court has excluded an entire group of humans from legal personhood and with it their right to life. . . . How long will it be before other groups of humans will be defined out of legal existence when it has been decided that they too have become socially burdensome? Senior citizens beware! Minority races beware! Crippled children beware! It did happen once before in this century you know. Remember Germany? Are you going to stand for this?[26]

William Rusher, publisher of the conservative *National Review*, painted a bleak picture of America's future in 1975:

> If we succeed, we will have accomplished a mighty thing. We will have reversed . . . the whole downward-spiraling tide of the 20th century. There is no reason why this country's great experiment with freedom must end in failure. It was men and women who created the opportunity, and they who have botched it; and they can rescue it, even now, if they only will.[27]

In a similar vein, Senator Jesse Helms lamented that:

> For forty years an unending barrage of "deals" . . . have regimented our people and our economy and federalized almost every human enterprise. This onslaught has installed a gigantic scheme for redistributing the wealth that rewards the indolent and penalizes the hard-working.[28]

But, said Helms, this onslaught can be reversed: "I believe we can halt the long decline. There is nothing inevitable about it. There is a way back."[29]

Let us not presume from these examples that reversive arguments are heard only on the American Right. Several powerful pieces of reversive argument attack the Right itself. Liberal Republican Nelson Rockefeller, a defeated candidate for his party's presidential nomination, addressed the 1964 Republican Convention to propose that the platform condemn extremism:

> There is no place in the Republican Party for such hawkers of hate, such purveyors of prejudice, such fabricators of fear, whether Communist, Ku Klux Klan, or Bircher. . . . These people have nothing in common with Republicanism. These people have nothing in common with Americanism. The Republican Party must repudiate these people.[30]

Rockefeller's call to reverse the trend toward extremism of all sorts was drowned out by the boos of an audience unworried by what it regarded as the right kind of extremism. The next evening the audience cheered as conservative nominee presidential Barry Goldwater exclaimed, "Extremism in defense of liberty is no vice!"

Reversive argument may be near the middle of the typology, but it is hardly moderate in tone. Indeed, it is frequently quite vehement as befits its function of reversing societal direction. It is not unlike shifting into reverse at 65 mph.

Reversive argument must direct its audience to (1) see the current direction of society as dangerous, (2) see an alternative direction as desirable, and (3) provide some vehicle for facilitating the necessary change in direction. It cannot rely upon foot-dragging, stubbornness, or apathy. Instead, the willingness of the people simply to "go along" with trends is part of the problem. Reversive argument seeks action, and it can fail either because it sounds too "radical" to Standpatters and Conservatives, or because it is insufficiently inspiring to accomplish its three objectives.

Restorative Argument. Restorative argument urges a full-scale return to a previous state of affairs. The relative merits of that Golden Age are no longer debated: it is clearly preferable to the existing order. Restorative argument centers upon questions of when and why society went astray and how restoration can be accomplished. Reactionaries typically propose legislative or electoral solutions, a change in funding or enforcement of existing means, or a reconstitution of values to conform more closely to an earlier ideology. Revolutionary Reactionaries urge more abrupt tactics for the overthrow of the existing order and restoration of the Ancient Regime.

Believing that our national problems stemmed from the intrusion of the federal government into unnecessary ventures, a campaign was advanced during the 1960s on behalf of "The Liberty Amendment" to the U.S. Constitution which would have prohibited government engagement in "any business, professional, commercial, financial, or industrial enterprise except as specified in the Constitution."[31] All such enterprises would be sold to private entrepreneurs, and the federal government's right to tax would be repealed. Supporters of the Amendment argued that:

> We can renew the effectiveness of our Constitution. . . . We can restore the efficiency of our capitalist economy. The Liberty Amendment will accomplish both these purposes, by reducing the functions and powers of the Federal Government, and by restoring the abilities of people to take care of themselves, . . . and by curtailing destructive intervention in our free enterprise economy."[32]

For Jesse Helms, the critical turning point in our demise seems to have been the ban on prayer in public schools. He explains that:

> It is hardly coincidence that the banishment of the Lord from the public schools has resulted in their being taken over by a totally secularist philosophy. Christianity has been driven out. In its place has been enshrined a permissiveness in which the drug culture has flourished, as have pornography, crime, and fornication. . . . I think there is no more pressing duty facing the Congress than to restore the true spirit of the First Amendment.[33]

Robert Welch of the John Birch Society encouraged his followers to work toward restoration of the nature of America in the latter half of the 19th century. He prescribed that America:

> Push the Communists back, get out of the bed of a Europe that is dying with the cancer of collectivism, and breathe our own healthy air of opportunity,

enterprise, and freedom. . . . And despite the bad scars and the loss of some muscles, this young, strong, great new nation, restored to vigor, courage, ambition, and self-confidence, can still go ahead to fulfill its great destiny, and to become an even more glorious example for all the earth than it ever was before.[34]

Restorative argument, therefore, alludes to an era or condition which was preferable to the present in one or more respects. Like reversive argument, it is characteristically immoderate; unlike reversive argument, it often presents a goal to be pursued.

Revolutionary Argument. Revolutionary argument urges total overthrow of the existing order but disagrees as to the form and/or nature of the new regime. While Revolutionary Radical and Revolutionary Reactionary groups frequently terrorize one another, they agree that the existing order is intolerable, corrupt, and burdensome. They also agree that its despicable nature justifies violent overthrow. Thus, some reactionaries migrate from radical to reactionary variants of revolutionary argument, and back again. It is possible to become a Revolutionary Radical from either direction: a frustrated Radical or a disenchanted Revolutionary Reactionary. Revolutionary argument is clearly the most confrontational form of political argument. Here, the confrontation is more than symbolic; it relies heavily on brute force to destroy the persons and established institutions which it holds responsible for the problems of society.

Nevertheless, revolutionary argument depends upon dramatic rhetorical depictions of its violent acts for its effect. This is why several terrorist groups (often rivals) may claim responsibility for the same bombing—the destruction of property is generally less important than the symbolic mileage gained from it.

Perhaps the most prominent advocate of revolutionary argument was the anarchist Johann Most. While others simply blew buildings to pieces, Most savored violent acts through language. In a pamphlet on dynamite, he wrote:

> Dynamite! Of all the good stuff, that is the stuff! . . . Place this in the immediate vicinity of a lot of rich loafers who live by the sweat of other people's brows, and light the fuse. A most cheerful and gratifying result will follow. In giving dynamite to the downtrodden millions . . . science has done its best work. . . . A pound of this stuff beats a bushel of ballots all hollow—and don't you forget it.[35]

On another occasion, Most proclaimed in his famous speech, "The Beast of Property," that:

> If the people do not crush them, they will crush the people, drown the revolution in the blood of the best, and rivet the chains of slavery more firmly than ever. Kill or be killed is the alternative. Therefore massacres of the people's enemies must be instituted.[36]

Dennis Kearney, a California labor leader during the 1870s, sought to rid California of Orientals who constituted a source of cheap labor. But his violence was directed not only at the Orientals, but also at his own union:

> The first time you find a man in the ranks who is not true to the core take him by the nape of the neck and chuck him into the street and then take the bloody

shrimps by the throat and tell them you will put big stones around their necks
and throw them in the bay.[37]

Of course, exhorting people to violence entails risks—to both the speaker and
the audience. Anarchist Albert Parsons, who was hanged in connection with the
1886 Haymarket bombing in Chicago, was a master of revolutionary argument.
He told his audience that:

> If we would achieve our liberation from economic bondage and acquire our natural
> right to life and liberty, every man must lay by a part of his wages, buy a Colt's
> navy revolver, a Winchester rifle, and learn how to make and use dynamite. Then
> raise the flag of rebellion, the scarlet banner of liberty, fraternity, equality and
> strike down to the earth every tyrant that lives upon this globe.[38]

Lest his audience hesitate, Parsons reminds hearers that, "Until this is done you
will continue to be robbed, to be plundered, to be at the mercy of the privileged
few."[39]

Revolutionary argument recommends violent actions against the established
order. It is possible for such terrorist rhetoric to be largely devoid of social or
political ideology; such is the case today with the Irish Republican Army, the
skinheads in England, and the neo-Nazis in Germany. While the threat of violence
may pave the way for less extreme advocates, actual violence more often polarizes
negotiations and renders reasoned, moderate argument exceedingly difficult. Of
course, this is rarely important to the revolutionary, who sees moderation as part
of the problem.

Conclusions

Seven types of argument—Insurgent, Innovative, Progressive, Retentive,
Reversive, Restorative, and Revolutionary—are found throughout political
controversies. Various social movements have engaged in revolutionary terrorism,
insurgency, and progressive arguments, while others have sought to preserve the
status quo, reverse trends, or restore various Golden Ages. Each type of argument
serves a different purpose, and each is a response to a changing rhetorical situation.

Our illustrative examples show that each of the seven types of argument can
be found in the discourse of almost any social movement. But when a social
movement or a social movement organization relies disproportionately on one
type of argument, we can detect rhetorical patterns that differentiate it from other
movements or organizations. The important question is: Which types of argument
appear between which people at what points in the movement's development?

Endnotes

[1] Herbert W. Simons, "Persuasion in Social Conflicts: A Critique of Prevailing Conceptions and
a Framework for Future Research," *Speech Monographs* 39 (November 1972), 227,247.
[2] Unless otherwise noted, all references to Rossiter's typology refer to Clinton Rossiter, *Conservatism*

in America, 2nd rev. ed. (New York: Vintage Books, 1962), 11, 14.

[3] See Stephen W. Littlejohn, ed. *Theories of Human Communication*, 4th ed. (Belmont, CA: Wadsworth Publishing, 1992), 162, 164 for a helpful summary of social judgment theory, or Muzafer Sherif and Carl Hovland, *Social Judgment: Assimilation and Contrast Effects in Communication and Attitude Change* (New Haven: Yale University Press, 1961).

[4] Michael Billig, *Ideology and Opinions: Studies in Rhetorical Psychology* (Newbury Park, CA: Sage Publications, 1991), 17.

[5] "Preamble of the I.W.W. Constitution as amended in 1908," *The American Labor Movement*, Leon Litwack, ed. (Englewood Cliffs, NJ: Prentice-Hall, 1962), 42.

[6] John Swinton, *Striking for Life: Labor's Side of the Question* (Westport, CT: Greenwood Press, 1970), 104, 110.

[7] Malcolm X, "The Ballot or the Bullet?" *Malcolm X Speaks*, George Breitman, ed. (New York: Ballantine Books, 1965), 31.

[8] Eugene V. Debs, "Outlook for Socialism in the United States," *Debs*, Ronald Radosh, ed. (Englewood Cliffs, NJ: Prentice-Hall, 1971), 21.

[9] Clifford Odets, "Waiting for Lefty," *Modern American Plays*, Frederick Cassidy, ed. (Freeport, NY: Books for Libraries Press, 1949), 192.

[10] William Lloyd Garrison, "No Union with Slaveholders," *William Lloyd Garrison*, George M. Frederickson ed. (Englewood Cliffs, NJ: Prentice-Hall, 1968), 54.

[11] Odets, 195.

[12] Ralph Smith and Russell Windes, "The Innovational Movement: A Rhetorical Theory," *Quarterly Journal of Speech* 61 (April 1975), 143. Although we disagree with their conception of innovational movement, we find their characteristics of such movements useful for understanding innovational argument.

[13] Samuel Gompers, *Seventy Years of Life and Labor*, quoted in *Samuel Gompers Credo* (New York: American Federation of Labor Samuel Gompers Centennial Committee, 1950), 37.

[14] Martin Luther King, Jr. "I Have a Dream," *American Rhetoric from Roosevelt to Reagan*, Halford R. Ryan, ed. (Prospect Heights, IL: Waveland Press, Inc., 1983), 171, 172.

[15] Quoted in John C. Echowak, letter (Boulder, CO: Native American Rights Fund, n.d. [1993]).

[16] Echowak, 1.

[17] Echowak, 3.

[18] Henry Ford, "History Is More or Less Bunk," *Henry Ford*, John B. Rae, ed. (Englewood Cliffs, NJ: Prentice-Hall, 1969), 53.

[19] Robert S. Cathcart, "Movements: Confrontation as Rhetorical Form," *Southern Speech Communication Journal* 43 (Spring 1978), 237, 238.

[20] Lyndon B. Johnson, "Annual Message to the Congress on the State of the Union," *Public Papers of the Presidents of the United States: Lyndon B. Johnson*, 1963,1964, Book 1 (Washington, DC: U.S. Government Printing Office, 1965), 113.

[21] Lyndon B. Johnson, "Annual Message to the Congress on the State of the Union," *Public Papers of the Presidents of the United States: Lyndon B. Johnson*, Book 1 (Washington, DC: U.S. Government Printing Office, 1970), 31.

[22] Barbara C. Jordan, "Democratic Convention Keynote Address," reprinted in Ryan, 230, 231.

[23] Barry M. Goldwater, *With No Apologies* (New York: William Morrow, 1979), 14.

[24] Gary Allen, *Jimmy Carter, Jimmy Carter* (Seal Beach, CA: 76 Press, 1976), 68.

[25] Ronald Reagan, "Free Enterprise," in Ryan, 273.

[26] Dr. and Mrs. J. C. Wilke, "The U.S. Supreme Court Has Ruled It's Legal to Kill a Baby. . . ." (Cincinnati: Hayes Publishing, n.d.), 4.

[27] William A. Rusher, *The Making of the New Majority Party* (Ottawa, IL: Green Hill, 1975), 161, 162.

[28] Jesse Helms, *When Free Men Stand Tall* (Grand Rapids, MI: Zondervan, 1976), 11.

[29] Helms, 12.

[30] Nelson A. Rockefeller, "Address to the Third Session of the 1964 Republican National Convention in Moving Adoption of the Amendment to the Report of the Committee on Resolutions on the Subject of Extremism," Cow Palace, San Francisco, California, July 14, 1964," *Public Papers*

of Governor Nelson A. Rockefeller, 1964, 1330.

31 Lloyd G. Herbstreith and Gordan van B. King, *Action for Americans: The Liberty Amendment* (Los Angeles: Operation America, 1963), inside cover.

32 Herbstreith and King, 105.

33 Helms, 108.

34 Robert H. W. Welch, *The Blue Book of the John Birch Society* (Boston: Western Islands, 1961), 39.

35 Quoted in Louis Adamic, *Dynamite: The Story of Class Violence in America* (New York: Chelsea House, 1958), 47.

36 Johann Most, "The Beast of Property," reprinted in Charles W. Lomas, *The Agitator in American Society* (Englewood Cliffs, NJ: Prentice-Hall, 1968), 39.

37 Dennis Kearney, "The Chinese Must Go!" reprinted in Lomas, 29.

38 Albert Parsons, "The Board of Trade: Legalized Theft," reprinted in Lomas, 44.

39 Parsons, in Lomas, 44.

Chapter Thirteen

Argument from Narrative Vision
The New Right and the
Panama Canal Treaties

This chapter examines how some people help other people to see the world "properly." It will consider how people cluster around frameworks for interpreting reality, how a social movement can challenge the establishment's narrative, how the interpretive frameworks and events are interdependent, and how a rhetorical form can become a political resource.

Narrative and Rhetorical Vision

Historian David Carr writes that, "Human existence and action . . . consist not in overcoming time, not in escaping it or arresting its flow, but in shaping and forming it."[1] Time matters as it is experienced by people, and people experience time through stories. Carr maintains that each person lives in a remembered past and acts in expectation of a future that is a projection of past and present. We cast ourselves in an unfolding story and act it out, and because we choose the story and our role in it, we can switch stories at any time.

Philosopher Howard Kamler explains that stories help us to "know" and to protect what we "know" from counterargument. Stories give structure to our lives by contextualizing otherwise ambiguous episodes, and they let us believe what we need to believe by defining what constitutes relevant evidence and what does not. Kamler also writes that we communicate by making our private stories public and public stories such as myths our own.[2] Moreover, storytelling invites audiences to agree for the sake of the story, in contrast to propositional arguments that invite debate. Thus, individuals search for self-understanding by imposing narrative structure on their lives.

In earlier chapters, we discussed the importance of perceived environments and the need for social movements to transform perceptions of reality and society. These functions are normally accomplished through narratives. Each narrative structures the past, projects a future, and prescribes a preferred course of conduct from a particular vantage point. Each narrative has an author, a narrator, a protagonist, and an audience, but the narrator's vantage point—in time, intellect, wisdom, values, and character—positions the story for the audience. The reader-narrator identification is central. Readers who identify with the narrator step into the story, enact it, and retain the experience. Stories that facilitate these processes, in turn, foster identification. Readers repelled by the narrator may use the narrative for its opposite lesson, and an ill-defined or unconvincing narrator can be ignored. The narrator's image and audience appeal are so important to the narrative that personal identification overpowers logical rigor.[3]

David Carr theorizes that we organize our social relationships and communities through the telling and retelling of stories. Stories or myths link us to our contemporaries and to our predecessors and successors.[4] The storytelling process engages people in a communicative relationship defined by the narrator-audience relationship. The narrator and listener create a "we" through their identification as "my story" becomes "our story" through the co-creation of the story. Interpretive communities coalesce around stories as each "we" acquires its own folklore and narrators. Narrators embellish the story by emphasizing different characters, motives, events, chronology, and plotlines. Carr distinguishes between stories that endure ("retentions") and those that can be remembered if necessary ("recollections").[5] Differences develop when one person's retention is another's mere recollection. Social movements often weave a variety of recollections into a new story to raise them to the level of retention.

If history is the creation of explanatory stories, and if communities form around their stories, then some of these narrative groups must inevitably conflict. Consider the historic conflicts among Christian denominations, all based upon their varying interpretations of the story of Jesus of Nazareth. Likewise, most American social movements offer conflicting narratives of the "meaning of America" and the essence of "the American Dream."

Walter Fisher suggests that each narrative enacts a set of values and that these enacted values govern the narrative's audience appeal. Each narrative is judged, according to Fisher, by its narrative coherence (does the story work?) and by its narrative fidelity (does the story use the audience's beliefs and values?). He says that audiences look for good reasons, which they regard as stories that are consistent with what they know and value, appropriate to the pending decision, promising in effects for themselves, and consistent with what they regard as an ideal basis for conduct.[6] This view of persuasion hinges less on changing beliefs, attitudes, or values than on integrating beliefs and behaviors into a story regarded as coherent, relevant, compatible, promising, and proper.

The narrative position is largely compatible with a popular rhetorical perspective of symbolic convergence, sometimes known as "fantasy theme analysis." Ernest Bormann's studies of small-group communication confirmed Robert F. Bales' observation that individuals working together frequently dramatize or act out a "fantasy" (a recollection or an estimation of the future).[7] The verbalizing, expressing, or dramatizing of a fantasy orients listeners to the present by drawing upon their pasts and futures. Some fantasies fall flat. But when listeners recognize the fantasy as one of their own, they respond emotionally as well as cognitively. They hitchhike on the original comment and extend the fantasy by polishing the image, adding examples, and extending it. Then a third person recognizes the shared fantasy and joins. Soon the individuals are drawing on their separate pasts and futures to create a shared present. Thus, they develop a common orientation to the present and are bound to one another by the shared vision and by the process of creating it. This process is called "chaining" (as in "they created an elaborate fantasy chain" or "the fantasy chained out to the entire group").

Bormann's primary contribution is his suggestion that fantasy-chaining transcends the small-group experience. If small groups create shared identities through group fantasizing, he reasons, so might large groups such as audiences, organizations, social movements, and societies. Bormann identifies rhetorical visions as "the composite dramas which catch up large groups of people in a symbolic reality."[8] They arise through communication and provide the themes, heroes, villains, values, and motivations which are invoked in later communication. Rhetorical visions are particularly pertinent where clear explanations are elusive. Bormann observes that:

> When the authentic record of events is clear and widely understood, the competing visions must take it into account . . . [But] Whenever occasions are so chaotic and indiscriminate that the community has no clear observational impression of the facts, people are given free rein to fantasize within the assumptions of their rhetorical vision.[9]

Narrative and rhetorical vision are not identical frameworks. The narrative model is more perceptually grounded, more cognitive, and offers more analytical guidance. Fantasy theme analysis draws rather more heavily upon imaginings than recollections, although most would agree that our fantasies and imaginings grow out of our experiences. But the connection between narrative and rhetorical vision should be evident. Fantasies and rhetorical visions are narrative in form. Some fantasies stimulate recognition and empathy, thereby enhancing audience-narrator identification, inviting the audience to join in the creative process by participating in the story itself, fostering identification with like-minded auditors, and motivating listeners to remember the story. We shall coin the term "narrative vision" to encompass both Carr's sense of configured time and Bormann's collective imagining with respect to the New Right movement's Panama Canal narrative of the 1970s.

The Politics of Renegotiation, 1964–1978

President Lyndon Johnson responded to protests in Panama by initiating a renegotiation of the treaties governing ownership and use of the canal, a process continued by President Nixon. Congressman Daniel Flood (R. PA) wrote several times during 1974 warning Nixon of threats to our navigational freedom: "In the current struggle for the domination of strategic waterways . . . a line must be drawn somewhere and I can think of no better place to do so than at Panama where Soviet agents are already ensconced in its government."[10] Nixon responded that, "at stake is not just our control of the canal—vital as that may be—but relations with the Republic of Panama, the nations of the Caribbean and Latin America, and by extension with much of the Third World, all of which feel a concern and involvement in the resolution of this matter."[11] Here Flood and Nixon expressed the core themes of the canal controversy four years and two presidents before the treaty would come to a vote: drawing a line in the dust versus nurturing relations with smaller nations.

When Gerald Ford succeeded Nixon, Henry Kissinger remained as Secretary of State, and Ambassador Ellsworth Bunker continued to negotiate. But the Ford administration was insecure. Nixon holdovers had little respect for the newcomers, and Ford's loyalists mistrusted both the holdovers and those jockeying for the 1976 presidential nomination. President Ford had never been endorsed by voters beyond Grand Rapids, Michigan, and the Presidency had been disgraced through the Watergate scandal. In this atmosphere, White House staffers avoided controversy by sidestepping questions, keeping few informal memoranda, and avoiding explanations.

One exchange of letters illustrates the impact of the bureaucratic process and the Ford administration's insecurity on the developing rhetorical situation. William Douglas Pawley of Miami, a former ambassador to Peru and Brazil, wrote President Ford to oppose renegotiation. His letter went to the White House, to the National Security Council, and then to the State Department for a draft reply, before going back to the National Security Council which returned it to the White House Director of Correspondence, Roland Elliott. Elliott's reply to Ambassador Pawley said in part:

> [our] interest in the Panama Canal, therefore, is that it continue to be efficiently operated on a nondiscriminatory basis and that it be secure. . . . The achievement of a cooperative relationship with Panama would constitute neither a surrender nor an apology to it, but rather would strengthen the mutual interests of both countries in maintaining a well run canal.[12]

But Elliott's letter omitted major portions of the State Department draft that would have illuminated the administration's thinking. For example, the ambassador was not told that:

> In this new treaty relationship we are seeking the specific treaty rights which allow the United States to operate and defend the canal effectively for an extended period of time and the option to expand canal capacity either by enlarging the current canal or constructing a new sea level canal. We believe that a new treaty embodying . . . such rights will fulfill our most basic interest in the Panama Canal and at the same time satisfy Panamanian aspirations for full sovereignty over their territory and for increased participation in the canal's operation and defense.[13]

The Ford administration withheld its rationale and missed its chance to tell the story in which treaty negotiation made sense. The Ford people knew why they were negotiating, but they failed to inform the public.

Consequently, few Americans learned much of the treaty process, and rumors ran rampant. The Veterans of Foreign Wars charged that "The Battle is now clearly joined between those who would cede our Canal to the Panamanians and those who would not" without pondering the reasons for "ceding our Canal."[14] Senator Jesse Helms (R. N.C.) characterized Secretary of State Kissinger as a diplomatic Santa Claus:

> After having given away our nuclear superiority, our wheat, our technology, our production capacity, and our money, Secretary Kissinger has now graduated to giving away our territory itself. The Panama Canal is ours, bought and paid for as indisputably as the Louisiana Purchase, or California or Alaska.[15]

And Phillip Harman of the American Education League railed that, "It is hardly the hallmark of diplomatic genius to consider surrendering our canal lifeline—vital for our national defense and economic health—to the specious claims of an unstable, totalitarian government closely tied to history's most dangerous tyranny?"[16] These and similar statements flourished among conservatives because they enunciated their latent concerns about Soviet influence, military security, insecure Third World countries, public demonstrations, and disrespect for the law. They also flourished because they had no competing narrative from the establishment which preferred to handle renegotiation as an administrative act.

When President Ford announced his intention to run for election, Republicans coalesced around Ford and Ronald Reagan. Their contrasting styles were most evident in their handling of Harman and his American Education League. Robert McFarlane of Ford's National Security Council scrawled "Don't answer it" on Harman's letter, while Reagan named Harman his advisor on the Panama Canal and Central America.[17] Reagan garnered considerable support, but Ford won his party's nomination. Reagan's best moment occurred in North Carolina where he used the canal issue to win the primary in Jesse Helms's state. Although Ford answered canal questions from reporters, he continued to avoid a major speech on the canal treaties, perhaps realizing that he could alienate conservatives in his party.

Reagan's problem was that most Americans were unconcerned about the Panama Canal. Americans agreed with Reagan that America should "retain" sovereignty over the canal, but Gallup's "most important issue" poll for May, 1976 indicated that they were worried about high prices (38 percent), unemployment (24 percent), government dishonesty (13 percent), and crime (8 percent). All foreign policy issues combined concerned only 5 percent of Gallup's respondents.[18] Reagan beat Ford on the canal issue, but only 5 percent of the public seemed to care.

Some people urged President Ford to take charge of the canal issue. Aide Terry O'Connell suggested a National Security Council paper on the canal "so we can catch Reagan in the midst of his lie." Godfrey Harriss, a consultant to Panama, suggested that the canal could be "used positively by the President to advance his position" against Reagan. He also pointed out, for the first time in the White House Central Files on Panama, what was to become a crucial semantic wedge: the original treaty did not grant the United States sovereignty over the canal; it granted all rights *as if* America had sovereignty. Ford's staffers recognized the delicacy of taking advice from a consultant to Panama and expressed their appreciation for the spirit in which Harriss had made the offer. They similarly appreciated the "active and constructive support" of a publisher who urged Ford "to explode Ronald Reagan's campaign myths about the Panama Canal in a nationwide television address."[19] Ford opted to handle the issue with administrative rhetoric. The treaties would be decided by the Senate, not by referendum, and Ford and Kissinger believed that these were delicate matters for skilled negotiators, not fodder for public campaigning.

The canal did not become an issue during the general election campaign because Ford and Carter agreed and the public was apathetic. Moreover, conservatives and Republicans were not uniformly opposed to the treaties. As influential a conservative as Senator Barry Goldwater found himself becoming less opposed to the new treaties. He told the *Arizona Republic* that "there is peril in refusing to look ahead to eventual relinquishment" of the canal, and in March of 1976 he wrote that "I have not firmly made up my mind on this and I am open to suggestions from the public."[20] Goldwater's reservations were quite specific: "I'm cosponsoring a Senate resolution that takes a stand against relinquishing any U.S. *right or jurisdiction* [italics added] over the Canal Zone without a treaty agreed to by the Senate, and *I feel certain that the matter will be presented in the form of a treaty* [italics added]". [21] Importantly, Goldwater sought to protect America's "right or jurisdiction" rather than sovereignty, and he regarded an acceptable treaty as the solution, not the problem.

When Ford lost the election, it fell to President Jimmy Carter and the Democrats to advocate ratification. Once the treaties were ready for debate, the public's interest began to increase. Republicans now saw ratification as a Democratic plan, and conservative opponents were ready to lead the fight against the treaties and, in the process, to wrest control of the Republican Party from the Nixon-Ford-Kissinger-Rockefeller wing.

The rhetorical situation was ripe for harvesting by an emerging social movement. First, the Panama Canal has a rich symbolic heritage that evokes stories of American know-how, Teddy Roosevelt and the Rough Riders, and American naval strength. Second, the established order—including the Pentagon—solidly supported renegotiation, but no one was taking the case for the treaties to the public. Third, the negotiations could be explained in stories of giveaway and surrender that dramatized the fears of people disaffected from national political institutions, and after Vietnam and Watergate, there were plenty of them. Fourth, the rationale for renegotiation centered around the important technicality that the United States had all the rights and privileges we would have if we had sovereignty over it. But this technicality was not part of the basic history that most people had learned in grade school, with the result that renegotiation was incompatible with what many people "knew" about the canal. Fifth, the situation was ripe because it was Jimmy Carter, a president of modest rhetorical skills, who would advocate ratification. Partisan Republicans who had supported renegotiation under Presidents Nixon and Ford were now prepared to reconsider.

The Emerging New Right, 1976–1977

Richard Viguerie boasted that "No political issue in the last 25 years so clearly divided the American establishment from the American people as the Panama Canal treaties." The proposed treaties were truly supported by the establishment: two Democratic and two Republican presidents, the Democratic leaders in both houses or Congress, the Joint Chiefs of Staff, "Big Labor, Big Business, Big Media, the big international banks, and just about every liberal political and cultural star you could name." Opposed to the treaties were "the American people—about 70 percent of them . . . probably 85 percent of registered Republicans" and a coterie of conservative spokespersons who would become known as the "New Right:" Senators Paul Laxalt, Jake Garn, and Bill Scott, Congressmen Philip Crane, Larry McDonald, and Mickey Edwards, and organizers Paul Weyrich, Howard Phillips, William Rhatican, Terry Dolan, and Viguerie himself.[22] The treaties passed the Senate by a two-vote margin, a significant victory for President Carter. But many Americans remained deeply opposed to the treaties.[23]

The "New Right" movement used the proposed Panama Canal treaties to energize the conservative imagination. By advancing a narrative that made treaty ratification illogical, rather than conceding the worldview and arguing technicalities, the New Right engaged less active conservatives in group fantasizing.

To defeat the treaties and/or mobilize a new conservative majority, the New Right needed a rhetoric that would appeal to a variety of interpretive communities. Specifically, the New Right needed to meet four rhetorical goals. First, they needed to incorporate the enduring symbols and beliefs of foreign policy conservatives, many of them Democrats, as the core of the anti-treaty coalition. Second, they needed to enhance Americans' recollections of the Panama Canal. Third, they needed to dramatize latent fantasies about the perilous world to keep Americans from trusting other nations. Fourth, and most delicately, they had to link the Ford-Kissinger-Rockefeller-Nixon wing of the Republican party with Carter and the Democrats, while linking the Republican party, treaty opposition, the New Right, and public opinion.

Reagan's success in North Carolina had shown the way, and he continued to be a prominent anti-treaty voice. Although a private citizen in August 1977, he received a private briefing from the chief negotiators.[24] But Reagan was unconvinced by this briefing, and he told the Young Americans for Freedom that the treaties "would eliminate the rights of sovereignty we acquired in the original treaty. . . . Without these rights we must ask what is to prevent a Panamanian regime one day from simply nationalizing the canal and demanding our immediate withdrawal . . . Secrecy, of course, is no longer the issue. Security is.''[25] Here Reagan replaced the State Department's legal ''as if we had sovereignty'' premise with a simple and familiar ''actual sovereignty'' premise. He then shifted adroitly from propositional argument to a narrative structure that invited his young, unbriefed, conservative listeners to fantasize. Instead of telling them what he had learned from the negotiators, Reagan asked them to allay *his* fears.

Reagan's campaign against the treaties continued into the fall of 1977. An antitreaty letter in Reagan's name was sent out on Republican National Committee letterhead in late October. The letter advanced nine propositions:

1. In the process of giving up our Canal, Mr. Carter has also surrendered our rights to build a new one if needed.
2. There's no guarantee our Naval Fleet will have the right of priority passage in time of war.
3. The U.S. does *not* have the right to intervene to defend the Canal.
4. We must close down 10 of our military bases, Americans in the Zone will be under Panamanian rule, and we must pay [general Omar] Torrijos millions more each year for the Canal.
5. These treaties could cost Americans hundreds of millions . . . Plus we'll pay higher prices . . . [Torrijos] maintains close ties with Fidel Castro and the Soviet Union.
6. [Torrijos] seized power by gunpoint . . . [and] controls the press, he's outlawed all political parties but the Marxist party and he controls the military.
7. Once we pull out, what's to stop Torrijos or his successor from nationalizing the Canal and ordering us out at once?
8. Panama is one of the most unstable countries in Latin America.
9. From the beginning, Mr. Carter negotiated this treaty without consulting Congressional leaders.[26]

It is difficult to imagine the Republican National Committee sponsoring this same mailing if Ford had won the 1976 election. Indeed, five of the nine statements refer explicitly to Carter while none mention that Republicans Ford and Nixon also supported the negotiations. By coming out so strongly against the treaties, the Republican National Committee significantly disadvantaged the future prospects of Republican treaty supporters such as Ford.

The Reagan letter was the New Right's first major victory in its efforts to lead mainstream Republican opposition to the Carter administration. The Republican leadership had significant political and organizational needs that provided incentives for them to oppose the treaties now being advocated by the Democrats. Nevertheless, the Reagan letter was flawed because it was a propositional rather than a narrative argument. By detailing nine propositions, Reagan invited refutation, and this he received from many quarters because many Republican conservatives did not yet oppose the treaties.

The most trenchant response to Reagan's letter came in a letter from actor John Wayne, the icon of American patriotism and military heroism. Wayne's personal cover letter to "Ronnie" expressed his regrets: "If you had given time and thought on this issue, your attitude would have gained you the image of leadership that I wished for you, rather than, in the long run, a realization by the public that you are merely making statements for political expediency."[27] He told Reagan that "I'll show you point by God damn point in the Treaty where you are misinforming people." Wayne then gave an important warning: "If you continue these erroneous remarks, someone will publicize your letter to prove that you are not as thorough in your reviewing of the Treaty as you say or are damned obtuse when it comes to reading the English language."[28] Attached to the cover letter was a four-page cut-and-paste summary of Reagan's nine points under the title "SCARE LETTER FROM THE HONORABLE RONALD REAGAN" along with Wayne's quite specific and technical responses. His responses were replete with phrases such as "the *truth* is," "completely misleading," "complete untruth," and "How dare you continue to make these statements." Wayne's conclusion spoke directly to Reagan's use of the canal as a vehicle for fund raising. "Quite obviously," said Wayne, "you are using . . . [the Panama Canal Treaty] as a teaser to attract contributions to our party. I know of our party's need for money; but if your attitude in order to get it is as untruthful and misleading as your letter, we haven't a chance."[29] The tone of Wayne's letter may seem surprising in the post-Reagan era. But it must be read in the context of 1977 when the treaties had been supported by Nixon, Ford, and the Joint Chiefs of Staff, and Senator Goldwater was moving toward support.

John Wayne's letter highlights the rhetorical dilemmas facing the New Right in late 1977. Reagan was their best prospect for winning the presidency in 1980 and the Panama Canal Treaty was their best issue for mobilizing support. But Reagan's propositional arguments against the treaties might well destroy his credibility in the process. The rhetorical leadership of the anti-treaty forces passed from Reagan to Illinois Congressman Phillip Crane, a historian by profession, in January 1978.

President Carter spoke frequently about the canal, but did not go on national television in 1977. On September 14, shortly after the treaty signing, speechwriter James Fallows urged the President to go on television for a "Fireside Chat" about the treaties. Fallows feared that the public would conclude that "we've abandoned the fight. We're leaving all the public argumentation to the other side," he wrote, "and by letting their crazy charges go unanswered for the moment we suggest that we don't have any answers."[30]

Fallows had written a Fireside Chat for Carter by September 19, and he preferred to err in the direction of overexposure. He agreed with Harlan Strauss, legislative director of a Washington law firm, that the basic problem was "the McGuffey Reader Complex." Strauss explained that, "Since early this century . . . the myth that the Panama Canal and its surrounding territory was ours 'in perpetuity' was taught as a truism in the classroom and in the grammar school textbooks.'' Strauss's letter suggested that the President needed to re-educate "the over 50, the grade school only, and Republican" audiences about manifest destiny, the Monroe Doctrine, and the "in perpetuity" clause.[31]

Herein lay Carter's rhetorical predicament. The New Right was busy constructing a coherent anti-treaty narrative out of the recollections that older, conservative, Republican citizens had acquired early in life. Even if the narrative was as erroneous as Strauss and Wayne had said, it was consistent with everything this target audience had learned about the canal, and a narrative's persuasiveness hinges largely on its fidelity to its audience's experiences.[32] On the other hand, the President was being advised to tell this audience that the facts of American history they had learned in grade school were wrong—facts that were being used and reinforced almost daily by the anti-treaty advocates. To do so would be to step into the story being told by Reagan, Crane, and others. Although Fallows agreed with Strauss's analysis, he recognized this predicament. He responded to Strauss, "It is obviously true . . . But unless that point is made with extreme delicacy, it loses many more friends than it gains."[33]

The Fallows-Carter brand of rhetorical delicacy was largely defensive and lacking in either eloquence or creativity, and the Fireside Chat that Fallows had written in September 1977 was still in limbo when the New Year began. On January 25, 1978, Fallows prepared a revised outline for a Fireside Chat. It was to be a short (10 to 15 minute) address, "confident, positive, and forward looking" as well as "simple (7th grade this time)." But the proposed outline suggested twenty-eight points and sub-points distributed over four sections.[34] Moreover, subsequent discussions led to thirteen additional points, leaving Fallows with an average of fifteen to twenty seconds per point—not counting the introduction and conclusion. Carter's key aides, the speechwriting staff, negotiators Sol Linowitz and Ellsworth Bunker, Vice President Mondale, and First Lady Rosalyn Carter reviewed drafts of this Fireside Chat. Their advice did not prove helpful.

The Conflicting Narratives of Carter and Crane

By contrasting pro- and anti-treaty narratives from the 1974–1978, we can see how the New Right movement used the canal issue to weave diverse public recollections and fantasies into a narrative vision that aroused and united conservatives and, ultimately, reoriented American foreign policy. We will pay particular attention to the narratives advanced by the movement's primary spokesman and legitimizer, Illinois Republican Congressman Philip Crane, and by the addresses and remarks of the establishment's major advocate, President Jimmy Carter.[35] President Carter spoke for the foreign policy establishment: the leadership of both parties, the diplomatic corps, the State Department, the CIA, and the Pentagon. Crane's book was the New Right movement's definitive critique of that bipartisan foreign policy. Congressman Crane, like anti-Vietnam War Senators Eugene McCarthy, George McGovern, and Alan Cranston, served as an elected member of the established order while energetically advocating the position of an uninstitutionalized collectivity. Moreover, Carter and Crane advanced comparable narratives. Each recounted our past, depicted our present situation, envisioned desirable and undesirable futures, dramatized and reconciled significant American values and symbols, and espoused a preferred course of action consistent with the narrative and its values.

Narratives Depicting the Past: America's Claim to the Canal

President Carter's narrative contrasted characteristic American fairness and morality with the unfair 1903 Hay-Bunau-Varilla Treaty. He found it shameful that "No person from Panama ever saw that treaty before it was signed. No Panamanian, of course, was involved in the signing of that treaty."[36] But the new treaties would reaffirm America's fairness since ratification "is what is right for us and what is fair to others."[37] Carter further argued that even the unfair treaty failed to grant America sovereignty over the canal. He told a questioner that, "the treaty . . . gave Panama sovereignty over the Panama Canal Zone itself. It gave us control over the Panama Canal Zone as though we had sovereignty. So, we've always had a legal sharing of responsibility over the Panama Canal Zone."[38] Since Panama retained sovereignty even under an unfair treaty, we should affirm it with a fair treaty.

But Congressman Crane argued that America's claim to the canal was legally derived from the Hay-Bunau-Varilla Treaty. He did not, however, argue that the treaty was fair. He said the treaty was advantageous to America and disadvantageous to Panama because a clever and legal treaty had granted the United States sovereignty over the Canal Zone. Crane's narrative covered the negotiation of the treaty that enabled Panamanians to win their independence from Columbia so that they could relinquish their sovereignty over the Canal Zone to the United States.[39] Our claim to the canal stemmed from shrewdness and opportunism, because "When any nation goes to the bargaining table it does so with the determination to act in its own best interests and to derive as many benefits as possible." "Our 1903 agreement," he said, was "a shrewd bargain."[40] Crane's account of the original treaty's imbalance was fully consistent with that of its negotiator, Mr. Hay.[41]

Crane further maintained that the legal treaty ceded all sovereignty over the Canal Zone to the United States. He attempted to refute Carter's claim that America was granted control "as though" we had sovereignty with a 1904 memorandum from the Panamanian secretary of government to the effect that Panama ended its jurisdiction over the Canal Zone upon ratification in 1904.[42] But the thrust of Carter's argument was that the treaty provided for Panamanian sovereignty and American jurisdiction *as if* we had sovereignty. Crane cited Henry Kissinger's pro-treaty references to "restoring Panamanian sovereignty" and several examples of American acts usually associated with sovereignty, and he inferred that "the very yielding to Panama of certain small pieces of control proves that the United States has full control—de facto sovereignty—in the first place."[43]

Carter's concern was that very discrepancy between our *de facto* sovereignty and Panama's *de jure* sovereignty. His most authoritative and cogent handling of the sovereignty issue came three months before Crane's book and four months before his Fireside Chat. Carter explained to a Denver audience that:

> We [Americans] have never owned the Panama Canal Zone. We've never had title to it. We've never had sovereignty over it . . . the Supreme Court has confirmed since then [sic] that this is Panamanian territory. People born in the Panama Canal Zone are not American citizens. We've always paid them an annual fee, since the first year of the Panama Canal Treaty that presently exists, for the use of their property . . . People say we bought it; it's ours; we ought not to give it away. We've never bought it. It's not been ours. We are not giving it away.[44]

Although Carter and Crane built persuasive arguments on sovereignty, neither directly engaged the other's argument. Crane's account sidestepped the treaty's grant of control *as if* America held sovereignty—despite reprinting the text of Article III of the 1903 treaty in his book. It states that, "The Republic of Panama grants to the United States all the rights, power and authority within the zone . . . which the United States would possess and exercise *if* it were the sovereign of the territory within which said lands and waters are located" [emphasis added].[45] Crane chose to focus on signs of sovereignty and exploited the fact that few Americans knew that the original treaty preserved Panamanian sovereignty in principle. For his part, Carter too often summarized and asserted while Crane used detailed extrinsic support such as testimony and court decisions. Carter's claim that "the Supreme Court has confirmed since then that this is Panamanian territory," for example, seems to be refuted with Crane's specific references to *Wilson v. Shaw* (1907), *The United States v. Husband* (1972), and a "veteran American diplomat and international law authority."[46]

Carter and Crane presented strikingly divergent histories which constrained their audiences' reactions. If the treaty were grossly unjust and exploitive, even an explicit Panamanian grant of sovereignty to America might be discounted. But if the treaty were honorably negotiated, then even implicit Panamanian concessions should be binding. Moreover, if America held sovereign control over the Canal Zone, any sharing of that power could be construed as surrender, retreat, or a giveaway; but if Panama itself held sovereignty, there was nothing to surrender.

Crane's narrative dramatized an American success based on legality, shrewdness, pride, and self-interest. Carter's narrative dramatized an American embarrassment and intimated that our collective past was less noble than we had believed. Fisher's first test for "good reasons" is the degree to which the narrative is "true to and consistent with what we think we know and what we value."[47] Crane's history met the first narrative test better than did Carter's, even though it misused its own evidence.

Narratives Depicting the Present:
The Western Hemisphere Today

President Carter characterized Panama as one of our "historic allies and friends" headed by a "stable government which has encouraged the development of free enterprise" and will hold democratic elections.[48] But Crane described a "banana republic" dominated by "forty influential families" where "poverty is abysmal" and in which General Omar Torrijos runs a "corrupt, vicious police state . . . built with the help of his Marxist allies" and kept from bankruptcy only by "the New York banking community."[49]

Carter and Crane advanced contrasting views of Pan-American relations. Carter described legitimate disaffection in the hemisphere and depicted the canal as "the last vestige of alleged American colonialism."[50] Thirteen years of negotiations had "built up hopes of new friendship, new trade opportunities, and a new sense of commonality and equality of stature between their governments and our government that never existed before."[51] The cornerstone of these hopes and expectations was a "new sense . . . of improved friendship and common purpose . . . not based on grants or loans or financial aid from us to them but based on the fact that this treaty corrects a longstanding defect in our relationships with countries to the south."[52] Carter eagerly anticipated this "new partnership" and spoke of defending the canal with Panamanian forces "joined with us as brothers."[53] The Carter narrative dramatized Panamanian resentment of America against the background of America's uncharacteristic deceit.

But where President Carter saw our exploitation and injustice as contributors to Panamanian resentment, Crane saw only American generosity:

> The United States did for Panama what the Spanish, Simon Bolivar, the French Company, and the Colombians had all failed to do: built and operated a magnificent interoceanic canal that pumped commercial vitality and opportunity into the stagnant economic bloodstream of Panama. We also rid the country of the scourges of malaria and yellow fever, brought good jobs and opportunity to thousands of needy Panamanians, and promptly paid increasingly large subsidies to the Panamanian government—all after helping Panama to win independence in the first place.[54]

Thus, where Carter advanced a story of legitimate resentment, Crane told of childish ingratitude: "To the extent that Panama exists and is a viable state today, it is because a strong America, which could have taken what it wanted without giving anything in return, has been a generous friend of Panama from the moment of ratification of the 1903 treaty. But . . . gratitude soon grows old."[55] Crane's view of Pan-American relations was distinctly paternalistic: the American parents bestowed countless favors upon young Panama only to be resented. Crane implied that Panama needed to be taught a lesson.[56]

Carter and Crane agreed that the canal would be crucial to Panama's future. Crane's account highlighted the danger that Panama might close the canal as economic and political blackmail. General Torrijos was ready to seize the canal.[57]

He cited a speech in which Torrijos predicted his own violent death fighting for the canal, and warned that, "he might very well do so again . . . especially in the face of a passive, docile America that has demonstrated a pattern of yielding to threats instead of dealing from a position of strength."[58] Crane warned that it would be a "criminal blunder" to turn the canal zone over to a "corrupt dictator" who is "a flagrant violator of human rights" and is "surrounded by criminals and Marxists," "an intimate friend of Fidel Castro, a rabid anti-American, and a seeker after advice, technicians, and aid from the Soviet Union" because we would risk both blackmail and closure of the canal."[59] "The real threat of violence to the canal," he wrote, "would crest after the departure of American security forces, not while they were in place to protect the zone."[60]

Carter examined Panama's economic interests and argued that "Panama wants the canal open and neutral—perhaps even more than we do" because "Much of her economy flows directly or indirectly through the canal." For this reason "Panama would be no more likely to neglect or close the canal than we would be to close [our] Interstate Highway System." The threat to the canal comes "not from any government of Panama, but from misguided persons who may try to fan the flames of dissatisfaction with the terms of the old treaty."[61]

If Americans were concerned by the bleak picture Crane sketched, then President Carter might well have reiterated his October 22nd comments about defending the canal. The President compared a canal defense to our military involvements in Korea and Vietnam:

> With the passing of these two treaties . . . if we should later have to go into Panama, it will be with the endorsement of the Panamanian Government, the Panamanian people. It will be with the endorsement of 30 or 40 or 50 other nations who will sign the neutrality treaty going into effect after the year 2000 . . . So it gives us a legitimacy and an endorsement of the rest of the world to keep the canal open, well managed, and to meet the security needs, the trade needs of our own country.[62]

Carter's position was that any attempt to defend or recapture the canal under the existing treaty would be a violation of Panamanian sovereignty, whereas the proposed treaties would explicitly commit Panama to an open, neutral canal under international law.

The Carter and Crane narratives dramatized divergent values. President Carter's story was one of a friendly, honest, rational, democratic, capitalist nation worthy of being our military and economic partner. But Crane told of a hostile, corrupt, childish, socialist nation unworthy of partnership with America. Accuracy aside, Crane's story built upon his audience's belief in American superiority and generosity but asked them to be suspicious and protective in this particular case. Carter's account undermined his audience's perceptions of our traditions of fairness and military strength, and asked his audience to demonstrate its trusting and generous nature in this particular case.

Narratives Depicting the Future:
The Kind of Power We Wish to Be

President Carter and Congressman Crane agreed that the canal decision would demonstrate "the kind of great power we wish to be."[63] Carter claimed that Theodore Roosevelt "would join us in our pride for being a great and generous people, with the national strength and wisdom to do what is right for us and what is fair to others."[64] The President told reporters that ratification would be "a show of strength . . . national will . . . fairness and . . . confidence in ourselves." He explained that we need not "run over a little country. It's much better for us to show our strength and our ability by not being a bully and by saying to Panama, let's work in harmony."[65] Carter said that ratification would demonstrate that "we are able to deal fairly and honorably with a proud but smaller sovereign nation . . . [because] we believe in good will and fairness, as well as strength."[66] He spoke of the "new partnership" as a "source of national pride and self-respect."[67]

Panama was to be transformed from "a passive and sometimes deeply resentful bystander into an active and interested partner" who will "[join] with us as brothers against a common enemy" should the canal need military defense.[68] The treaties would not create a "power vacuum" but would "increase our nation's influence in this hemisphere, help to reduce any mistrust and disagreement, [and] remove a major source of anti-American feeling." In the Carter vision, the United States was a powerful, fair, generous neighbor ready and willing to demonstrate those admirable traits by sharing the canal with the Panamanians.

But Crane, arguing the case for the New Right movement, painted a different future based upon the nature of the world and the proper places of property and generosity. Crane bluntly differentiated his world from Carter's:

> The world is not a Sunday school classroom in Plains, Georgia. It is a violent, conflict-ridden place where peace and freedom only survive when they are protected . . . Peace comes only to the prepared and security only to the strong.[69]

Generosity among friends is noble; generosity in a jungle is foolish and cowardly.

Crane therefore argued that ratification would be "one more crucial American step in a descent into ignominy—to the end of America's credibility as a world power and a deterrent to aggression."[70] Crane's future envisioned neither friendship nor generosity but a reputation for cowardice and weakness. A "surrender in Panama would appear as not a noble act of magnanimity, but as the cowardly retreat of a tired, toothless paper tiger."[71]

The futures Carter and Crane envisioned diverged. Crane saw danger, Carter security. Crane wanted superiority, Carter partnership. Crane implied force and punishment, Carter generosity and kindness. Crane thought America weak; Carter thought us strong. Crane saw shame in "surrender," Carter in continued imperialism. Each believed that the other side in the controversy indirectly helped America's enemies.

In the end, the treaties were ratified. But the New Right aroused public sentiment and developed a massive public relations machine, defined its identity, created a list of villains, and transformed treaty ratification into a rhetorical success. As New Right organizer Richard Viguerie explains:

> Our campaign to save the Canal gained conservative converts around the country, added more than 400,000 new names to our lists—encouraged many of the movements' leading figures . . . to run for public office—and produced significant liberal defeats. The New Right came out of the Panama Canal fight with no casualties, not even a scar. Because of Panama we are better organized. We developed a great deal of confidence in ourselves, and our opponents became weaker. That November [1978] the New Right really came of age.[72]

In short, the New Right campaign accomplished four of the five functions of social movement persuasion despite losing the treaty vote. It enabled them to transform perceptions of reality, transform perceptions of society, prescribe courses of action, and mobilize for action.

Discussion

The Panama Canal controversy illustrates how a social movement can take exception to a bipartisan consensus and develop a coherent narrative that arouses and unites potential supporters by dramatizing their fears. The New Right's narrative enabled them to take over the rhetorical agenda of the Republican National Committee which hungered for a set of arguments with which to mobilize Republicans against Carter and the Democrats.

New Right organizers saw the canal issue as a symbolic vehicle for energizing their movement. Because the debate was between narrative visions, defenders of the establishment narrative risked losing, and in fact did lose, their entire policy framework. The New Right undermined public confidence in the assumptions underlying our foreign policy and provided an alternative narrative framework through which subsequent events in Iran, Afghanistan, Nicaragua, Grenada, El Salvador, and the Persian Gulf would be interpreted.

Dramatic rhetorical narratives that excite the imagination are more persuasive than those that are more technical in nature. Both Crane and Carter claimed to have "the facts," and both established their authority and expertise. But Crane was better able than Carter to involve his audience in the process of collective fantasizing because his narrative provided themes that his audience interpreted as "good reasons."

Let us appraise the narratives with respect to Fisher's four criteria of narrative rationality.[73] First, Crane's narrative dramatized American heroism, strength, generosity, legality, and cleverness while Carter's narrative required us to revise our sense of history and national character to admit that our "Bully President" Teddy Roosevelt had himself been a bully who had tricked our unsuspecting neighbors. Crane's narrative was therefore more true to and consistent with what we "knew," "believed," and "valued" than Carter's. Ironically and importantly, the social movement used existing perceptions of history while the President sought to transform them.

Second, both narratives were appropriate to the ratification decision because they framed the issues and compelled a conclusion. Neither left its audience to ask, "So how does this affect treaty ratification?" But Crane's account was self-supporting. His conflict with the President and defense establishment clouded the decision and made caution seem more prudent than trust. Carter, like Ford, tried to respond to aroused concern with administrative rhetoric, but even this required him to allay the fears aroused by the social movement. This left Americans to ask two questions: "After fourteen years of negotiating, what's the hurry?" and "If you are right, Mr. President, why is this convincing congressman so worried?"

Third, Crane's narrative was the more promising in effects for his audience. It promised that the choice of cowardice and weakness would lead to the possibility of a friendship devoid of respect, while stern resolve would lead to power and respect. Carter's narrative promised that the choice of generosity and honor would lead to friendship, respect, and security while intransigence would lead to greater antagonism and vulnerability. Crane's account invites audience fantasizing because its stakes were so dramatic.

And fourth, Crane's narrative was the more internally consistent because of its simplicity. Carter's narrative presented several apparent inconsistencies. Why should we grant anything to people who are increasingly resentful? How are these resentful people developing this new sense of mutual purpose and trust with America? If Panama is friendly and stable, why need we worry about defending the canal? If we need to worry about defending the canal, why voluntarily relinquish any of our claim to it? Carter answered these questions reasonably well, but his answers were complex and strung-out over several months. Crane's narrative provided few apparent inconsistencies. He did commit a critical logical error by arguing that the presence of all the signs of American sovereignty over the canal proved American sovereignty, since the treaty preserved Panamanian sovereignty in principle. But this inconsistency was buried deep in his argument and it was obscured by his references to memoranda and court decisions on related points.

In short, President Carter advanced a technically sound argument for treaty ratification that did not meet the tests of good narrative. Crane's arguments against ratification, flawed as they were, met the narrative tests and involved audience members in the social movement. The treaty was ratified on administrative and technical grounds, but the social movement established its narrative framework as a viable alternative and used it a year later to frame events in Iran and Afghanistan and overthrew the Ford-Carter-Kissinger "friendly giant" scenario.

Conclusions

A choice between narrative frameworks ultimately boils down to the question of believability, and believability hinges on the individual's personal inventory of words, meanings, experiences, associations, social influences, values, needs, and sense of causation. People believe what they need to believe to keep themselves afloat in the world. A narrative that embodies and dramatizes our experiences and fantasies "makes sense" to us, as Fisher suggests, because it has coherence and fidelity. It excites us, and we wonder why no one noticed it before. We share it excitedly with our associates and, as Bormann explains, create through the act of collective fantasizing a sense of community that is embodied in the shared vision.

President Carter sought support for treaty ratification on technical grounds, relying upon the testimony of establishment figures to create a bandwagon of support. But the New Right transformed the controversy into a social movement vs. establishment conflict. Crane's office legitimized his advocacy and his reliance upon old memoranda, court cases, testimony, and reprinted treaties created what Barnet Baskerville once called "the illusion of proof."[74] When Crane's narrative accounted for subsequent developments in Iran and Nicaragua, moderate Republicans like Richard Nixon and Gerald Ford were perceptually exiled to the Carter position.

In a debate between narratives, the struggle over images, heroes, villains, values, and motives is central. These symbolic struggles determine how Americans, whether policymakers or ordinary citizens, will order the world around them and how they will perceive their policy alternatives. Narrative visions are the frameworks within which specific people, motives, and incidents are interpreted. As people recognize, share, and apply their vision, they recruit members and consolidate them into a working group.

This analysis of the New Right's Panama Canal campaign illustrates four important points about social movements and argument from narrative vision. First, activists coalesce around a narrative framework for interpreting political realities. Second, even a logical establishment narrative advanced by the president can be credibly challenged by an emerging social movement with a clear and convincing narrative. Third, the movement's narrative transcends its particular focus, and short-term losses become long-term wins. Fourth, because narratives help us to interpret events, and because events help us to validate our choice of narrative, political history is a series of narrative visions.

Endnotes

[1] David Carr, *Time, Narrative, and History* (Bloomington: Indiana University Press, 1986), 89.

[2] Howard Kemler, *Communication: Sharing Our Stories of Experience* (Seattle: Psychological Press, 1983), 27–58.

[3] Walter R. Fisher, *Human Communication As Narration: Toward a Philosophy of Reason, Value, and Action* (Columbia: University of South Carolina Press, 1987), 66–67.

[4] Carr, 1–113.

[5] Carr, 23.

[6] Fisher, 194.

[7] Ernest G. Bormann, "Fantasy and Rhetorical Vision: The Rhetorical Criticism of Social Reality," *Quarterly Journal of Speech* 58 (December 1972), 396–407; and "Fantasy and Rhetorical Vision:

Ten Years Later," *Quarterly Journal of Speech* 68 (August 1982), 288–305. See also Dan Nimmo and James E. Combs, *Mediated Political Realities* (New York: Longman, 1983); and Murray Edelman, *Constructing the Political Spectacle* (Chicago: University of Chicago Press, 1988).

8 Bormann (1971), 398.

9 Bormann (1972), 405.

10 Daniel J. Flood, Letter to President Richard M. Nixon, June 3, 1974, White House Central Files: Foreign Policy, Panama Canal (Ann Arbor, MI: Gerald R. Ford Presidential Library). Hereafter referred to as Ford Central Files.

11 Richard M. Nixon, Response to Congressman Flood, May 29, 1974, Ford Central Files.

12 William Douglas Pawley, Letter to President Ford, July 2, 1975, Ford Central Files.

13 Roland Elliott, Response to William Douglas Pawley, October 6, 1975, Ford Central Files.

14 Col. F. P. Jones (Ret.), "The United States Canal on the Isthmus of Panama: The Showdown Approaches" (Washington, DC: Official Memorandum to officers and publications of the Veterans of Foreign Wars, September 25, 1975), Ford Central Files.

15 Quoted in Jones, "The United States Canal . . ."

16 Phillip Harman, "Our Panama Canal: A Vital Asset" (Buena Park, CA: mimeographed flier, December 16, 1975), Ford Central Files.

17 Robert McFarlane, memorandum attached to the Harman flier, Ford Central Files.

18 Although available from other sources, these data are from the files of Foster Channock who tracked issues for the administration and suggested strategy. They represent not just what pollsters saw in America but what the Ford White House saw in America. See White House Staff Files, White House Operations, Foster Channock Files, 1975–1976, Gallup Polls of May 16, 1976.

19 See the Memorandum from Terry O'Donnell to Jerry Jones on May 5, 1976; the letter from Godfrey Harriss to John Marsh on May 5, 1976; Marsh's reply to Harriss; and the telegram from Stan Rose to Robert Dole. All of these are in the Ford Central Files.

20 Barry Goldwater, Letter to Robert Pastor, March , 1976. Staff Office Files, Speechwriters' Office, James Fallows Files. Jimmy Carter Library.

21 Goldwater, letter.

22 Richard A. Viguerie, *The New Right: We're Ready to Lead* (Falls Church, VA: The Viguerie Company, 1981), 65–67.

23 Although both Carter and Crane refer to 70–80% public opposition to the treaties, an August, 1977 Gallup Poll reports only 47% opposition. See American Institute of Public Opinion, *The Gallup Poll: Public Opinion, 1972–1977*, Vol. 2 (Wilmington, DE: Scholarly Resources, 1978), 1181–1183. In his memoirs, *Keeping the Faith* (New York: Bantam Books, 1982), Carter calls his efforts to win support for the Canal treaties his most difficult political battle (184).

24 E. Pace, "Reagan Declares Canal Treaties Should Be Rejected by the Senate," *New York Times*, August 26, 1977, 1.

25 Pace, 6.

26 John Wayne, "Scare Letter from the Honorable Ronald Reagan," November 11, 1977. Fireside Chat, 2-1-78, Box 17, Staff Office Files, Speechwriters' Chronological, Jimmy Carter Library.

27 Wayne, letter.

28 Wayne, letter.

29 Wayne, letter.

30 James Fallows, Memo to Hamilton Jordan, September 4, 1977. Fireside Chat, 2-1-78, Box 17, Staff Office Files, Speechwriters' Chronological, Jimmy Carter Library.

31 Harlan J. Strauss, Letter to Jim Fallows, September 6, 1977. Staff Office Files, Speechwriters, James Fallows Files, Jimmy Carter Library.

32 Fisher, 105–8.

33 James Fallows, Letter to Harlan Strauss, September 19, 1977. Staff Office Files, Speech Writers, James Fallows Files, Jimmy Carter Library.

34 James Fallows, Memorandum to Zbigniew Brzezinski, January 27, 1978 and Suggested Outline: Panama Canal Speech, 1-25-78. Fireside Chat, 2-1-78, Box 17, Staff Office Files, Speechwriters'

Chronological, Jimmy Carter Library.

35 Phillip M. Crane, *Surrender in Panama: The Case Against the Treaty* (New York: Dale Books, 1978), 1–2; and Jimmy Carter, "Panama Canal Treaties," *Public Papers of the President of the United States: Jimmy Carter*, 1978 (Washington, DC: United States Government Printing Office, 1979), 259. About 100,000 copies of Crane's book were distributed in January, 1978 by Richard Viguerie's associates.

36 Jimmy Carter, "Radio-Television News Directors Association," *Public Papers of the Presidents: Jimmy Carter*, 1977 (Washington, DC: United States Government Printing Office, 1978), 1597 (referred to hereafter as 9–15–77).

37 Carter, "Fireside Chat," 262 and 263.

38 Jimmy Carter, "'Ask President Carter' on CBS Radio," *Public Papers of the Presidents: Jimmy Carter*, 1977 (Washington, DC: United States Government Printing Office, 1978), 325 (referred to hereafter as 3–5–77).

39 The treaty chain included the 1901 Hay-Paunceforte Treaty with Britain permitting American involvement in any Central American canal, the 1903 Hay-Herran Treaty (unanimously rejected by the Colombian Senate) which would have granted America complete control over the canal area to build and operate a canal, and the 1903 Panamanian secession from Colombia in which America played "a secondary role." See Crane, 23–33.

40 Crane, 41.

41 Crane quotes a Hay warning that American failure to ratify the Hay-Bunau-Varilla Treaty could mean the failure of any American canal effort: "As it stands now as soon as the Senate votes we shall have a treaty in the main very satisfactory, vastly advantageous to the United States . . . not so advantageous to Panama. If we amend the treaty and send it back some time next month, the . . . period of enthusiastic unanimity, which . . . comes only once in the lifetime of a revolution, will have passed away, and they will have entered on the new fields of politics and dispute. . . . If it is again submitted to their consideration they will attempt to amend it in many places, no man can say with what result." Quoted in Crane, 38.

42 Crane, 36.

43 Crane, 37.

44 Jimmy Carter, "Denver, Colorado," *Public Papers of the Presidents: Jimmy Carter*, 1977 (Washington, DC: United States Government Printing Office, 1978), 1886 (referred to hereafter as 10–22–77)

45 Quoted by Crane, 136.

46 Crane, 36–37.

47 Fisher, 194.

48 Carter, "Fireside Chat," 262.

49 Crane, 56–57, 71, and 66.

50 Carter, "Fireside Chat," 258 and 261.

51 Jimmy Carter, "Interview with the President," Public Papers of the Presidents: Jimmy Carter, 1977 (Washington, DC: United States Government Printing Office, 1978), 1513 (referred to hereafter as 8–27–77).

52 Carter, 9–15–77, 1597.

53 Carter, "Fireside Chat," 260 and 262.

54 Crane, 41.

55 Crane, 41.

56 Carter disdained Crane's sort of South American policy as "kind of like a big brother giving handouts to small nations to the south to buy their friendship," Carter, 10–22–77, 1886.

57 Crane, 93.

58 Crane, 93.

59 Crane, 82.

60 Crane, 102.

61 Carter, "Fireside Chat," 262.

[62] Carter, 10–22–77, 1888.

[63] Carter, "Fireside Chat," 262.

[64] Carter, "Fireside Chat," 263, emphasis added.

[65] Carter, 10–22–77, 1890.

[66] Carter, "Fireside Chat," 259 and 262.

[67] Carter, "Fireside Chat," 262.

[68] Carter, "Fireside Chat," 260.

[69] Crane, 113–114.

[70] Crane, 113.

[71] Crane, 1.

[72] Viguerie, 70–71.

[73] Fisher, 194.

[74] Barnet Baskerville, "The Illusion of Proof," *Western Speech* 25 (Fall 1961), 236–242.

Chapter Fourteen

Argument from Transcendence
Pro-Life Versus Pro-Choice

As a social movement challenges established norms, values, hierarchical relationships, symbols, and rhetorical strategies and as it proceeds from the genesis and social unrest stages to the enthusiastic mobilization stage, its newfound strength "creates doubts about the legitimacy and morality of the establishment."[1] Established institutions cannot ignore this threat. They respond, often in conjunction with resistance or countermovements, to the social movement's provocations by challenging its fragile claim of legitimacy, means and ends, norms and values, and credibility.

Confrontations with institutional forces and countermovements serve three essential functions for social movements. They establish the social movement as a serious threat; they contrast the two collectives; and they reveal the ugly side of the establishment and its collaborators. Robert Cathcart claims that confrontation is "the necessary ingredient" for a social movement to come into being and to proceed with its cause, while Kenneth Burke notes that "drama requires a conflict."[2] And Leland Griffin, building on Burke's writings, argues that "The development of a countermovement is vital: for it 'is the bad side that produces the movement which makes history, by providing a struggle.'"[3]

As necessary as confrontation appears to be for social movements, however, its results are often a mixture of blessings and curses. Resistance rhetoric from institutions and countermovements threatens the social movement's existence by attacking its foundations: ideology, methods, ends, structure, and legitimacy. Unless the social movement is able to develop an effective rebuttal strategy, it may be pushed back to an earlier stage, may stall, or may perish. If for every persuasive action there is a reaction, it is always possible that the reaction may overwhelm the social movement's action.

Argument from Transcendence

Social movements (innovative, revivalistic, and resistance) appear to rely heavily upon a "rhetoric of transcendence" to challenge and counter the persuasive efforts of institutions and other movements. In a rhetoric of transcendence, persuaders argue that a person, group, goal, thing, right, action, or proposal *surpasses*, is *superior* to, or was *prior* to related choices. Karl Wallace notes that "In deliberatives the point is, what is good and what is evil, and of good what is greater, and of evil what is the less."[4]

When operating at the *highest level* of transcendence, persuaders claim that a goal, group, or right, for instance, is superior to or greater than *all* other options. The goal, group, or right has attained (through development, achievement, statute, discovery, or dogma) the *ultimate* state of perfection. When operating at the *lowest level* of transcendence, persuaders argue that a goal, group, or right is superior to or greater than *one* or *some* of its kind.[5] Aristotle wrote many centuries ago that "The acquisition of a greater in place of a lesser good, or of a lesser in place of a greater evil, is also good, for in proportion as the greater exceeds the lesser there is acquisition of good or removal of evil."[6] Thus, the goal, group, or right has not reached an ultimate state of perfection but is *more perfect* than its competitors.

Kenneth Burke describes transcendence as the building of a language "*bridge* whereby one realm is *transcended* by being viewed *in terms of* a realm 'beyond it.' "[7] Theorists from Cicero in ancient Rome to the twentieth century have identified four common points of comparison in establishing transcendence, Burke's language bridge: quantity (more-less, large-small), quality (good-bad, excellent-poor), value (important-unimportant, desirable-undesirable), and hierarchy (high-low, above-below).[8] Persuaders base arguments on *quantity*, writes Kenneth Burke, when contending that one group is larger than a competing group or that one organization is more inclusive than one or more organizations with which it is identified.[9] For instance, Planned Parenthood claims to be "America's oldest, largest and most respected family planning organization."[10] A person advocating censorship may claim a right to speak for the "American people" that transcends political parties, special interest groups, or liberals. Leaders of an "industrial union" that is open to all workers may claim that their organization transcends a "trade union" that represents only one trade such as carpenters, plumbers, or control tower operators. Thus, many protest groups struggle to become (or claim to be) the largest or most inclusive of all grassroots, people's, workers', professional, reform, or political organizations.

Persuaders use the comparative point of *quality* when arguing that one goal, proposal, or strategy, for instance, is good while a competing goal, proposal, or strategy is bad or evil. Truth is contrasted with falsehood, justice with injustice, freedom with slavery, equality with inequality, nonviolence with violence, rationality with irrationality, reason with emotion, prejudice with tolerance or respect, moral development with moral underdevelopment. Aristotle has noted, however, that "it often happens that people agree that two things are both useful but do not agree about which is the more so, the next step will be to treat of relative goodness and relative utility."[11] Thus, a persuader may contend that one proposal promises a *greater good* than a competing proposal or that one strategy is *less evil* than another strategy. Debaters, litigants, and legislators often argue about "comparative advantages" or "comparative disadvantages" of proposals and actions. For instance, persons warning of the potential catastrophic results of acid rain may recognize that solutions will cause economic hardships for some companies and workers; persons advocating censorship of textbooks or gun control measures may admit that their proposals will place some limits on constitutional rights; and persons arguing against using animals for medical research may admit that some research might be more difficult to perform without animals. But in each case, persuaders argue that the potential benefits outweigh the potential harms.

Persuaders use the point of *value* when arguing that a group's ends are so important that any means (vilification, dishonesty, obscenity, espionage, disruptions, violence, terrorism) are justified or that the need to meet a crisis takes precedence over factional differences. For example, government agencies use "national security" to justify spying on American citizens and the issuance of "disinformation." Political parties justify mudslinging and dirty campaign tricks by arguing it is for "the good of the people." Militant elements of social movements may use justice, freedom, equality, and independence to rationalize bombings, assassinations, and terrorism. Attaining a goal or preventing a change, persuaders argue, is more important—is of greater value—than the means used, factional differences, ideological disputes, or which movement leader or organization takes the lead or gets the credit. Barry Brummett notes that "one may *avoid* guilt by engaging in *transcendence*. This avoidance of guilt puts the sin into a perspective which redefines it as 'not a sin,' as a virtue or as the requirement of some higher or nobler hierarchy."[12] All kinds of questionable actions are taken by both institutions and social movements "in the name of God."

Persuaders use the point of *hierarchy* when attempting to establish that one thing, act, right, or ideal exceeds another because it is of a higher order along a gradation or continuum: human above animal, animal life over comfort or style, spiritual over temporal, supernatural over natural, universal over the individual or local, ethical over utilitarian.[13] Medical scientists, for example, argue that it is ethical to experiment on animals because these experiments will eventually help save the lives of humans, a higher order of life. Animal rights activists, on the other hand, argue that the suffering and mutilation of animals is evil for what it does to living, feeling beings superior to inanimate objects and plants. Persons of some religious organizations refuse to recite the "Pledge of Allegiance" or go to war for their country because these human, political acts violate religious principles that are of a higher order. The notion of "hierarchy" is a versatile argumentative tactic for collectives such as social movements. For instance, if a member or leader does something to discredit the movement, a persuader might argue that the "power of truth" for which the movement is fighting "transcends the limitations of the personal agent who propounds it."[14] To counteract feelings of guilt or accusations of blame for the consequences of a movement's actions, a persuader might argue that the act was not an "inferior kind of crime" (breaking-and-entering, trespassing, petty theft, vandalism, killing in a drunken brawl) but a "transcendent kind of crime" actually "required by traditional values" or to further a just cause.[15]

The strategy of transcendence provides social movements with a variety of lines of argument for defending organizations, enhancing positions, countering other movements, and avoiding the necessity of denying the undeniable. Argument from transcendence may strengthen a movement's support among "the people" and important legitimizers because it refutes the opposition by identifying the movement symbolically (including its ideology, prescribed course of action, mobilization efforts, and claims to legitimacy) with what is large, good, important, and of the highest order and the opposition with what is small, evil, unimportant, and of a lower order. Kenneth Burke writes:

> Hence, to some degree, solution of conflict must always be done purely in the symbolic realm (by "transcendence") if it is to be done at all. Persons of moral and imaginative depth require great enterprise and resourcefulness in such purely "symbolic" solutions of conflict (by the formation of appropriate "attitudes").[16]

The Abortion Conflict as a Case Study

The conflict over abortion is centuries old, but the current conflict in the United States began with the forming of "right-to-life" committees during the late 1960s to resist increasing efforts to liberalize state laws governing abortion.[17] On January 22, 1973, the United States Supreme Court dealt this fledgling resistance movement an "unqualified legal defeat."[18] In *Roe v. Wade*, the Supreme Court decided (1) that a woman's constitutional right of privacy precludes a state from prohibiting her from obtaining an abortion on demand during the first trimester of pregnancy, (2) that a state could regulate abortions during the second trimester only for the purpose of protecting the woman's life, and (3) that a state could regulate abortions during the third trimester to preserve the life of the child.[19] Thus, the Supreme Court viewed fetal life as human (viable) only after the first six months of pregnancy.

Right-to-life groups recovered quickly from the shock of this defeat and began to create a revivalistic social movement to make abortion unlawful once again and to reaffirm society's respect for all human life. The primary solution proposed and the means of obtaining it, particularly during the early years, is a constitutional amendment defining human life as beginning at the moment of conception and prohibiting the termination of a "child's" life except in situations in which the "mother's" life is in grave danger. This amendment would overturn the Supreme Court decision and preclude further court and legislative actions (state and national) to liberalize abortion. The National Right to Life Committee, its affiliates in all fifty states, Baptists for Life, American Life League, Women Exploited By Abortion, American Life Lobby, Americans Against Abortion, Catholic and evangelical churches, the Moral Majority, and allied groups have mobilized massive political pressure from the "grassroots level" to move an amendment through the Congress, to pass restrictive federal and state laws, to elect candidates at all levels (including Presidents Reagan and Bush) who would support their positions and appoint anti-abortion justices to the Supreme Court to overturn *Roe v. Wade*. More militant tactics have become common since the mid-1980s, particularly Operation Rescue's efforts to blockade abortion clinics, discourage pregnant women from obtaining abortions through "sidewalk counseling," pressure hospitals and physicians into refusing to perform abortions, and clog the jails by prompting police officers into massive arrests. Violence such as bombings, arson, vandalism, and shooting into clinics have become commonplace. The ultimate violence occurred on March 10, 1993 when Dr. David Gunn was murdered by a pro-life militant in Pensacola, Florida.[20]

A "pro-choice" resistance—and now countermovement—organized quickly to resist the efforts to overturn *Roe v. Wade* and restrict access to abortion through municipal, state, congressional, and presidential actions. NARAL had been a major participant in the pre-1973 years and was then known as the National Association for Repeal of Abortion Laws. After *Roe v. Wade*, it changed its name to the National Abortion Rights Action League and has worked closely with the Religious Coalition for Abortion Rights (RCAR), Planned Parenthood, the National Organization for Women (NOW), and allied organizations to protect the "woman's right to choose." For several years these groups presented their cases primarily through leaflets, mailings, and advertisements in magazines and newspapers. As the pro-life movement pressured physicians and hospitals into refusing to perform abortions, achieved many legislative successes, and seemed near victory with conservative, pro-life appointments to the Supreme Court, pro-choice became more active. The movement has held mass rallies in Washington, D.C. and other cities, campaigned actively for pro-choice candidates, brought pressure on state legislatures and Congress, presented court cases, protected abortion clinics, and formed escorts for women trying to enter clinics surrounded by pro-life activists.

The election of President Clinton in 1992, and the possibility of appointment of pro-choice justices to the Supreme Court, has apparently tilted the conflict once more toward the pro-choice countermovement. This election and other electoral setbacks have spurred the pro-life movement into greater efforts to end legalized abortion. Rather than the struggle lessening, it has seemingly entered a new and perhaps more militant phase.

The raging conflict over legalized abortion in the United States provides us with an excellent case study of how movements and countermovements use argument from transcendence. Although the conflict has increasingly been punctuated by violence, disruptions, coercive tactics, terrorism, and even murder, both movement and countermovement have relied primarily on symbols and symbolic actions to attain and maintain public support and to win victories in living rooms, voting booths, courtrooms, legislative chambers, and executive offices.[21] An analysis of dozens of leaflets, pamphlets, mailings, books, newspaper essays, and advertisements reveals that, for over thirty years, the pro-life and pro-choice movements have relied heavily on arguments from transcendence.[22]

These movements use the four points of comparison to define fundamental issues, to present and defend cases, to resolve dilemmas, to enhance their credibilities, to attack one another, and to refute charges made against their ideologies, tactics, organizations, and memberships. In the remainder of this chapter, we will focus on how both social movements have used arguments from transcendence in their clashes over personhood, rights, reality, and respective movements.

The Clash Over Personhood.   The key premise on which all pro-life and pro-choice arguments from transcendence rest is when a "life" or a "person" comes into existence. Both movements expend a great deal of rhetorical energy trying to establish the moment of "personhood" and to discount the other's claims. If a person exists at the moment of conception, abortion is murder; if a person does not exist until the moment of birth or viability, abortion is not murder but a medical procedure to terminate an unwanted pregnancy.

Pro-Choice   The first tenet of this movement is that the fetus has never been recognized legally, constitutionally, or historically as a "full-fledged person" but only as a "potential human being."[23] Persuaders contend that even the Bible declines to identify the fetus as a person. Exodus 21:22 regards the fetus not as a person but as belonging to the father; the New Testament does not address the issue.[24] Second, the pro-choice movement claims that no one really knows when personhood begins. Persuaders assert that "medical, legal, and religious experts cannot, and will never, agree!"[25] The belief that personhood begins at conception, they contend, has been "disputed by theologians for centuries"; even the Roman Catholic church did not espouse this belief until the mid-nineteenth century.[26] Third, the pro-choice movement points out that the lack of agreement "means determining when life begins—which no one knows—must ultimately rest on man-made definitions more arbitrary, philosophical and religious than scientific."[27] Contrary opinions are theological or religious beliefs held by the Roman Catholic church and a few other denominations, not biological or absolute facts.[28] These three claims place the opposition's belief of personhood at the moment of conception at the bottom of a hierarchy of beliefs: below scientific or biological facts, legal or constitutional statutes and decisions, biblical teachings, and prevailing theological beliefs. It is reduced in *importance* and in a *hierarchy* of beliefs to *merely* an arbitrary, man-made, religious issue among *some* denominations.[29] Thus, pro-choice persuaders conclude that anti-abortion advocates give "a fertilized egg or a fetus legal standing equal to that of a pregnant woman" whose personhood is undisputed.[30] They argue that "a qualitative distinction must be made between its [the fetus] claims and the rights of a responsible person made in God's image who is living relationships with God and other human beings;" to do otherwise would be "to dehumanize the woman, to consider her a mere 'thing' through which the fetus is passing."[31] The woman (a recognized person) is clearly superior to the fetus (recognized arbitrarily as a person only by a few religious denominations) she is carrying and thus deserves higher legal and constitutional standing and concern.

Pro-Life This movement argues that life begins at the moment of conception, that "Human life is a continuous developmental process that begins at conception and ceases at death."[32] In support of this claim, pro-life persuaders offer detailed chronologies (often with photographs) of development from conception, through three weeks when the heart starts beating, to the moment of birth.[33] They argue that, contrary to pro-choice claims and the Supreme Court decision that declared the unborn to be "not persons at all," scientists, medical authorities, every Protestant theologian since Calvin, the Catholic church and most Protestant denominations, and the Bible agree that life begins at conception, the moment the sperm and egg meet.[34] Thus, the pro-life position is not *merely* church dogma or a religious issue, but is a scientific fact, a basic human issue.[35] If human life exists from the moment of conception, persuaders conclude, the fetus is a person, one of us, and not a "poorly functioning adult" but a "splendidly functioning baby."[36] The act of abortion, then, is not removing, as pro-choice claims, "a mass or blob of tissue," a "POC—product of conception," or a "clump of cells" but the destruction, killing, murdering of "an innocent human life," "pre-born children," and the "defenseless little child living in the mother's womb."[37] In the hierarchy of living beings, the fetus or baby is equal to its mother and higher than all nonpersons. Because the fetus is both innocent and defenseless, it deserves special protection against its mother's (an equal but not superior) desire to kill it.

The Clash Over Rights. The establishment of the personhood and hierarchical status of the woman or the fetus allows each movement to develop a case for which rights are most important and which are being violated or are in danger of being violated. Persuaders use the comparative points of value and hierarchy in their clashes over rights.

Pro-Choice argues that "every woman in a free society" has the fundamental, constitutional right guaranteed by the Supreme Court to a safe, legal abortion because it is crucial to her health and well-being.[38] "The welfare of the mother," a universally recognized person, "must always be our primary concern," pro-choice advocates argue, and freedom of choice (reproductive freedom) is fundamental.[39] This choice, free from unwarranted governmental intrusion into our private lives, is the "most precious of individual rights."[40] Persuaders claim that the right to privacy, upon which the Supreme Court based its decision in *Roe v. Wade* in 1973, is guaranteed by the 1st, 9th, and 14th amendments to the constitution. Any effort by religious groups to limit this choice is a direct threat to religious liberty and the constitutional provision of separation of church and state. This position is summed up in the pro-choice slogan, "Not the church, not the state, women must decide their fate."[41] Pro-choice advocates contend, then, that the value of the woman's health and well-being exceeds that of a nonperson, and the rights of privacy and freedom of choice are the most important of all human rights. These rights are essential to our religious liberty and reproductive freedom. All other rights are lower in the hierarchy and of less importance.

Pro-Life argues that since the fetus is without doubt a person, a living human being, it must be guaranteed the right to life that is the "most basic value of our society," the "most fundamental right," the "paramount right," "the most basic human right bestowed on us by God."[42] This premise allows pro-life persuaders to argue from the highest level of transcendence and to claim that "If all of our rights are to be protected, we must defend this first and most basic right—the right to life."[43] They do not argue against women's rights, the freedom of choice, or religious liberty, but place these lower on the rights hierarchy and dependent upon the right to life. A leaflet entitled *The Abortion Connection* exclaims that in contrast to the right to life, "There is *NO* 'constitutional' right to abortion. There is only a Supreme Court-created right from a split decision in *Roe v. Wade* on January 22, 1973."[44] In a leaflet bearing a picture of an unborn but fully developed fetus, the author asks, "But does her [the woman's] rights include dealing out a death sentence to another human being who is completely defenseless?"[45] The point appears to be a reverse value argument: the end (preserving a woman's right of privacy or choice) does not justify the means (depriving the fetus of the right to life).

Pro-life persuaders also point to state and federal laws designed to guarantee lesser rights and the rights of lower beings, a combination value and hierarchy argument. For example, one writer notes that state laws guarantee "the right of inheritance, to damages received while yet unborn, to get a blood transfusion over the mother's objection, to have a guardian appointed, and other rights of citizenship" but not the "most basic right of all—the right to life."[46] Newspaper advertisements entitled "Eagles, Beagles, Babies and 'There Oughta Be a Law' " contain large pictures of a bald eagle, two beagle puppies, and a fetus. A caption reads: "Ours is a peculiar society. We have laws protecting wildlife and dogs, but not defenseless human beings."[47] The advertisements report that stealing one eagle egg may result in a $5,000 fine, one year in jail, or both and that both houses of Congress overwhelmingly approved a federal law prohibiting the use of dogs in tests of chemical, biological, and radioactive warfare materials. While these laws protect the life and rights of eagles and beagles, the advertisements note, "Last year . . . more than 1,000,000 unborn babies were 'terminated' through 'abortion on demand.' Terminated means killed. Killed without penalty. Unless someone got a parking ticket in front of an abortion mill." The lines of argument are clear. Although states and the federal government have laws to protect the rights of privacy and choice for the mother, civil rights for the unborn child, and life and well-being of animals, no laws guarantee the human right to life—the right at the pinnacle of the human rights hierarchy.

The Clash Over Realities. The pro-choice and pro-life movements offer very different views of reality. Essentially the first portrays the present as the best of times and the second portrays the present as the worst of times, but each also takes a look backward and a look forward in presenting their cases for resisting or bringing about change. Arguments tend to be from quality and value.

Pro-Choice traces abortion practices back to ancient Egypt and concludes that there have always been and always will be abortions.[48] The only issue, persuaders argue, is whether abortions will be legal and safe or illegal and brutal. Early pro-choice leaflets contain police photographs of mutilated women on bathroom floors from self-induced and "back-alley" abortions and abused or murdered unwanted babies.[49] Later leaflets and mailings write of the "horror," "slaughter," and "butchery" of past abortions in which knitting needles, coat hangers, Lysol, and soap suds were used to induce abortions in filthy conditions.[50] Actress Joanne Woodward writes of a haunting part she played in which a woman faced the evils of a back-alley abortion. Kate Michelman (Executive Director of NARAL) relates her personal story about receiving an abortion. First, she was treated in the most demeaning fashion by medical and legal officials; second, she had to be declared an unfit mother even though she had three small children and; third, she had to receive her husband's permission even though he had abandoned the family and refused to pay child support.[51] In the past, persuaders claim, the wealthy could get hospital abortions because they could afford to travel long distances and pay large sums of money. The poor, on the other hand, had to turn to the butchery of the back alley even when they were the "innocent victims of rage and violence" such as child abuse, rape, and incest.[52]

The pro-choice movement contrasts the horrors of the past with safe, legal abortions since 1973. All women, including the poor, now receive "safe and skilled treatment in hospitals and clinics," children are wanted and eagerly awaited, maternal and infant health has improved markedly, and countless women have been saved from injury and death.[53] Advocates claim that death from legal abortion is rare, actually safer than childbirth, and that there has been no detectable increase in mental illness or psychological stress resulting from abortions.[54] Clearly the *quality* of life for women and infants since *Roe v. Wade* transcends the past to which the pro-life movement would return. Pro-choice persuaders have increasingly warned audiences that the Reagan and Bush administrations and state governments, in support of the pro-life cause, have placed unwarranted and evil restrictions on the woman's right to choose. They cite gag rules on counselors, parental and spouse consent laws, class discrimination against the poor who cannot get federal funds for abortions, and denial of abortions to institutionalized women, military wives and women, Peace Corps workers, and even children pregnant from incest.[55] The present, they warn, is slipping slowly back to the butchery of the past.

The pro-choice movement increasingly peers into the future and describes the horrors that will take place if its resistance efforts fail. Since laws and constitutional amendments will not eliminate abortions, persuaders claim, women will be "dragged back" to the untold suffering—the nightmare—of illegal abortions. Women would have to choose between compulsory pregnancy or death at the hands of quack abortionists.[56] Extending the opposition's argument about protecting the rights of the fetus legally, persuaders describe the chaotic impact such laws might have on our "entire system of civil and criminal laws." The woman would have to register her fetus with a "fetus-protection agency," and if the fetus were to die from disease, be miscarried, or be killed in an auto or sporting accident, the woman could be charged with premeditated murder and be jailed for life or executed. Physicians could be convicted of homicide for performing an abortion and suffer the same fate.[57] Coinciding with all of these horrors, advocates warn, infant and maternal mortality would increase, intolerable governmental intrusion into the private lives of pregnant women would be legal, and religious liberty would diminish because "one particular theology would become civil law."[58] The rhetoric of the pro-choice movement attempts to do what a resistance movement must do—convince audiences that the present must be preserved at all cost because it is *far better* than the past or the future desired by the opposition.

Pro-Life dwells little on the past and never claims there were few or no abortions prior to *Roe v. Wade* in 1973. A publication by Americans Against Abortion does argue that 84 percent to 87 percent of so-called "back-alley" abortions of the past "were not done in back alleys at all" but by "reputable physicians" in medical facilities.[59] Pro-life persuaders dwell most on what has happened in the past when humans were labeled as nonpersons. They offer Nazi Germany and the extermination of six million Jews as indisputable evidence of what happens when some humans are judged to be inferior.[60] A number of sources refer to the treatment of native Americans as "savages" and of African Americans who, as nonpersons, could be bought, sold, or killed, particularly after the Dred Scott decision of 1857.[61] Thus, pro-life implies that the instances of abortion prior to 1973 were inconsequential and uses historical accounts of native Americans, slavery, and Nazi Germany as lead-ins to its lengthy accounts of the horrors of the present. The past was obviously better than the present, at least for the unborn.

Pro-life materials abound with accounts and pictures of the cruel, barbarous slaughter and even cannibalism of the unborn, what is called the "hidden holocaust." This evil is perpetrated for insignificant or unimportant reasons. Persuaders claim that 98 percent of abortions are for social and professional reasons, literally killing unborn humans "on whim."[62] Millions die every year merely because pregnancy is inconvenient or the mother wants to get rid of an annoying problem. Nurses and physicians tell stories about when they had to starve, smother, or bash in the head of an aborted fetus when it refused to die, and these stories are often accompanied by gory, full-color pictures of tiny bodies torn apart by a variety of abortion methods and dumped in buckets and trash cans.[63] The most spectacular and controversial effort to show life and death in the womb is the video entitled "The Silent Scream" that purports to show the struggle for life of a fetus being "murdered" by a vacuum aspirator. Joseph Scheidler, founder and director of the Pro-Life Action League, often narrates this struggle: "She retreats frantically from the device. But it pulls her legs off. Then it disembowels her. She struggles violently with her arms. Her head falls back; her mouth opens in anguish."[64] Pro-life advocates claim that the act is so heinous that pro-abortion forces have created euphemisms to mask reality: "terminating a pregnancy," "post-conceptual planning," "menstrual extraction," and "exercising a woman's right to choose." And they claim that the tragedies of the present, largely unreported and covered up, go beyond the unborn. Women who have been "exploited by abortion" suffer life-threatening complications and even death, serious mental and psychological problems, and increases in sterility, miscarriages, tubal pregnancies, and premature babies. Persuaders argue that abortion-on-demand has caused child abuse to increase by 500 percent.[65] The conclusion is obvious: this is the worst of times. The past may not have been perfect, but it was better than the present with its hidden tragedies for both the unborn and the mothers that destroy them.

What about the future? Pro-life persuaders predict a chain reaction because, "Once we permit killing of the unborn child, there will be no stopping."[66] The list of nonpersons may grow to include anyone considered to be a burden because if the state can legalize murder of some, it can do so for the many. One leaflet warns:

> How long will it be before other groups of humans will be defined out of legal existence when it has been decided that they too have become socially burdensome?

> SENIOR CITIZENS BEWARE

> MINORITY RACES BEWARE

> CRIPPLED CHILDREN BEWARE

> Once the decision has been made that all human life is no longer an unalienable right, but that some can be killed because they are a social burden, then the senile, the weak, the physically and mentally inadequate and perhaps someday even the politically troublesome are in danger.

> It did happen once before in this century you know. Remember Germany?[67]

The United States must return to a better past to stop the evils of the present and to avoid even greater evils of the future.

The Clash Over Competing Social Movements. Each movement uses a variety of arguments from transcendence to establish its size and stature and to justify its motives and methods while shrinking the other and painting it in dark-hued colors of evil. The transcendent points of quantity, quality, and hierarchy are common in these competing rhetorical efforts.

Pro-Choice advocates describe their movement as a "massive state-by-state grassroots campaign" and mobilization that has the "overwhelming support" of the "vast majority" of Americans. They claim that polls continually show that four out of five Americans, including the majority of Roman Catholics and almost all Protestant and Jewish groups, support the pro-choice position that "there are situations in which abortion may be a moral alternative."[68] They talk about the size of NARAL's membership, the hundreds of thousands who have marched for pro-choice in Washington, D.C., and the 27–35 religious organizations that belong to the Religious Coalition for Abortion Rights. In contrast, the pro-life movement is an "anti-choice minority," a "tiny, fanatical minority," a "vocal, powerful minority."[69] Compared to pro-choice that represents most Americans and mainline religious groups, pro-life consists of a small group of religious zealots, a few small Protestant denominations, Orthodox Jews, and the Roman

Catholic hierarchy allied with the political right-wing and anti-women's rights organizations.[70] Thus, they argue pro-choice is superior in both size (quantity) and stature (hierarchy).

Advocates claim the pro-choice community is being heard and heeded in elections throughout the country because its motives, goals, and methods are virtuous (quality) and desirable (value). The pro-choice movement disputes opposition claims that the movement advocates abortion. In fact, some sources claim, we "don't know *anyone*" connected with the movement "who is 'pro-abortion.' "[71] Instead, the movement is pro-family, for peace among nations, and an advocate of help for the poor, a sound educational system, and a clean environment while struggling against racism, classism, and sexism. Its methods are limited to electing pro-choice candidates and preserving abortion rights through the courts. As a result, its position has received the endorsement of such highly credible groups as the American Medical Association, the American Bar Association, hundreds of doctors of obstetrics and gynecology, the President's Commission on Population Growth and the American Future, the National Conference of Commissioners on Uniform State Laws, the U.S. Commission on Civil Rights, and the National Academy of Scientists Institute on Medicine.[72]

Pro-choice contrasts their membership with that of the pro-life movement which consists of religious sects, church-supported lobbying groups, the hierarchy of the Roman Catholic Church (not Catholics themselves), the ultra right, spineless politicians, and arch conservatives such as Senators Jesse Helms of North Carolina and Orin Hatch of Utah and the reverends Jerry Falwell and Jimmy Swaggart. The cover of one leaflet is the picture of weeping, pro-life advocate Reverend Jimmy Swaggart on television admitting to having consorted with prostitutes.[73] Pro-life advocates are identified as dangerous extremists, ruthless fanatics, mobs, terrorists, and irrational, moral zealots who will stop at nothing until they achieve their evil, self-serving goals: return women to a position of subservience, force their religious dogma on the American people, foster class discrimination, end sex education in the schools, and outlaw all forms of birth control.[74] Pro-choice literature chronicles the guerrilla, ruthless, and terrorist tactics of so-called right-to-life groups who "have an iron disregard for life" and are often in "a frenzy amounting to hysteria."[75] These include death threats, threats to kidnap children, arson, bombings, shootings into clinics while patients and staff are inside, acid sprayed into clinics, hate campaigns, obscenity shouting, blockades of clinics, stalking of physicians and physicians' families, and threats to hospitals where abortions might take place. After Dr. David Gunn was murdered by a pro-life advocate outside a clinic in Pensacola, Florida in March 1993, pro-choice supporters said they had been expecting this to happen as terrorist tactics had escalated:

> Anyone who wants to check the fertile soil in which fanaticism grows has only to listen to the leaders' responses to the assassination of the 47-year-old doctor and father of two: "While Gunn's death is unfortunate," said Don Treshman of "Rescue America," "it's also true that quite a number of babies' lives will be saved." While it is wrong to kill, said Randall Terry [leader of Operation

Rescue], "we have to recognize that this doctor was a mass murderer." "Praise God," said a protestor at a clinic in Melbourne, Florida, "one of the (baby) killers is dead!"[76]

Thus, the pro-choice movement concludes that the pro-life movement is smaller (quantity), consists of and is supported by evil persons and groups (quality), and employs evil means to achieve evil and self-centered goals (quality).

Pro-Life advocates claim their movement is not a narrow, conservative, religious and political movement but a "great people's movement," "the largest grassroots citizens movement in recent history," a "majority movement" that transcends all religions and political parties. "Millions have joined the National Right to Life Committee and many more millions will join when they realize how big the problem is."[77] Persuaders argue that polls cited in pro-choice literature are highly misleading and present their own interpretations of results: 65 percent of Americans believe abortion is morally wrong, 52–55 percent approve of abortion only for "hard cases," 77 percent of Americans oppose abortion for social, non-medical reasons, and most Americans approve of only 2 percent of abortions performed today. One writer notes that if the following question were asked, results would favor the pro-life position: "Should an innocent human being be killed for the crime of another?"[78] They believe their movement is not a small political-religious coalition, but a massive movement that represents the true beliefs of America. This "majority movement," advocates claim, is supported by "some of the finest minds in the country," "people from all across the country and in every walk of life," moms, dads, business people, retired people and children," nurses, physicians, lawyers, courts, state and federal legislators of both parties, and presidents Reagan and Bush.[79] In contrast, they portray the pro-choice movement, nearly always referred to as "abortionists," as "social engineering advocacy groups," tiny minorities, and the "abortion industry." One leaflet argues that, since it is possible for eleven people in the National Council of Churches to convey an "official stand" for thirty-three denominations with forty-two million members, the pro-choice stance should be discounted.[80] Thus, they argue pro-life exceeds pro-choice in both quantity and quality.

The pro-life movement also argues that it is superior to the pro-choice movement in motives for acting. In a "VERY URGENT" "action-gram" to National Right to Life Committee members in 1987, president Dr. John Willke declared that the NLRC's sole purpose was to "stop the wholesale slaughter of unborn babies in their mother's wombs," while "Planned Parenthood, NARAL and the National Organization for Women exist to make sure that unborn babies don't live. That's a very sorry reason."[81] Persuaders contrast their unselfish crusade to save unborn lives with the "abortionists' " motive to maintain "abortion-on-demand industry for financial profit, alleging that pro-choice is only interested in the $700 million dollars a year they get from killing babies and selling these bodies for soap and cosmetics.[82] David Mall, in his book entitled *In Good Conscience: Abortion and Moral Necessity*, reviews the moral development principles and theories of philosopher Jean Piaget and psychologist Lawrence Kohlberg and asserts that pro-life advocates have reached a high level of moral development in which they struggle for the rights and welfare of others while pro-choice advocates never advance beyond an immature, self-centered stage of moral development and are willing to kill their unborn to achieve social and professional benefits. Mall writes:

> There appear to be two contrary psychological forces at work in the abortion debate: one pulls toward genuine moral growth and development and the other toward moral decay and dissolution. The struggle is really between a moralizing process that is authentic and one that is not. Moralizing that favors abortion is really an anti-development. A parallel is to be found in the relationship between the symbolic and the diabolic, a relationship with deep religious significance. . . . One leads to life and the other leads to death.[83]

Perhaps the greatest rhetorical dilemma facing the pro-life movement is the growing militancy that culminated in the killing of Dr. David Gunn in Pensacola in March 1993. At least 1,000 cases of violent acts were reported between 1984 and 1992, but it is risky for movement members to condemn violence unconditionally. They risk fragmenting the movement.[84] Some pro-life groups take this risk. For example, a consortium of pro-life groups in New York offered a $5,000 reward for information leading to those responsible for bombing an abortion clinic, and the Reverend Jerry Falwell (founder and leader of the Moral Majority) called violent elements "common criminals" and warned that violence does "great damage to the anti-abortion cause."[85] Helen Alvare, director of planning and information for the U.S. Bishop's Secretariat for Pro-Life Activities, declared in a statement following the murder of Dr. Gunn, "As we abhor the violence of abortion, we abhor violence as a dangerous and deplorable means to stop abortion. In the name and in the true spirit of pro-life, we call on all in the pro-life movement to condemn such violence in no uncertain terms."[86] Some leaders of pro-life organizations deny that their members have committed violent acts and urge followers to refrain from violence. Willke of the NLRC issued this appear to members: "Let us witness peacefully in work, in picketing, by sit-ins, in letters, by prayers, and at the ballot box. It is they who live by violence and the modern sword, the suction curette. Violence is not our way."[87] Some pro-life leaders in statements following the death of Dr. Gunn blamed the pro-choice movement for having created the violent climate through abortion. John Burt, regional director of Rescue America, remarked: "I think all life is sacred, and Dr. Gunn and Michael Griffin [Gunn's confessed killer] are both victims of abortion."[88]

Although many moderate movement leaders and followers condemn militancy, some use arguments from transcendence to justify militancy for the cause of life. First, they vindicate militant pro-lifers because militants defend *higher principles* and do not act through self-interest. A writer in the *National Right to Life News* claims "the appeal of the pro-life movement is to those principles of justice and nondiscrimination which transcend self-seeking."[89] Second, pro-life apologists argue that violence for *noble purposes* transcends violence for ignoble purposes and, thus, is acceptable. Cal Thomas of the Moral Majority compares pro-life violence with the civil rights riots of the 1960s and concludes that both were "equally wrong, but served a higher and nobler purpose in that they moved lethargic government leaders to action."[90] Third, pro-life argues that militancy is justified in defense of a *higher law*. For example, Monsignor Thomas C. Corrigan defended the "Cleveland Eleven" by contending that when "the laws of God (which say that abortion is wrong) are in opposition to the laws of man (which say abortion is legal), people are justified in siding with the Gospels and challenging man-made laws."[91] Fourth, persuaders claim that the *end justifies or transcends the means used*. During his trial for trespassing in an abortion clinic sit-in, Dabien Avila of Fort Wayne, Indiana, declared that "when life or property is in danger . . . a person does have a right to go in. He has a right to attempt in a reasonable manner to stop the destruction of life or property."[92] The Cleveland Eleven, arrested for disrupting an abortion clinic, concluded, "It's a small price to pay in view of the millions of lives annually being snuffed out."[93] Fifth, advocates argue that *lesser violence* is justified if it stops a *greater violence*. Jan Carroll of the National Right to Life Committee refuses to apologize for violence because "violence that goes on inside the clinic is much more damaging to the moral fiber of the nation."[94] This is how some pro-life leaders reacted to the death of Dr. Gunn; it was the lesser of two evils. Others seemed to argue this way with reluctance. John Burt said, "We don't condone this, but we have to remember that Dr. Gunn has killed thousands and thousands of babies."[95] And sixth, some advocates contend that *extraordinary circumstances* justify violent means that are ordinarily considered unacceptable in society. Elsie Lewis, active in the American Life League, explains that:

> For the most part, where there is an unjust law, you obey it, and you try to change it. But when they are killing two million babies a year—it is so heinous an injustice. While working to change the law, many lives are being lost. Since 1973 a holocaust has been going on . . . If you believe that an abortuary is murdering thousands of babies and thirty are scheduled for tomorrow, how can you condemn someone for destroying it?[96]

Thus, pro-life persuaders defend militant tactics ranging from trespassing to murder by using six lines of argument that develop three of the four points of comparison that establish transcendence: hierarchy (higher principles, higher law), quality (noble purposes, lesser crime or evil), and value (end over means, extraordinary circumstances, life over a building). These points allow persuaders both to condemn and to praise militant actions and thereby to answer challenges from pro-choice and avoid factionalizing the movement over tactics. Violence, like war, is generally to be condemned, they argue, but there are circumstances when violence is the lesser of two evils and the only viable course of action.

Conclusions

The pro-choice and pro-life movements rely heavily upon argument from transcendence to establish their positions on fundamental issues, to attack one another, and to defend themselves. They employ the comparative points of value and hierarchy when establishing their positions on personhood (the issue upon which all subsequent arguments rest) and to attack opposition claims regarding personhood of the fetus or woman. They employ hierarchy and value points when arguing which rights are most basic (at the top of the rights hierarchy) and which are most important (religious liberty over denominational dogma and life over civil rights, for instance). They employ the points of value and quality when presenting their versions of reality: the past, present, and future. Pro-choice, as a resistance social movement, claims that the present is the best of times while both the past and future have been or might be full of horrors. Pro-life, as a revivalistic social movement, implies that the past was the best of times while the present is full of horrors and the future is likely to be worse. They employ the points of quantity, quality, and hierarchy when establishing themselves (including size, motives, morals, and methods) as the superior movement in the abortion conflict.

Each movement's argument from transcendence is a fragile interdependent network of premises based on a single major premise: either the woman is a full-fledged person while the fetus is a potential person or the fetus is a person from the moment of conception and deserves special protection because of its innocence and vulnerability. The majority of Americans, including many of each movement's sympathizers, have reservations about and support exceptions to or qualifications of these premises. If the recipient of a pro-choice or pro-life message seriously questions or denies the central premise, the network of transcendent arguments crumbles. Thus, neither the woman nor the fetus has the inalienable rights claimed. The past, present, and future was not, is not, and will not be as bright or dark as portrayed. Neither movement rests on the moral high ground to which it has laid claim.

Argument from transcendence is a highly functional rhetorical strategy for social movements. For instance, social movements take moralistic stances portraying their causes and members as being *above* or *superior* to established or proposed norms, values, and institutions. Social movements suffer from limited resources and often find it difficult to *prove* that an institution, competing movement, norm, or value is utterly without value. Transcendence allows a movement to address *degrees* of size, importance, goodness, or risk. For instance, a social movement need not establish that it, its cause, or its methods are without flaw but only that it is larger than an establishment or an opposing movement claims, that it is more honorable than established institutions or a countermovement, that its plan is safer than current or proposed policies, or that its tactics are less evil than ones employed by established institutions or countermovements. Social movements must also strive to maintain unity among supporters of the cause and attract support from the public, legitimizers, and established institutions. Argument from transcendence allows a social movement, or a faction of a movement, to stress its superiority, explain its ideology, and justify its tactics without having to destroy other factions or antagonize institutions that might be potential allies. A social movement does not have to deny competing rights but only to claim that such rights are less important or lower on a hierarchy of rights. Thus, a movement may reduce the risk of factionalizing the movement by scaring away potential supporters.

This chapter has illustrated how the pro-choice and pro-life movements have employed argument from transcendence in their continual conflict over legalized abortion. The four points of comparison—quality, quantity, value, and hierarchy—have enabled them to establish, attack, and defend their positions on personhood, competing rights, visions of reality, and organization (including membership, motives, and tactics). It is difficult to imagine how social movements could carry forward their struggles and meet oppositions without relying upon this essential language "bridge."

Endnotes

[1] Robert S. Cathcart, "Defining Social Movements by Their Rhetorical Form," *Central States Speech Journal* 31 (Winter 1980), 271.

[2] Robert S. Cathcart, "New Approaches to the Study of Social Movements," *Western Speech Communication Journal* 36 (Spring 1972), 88; Kenneth Burke, "Catharsis—Second View," *Centennial Review* 5 (1961), 130; Leland M. Griffin, "A Dramatistic Theory of the Rhetoric of Movements," *Critical Responses to Kenneth Burke*, William Rueckert, ed. (Minneapolis: University of Minnesota Press, 1969), 456.

[3] Griffin, 464.

[4] Karl R. Wallace, *Francis Bacon on Communication and Rhetoric* (Chapel Hill, NC: University of North Carolina Press, 1943), 65.

[5] These levels are apparent in Kenneth Burke's usage of the term transcendence and many synonyms in *Roget's International Thesaurus* (New York: Crowell, 1958), entries 33.5 and 33.8.

[6] Aristotle, *The Rhetoric*, W. Rhys Roberts, trans. (New York: Modern Library, 1954), Book I, 1362a37–1362b2.

[7] Kenneth Burke, *Language as Symbolic Action* (Berkeley: University of California Press, 1966), 187.

[8] Marcus Tullius Cicero, *Topics*, H. M. Hubbell, trans. (Cambridge: Harvard University Press, 1959), 433; Aristotle, Book I, 1363b5–13; Kenneth Burke, *A Rhetoric of Motives* (Berkeley: University of California Press, 1969), 231–279.

[9] Burke, *Rhetoric of Motives*, pp. 11–12; Kenneth Burke, *Dramatism and Development* (Barre, MA: Clark University Press, 1972), 23–24.

[10] Mailing 2 from Faye Wattleton, President, Planned Parenthood Federation of America, n.d., 1.

[11] Aristotle, Book I, 1362a37–b2 and 1363b5–13; Wallace, 60–65.

[12] Barry Brummett, "Burkeian Scapegoating, Mortification, and Transcendence in Presidential Campaign Rhetoric," *Central States Speech Journal* 32 (Winter 1981), 256.

[13] Kenneth Burke, *A Grammar of Motives* (Berkeley: University of California Press, 1969), 424, 425, and 428; Burke, *Rhetoric of Motives*, 14, 16, 76, and 138; Kenneth Burke, *The Rhetoric of Religion* (Berkeley: University of California Press, 1970), 58, 83, and 156.

[14] Burke, *Rhetoric of Motives*, 76.

[15] Burke, *Rhetoric of Religion*, 230; Brummett, 256 and 259.

[16] Kenneth Burke, *The Philosophy of Literary Form* (Berkeley: University of California Press, 1973), 312.

[17] See for example, Frederick S. Jaffe, Barbara L. Lindheim, and Philip R. Lee, *Abortion Politics:*

Private Morality and Public Policy (New York: McGraw-Hill, 1981); Marilyn Falik, *Ideology and Abortion Policy Politics* (New York: Praeger, 1983); "America's Abortion Dilemma," *Newsweek*, January 14, 1985, 20–29; "The Future of Abortion," *Newsweek*, July 17, 1989, 14–20; "Abortion Angst," *Newsweek*, July 13, 1992; 16–20.

[18] Richard D. Orlaski, "Abortion: Legal Questions and Legislative Alternatives," *America*, August 10, 1974, 50.

[19] *United States Supreme Court Reports*, vol. 35 (Rochester, NY: Lawyers Co-Operative Publishing Company, 1974), 147–149.

[20] "The Death of Doctor Gunn," *Newsweek*, March 22, 1993, 34–35.

[21] Randall A. Lake, "Order and Disorder in Anti-Abortion Rhetoric: A Logological View," *Quarterly Journal of Speech* 70 (November 1984), 425–443; Celeste Condit Railsback, "The Contemporary American Abortion Controversy: Stages in the Argument," *Quarterly Journal of Speech* 70 (November 1984), 410–424; Marsha L. Vanderford, "Vilification and Social Movements: A Case Study of Pro-Life and Pro-Choice Rhetoric," *Quarterly Journal of Speech* 75 (May 1989), 166–182; Celeste M. Condit, *Decoding Abortion Rhetoric: Communicating Social Change* (Urbana: University of Illinois Press, 1990); Faye D. Ginsburg, *Contested Lives: The Abortion Debate in an American Community* (Berkeley: University of California Press, 1989).

[22] Fifty leaflets, pamphlets, mailings, and newspaper advertisements produced by each movement from 1970–1992 were the primary sources for this study. Additional materials included thirty issues of The *Communicator*, the Indiana Right to Life newspaper, thirty issues of the Tippecanoe County Right to Life newsletter, and magazine articles dealing with the abortion issue.

[23] *Saving Abortion* (New York: Association for the Study of Abortion, n.d.), 2; *Legal Abortion: Arguments Pro & Con* (New York: Westchester Coalition for Legal Abortion, 1978), n.pag.; *Sponsors & Members* (Washington, D.C.: Religious Coalition for Abortion Rights, 1978), n.pag.

[24] *The Abortion Dilemma* (Washington, D.C.: Religious Coalition for Abortion Rights, n.d.), n.pag.

[25] Mailing from the Religious Coalition for Abortion Rights, n.d., n.pag.

[26] *Abortion: Why Religious Organizations in the United States Want to Keep It Legal* (Washington, D.C.: Religious Coalition for Abortion Rights, 1979), n.pag.

[27] *Saving Abortion*, 2–3; mailing from the Religious Coalition for Abortion Rights, n.d., n.pag.

[28] *What Is the RCAR?* (Washington, D.C.: Religious Coalition for Abortion Rights, 1979), n.pag.; *The Abortion Dilemma*, n.pag.; *Sponsors & Members*, n.p.; *Legal Abortion: Arguments Pro & Con*, n.pag.

[29] *Abortion: Why Religious Organizations in the United States Want to Keep It Legal*, n.pag.; mailing from Fredrica F. Hodges, Executive Director of the Religious Coalition for Abortion Rights, n.d., n.pag.; *Wouldn't a Law Prohibiting Abortion Violate Religious Liberty?* (Washington: D.C.: Religious Coalition for Abortion Rights, n.d.), n.pag.

[30] *Sponsors & Members*, n.pag.; *What Is the RCAR?*, n.pag.

[31] *We Affirm: Excerpts from Statements about Abortion Rights as Expressed by National Religious Organizations* (Washington, D.C.: Religious Coalition for Abortion Rights, 1978), n.pag.; *Abortion: Why Religious Organizations in the United States Want to Keep It Legal*, n.pag.

[32] *Abortion: Questions and Answers* (Washington, D.C.: Committee for Pro-Life Activities, 1983), n.pag.; *Abortion: Death Before Life* (Washington, D.C.: NRL Educational Trust Fund, 1985), n.pag.; *Some Surprising Facts . . . about Your Right to Life* (Washington, D.C.: National Right to Life Committee, n.d.), n.pag.

[33] *We Care, We Love, We Are PRO-LIFE* (Conway, AR: Conway Mother & Unborn Baby Care, n.d.), n.pag.; *The U.S. Supreme Court Has Ruled It's Legal to Kill a Baby . . .* (Cincinnati: Hayes Publishing Company, 1976), n.pag.; *Where Do You Stand?* (Cincinnati: Willke & Hiltz Publishing Company, n.d.), n.pag.

[34] *Why Vote Pro-Life* (Lafayette, IN: Tippecanoe County Right to Life, n.d.), n.pag.; *Aborted Baby Discarded in Hospital Bucket* (n.p., n.d.), n.pag.; Melody Green, *Children—Things We Throw Away?* (Lindale, TX: Last Days Lifeline, 1979), n.pag.

[35] *Abortion: Death Before Life*, n.pag.; *Abortion: A Catholic Issue* (Minneapolis: For LIFE, 1977).

[36] *Abortion: Questions and Answers*, n.pag.; *What Is the Key Question?* (Minneapolis: For LIFE,

1977), n.pag.; *The Facts of Death* (Glendale, CA: Committee of Ten Million, 1973), n.pag.

[37] *The Hidden Holocaust* (Taylor, AZ: The Precious Feet People, n.d.), n.pag.; *Their Life Is in Your Hand* (Lafayette, IN: Tippecanoe County Right to Life, n.d.), n.pag.; mailing from Judie Brown, President, American Life Lobby, Stafford, VA, n.d., n.pag.

[38] *Do You Want to Return to the Butchery of Back-Alley Abortion?* (New York: NARAL, n.d.), n.pag.; "Mobilization Bulletin" (Washington: National Organization for Women, n.d.), 1; mailing from Patricia Ireland, President, National Organization for Women, n.d., 1–2.

[39] Mailing from Kenneth Edelin, Planned Parenthood Federation of America, n.d., 1; *We Affirm*, n.pag.; mailing 4 from Faye Wattleton, President, Planned Parenthood Federation of America, n.d., 1.

[40] "Special Advisory Memorandum" from Kate Michelman, Executive Director, NARAL, April 19, 1988, 1–4.

[41] *Constitutional Aspects of the Right to Limit Childbearing* (Washington: NARAL, n.d.), n.pag.; mailing 1 from Molly Yard, President, National Organization for Women, n.d., 1–4; mailing from Sarah Weddington, RCAR, n.d., n.pag.

[42] *We Care, We Love, We Are Pro-Life*, n.pag.; mailing from Judie Brown, 2–4; *Abortion: A Catholic Issue*, n.pag.

[43] *Why Vote Pro-Life*, n.pag.; *Abortion: A Catholic Issue*, n.pag.

[44] *The Abortion Connection*, n.p., n.d., n.pag.

[45] *Is This Life Worth a Postage Stamp?*, n.p., n.d., n. pag.

[46] Ken Unger, *What You Don't Know Can Hurt You* (Ashtabula, OH: Protestants Protesting Abortion, n.d.), n.pag.; *Children—Things We Throw Away?*, n.pag.; *The Facts of Death*, n.pag.

[47] Lafayette, Indiana *Journal and Courier*, January 22, 1979, A–8; January 22, 1980, B–4; May 11, 1980, B–7.

[48] Mailing 1 from Molly Yard, President, National Organization for Women, 1990, 1–2; mailing 2 from Molly Yard, President, National Organization for Women, 1991, 2–3; Mailing from Edelin, 2.

[49] *Do You Want to Return to the Butchery of Back-Alley Abortion?*, n.pag.

[50] Mailing from Edelin, 1; mailing 1 from Joanne Woodward, n.d., 1; *Congressional Action in Violation of Reproductive Freedom: 1978* (Washington, D.C.: NARAL, 1978), 1.

[51] Mailing 2 from Joanne Woodward, n.d., 1; Mailing from Kate Michelman, Executive Director, NARAL, July 25, 1988, 1–2.

[52] *What Is RCAR?*, n.pag.; *Abortion: Why Religious Organizations in the United States Want to Keep It Legal*, n.pag.; *Legal Abortion: Arguments Pro & Con*, n.pag.; *We Affirm*, n.pag.

[53] *Abortion Q & A* (Washington, D.C.: NARAL, n.d.), n.pag.; *Abortion Fact Sheet* (New York: NARAL, n.d.), n. pag.; mailing from Edelin, 3–4.

[54] *The Abortion Dilemma*, n.pag.; *Legal Abortion: Arguments Pro & Con*, n.pag.; Abortion Q & A, n.pag.

[55] Mailing 2 from Faye Wattleton, President, Planned Parenthood Federation of America, n.d., 1–4; mailing 3 from Faye Wattleton, President, Planned Parenthood Federation of America, n.d., 1–3; mailing from Karen Mulhauser, Executive Director, NARAL, n.d., 2.

[56] Mailing from Gloria Steinem, n.d., 1; mailing 2 from Molly Yard, 1–2; mailing 1 from Joanne Woodward, 1.

[57] Mailing 3 from Molly Yard, President, National Organization for Women, n.d., 2–3; *Saving Abortion*, 1–3; *Constitutional Aspects of the Right to Limit Childbearing*, n.pag.

[58] *Sponsors & Members*, n.pag.; *Abortion: Why Religious Organizations in the United States Want to Keep It Legal*, n.pag.

[59] *Americans Against Abortion*, Summer, 1986, 2.

[60] *Life or Death* (Cincinnati: Hayes Publishing, n.d.), n.pag.; *Children—Things We Throw Away?*, n. pag.; *The Hidden Holocaust*, p.pag.

[61] *What Is the Key Question?* (Minneapolis: ForLife, 1977), n.pag.; *Heartbeat*, September/October 1991, 2–3; Paul Marx, *The Mercy Killers* (Palos Verdes Estates, CA: Right to Life, 1974), 1–11.

[62] *Abortion: Public Opinion* (Washington, D.C.: NRL Educational Trust Fund, 1985), n.pag.; *The*

Hidden Holocaust, n.pag.; *Sex Discrimination Before Birth* (Jefferson City, MO: Easton Publishing, 1985), n.pag.

63 See for example, *Aborted Baby Discarded in Hospital Bucket*, n.p., 1973, n.pag.; *Children—Things We Throw Away?*, n.pag., Gary Bergel, *Abortion in America* (Washington, D.C.: National Right to Life, 1990), 11–5.

64 *Newsweek*, January 14, 1985, 25.

65 *Before You Make the Decision* (Moreno Valley, CA: Women Exploited by Abortion, 1984), n.pag.; *Abortion: Death Before Life*, n.pag.; *Aborted Baby Discarded in Hospital Bucket*, n.pag.; *Rape* (Jefferson City, MO: Easton Publishing, 1986), n.pag; *Incest* (Jefferson City, MO: Easton Publishing, 1987), n.pag.

66 Marx, 16.

67 *The U.S. Supreme Court Has Ruled It's Legal to Kill a Baby . . .*, n.pag.

68 *Religious Freedom and the Abortion Controversy* (Washington, D.C.: RCAR, 1978), n.pag.; mailing #3 from Kate Michelman, Executive Director, NARAL, n.d., 2; Woodward, mailing 2, 2; Yard mailing #2, 2–4.

69 *Abortion Q & A*, n.pag.; Weddington mailing, n.pag.; Wattleton mailing 4, 1–3.

70 Wattleton mailing 1, 1–2; *What Is the RCAR?*, n.pag.; Ireland mailing, 1–4.

71 *You Know Them as the 'Right to Life' People. They Oppose Abortion. But Did You Know . . .* (Washington, D.C.: NARAL, n.d.), n. pag.; *The Abortion Dilemma*, n.pag.

72 *How to Become a Pro-Choice Activist*, n.pag.; *Twelve Abortion Facts* (Washington, D.C.: NARAL, n.d.), n.pag.; *Saving Abortion*, 3.

73 Yard, mailing 3, 1–4; *Legal Abortion: Arguments Pro & Con*, n.pag.; *Listen to the Anti-Choice Leaders—Then Help Us Stop Them Before It's Too Late* (New York: Planned Parenthood Federation of America, n.d.).

74 *You Know Them as the 'Right to Life' People*, n.pag.; Steinem, 1; Edelin, 1–4.

75 Mulhauser, 1; Steinem, 1–4.

76 Ellen Goodman, "This Time, However, the Word 'Terrorism' Is Perhaps too Mild," Lafayette, Indiana *Journal and Courier*, March 16, 1993, A4.

77 *The Communicator*, June 1978, 2; and May 1977, 2.

78 *Abortion: Public Opinion*, n.pag.; Brown, 1–3; *Americans Against Abortion*, 3 & 16.

79 *The Communicator*, September 1978, 2; November/December 1977, 2; October/November, 1980, 3.

80 *Abortion: Public Opinion*, n.pag.; Heartbeat, 1–3; *Abortion: A Catholic Issue,* n.pag.

81 John Willke, President, National Right to Life Committee, "Action-Gram," February 9, 1987, n.pag.

82 *Abortion: Death Before Life*, n.pag.; *The Hidden Holocaust*, n.pag.

83 David Mall, *In Good Conscience: Abortion and Moral Necessity* (Libertyville, IL: Kairos Books, 1982), 41.

84 *New York Times*, March 11, 1993, B10.

85 "More Ads, No More Bombs," *America*, February 8, 1968, 82; "Violence Against Abortion Clinics Escalates Despite the Opposition of Prolife Leaders," *Christianity Today*, February 1, 1985, 45.

86 *The Sunday Visitor*, March 21, 1993, 1 & 4; see also Bill Price, President, Texans United for Life, *New York Times*, March 12, 1993, A17.

87 John Willke, "Violence—The Answer?" *The Communicator*, May, 1978, 2.

88 *The Sunday Visitor*, March 21, 1993, 1; *Newsweek*, March 22, 1993, 34–35; *New York Times*, March 11, 1993, B10.

89 *Indiana Right to Life*, n.p., n.d., 3, reprinted from *National Right to Life News*, Feb., 1980, n.pag.

90 "Violence Against Abortion Clinics," 45–46.

91 Cleveland, Ohio *Catholic Universe Bulletin*, September 17, 1976, 2, col. 4.

92 *The Communicator*, January, 1978, 3.

93 *Catholic Universe Bulletin*, September 17, 1976, 2, col. 2.

94 "Violence Against Abortion Clinics," 46.

95 *Newsweek*, March 22, 1993, 34–35.

96 Judith Adler Hennessee, "Inside a Right-to-Life Mind," *Mademoiselle*, April, 1986, 261.

Chapter Fifteen
Summary and Conclusions

We undertook the first edition of this book to synthesize, to extend, and to apply many of the findings, theories, and approaches to persuasion and social movements generated since the 1960s. It seems appropriate to close the third edition by summarizing our view of social movement persuasion.

We defined a social movement as "an organized, uninstitutionalized, and large collectivity that emerges to bring about or to resist a program of change in societal norms and values, operates primarily through persuasive strategies, and encounters opposition in a moral struggle." Although this definition is difficult to operationalize, it neatly distinguishes our conception of social movements from political parties, political action committees, riots, trends, campaigns, and revolutions. Social phenomena such as riots, individual protests, isolated demonstrations, and benefit concerts are important symbolic acts. They are persuasion and they do have important influences in American society, but they are not social movements. Social movements face a unique set of rhetorical problems stemming from their need to attract, to unify, to mobilize, and to sustain large numbers of people over time in the absence of institutionalized resources, authority, or sanctions.

Social movements "encounter opposition" from many sources ranging from fearful and disgruntled individuals and groups, sometimes acting as surrogates for established orders, to institutions such as schools, churches, governmental agents and agencies, political parties, labor unions, and competing social movements. They encounter indifference, inertia, evasion, counter-persuasion, coercive persuasion, and coercion.

A social movement does not emerge from quiet times unless its needs and interests have been frustrated by opposition. That frustration invites movement adherents to reexamine their purposes and motives. Having lost on the grounds of practicality and legality, social movements turn to a general sense of rightness. Most movements soon ground their objectives in a superior morality which necessarily defines established institutions as morally corrupt and generates conflict that is moral in tone. Certainly most American political, social, and religious rhetoric is moral in tone, and one can argue that every argument contains a moral dimension. Social movements have few resources at their disposal, and they need moral arguments as the cores of their ideologies. Moreover, opponents typically characterize movements as evil threats to the prevailing morality. Rhetoric that is moral in tone need not come from a social movement, but every social movement will find itself locked in a rhetorical struggle that is moral in tone. We see in social movement persuasion the evolution of political communities. Representative democracy does not guarantee policy satisfaction, and the dissatisfied may find one another and develop sufficient dissatisfaction to confront the established order and the interests it has seen fit to represent. The emerging dialectic between movement and institution eventually results in a revised political community supported by a new consensus. Sometimes the social movement overthrows the establishment, sometimes they win minor concessions, and sometimes they are disenfranchised. The struggle usually results in new distinctions, priorities, and relationships.

The social systems perspective emphasizes the social evolution of political communities through interpretation and depiction. It seeks to discover and to explain the interdependent, adaptive, and growing nature of the social organism. Conflict is seen as a sign of system-environment adaptation, not as an evil to be avoided or suppressed. A social systems perspective enables us to pursue the all-important question, "Which individuals, conceiving themselves to be what 'people' in what environment, use what relational patterns and what adaptive strategies with what evolutionary results?"

Social movements must perform a number of essential persuasive functions if they are to come into existence, grow in size and influence, and bring about or resist change in societal norms and values. They must transform perceptions of reality, transform perceptions of society, prescribe courses of action, mobilize the discontented, and sustain the movement until victory is achieved. As we study how social movements attempt to perform these functions, we can answer such questions as: How do social movements revise versions of reality as they age, confront opposition, and meet successes and failures? How does degree of desired change affect consciousness-raising rhetoric and attacks on the opposition? How do social movement ideologies define or obscure, stabilize or upset, strengthen or weaken, relieve or exacerbate situations? How do social movements adapt persuasive efforts to various and changing relationships? How do social movements sustain the zeal created during the early days of the movement when it was personal, visible, and active?

The efforts of social movements to tackle their unique rhetorical problems creates a characteristic life cycle: genesis, social unrest, enthusiastic mobilization, maintenance, and termination. We see in the women's, civil rights, and labor movements examples of this life cycle and the ability of social movements to turn maintenance into remobilization. We have also seen cases where movements have stalled in a particular stage for decades because they failed to enter the next phase, and we have seen cases where movements failed to handle the rhetorical problems presented by a new stage. Indeed, non-institutionalization itself forces this constant adaptation upon social movements. For social movements that reach the final stage of termination, the results are usually disappointing and disillusioning. Rarely does a social movement reach the state of perfection envisioned by its creators.

Two particular problems facing social movements concern leadership and legitimacy. We have argued that popular images of movement leaders are misleading. Social movements are led by editors, clergy, business people, teachers, and lawyers so frustrated by the injustices they perceive in the world that they take extraordinary action; movements are not spearheaded by some thoughtless, irresponsible, possibly psychotic "lunatic fringe." The leaders are both decision makers and symbols of their movements. They may attain leadership because of their charisma, prophecy, or pragmatism; they keep it by blending multiple attributes, by adapting to events, by handling diverse or conflicting leadership roles, by changing as the movement changes, by adapting to events, and by not falling behind or getting ahead of their followers.

Political, religious, and social institutions have the presumption of legitimacy, and those who attack such institutions need to prove the legitimacy of their causes and their organizations. Social movements can draw upon constitutional rights such as freedom of speech, freedom to assemble, and the consent of the governed to legitimize their positions. The point is that established institutions need not bother to prove their legitimacy. We have set forth some of the problems and strategies facing social movements as they search for legitimacy through coactive and confrontational strategies, the first employed to establish their worthiness of legitimacy and the second employed to strip institutions of the legitimacy society has granted them.

Social movement organizations recruit people suited to their organizational efforts and exclude people who will not fit. For example, John Birch Society and Gray Panther rhetoric provided people with gratifications that were primarily psychological rather than political, social, or philosophical. John Birch Society rhetoric spoke directly to the needs of a classic authoritarian character structure, and Gray Panther rhetoric spoke to the needs of a democratic character structure.

Established institutions cannot long ignore growing social movements because they inevitably pose threats to their ideologies, powers, and legitimacy. Institutions and their surrogates employ a combination of strategies to meet these threats: evasion, counter-persuasion, coercive persuasion, adjustment, and capitulation. They must select the best strategy for the situation and avoid the appearance of overreacting or abusing the powers granted to them by "the people."

Kenneth Burke's dramatistic approach to human communication emphasizes the attribution and the resolution of guilt in conflicts between opposing groups. At the heart of Burke's perspective is the discovery of how motives and behavior arise and exist through communication. In his terms, a social movement is a transformation from order, division, drama, conflict, victimage, transcendence, redemption, and reestablished order. Burke's theories can help to answer questions such as: How did the social movement assign blame for the problem? How did the social movement and establishment characterize their conflict? Through what means was societal redemption achieved? Which key term of Burke's pentad (act, scene, agent, agency, purpose) is favored and thus defines a situation for the social movement or institution?

Social movements use language strategies such as slogans, obscenity, and ridicule to control their worlds. The ambiguity of words and phrases allow them to serve as verbal bridges from one meaning to another and permit individuals and groups to interpret them according to their own perceptions and needs. Words help to determine how we see ourselves and others, and they simplify complex problems, solutions, and situations while demanding instant corrective actions.

The verbal and nonverbal elements of protest songs enable them to serve multiple persuasive functions for social movements. Although they are simplistic, brief, and poetic in nature, they are complex persuasive channels. The majority of songs describe the present state of affairs, identify the social movement's devils, list demands and solutions, and urge members to act and remain committed to the cause. Nonverbal elements complement the verbal. Instruments create somber and haunting views of reality; rhythm reduces inhibitions and defense mechanisms; repetition "drums in" visions of reality, the evil of institutions, and the plight of victims; and group singing promotes togetherness and self-persuasion.

We have offered a typology of political arguments related to the desirability of change: insurgent, innovative, progressive, retentive, reversive, restorative, and revolutionary. It may be that "ultra-conservative" movements want to go back to an earlier time and that "ultra-liberal" movements want to move ahead. But these social movements pursue their objectives through a kaleidoscopic array of arguments. Rather than classifying a social movement and deducing its rhetorical style, we should comparatively study the array of arguments across the political spectrum and infer types of social movement persuasion accordingly. The important question is: Which types of argument appear between which people at what points in the social movement's development?

The New Right movement's Panama Canal campaign illustrates four important points about social movements and argument from narrative vision. Activists coalesce around a narrative framework for interpreting political realities. Even a logical establishment narrative advanced by a president can be credibly challenged by an emerging social movement with a clear and convincing narrative. The social movement's narrative transcends its particular focus, and short-term losses become long-term wins. Finally, narratives help us to interpret events. Because events help us to validate our choice of narrative, political history is a series of narrative visions.

Argument from transcendence is a highly functional strategy for social movements. It allows them to take moralistic stances portraying their causes as being above or superior to established norms and values. Argument from transcendence allows social movements to address degrees of size, importance, goodness, or risk. It allows social movements to stress their superiority, explain their ideology, and justify their tactics without having to disprove or destroy other factions or antagonize institutions that might be potential allies. The pro-life and pro-choice movements have employed arguments from transcendence in their conflict over legalized abortion. They have used all four points of comparison—quality, quantity, value, and hierarchy—to establish, attack, and defend their positions.

In this book, we have tried to present and validate a theoretical framework appropriate for the study of social movement persuasion. Concepts such as legitimacy, moral argument, leadership, resistance, evolution, dramatism, and depiction are not unique to social movements. The decision to cross the threshold of societal norms takes persuader and audience into a different dimension in which unifying symbolic resources such as norms, myths, and values can no longer be used. Old presumptions that support the established order become conceptual trapdoors leading back to the mainstream. The right to speak and the right to assemble become difficult to exercise in opposition to the agents of authority. For these and other reasons already discussed, social movement persuasion is a unique kind of rhetoric that requires a shift in analytical perspective.

An old friend of one of the authors read the first edition and said, "Hitler would have kept this book at his bedside." Students of rhetoric are well-acquainted with the charge that persuasion can be used for undesirable purposes, and it is worth recalling Plato's answer to that charge nearly two thousand years ago. In his treatise *The Gorgias*, Plato conceded that rhetoric could be used for undesirable purposes, but he argued that it would be impossible to expose immorality, illegality, undesirability, or impropriety without it. Rhetoric is a process of adjusting your own experience to your audience's experience, and it will be used for good or ill in accordance with the persuader's sense of morality and ethics. Perhaps some future Hitler may benefit from books like this one. If so, some future Thomas Jefferson, Susan B. Anthony, Samuel Gompers, Mohandas Gandhi, Martin Luther King, Cesar Chavez, or Maggie Kuhn should benefit as well. More importantly, we believe that a fuller understanding of social movement persuasion will enable citizens to understand better the important evolutionary role of social movements in American society. The more clearly we hear and understand, the more clearly we can choose from the persuasion presented.

Selected Bibliography

Articles

Abbott, Don. "Ian Paisley: Evangelism and Confrontation in Northern Ireland," *Today's Speech* 21 (Fall 1973), 49–55.

Anderson, Judith. "Sexual Politics: Chauvinism and Backlash?" *Today's Speech* 21 (Fall 1973), 11–16.

Andrews, James R. "The Ethos of Pacifism: The Problem of Image in the Early British Peace Movement," *Quarterly Journal of Speech* 53 (February 1967), 28–33.

_____. "Piety and Pragmatism: Rhetorical Aspects of the Early British Peace Movement," *Speech Monographs* 34 (November 1967), 423–436.

_____. "Confrontation at Columbia: A Case Study in Coercive Rhetoric," *Quarterly Journal of Speech* 55 (February 1969), 9–16.

_____. "The Rhetoric of Coercion and Persuasion: The Reform Bill of 1832," *Quarterly Journal of Speech* 56 (April 1970), 187–195.

_____. "Reflections of the National Character in American Rhetoric," *Quarterly Journal of Speech* 57 (October, 1971) 316–324.

_____. "The Passionate Negation: The Chartist Movement in Rhetorical Perspective," *Quarterly Journal of Speech* 59 (April 1973), 196–208.

_____. "*Spindles vs. Acres*: Rhetorical Perceptions on the British Free Trade Movement," *Western Speech* 38 (Winter 1974), 41–52.

_____. "History and Theory in the Study of the Rhetoric of Social Movements," *Central States Speech Journal* 31 (Winter 1980), 274–281.

_____. "An Historical Perspective on the Study of Social Movements," *Central States Speech Journal* 34 (Spring 1983), 67–69.

Asinaf, Eliot. "Dick Gregory Is Not So Funny Now," *The New York Times Magazine* 17 (March, 1968) 37–45.

Banninga, Jerald L. "John Quincy Adams on the Right of a Slave to Petition Congress," *Southern Speech Communication Journal* 38 (Winter 1972), 151–163.

Baskerville, Barnet. "The Cross and the Flag: Evangelists of the Far Right," *Western Speech* 27 (Fall 1963), 197–206.

Benson, Thomas W. "Rhetoric and Autobiography: The Case of Malcolm X," *Quarterly Journal of Speech* 60 (February 1974), 1–13.

Benson, Thomas W. and Bonnie Johnson. "The Rhetoric of Resistance: Confrontation with the Warmakers, Washington, DC, October 1967," *Today's Speech* 16 (September 1968), 35–42.

Berg, David M. "Rhetoric, Reality, and the Mass Media," *Quarterly Journal of Speech* 58 (October 1972), 255–263.

Betz, Brian R. "Eric Fromm and the Rhetoric of Prophecy," *Central States Speech Journal* 26 (Winter 1975), 310–315.

Bezayiff, David. "Legal Oratory of John Adams: An Early Instrument of Protest," *Western Journal of Speech Communication* 40 (Winter 1976), 63–71.

Black, Edwin. "Secrecy and Disclosure as Rhetorical Forms," *Quarterly Journal of Speech* 74 (May 1988), 133–150.

Bloodworth, John D. "Communication in the Youth Counter Culture: Music as Expression," *Central States Speech Journal* 26 (Winter 1975), 304–309.

Bormann, Ernest G. "The Southern Senator's Filibuster on Civil Rights: Speechmaking as Parliamentary Stratagem," *Southern Speech Journal* 27 (Spring 1962), 183–194.

_____. "Fantasy and Rhetorical Vision: The Rhetorical Criticism of Social Reality," *Quarterly Journal of Speech* 58 (December 1972), 396–407.

_____. "Fetching Good Out of Evil: A Rhetorical Use of Calamity," *Quarterly Journal of Speech* 63 (April 1977), 130–139.

Bosmajian, Haig A. "The Nazi Speaker's Rhetoric," *Quarterly Journal of Speech* 46 (December 1960), 365–371.

_____. "Nazi Meetings: The *Sprechabend*, the *Versaamlung*, the *Kundgebung*, the *Feierstunde*," *Southern Speech Journal* 31 (Summer 1966), 324–337.

_____. "The Persuasiveness of Nazi Marching and *Der Kampf um Die Strasse*," *Today's Speech* 16 (November 1968), 17–22.

_____. " 'Speech' and the First Amendment," *Today's Speech* 18 (Fall 1970), 3–11.

_____. "Obscenity and Protest," *Today's Speech* 18 (Winter 1970), 9–14.

_____. "Freedom of Speech and the Heckler," *Western Speech* 36 (Fall 1972), 218–232.

_____. "Defining the 'American Indian': A Case Study in the Language of Suppression," *Speech Teacher* 22 (March 1973), 89–99.

_____. "The Abrogation of the Suffragists' First Amendment Rights," *Western Speech* 38 (Fall 1974), 218–232.

_____. "The Sources and Nature of Adolf Hitler's Technique of Persuasion," *Central States Speech Journal* 25 (Winter 1974), 240–248.

_____. "Freedom of Speech and the Language of Oppression," *Western Journal of Speech Communication* 42 (Fall 1978), 209–221.

Bowen, Harry W. "Does Non-Violence Persuade?" *Today's Speech* 11 (April 1963), 10–11, 31.

_____. "The Future of Non-Violence," *Today's Speech* 11 (September 1963), 3–4.

_____. "A Realistic View of Non-Violent Assumptions," *Today's Speech* 15 (September 1967), 9–10.

Booth, Wayne. " 'Now Don't Try to Reason With Me': Rhetoric Today, Left, Right, and Center," *The University of Chicago Magazine* 60 (November 1967), 12.

Branham, Robert James. "Speaking Itself: Susan Sontag's Town Hall Address," *Quarterly Journal of Speech* 75 (August 1989), 259–276.

_____. "The Role of the Convert in *Eclipse of Reason* and *The Silent Scream*," *Quarterly Journal of Speech* 77 (November 1991), 407–426.

Brock, Bernard L. "A Special Report on Social Movement Theory and Research: Editor's Commentary," *Central States Speech Journal* 34 (Spring 1983), 80–82.

Brock, Bernard L. and Sharon Howell, "The Evolution of the PLO: A Rhetoric of Terrorism," *Central States Speech Journal* 39 (Fall/Winter, 1988), 281–292.

Brockriede, Wayne E. and Robert L. Scott. "Stokely Carmichael: Two Speeches on Black Power," *Central States Speech Journal* 19 (Spring 1968), 3–13.

Brommel, Bernard J. "The Pacifist Speechmaking of Eugene V. Debs," *Quarterly Journal of Speech* 52 (April 1966), 146–154.

———. "Eugene V. Debs: The Agitator as Speaker," *Central States Speech Journal* 20 (Fall 1969), 202–214.

Brooks, Robert D. "Black Power: The Dimensions of a Slogan," *Western Speech* 34 (Spring 1970), 108–114.

Brown, William J. "The Persuasive Appeal of Mediated Terrorism: The Case of the TWA Flight 847 Hijacking," *Western Journal of Speech Communication* 54 (Spring 1990), 219–236.

Brummett, Barry. "The Skeptical Critic," *Western Journal of Speech Communication* 46 (Fall 1982), 379–382.

———. "Premillennial Apocalyptic as a Rhetorical Genre," *Central States Speech Journal* 35 (Summer 1984), 84–93.

Burgchardt, Carl R. "Two Faces of American Communism: Pamphlet Rhetoric of the Third Period and the Popular Front," *Quarterly Journal of Speech* 66 (December 1980), 375–391.

Burgess, Parke G. "The Rhetoric of Black Power: A Moral Demand," *Quarterly Journal of Speech* 54 (April 1968), 122–133.

———. "The Rhetoric of Moral Conflict: Two Critical Dimensions," *Quarterly Journal of Speech* 56 (April 1970), 120–130.

———. "Crisis Rhetoric: Coercion vs. Force," *Quarterly Journal of Speech* 59 (February 1973), 61–73.

Burgoon, Michael. "A Factor-Analytic Examination of Messages Advocating Social Change," *Speech Monographs* 39 (November 1972), 290–295.

Burkholder, Thomas R. "Kansas Populism, Woman Suffrage, and the Agrarian Myth: A Case Study in the Limits of Mythic Transcendence," *Communication Studies* 40 (Winter 1989), 292–307.

Bytwerk, Randall L. "Rhetorical Aspects of the Nazi Meeting: 1926–1933," *Quarterly Journal of Speech* 61 (October 1975), 307–318

Campbell, Finley C. "Voices of Thunder, Voices of Rage: A Symbolic Analysis of a Selection from Malcolm X's Speech 'Message to the Grass Roots'," *Speech Teacher* 19 (March 1970), 101–110.

Campbell, Karlyn Kohrs. "The Rhetoric of Radical Black Nationalism: A Case Study in Self-Conscious Criticism," *Central States Speech Journal* 22 (Fall 1971), 151–160.

———. "The Rhetoric of Women's Liberation: An Oxymoron," *Quarterly Journal of Speech* 59 (February 1973), 74–86.

———. "Femininity and Feminism: To Be or Not To Be a Woman," *Communication Quarterly* 31 (Spring 1983), 101–108.

———. "Style and Content in the Rhetoric of Early Afro-American Feminists," *Quarterly Journal of Speech* 72 (November 1986), 434–445.

Carlson, A. Cheree. "Gandhi and the Comic Frame: 'Ad Bellum Purificandum'," *Quarterly Journal of Speech* 72 (November 1986), 446–455.

_____. "Albert J. Beveridge as Imperialist and Progressive: The Means Justify the End,"
Western Journal of Speech Communication 52 (Winter 1988), 46–62.

_____. "The Rhetoric of the Know-Nothing Party: Nativism as a Response to the
Rhetorical Situation," *Southern Communication Journal* 54 (Summer 1989), 364–383.

_____. "Creative Casuistry and Feminist Consciousness: A Rhetoric of Moral Reform,"
Quarterly Journal of Speech 78 (February 1992), 16–32.

Carpenter, Ronald H. and Robert V. Stelzer. "Nixon, *Patton*, and a Silent Majority
Sentiment about the Vietnam War: The Cinematographic Bases of a Rhetorical
Stance," *Central States Speech Journal* 25 (Summer 1974), 105–110.

Carson, Herbert L. "An Eccentric Kinship: Henry David Thoreau's 'A Plea for Captain
John Brown'," *Southern Speech Journal* 27 (Winter 1961), 151–166.

Carter, David A. "The Industrial Workers of the World and the Rhetoric of Song,"
Quarterly Journal of Speech 66 (December 1980), 365–374.

Cathcart, Robert S. "New Approaches to the Study of Movements: Defining Movements
Rhetorically," *Western Speech* 36 (Spring 1972), 82–88.

_____. "Movements: Confrontation as Rhetorical Form," *Southern Speech
Communication Journal* 43 (Spring 1978), 233–247.

_____. "Defining Social Movements by Their Rhetorical Form," *Central States Speech
Journal* 31 (Winter 1980), 267–273.

_____. "A Confrontation Perspective on the Study of Social Movements," *Central States
Speech Journal* 34 (Spring 1983), 69–74.

Chapel, Cage William. "Christian Science and the Nineteenth Century Woman's
Movement," *Central States Speech Journal* 26 (Summer 1975), 142–149.

Charland, Maurice. "Constitutive Rhetoric: The Case of the *People Quebecois*," *Quarterly
Journal of Speech* 73 (May 1987), 133–150.

Chesebro, James W. "Rhetorical Strategies of the Radical Revolutionary," *Today's Speech*
20 (Winter 1972), 37–48.

_____. "Cultures in Conflict—A Generic and Axiological View," *Today's Speech* 21
(Spring 1973), 11–20.

Chesebro, James W., John F. Cragan, and Patricia McCullough. "The Small Group
Technique of the Radical Revolutionary: A Synthetic Study of Consciousness Raising,"
Speech Monographs 40 (June 1973), 136–146.

Clark, Thomas D. "Rhetorical Image-Making: A Case Study of the Thomas Paine-William
Smith Propaganda Debates," *Southern Speech Communication Journal* 40 (Spring
1975), 248–261.

_____. "Rhetoric, Reality, and Rationalization: A Study of the Masking Function of
Rhetoric in the London Theosophical Movement," *Communication Quarterly* 26 (Fall
1978), 24–30.

Condit, Celeste Michelle. "The Functions of Epideictic: The Boston Massacre Orations
as Exemplar," *Communication Quarterly* 33 (Fall 1985), 284–299.

_____. "Crafting Virtue: The Rhetorical Construction of Public Morality," *Quarterly
Journal of Speech* 73 (February 1987), 79–97.

_____. "Democracy and Civil Rights: The Universalizing Influence of Public
Argumentation," *Communication Monographs* 54 (March 1987), 1–18.

Condit, Celeste Michelle and John Louis Lucaites, "The Rhetoric of Equality and the
Expatriation of African-Americans, 1776–1826," *Communication Studies* 42 (Spring
1991), 1–21.

Conrad, Charles. "The Transformation of the 'Old Feminist' Movement," *Quarterly
Journal of Speech* 67 (August 1981), 284–297.

_____. "The Rhetoric of the Moral Majority: An Analysis of Romantic Form," *Quarterly Journal of Speech* 69 (May 1983), 159–170.

Corbett, Edward P. J. "The Rhetoric of the Open Hand and the Rhetoric of the Closed Fist," *College Composition and Communication* 20 (December 1969), 288–296.

Coughlin, Elizabeth M. and Charles E. Coughlin. "Convention in Petticoats: The Seneca Falls Declaration of Women's Rights," *Today's Speech* 21 (Fall 1973), 17–23.

Cox, J. Robert. "The Rhetoric of Child Labor Reform: An Efficacy-Utility Analysis," *Quarterly Journal of Speech* 60 (October 1974), 359–370.

_____. "Perspectives on Rhetorical Criticism of Movements: Antiwar Dissent, 1964–1970," *Western Speech* 38 (Fall 1974), 254–268.

Cragan, John F. "Rhetorical Strategy: A Dramatistic Interpretation and Application," *Central States Speech Journal* 26 (Spring 1975), 4–11.

Crandell, S. Judson. "The Beginnings of a Methodology for Social Control Studies in Public Address," *Quarterly Journal of Speech* 33 (February 1947), 36–39.

Crocker, James W. "A Rhetoric of Encounter Following the May 4th, 1970, Disturbances at Kent State University," *Communication Quarterly* 25 (Fall 1977), 47–56.

Cusella, Louis P. "Real-Fiction Versus Historical Reality: Rhetorical Purification in 'Kent State'—The Docudrama," *Communication Quarterly* 30 (Summer 1982), 159–164.

Darsey, James. "The Legend of Eugene V. Debs: Prophetic *Ethos* as Radical Argument," *Quarterly Journal of Speech* 74 (November 1988), 434–452.

_____. "From 'Gay Is Good' to the Scourge of AIDS: The Evolution of Gay Liberation Rhetoric, 1977–1990," *Communication Studies* 42 (Spring 1991), 43–66.

Dees, Diane. "Bernadette Devlin's Maiden Speech: A Rhetoric of Sacrifice," *Southern Speech Communication Journal* 38 (Summer 1973), 326–339.

Denton, Robert E. "The Rhetorical Functions of Slogans: Classifications and Characteristics," *Communication Quarterly* 28 (Spring 1980), 10–18.

Delia, Jesse G. "Rhetoric in the Nazi Mind: Hitler's Theory of Persuasion," *Southern Speech Communication Journal* 37 (Winter 1971), 136–149.

Dick, Robert C. "Negro Oratory in the Anti-Slavery Societies: 1830–1860," *Western Speech* 28 (Winter 1964), 5–14.

Dionisopoulos, George N.; Victoria J. Gallagher; Steven R. Goldzwig; and David Zarefsky. "Martin Luther King, the American Dream and Vietnam: A Collision of Rhetorical Trajectories," *Western Journal of Communication* 56 (Spring 1992), 91–107.

Doolittle, Robert J. "Riots as Symbolic: A Criticism and Approach," *Central States Speech Journal* 27 (Winter 1976), 310–317.

Dow, Bonnie J. "The 'Womanhood' Rationale in the Woman Suffrage Rhetoric of Frances E. Willard," *Southern Communication Journal* 56 (Summer 1991), 298–307.

Duffy, Bernard K. "The Anti-Humanist Rhetoric of the New Religious Right," *Southern Speech Communication Journal* 49 (Summer 1984), 339–360.

Duncan, Rodger D. "Rhetoric of the Kidvid Movement: Ideology, Strategies, and Tactics," *Central States Speech Journal* 27 (Summer 1976), 129–135.

Edwards, Michael L. "A Resource Unit on Black Rhetoric," *Speech Teacher* 22 (September 1973), 183–188.

Eich, Ritch K. and Donald Goldmann. "Communication, Confrontation, and Coercion: Agitation at Michigan," *Central States Speech Journal* 27 (Summer 1976), 120–128.

Erickson, Keith V. "Black Messiah: The Father Divine Peace Mission Movement," *Quarterly Journal of Speech* 63 (December 1977), 428–438.

Erlich, Howard S. "Populist Rhetoric Reassessed: A Paradox," *Quarterly Journal of Speech* 63 (April 1977), 140–151.

Ferris, Maxine Schnitzer. "The Speaking of Roy Wilkins," *Central States Speech Journal* 16 (May 1965), 91–98.

Fletcher, Winona L. "Knight Errant or Screaming Eagle? E. L. Godkin's Criticism of Wendell Phillips," *Southern Speech Journal* 29 (Spring 1964), 214–223.

Flynt, Wayne. "The Ethics of Democratic Persuasion and the Birmingham Crisis," *Southern Speech Journal* 35 (Fall 1969), 40–53.

Flynt, Wayne and William Warren Rogers. "Reform Oratory in Alabama, 1890–1896," *Southern Speech Journal* 29 (Winter 1963), 94–106.

Foss, Karen A. "Out from Underground: The Discourse of Emerging Fugitives," *Western Journal of Communication* 56 (Spring 1992), 125–142.

Foss, Sonya K. "Teaching Contemporary Feminist Rhetoric: An Illustrative Syllabus," *Communication Education* 27 (November 1978), 328–335.

Frank, David A. "*Shalem Achschav*—Rituals of the Israeli Peace Movement," *Communication Monographs* 48 (September 1981), 165–182.

Freeman, Sally A; Stephen Littlejohn; and W. Barnett Pearce. "Communication and Moral Conflict," *Western Journal of Communication* 56 (Fall 1992), 311–329.

Fulkerson, Gerald. "Exile as Emergence: Frederick Douglass in Great Britain, 1845–1847," *Quarterly Journal of Speech* 60 (February 1974), 69–82.

Fulkerson, Richard P. "The Public Letter as a Rhetorical Form: Structure, Logic, and Style in King's 'Letter from Birmingham Jail'," *Quarterly Journal of Speech* 65 (April 1979), 121–136.

Gallagher, Mary Brigid. "John L. Lewis: The Oratory of Pity and Indignation," *Today's Speech* 9 (September 1961), 15–16, 29.

Gilder, Eric. "The Process of Political *Praxis*: Efforts of the Gay Community to Transform the Social Significance of AIDS," *Communication Quarterly* 37 (Winter 1989), 27–38.

Gillespie, Patti P. "Feminist Theatre: A Rhetorical Phenomenon," *Quarterly Journal of Speech* 64 (October 1978), 284–294.

Glancy, Donald R. "Socialist with a Valet: Jack London's 'First, Last, and Only' Lecture Tour," *Quarterly Journal of Speech* 49 (February 1963), 31–39.

Goldzwig, Steven R. "A Rhetoric of Public Theology: The Religious Rhetor and Public Policy," *Southern Speech Communication Journal* 52 (Winter 1987), 128–150.

————. "A Social Movement Perspective on Demagoguery: Achieving Symbolic Realignment," *Communication Studies* 40 (Fall 1989), 202–228.

Goodman, Richard J. and William I. Gorden. "The Rhetoric of Desecration," *Quarterly Journal of Speech* 57 (February 1971), 23–31.

Goodnight, G. Thomas and John Poluakos. "Conspiracy Rhetoric: From Pragmatism to Fantasy in Public Discourse," *Western Journal of Speech Communication* 45 (Fall 1981), 299–316.

Gravlee, G. Jack and James R. Irvine. "Watts' Dissenting Rhetoric of Prayer," *Quarterly Journal of Speech* 59 (December 1973), 463–473.

Gregg, Richard B. "A Phenomenologically Oriented Approach to Rhetorical Criticism," *Central States Speech Journal* 17 (May 1966), 83–90.

————. "The Ego-Function of the Rhetoric of Protest," *Philosophy and Rhetoric* 4 (Spring 1971), 71–91.

Gregg, Richard B. and A. Jackson McCormack. " 'Whitey' Goes to the Ghetto: A Personal Chronicle of a Communication Experience with Black Youths," *Today's Speech* 16 (September 1968), 25–30.

Gregg, Richard B.; A. Jackson McCormack; and Douglas J. Pederson. "The Rhetoric of Black Power: A Street-Level Interpretation," *Quarterly Journal of Speech* 55

(April 1969), 151–160.

Griffin, Charles J. G. "Jedidiah Morse and the Bavarian Illuminati: An Essay in the Rhetoric of Conspiracy," *Central States Speech Journal* 39 (Fall/Winter, 1988), 293–303.

Griffin, Leland M. "The Rhetoric of Historical Movements," *Quarterly Journal of Speech* 38 (April 1951), 184–188.

_____. "The Rhetorical Structure of the 'New Left' Movement: Part I," *Quarterly Journal of Speech* 50 (April 1964), 113–135.

_____. "On Studying Social Movements," *Central States Speech Journal* 31 (Winter 1980), 225–232.

Gunter, Mary F. and James S. Taylor. "Loyalist Propaganda in the Sermons of Charles Inglis, 1717–1780," *Western Speech* 37 (Winter 1973), 47–55.

Gustainis, J. Justin and Dan F. Hahn, "While the Whole World Watched: Rhetorical Failures of Anti-War Protest," *Communication Quarterly* 36 (Summer 1988), 203–216.

Hagan, Martha. "The Antisuffragists' Rhetorical Dilemma: Reconciling the Private and Public Spheres," *Communication Reports* 5 (Summer 1992), 73–81.

Hagen, Michael R. "*Roe vs. Wade*: The Rhetoric of Fetal Life," *Central States Speech Journal* 27 (Fall 1976), 192–199.

Hahn, Dan F. "Social Movement Theory: A Dead End," *Communication Quarterly* 28 (Winter 1980), 60–64.

Hahn, Dan F. and Ruth M. Gonchar, "Studying Social Movements: A Rhetorical Methodology," *Speech Teacher* 20 (January 1971), 44–52.

Haiman, Franklyn S. "The Rhetoric of the Streets: Some Legal and Ethical Considerations," *Quarterly Journal of Speech* 53 (April 1967), 99–114.

_____. "Nonverbal Communication and the First Amendment: The Rhetoric of the Streets Revisited," *Quarterly Journal of Speech* 68 (November 1982), 371–383.

Hammerback, John C. "The Rhetoric of Righteous Reform: George Washington Julian's 1852 Campaign against Slavery," *Central States Speech Journal* 22 (Summer 1971), 85–93.

_____. "George W. Julian's Antislavery Campaign," *Western Speech* 37 (Summer 1973), 157–165.

Hancock, Brenda Robinson. "Affirmation by Negation in the Women's Liberation Movement," *Quarterly Journal of Speech* 58 (October 1972), 264–271.

Hart, Roderick P. "The Rhetoric of the True Believer," *Speech Monographs* 38 (November 1971), 249–261.

_____. "An Unquiet Desperation: Rhetorical Aspects of 'Popular' Atheism in the United States," *Quarterly Journal of Speech* 62 (October 1976), 256–266.

Heath, Robert L. "Dialectical Confrontation: A Strategy of Black Radicalism," *Central States Speech Journal* 24 (Fall 1973), 168–177.

_____. "Black Rhetoric: An Example of the Poverty of Values," *Southern Speech Communication Journal* 39 (Winter 1973), 145–160.

_____. "Alexander Crummell and the Strategy of Challenge by Adaptation," *Central States Speech Journal* 26 (Fall 1975), 178–187.

Heisey, D. Ray and J. David Trebing. "A Comparison of the Rhetorical Visions and Strategies of the Shah's White Revolution and the Ayatollah's Islamic Revolution," *Communication Monographs* 50 (June 1983), 158–174.

_____. "Authority and Legitimacy: A Rhetorical Case Study of the Iranian Revolution," *Communication Monographs* 53 (December 1986), 295–310.

Henry, David. "Recalling the 1960s: The New Left and Social Movement Criticism," *Quarterly Journal of Speech* 75 (February 1989), 97–128.

Henry, David and Richard J. Jensen. "Social Movement Criticism and the Renaissance of Public Address," *Communication Studies* 42 (Spring 1991), 83–93.

Hensley, Carl Wayne. "Rhetorical Vision and the Persuasion of a Historical Movement: The Disciples of Christ in Nineteenth Century American Culture," *Quarterly Journal of Speech* 61 (October 1975), 250–264.

Hillbruner, Anthony. "Inequality, the Great Chain of Being, and Ante Bellum Southern Oratory," *Southern Speech Journal* 25 (Spring 1960), 172–189.

Hogan, J. Michael. "Wallace and the Wallacites: A Reexamination," *Southern Speech Communication Journal* 50 (Fall 1984), 24–48.

Holtan, Orley I. "A. C. Townly, Political Firebrand of North Dakota," *Western Speech* 35 (Winter 1971), 30–41.

Hong, Nathaniel. "Constructing the Anarchist Beast in American Periodical Literature, 1880–1903," *Critical Studies of Mass Communication* 9 (March 1992), 110–130.

Hope, Diana Schaich. "Redefinition of Self: A Comparison of the Rhetoric of the Women's Liberation and the Black Liberation Movements," *Today's Speech* 23 (Winter 1975), 17–25.

Howe, Roger J. "The Rhetoric of the Death of God Theology," *Southern Speech Communication Journal* 37 (Winter 1971), 150–162.

Hunsaker, David M. "The Rhetoric of Brown v. Board of Education: Paradigm for Contemporary Social Protest," *Southern Speech Communication Journal* 43 (Winter 1978), 91–109.

Hynes, Sandra S. "Dramatic Propaganda: Mercy Otis Warren's 'The Defeat,' 1773," *Today's Speech* 23 (Fall 1975), 21–27.

Ilkka, Richard J. "Rhetorical Dramatization in the Development of American Communism," *Quarterly Journal of Speech* 63 (December 1977), 413–427.

Jablonski, Carol J. "Rhetoric, Paradox, and the Movement for Women's Ordination in the Roman Catholic Church," *Quarterly Journal of Speech* 74 (May 1988), 164–183.

Jabusch, David M. "The Rhetoric of Civil Rights," *Western Speech* 30 (Summer 1966), 176–183.

Japp, Phyllis M. "Esther or Isaiah?: The Abolitionist-Feminist Rhetoric of Angelina Grimke," *Quarterly Journal of Speech* 71 (August 1985), 335–348.

Jefferson, Pat. "The Magnificent Barbarian in Nashville," *Southern Speech Journal* 33 (Winter 1967), 77–87.

———. "Stokely's 'Cool:' Style," *Today's Speech* 16 (September 1968), 19–24.

Jensen, J. Vernon. "British Voices on the Eve of the American Revolution: Trapped by the Family Metaphor," *Quarterly Journal of Speech* 63 (February 1977), 43–50.

Jensen, Richard J. and John C. Hammerback. " 'No Revolutions without Poets:' The Rhetoric of Rodolfo 'Corky' Gonzales," *Western Journal of Speech Communication* 46 (Winter 1982), 72–91.

———. "Feminists of Faith: Sonia Johnson and the Mormons for ERA," *Central States Speech Journal* 36 (Fall 1985), 123–137.

———. "From Muslim to Mormon: Eldridge Cleaver's Rhetorical Crusade," *Communication Quarterly* 34 (Winter 1986), 24–40.

Jensen, Richard J. and Cara J. Abeyta. "The Minority in the Middle: Asian-American Dissent in the 1960s and 1970s," *Western Journal of Speech Communication* 51 (Fall 1987), 402–416.

Jorgensen-Earp, Cheryl R. " 'Toys of Desperation'—Suicide as Protest Rhetoric," The *Southern Speech Communication Journal* 53 (Fall 1987), 80–96.

Jurma, William E. "Moderate Movement Leadership and the Vietnam Moratorium Committee," *Quarterly Journal of Speech* 68 (August 1982), 262–272.

Katz, Daniel. "Factors Affecting Social Change: A Social-Psychological Perspective," *Journal of Social Issues* 30 (1974), 159–180.

———. "Group Process and Social Integration: A System Analysis of Two Movements of Social Protest," *Journal of Social Issues* 39 (Winter 1983), 109–128.

Kendall, Kathleen E. and Jeanne Y. Fisher. "Frances Wright on Women's Rights: Eloquence versus Ethos," *Quarterly Journal of Speech* 60 (February 1974), 58–68.

Kennicott, Patrick C. "Black Persuaders in the Antislavery Movement," *Speech Monographs* 37 (March 1970), 15–24.

Kennicott, Patrick C. and Wayne E. Page. "H. Rap Brown: The Cambridge Incident," *Quarterly Journal of Speech* 57 (October 1971), 325–334.

Killian, L. "Organization, Rationality, and Spontaneity in the Civil Rights Movement," *American Sociological Review* 49 (December 1984), 770–783.

King, Andrew A. "The Rhetorical Legacy of the Black Church," *Central States Speech Journal* 22 (Fall 1971), 179–185.

———. "The Rhetoric of Power Maintenance: Elites at the Precipice," *Quarterly Journal of Speech* 62 (April 1976), 127–134.

King, Andrew A. and Floyd D. Anderson. "Nixon, Agnew, and the 'Silent Majority': A Case Study in the Rhetoric of Polarization," *Western Speech* 35 (Fall 1971), 243–255.

King, Andrew A. and Kenneth Petress. "Universal Public Argument and the Failure of Nuclear Freeze," *Southern Communication Journal* 55 (Winter 1990), 162–174.

Klumpp, James F. "Challenge of Radical Rhetoric: Radicalism at Columbia," *Western Speech* 37 (Summer 1973), 146–156.

Klumpp, James F. and Thomas A. Hollihan. "Rhetorical Criticism as Moral Action," *Quarterly Journal of Speech* 75 (February 1989), 84–96.

Knupp, Ralph E. "A Time for Every Purpose Under Heaven: Rhetorical Dimensions of Protest Music," *Southern Speech Communication Journal* 46 (Summer 1981), 377–389.

Kosokoff, Stephen and Carl W. Carmichael. "The Rhetoric of Protest: Song, Speech, and Attitude Change," *Southern Speech Journal* 35 (Summer 1970), 295–302.

Kroll, Becky Swanson. "From Small Group to Public View: Mainstreaming the Women's Movement," *Communication Quarterly* 31 (Spring 1983), 139–147.

Lake, Randall A. "Enacting Red Power: The Consummatory Function in Native American Protest Rhetoric," *Quarterly Journal of Speech* 69 (May 1983), 127–142.

———. "Order and Disorder in Anti-Abortion Rhetoric: A Logological View," *Quarterly Journal of Speech* 70 (November 1984), 425–443.

Lange, Jonathan I. "Refusal to Compromise: The Case of Earth First!" *Western Journal of Speech Communication* 54 (Fall 1990), 473–494.

Larson, Barbara A. "Samuel Davies and the Rhetoric of the New Light," *Speech Monographs* 38 (August 1971), 207–216.

Larson, Charles U. "The Trust Establishing Function of the Rhetoric of Black Power," *Central States Speech Journal* 21 (Spring 1970), 52–56.

Laufer, Robert S. and Vern L. Bengston. "Generations, Aging, and Social Stratification: On the Development of Generational Units," *Journal of Social Issues* 30 (1974), 181–205.

Lawson, R. "The Rent Strike in New York City, 1904-1980: The Evolution of a Social Movement Strategy," *Journal of Urban History* 10 (May 1984), 235-258.

Lawton, Cynthia Whalen. "Thoreau and the Rhetoric of Dissent," *Today's Speech* 16 (April 1968), 23-25.

Leathers, Dale G. "Fundamentalism of the Radical Right," *Southern Speech Journal* 33 (Summer 1968), 245-258.

Lee, Ronald E. "Moralizing and Ideologizing: An Analysis of Political Illocutions," *Western Journal of Speech Communication* 52 (Fall 1988), 291-307.

_____. "The Rhetorical Construction of Time in Martin Luther King, Jr.'s 'Letter from Birmingham Jail'," *Southern Communication Journal* 56 (Summer 1991), 279-288.

Lee, Ronald E. and James R. Andrews. "A Story of Rhetorical-Ideological Transformation: Eugene V. Debs as Liberal Hero," *Quarterly Journal of Speech* 77 (February 1991), 20-37.

Linkugel, Wil A. "The Speech Style of Anna Howard Shaw," *Central States Speech Journal* 13 (Spring 1962), 171-178.

_____. "The Woman Suffrage Argument of Anna Howard Shaw," *Quarterly Journal of Speech* 49 (April 1963), 165-174.

_____. "The Rhetoric of American Feminism: A Social Movement Course," *Speech Teacher* 23 (March 1974), 121-130.

Lippman, Monroe. "Uncle Tom and His Poor Relations: American Slavery Plays," *Southern Speech Journal* 28 (Spring 1963), 183-197.

Lipsky, Michael. "Protest as a Political Resource," *American Political Science Review* 52 (1968), 1144-1158.

Lomas, Charles W. "The Agitator in American Society," *Western Speech* 24 (Spring 1960), 76-83.

_____. "Kearney and George: The Demagogue and the Prophet," *Speech Monographs* 28 (March 1961), 50-59.

_____. "Agitator in a Cassock," *Western Speech* 27 (Winter 1963), 16-24.

Lucaites, John Lois and Celeste Michelle Condit. "Reconstructing Equality: Culturetypal and Counter-Cultural Rhetorics in the Martyred Black Vision," *Communication Monographs* 57 (March 1990), 4-24.

Lucas, Stephen E. "Coming to Terms with Movement Studies," *Central States Speech Journal* 31 (Winter 1981), 255-266.

Makay, John J. "George C. Wallace: Southern Spokesman with a Northern Audience," *Central States Speech Journal* 19 (Fall 1968), 202-208.

Makay, John J. and Alberto Gonzalez. "Dylan's Biographical Rhetoric and the Myth of the Outlaw Hero," *Southern Speech Communication Journal* 52 (Winter 1987), 165-180.

Mann, Kenneth Eugene. "Nineteenth Century Black Militant: Henry Highland Garnet's Address to the Slaves," *Southern Speech Journal* 36 (Fall 1970), 11-21.

Mansfield, Dorothy M. "Abigail S. Duniway: Suffragette with Not-so-common Sense," *Western Speech* 35 (Winter 1971), 24-29.

Martin, Howard H. "The Rhetoric of Academic Protest," *Central States Speech Journal* 17 (November 1966), 244-250.

Martin, Kathryn. "The Relationship of Theatre of Revolution and Theology of Revolution to the Black Experience, *Today's Speech* 19 (Spring 1971), 35-41.

McEdwards, Mary G. "Agitative Rhetoric: Its Nature and Effect," *Western Speech* 32 (Winter 1968), 36-43.

McGaffey, Ruth. "Group Libel Revised," *Quarterly Journal of Speech* 65 (April 1979), 157–170.

McGee, Michael C. "In Search of 'The People': A Rhetorical Alternative," *Quarterly Journal of Speech* 61 (October 1975), 235–249.

_____. " 'Social Movement': Phenomenon or Meaning," *Central States Speech Journal* 31 (Winter 1980), 233–244.

_____. "Social Movement as Meaning," *Central States Speech Journal* 34 (Spring 1983), 74–77.

McGee, Michael C. and Martha A. Martin. "Public Knowledge and Ideological Argumentation," *Communication Monographs* 50 (March 1983), 45–65.

McGuire, Michael. "Mythic Rhetoric in *Mein Kampf*: A Structuralist Critique," *Quarterly Journal of Speech* 63 (February 1977), 1–13.

McKerrow, Raymie E. "Antimasonic Rhetoric: The Strategy of Excommunication," *Communication Quarterly* 37 (Fall 1989), 276–290.

McPherson, Louise. "Communication Techniques of the Women's Liberation Front," *Today's Speech* 21 (Spring 1973), 33–38.

Mechling, Elizabeth W. and Gale Auletta. "Beyond War: A Socio-Rhetorical Analysis of a New Class Revitalization Movement," *Western Journal of Speech Communication* 50 (Fall 1986), 388–404.

Mechling, Elizabeth W. and Jay Mechling. "Hot Pacifism and Cold War: The American Friends Service Committee's Witness for Peace in 1950s America," *Quarterly Journal of Speech* 78 (May 1992), 173–196.

Medhurst, Martin J. "The Sword of Division: A Reply to Brummett and Warnick," *Western Journal of Speech Communication* 46 (Fall 1982), 383–390.

_____. "The First Amendment vs. Human Rights: A Case Study in Human Sentiment and Argument from Definition," *Western Journal of Speech Communication* 46 (Winter 1982), 1–19.

_____. "Resistance, Conservatism, and Theory Building," *Western Journal of Speech Communication* 49 (Spring 1985), 103–115.

Mele, Joseph C. "Edward Douglas White's Influence on the Louisiana Anti-Lottery Movement," *Southern Speech Journal* 28 (Fall 1962), 36–43.

Merriam, Allen H. "Symbolic Action in India: Gandhi's Nonverbal Persuasion," *Quarterly Journal of Speech* 61 (October 1975), 290–306.

Mixon, Harold D. "Boston's Artillery Election Sermons and the American Revolution," *Speech Monographs* 34 (March 1967), 43–50.

Monsma, John W., Jr. "John Brown: The Two Edged Sword of Abolition," *Central States Speech Journal* 13 (Autumn 1961), 22–29.

Morris, Richard and Philip Wander. "Narrative American Rhetoric: Dancing in the Shadows of the Ghost Dance," *Quarterly Journal of Speech* 76 (May 1990), 164–191.

Murphy, John M. "Domesticating Dissent: The Kennedys and the Freedom Rides," *Communication Monographs* 59 (March 1992), 61–78.

Nelson, Elizabeth, Jean. " 'Nothing Ever Goes Well Enough': Mussolini and the Rhetoric of Perpetual Struggle," *Communication Studies* 42 (Spring, 1991), 22–42.

Nelson, Jeffrey and Mary Ann Flannery. "The Sanctuary Movement: A Study in Religious Confrontation," *Southern Communication Journal* 55 (Summer 1990), 372–387.

Newman, Robert P. "Under the Veneer: Nixon's Vietnam Speech of November 3, 1969," *Quarterly Journal of Speech* 56 (April 1970), 168–178.

Newsom, Lionel and William Gorden. "A Stormy Rally in Atlanta," *Today's Speech* 11 (April 1963), 18–21.

Norton, Robert. "The Propaganda of Bodies," *Today's Speech* 18 (Spring 1970), 39–41.

O'Brien, Harold J. "Slavery Sentiments that Led to War," *Today's Speech* 9 (November 1961), 5–7.

Olien, C. N.; G. A. Donohue; and P. T. Tichenor. "Media and Stages of Social Conflict," *Journalism Monographs* (November 1984), 1–31.

Orban, Donald K. "Billy James Hargis: Auctioneer of Political Evangelism," *Central States Speech Journal* 20 (Summer 1969), 83–91.

Patton, John H. "Rhetoric at Catonsville: Daniel Berrigan, Conscience and Image Alteration," *Today's Speech* 23 (Winter 1975), 3–12.

Pearce, W. Barnett, Stephen W. Littlejohn, and Alison Alexander. "The New Christian Right and the Humanist Response: Reciprocated Diatribe," *Communication Quarterly* 35 (Spring 1987), 171–192.

Perkins, Sally J. "The Rhetoric of Androgyny as Revealed in The Feminine Mystique," *Communication Studies* 40 (Summer 1989), 69–80.

Phifer, Elizabeth F. and Dencil R. Taylor. "Carmichael in Tallahassee," *Southern Speech Journal* 33 (Winter 1967), 88–92.

Pollock, Arthur. "Stokely Carmichael's New Black Rhetoric," *Southern Speech Journal* 37 (Fall 1971), 92–94.

Powers, Lloyd D. "Chicago Rhetoric: Some Basic Concepts," *Southern Speech Journal* 38 (Summer 1973), 340–346.

Press, Andrea L. "The Impact of Television on Modes of Reasoning about Abortion," *Critical Studies of Mass Communication* 8 (December 1991), 421–441.

Railsback, Celeste Condit. "The Contemporary American Abortion Controversy: Stages in the Argument," *Quarterly Journal of Speech* 70 (November 1984), 410–424.

Reed, Robert Michael. "The Case of Missionary Smith: A Crucial Incident in the Rhetoric of the British Anti-Slavery Movement," *Central States Speech Journal* 29 (Spring 1978), 61–71.

Reid, Ronald F. "Varying Historical Interpretations of the American Revolution: Some Rhetorical Perspectives," *Today's Speech* 23 (Spring 1975), 5–15.

Reynolds, Beatrice K. "Mao Tse-Tung: Rhetoric of a Revolutionary," *Central States Speech Journal* 27 (Fall 1976), 212–217.

Riach, W. A. D. "'Telling It Like It Is': An Examination of Black Theatre as Rhetoric," *Quarterly Journal of Speech* 56 (April 1970), 179–186.

Rice, George P., Jr. "Freedom of Speech and the 'New Left'," *Central States Speech Journal* 21 (Fall 1970), 139–145.

Richardson, Larry S. "Stokely Carmichael: Jazz Artist," *Western Speech* 34 (Summer 1970), 212–218.

Riches, Suzanne V. and Malcolm O. Sillars. "The Status of Movement Criticism," *Western Journal of Speech Communication* 44 (Fall 1980), 275–287.

Ritchie, Gladys. "The Sit-In: A Rhetoric of Human Action," *Today's Speech* 18 (Winter 1970), 22–25.

Ritter, Ellen M. "Elizabeth Morgan: Pioneer Female Labor Agitator," *Central States Speech Journal* 22 (Winter 1971), 242–251.

Ritter, Kurt W. "Confrontation as Moral Drama: The Boston Massacre in Rhetorical Perspective," *Southern Speech Communication Journal* 42 (Winter 1977), 114–136.

Robinson, John P., Robert Pilskaln, and Paul Hirsh. "Protest Rock and Drugs," *Journal of Communication* 26 (Autumn 1976), 125–136.

Rogers, Richard S. "The Rhetoric of Militant Deism," *Quarterly Journal of Speech* 54 (October 1968), 247–251.

Rollins, J. "Part of the Whole: The Interdependence of the Civil Rights Movement and Other Social Movements," *Phylon* 47 (March 1986), 61–70.

Rosenfeld, Lawrence B. "The Confrontation Politics of S. I. Hayakawa: A Case Study in Coercive Semantics," *Today's Speech* 18 (Spring 1970), 18–22.

Rosenthal, N. B., *et al.* "Social Movements and Network Analysis: A Case Study of Nineteenth-Century Women's Reform in New York State," *American Journal of Sociology* 90 (March 1985), 1022–1054.

Rosenwasser, Marie J. "Rhetoric and the Progress of the Women's Liberation Movement," *Today's Speech* 20 (Summer 1972), 45–56.

Rossiter, Charles M. and Ruth McGaffey. "Freedom of Speech and the 'New Left': A Response," *Central States Speech Journal* 22 (Spring 1971), 5–10.

Rosteck, Thomas. "Irony, Argument, and Reportage in Television Documentary: *See It Now* Versus Senator McCarthy," *Quarterly Journal of Speech* 75 (August 1989), 277–298.

Rothman, Richard. "On the Speaking of John L. Lewis," *Central States Speech Journal* 14 (August 1963), 177–185.

Rothwell, J. Dan. "Verbal Obscenity: Time for Second Thoughts," *Western Speech* 35 (Fall 1971), 231–242.

Rude, Leslie G. "The Rhetoric of Farmer Labor Agitators," *Central States Speech Journal* 20 (Winter 1969), 280–285.

Scott, F. Eugene. "The Political Preaching Tradition in Ulster: Prelude to Paisley," *Western Speech* 40 (Fall 1976), 249–259.

Scott, Robert L. "Justifying Violence—The Rhetoric of Militant Black Power," *Central States Speech Journal* 19 (Summer 1968), 96–104.

———. "The Conservative Voice in Radical Rhetoric: A Common Response to Division," *Speech Monographs* 40 (June 1973), 123–135.

Scott, Robert L. and Donald K. Smith. "The Rhetoric of Confrontation," *Quarterly Journal of Speech* 55 (February 1969), 1–8.

Seibold, David. "Jewish Defense League: The Rhetoric of Resistance," *Today's Speech* 21 (Fall 1973), 39–48.

Shafer, George. "The Dramaturgy of Fact: The Treatment of History in Two Anti-War Plays," *Central States Speech Journal* 29 (Spring 1978), 25–35.

Short, Brant. "Earth First! and the Rhetoric of Moral Confrontation," *Communication Studies* 42 (Summer 1991), 172–188.

Sillars, Malcolm O. "The Rhetoric of the Petition in Boots," *Speech Monographs* 39 (June 1972), 92–104.

———. "Defining Movement Rhetorically: Casting the Widest Net," *Southern Speech Communication Journal* 46 (Fall 1980), 17–32.

Silvestri, Vito N. "Emma Goldman, Enduring Voice of Anarchism," *Today's Speech* 17 (September 1969), 20–25.

Simons, Herbert W. "Patterns of Persuasion in the Civil Rights Movement," *Today's Speech* 15 (February 1967), 25–27.

———. "Confrontation as a Pattern of Persuasion in University Settings," *Central States Speech Journal* 20 (Fall 1969), 163–169.

———. "Requirements, Problems, and Strategies: A Theory of Persuasion for Social Movements," *Quarterly Journal of Speech* 56 (February 1970), 1–11.

———. "Persuasion in Social Conflicts: A Critique of Prevailing Conceptions and a Framework for Future Research," *Speech Monographs* 39 (November 1972), 227–247.

_____. "Changing Notions about Social Movements," *Quarterly Journal of Speech* 62 (December 1976), 425–430.

_____. "On Terms, Definitions and Theoretical Distinctiveness: Comments on Papers by McGee and Zarefsky," *Central States Speech Journal* 31 (Winter 1980), 306–315.

_____. "Genres, Rules, and Collective Rhetorics: Applying the Requirements-Problems-Strategies Approach," *Communication Quarterly* 30 (Summer 1982), 181–188.

_____. "On the Rhetoric of Social Movements, Historical Movements, and 'Top Down' Movements: A Commentary," *Communication Studies* 42 (Spring 1991), 94–101.

Simons, Herbert W., James W. Chesebro, and C. Jack Orr, "A Movement Perspective on the 1972 Presidential Campaign," *Quarterly Journal of Speech* 59 (April 1973), 168–179.

Simpson, Tessa and Stephen King. "The Sanctuary Movement: Criminal Trials and Religious Dissent," Journal of Communication and Religion 15 (March 1992), 15–28.

Smiley, Sam. "Peace on Earth: Four Anti-War Dramas of the Thirties," *Central States Speech Journal* 21 (Spring 1970), 30–39.

Smith, Arthur L. "Henry Highland Garnet: Black Revolutionary in Sheep's Vestments," *Central States Speech Journal* 21 (Summer 1970), 93–98.

Smith, Craig Allen. "The Hofstadter Hypothesis Revisited: The Nature of Evidence in Politically 'Paranoid' Discourse," *Southern Speech Communication Journal* 42 (Spring 1977), 274–289.

_____. "An Organic Systems Analysis of Persuasion and Social Movement: The John Birch Society, 1958–1966," *Southern Speech Communication Journal* 59 (Winter 1984), 155–176.

Smith, Craig R. "Television News as Rhetoric," *Western Speech* 41 (Summer 1977), 147–159.

Smith, Donald H. "Social Protest . . . and the Oratory of Human Rights," *Today's Speech* 15 (September 1967), 2–8.

_____. "Martin Luther King, Jr.: In the Beginning at Montgomery," *Southern Speech Journal* 34 (Fall 1968), 8–17.

Smith, Ralph R. and Russell Windes. "The Innovational Movement: A Rhetorical Theory," *Quarterly Journal of Speech* 61 (April 1975), 140–153.

_____. "The Rhetoric of Mobilization: Implications for the Study of Movements," *Southern Speech Communication Journal* 42 (Fall 1976), 1–19.

_____. "Collective Action and the Single Text," *Southern Speech Communication Journal* 43 (Winter 1978), 110–128.

Smith, Ralph R. "The Historical Criticism of Social Movements," *Central States Speech Journal* 31 (Winter 1980), 290–297.

Snow, Malinda. "Martin Luther King's 'Letter from Birmingham Jail' as Pauline Epistle," *Quarterly Journal of Speech* 71 (August 1985), 318–334.

Solomon, Martha. "The Rhetoric of STOP ERA: Fatalistic Reaffirmation," *Southern Speech Communication Journal* 44 (Fall 1978), 42–59.

_____. "Stopping ERA: A Pyrrhic Victory," *Communication Quarterly* 31 (Spring 1983), 109–117.

_____. "Ideology as Rhetorical Constraint: The Anarchist Agitation of 'Red Emma' Goldman," *Quarterly Journal of Speech* 74 (May 1988), 184–200.

_____. "Autobiographies as Rhetorical Narratives: Elizabeth Cady Stanton and Anna Howard Shaw as 'New Women'," *Communication Studies* 42 (Winter 1991), 354–370.

Sproule, J. Michael. "An Emerging Rationale for Revolution: Argument from Circumstance and Definition in Polemics Against the Stamp Act, 1765–1766," *Today's Speech*

23 (Spring 1975), 17–23.

Stewart, Charles J. "A Functional Approach to the Rhetoric of Social Movements," *Central States Speech Journal* 31 (Winter 1980), 298–305.

———. "A Functional Perspective on the Study of Social Movements," *Central States Speech Journal* 34 (Spring 1983), 77–80.

———. "The Internal Rhetoric of the Knights of Labor," *Communication Studies* 42 (Spring 1991), 67–82.

———. "The Ego Function of Protest Songs: An Application of Gregg's Theory of Protest Rhetoric," *Communication Studies* 42 (Fall 1991), 240–253.

Stitzel, James A. "Inflammatory Speaking in the Victor, Colorado, Mass Meeting, June 6, 1904," *Western Speech* 32 (Winter 1968), 11–18.

Strother, David B. "Polemics and the Reversal of the 'Separate but Equal' Doctrine," *Quarterly Journal of Speech* 49 (February 1963), 50–56.

Talmon, Yonina. "Pursuit of the Millennium: The Relation between Religious and Social Change," *The European Journal of Sociology* 2 (1962), 140–141.

Tedesco, John L. "The White Character in Black Drama, 1955–1970: Description and Rhetorical Function," *Communication Monographs* 45 (March 1978), 64–74.

Thomas, Cheryl Irwin. " 'Look What They've Done to My Song, Ma': The Persuasiveness of Song," *Southern Speech Communication Journal* 39 (Spring 1974), 260–268.

Thomas, Gordon L. "John Brown's Courtroom Speech," *Quarterly Journal of Speech* 48 (October 1962), 291–296.

Thurber, John H. and John L. Petelle. "The Negro Pulpit and Civil Rights," *Central States Speech Journal* 19 (Winter 1968), 273–278.

Veenstra, Charles. "The House Un-American Activities Committee's Restriction of Free Speech," *Today's Speech* 22 (Winter 1974), 15–22.

Veninga, Robert. "The Functions of Symbols in Legend Construction . . . Some Exploratory Comments," *Central States Speech Journal* 22 (Fall 1971), 161–170.

Wagner, Gerard A. "Sojourner Truth: God's Appointed Apostle of Reform," *Southern Speech Journal* 28 (Winter 1962), 123–130.

Walsh, James F., Jr. "The Rhetoric of Social Movements: The Selection and Use of Mass Media by Maoist Mobilizers," *Indiana Speech Journal* 22 (November 1991), 17–34.

Wander, Philip C. "Salvation Through Separation: The Image of the Negro in the American Colonization Society," *Quarterly Journal of Speech* 57 (February 1971), 57–67.

———. "The John Birch and Martin Luther King Symbols in the Radical Right," *Western Speech* 35 (Winter 1971), 4–14.

———. "The Savage Child: The Image of the Negro in the Pro-Slavery Movement," *Southern Speech Communication Journal* 37 (Summer 1972), 335–360.

Ware, B. L. and Wil A. Linkugel. "The Rhetorical *Persona*: Marcus Garvey as Black Moses," *Communication Monographs* 49 (March 1982), 50–62.

Warnick, Barbara. "The Rhetoric of Conservative Resistance," *Southern Speech Communication Journal* 42 (Spring 1977), 256–273.

———. "Conservative Resistance Revisited," *Western Journal of Speech Communication* 46 (Fall 1982), 373–378.

Weatherly, Michael. "Propaganda and the Rhetoric of the American Revolution," *Southern Speech Journal* 36 (Summer 1971), 352–363.

Weaver, Richard L., II. "The Negro Issue: Agitation in the Michigan Lyceum," *Central States Speech Journal* 22 (Fall 1971), 196–201.

Weisman, Martha. "Ambivalence Toward War in Anti-War Plays," *Today's Speech* 17 (September 1969), 9–14.

Weithoff, William E. "Rhetorical Strategy in the Birmingham Political Union, 1830–1832," *Central States Speech Journal* 29 (Spring 1978), 53–60.

Whitfield, George. "Frederick Douglass: Negro Abolitionist," *Today's Speech* 11 (February 1963), 6–8, 24.

Wilkie, Richard W. "The Self-Taught Agitator: Hitler 1907–1920," *Quarterly Journal of Speech* 52 (December 1966), 371–377.

———. "The Marxian Rhetoric of Angelica Balabanoff," *Quarterly Journal of Speech* 60 (December 1974), 450–458.

Wilkinson, Charles A. "A Rhetorical Definition of Movements," *Central States Speech Journal* 27 (Summer 1976), 88–94.

Williams, Donald E. "Protest Under the Cross: The Ku Klux Klan Presents Its Case to the People," *Southern Speech Journal* 27 (Fall 1961), 43–55.

Wimmer, E. "Ideology of 'New Social Movements'," *World Marx Review,* (July 1985), 36–44.

Windt, Theodore O. "The Diatribe: Last Resort for Protest," *Quarterly Journal of Speech* 58 (February 1972), 1–14.

———. "Administrative Rhetoric: An Undemocratic Response to Protest," *Communication Quarterly* 30 (Summer 1982), 245–250.

Woodward, Gary C. "Mystifications in the Rhetoric of Cultural Dominance and Colonial Control," *Central States Speech Journal* 26 (Winter 1975), 298–303.

Wurthman, Leonard B. "The Militant-Moderate Agitator: Daniel O'Connell and Catholic Emancipation in Ireland," *Communication Quarterly* 30 (Summer 1982), 225–231.

Wuthnow, R. "The Growth of Religious Reform Movements," Annals of the American Academy of Political and Social Sciences 480 (July 1985), 106–116.

Yoder, Jess. "The Protest of the American Clergy in Opposition to the War in Vietnam," *Today's Speech* 17 (September 1969), 51–59.

———. "Communication Between Catholics and Protestants in Northern Ireland," *Religious Communication Today* 4 (September 1981), 15–20.

Zacharis, John C. "Emmeline Pankhurst: An English Suffragette Influences America," *Speech Monographs* 38 (August 1971), 198–206.

Zarefsky, David. "President Johnson's War on Poverty: The Rhetoric of Three 'Establishment' Movements," *Communication Monographs* 44 (November 1977), 352–373.

———. "A Skeptical View of Movement Studies," *Central States Speech Journal* 31 (Winter 1980), 245–254.

Book Chapters

Blumer, Herbert. "Social Movements," *Principles of Sociology*, A. M. Lee, ed. New York: Barnes and Noble, 1951.

Boettinger, L.A. "Organic Theory of Social Reform Movements," *Analyzing Social Problems*, John Nordskog, *et al.*, eds. New York: Dryden, 1950.

Griffin, Leland M. "The Rhetorical Structure of the Antimasonic Movement," *The Rhetorical Idiom*, Donald Bryant, ed. Ithaca, NY: Cornell University Press, 1958.

———. "A Dramatistic Theory of the Rhetoric of Movements," *Critical Responses to Kenneth Burke*, William Rueckert, ed. Minneapolis: University of Minnesota Press, 1969.

Gronbeck, Bruce E. "The Rhetoric of Social-Institutional Change: Black Action at Michigan," *Explorations in Rhetorical Criticism*, Gerald Mohrmann, Charles Stewart, and Donovan Ochs, eds. University Park, PA: Pennsylvania State University Press, 1973.

Hughes, Everett C. "Institutions Defined," *Principles of Sociology*, A. M. Lee, ed. New York: Barnes and Noble, 1951.

Killian, Lewis M. "Social Movements," *Handbook of Modern Sociology*, R. E. Faris, ed. Chicago: Rand McNally, 1964.

Leathers, Dale G. "Belief-Disbelief Systems: The Communicative Vacuum of the Radical Right," *Explorations in Rhetorical Criticism*, Gerald Mohrmann, Charles Stewart, Donovan Ochs, eds. University Park, PA: Pennsylvania State University Press, 1973.

Simons, Herbert W. and Elizabeth W. Mechling. "The Rhetoric of Political Movements," *Handbook of Political Communication*, Dan Nimmo and Keith Sanders, eds. Beverly Hills, CA: Sage, 1981.

Simons, Herbert W., Elizabeth Mechling, and Howard Schreier. "Functions of Communication in Mobilizing for Action from the Bottom Up: The Rhetoric of Social Movements," *Handbook on Rhetorical and Communication Theory*, Carroll C. Arnold and John W. Bowers, eds. Boston: Allyn and Bacon, 1984.

Stewart, Charles J. "Labor Agitation in America: 1865–1915," *America in Controversy: History of American Public Address*, DeWitte T. Holland, ed. Dubuque, IA: Brown, 1973.

Van Graber, Marilyn. "Functional Criticism: A Rhetoric of Black Power," *Explorations in Rhetorical Criticism*, Gerald Mohrmann, Charles Stewart, and Donovan Ochs, eds. University Park, PA: Pennsylvania State University Press, 1973.

Books

Alinsky, Saul D. *Reveille for Radicals*. New York: Vintage, 1969.

_____. *Rules for Radicals: A Practical Primer for Realistic Radicals*. New York: Vintage, 1972.

Amter, Joseph A. *Vietnam Verdict: A Citizen's History*. New York: Continuum, 1982.

Anderson, Walt, ed. *The Age of Protest*. Pacific Palisades, CA: Goodyear Publishing, 1969.

Apter, David, ed. *Ideology and Discontent*. London: Collier-MacMillan, 1964.

Arendt, Hannah. *The Origins of Totalitarianism*. New York: World, 1958.

_____. *On Revolution*. New York: Viking, 1965.

Arlen, Michael J. *Living-Room War*. New York: Penguin Books, 1969.

Armstrong, Gregory. *Protest: Man Against Society*. New York: Bantam Books, 1969.

Auer, J. Jeffrey, ed. *Antislavery and Disunion: 1858–1861*. New York: Harper and Row, 1963.

_____. *The Rhetoric of Our Times*. New York: Appleton-Century-Crofts, 1969.

Baechler, Jean. *Revolution*, trans. Joan Vickers. New York: Harper and Row, 1975.

Barbrook, Alec and Christine Bolt. *Power and Protest in American Life*. New York: St. Martin's Press, 1980.

Barkan, Steven E. *Protestors on Trial: Criminal Justice in the Southern Civil Rights and Vietnam Antiwar Movements*. New Brunswick, NJ: Rutgers University Press, 1986.

Bell, Daniel, ed. *The Radical Right*. New York: Doubleday Anchor, 1964.

Bell, J. Bowyer. *Transnational Terror*. Washington, DC: Hoover, 1975.

_____. *A Time of Terror*. Cambridge: Cambridge University Press, 1982.

Blaustein, Albert P. and Robert Zangrando, eds. *Civil Rights and the American Negro*. New York: Trident Press, 1968.

Blocker, Jack S. *"Give to the Minds Thy Fears": The Women's Temperance Crusade, 1873–1874*. Westport, CT: 1985.

Boase, Paul H. *The Rhetoric of Christian Socialism*. New York: Random House, 1969.

Boase, Paul H., ed. *The Rhetoric of Protest and Reform: 1878–1898*. Athens, OH: Ohio University Press, 1980.

Booth, Wayne. *Modern Dogma and the Rhetoric of Assent*. Chicago: University of Chicago Press, 1974.

Bosmajian, Haig A., ed. *Dissent: Symbolic Behavior and Rhetorical Strategies*. Boston: Allyn and Bacon, 1972.

Bosmajian, Haig A. and Hamida Bosmajian. *The Rhetoric of the Civil Rights Movement*. New York: Random House, 1969.

Bowers, John W.; Donovan J. Ochs; and Richard J. Jensen. *The Rhetoric of Agitation and Control*, 2/E. Prospect Heights, IL: Waveland Press, 1993.

Branch, *Parting the Waters: America in the King Years*. New York: Simon and Schuster, 1988.

Brandes, Paul D. *The Rhetoric of Revolt*. Englewood Cliffs, NJ: Prentice-Hall, 1971.

Brinkley, Alan. *Voices of Protest: Huey Long, Father Coughlin, and the Great Depression*. New York: Random House, 1983.

Brinton, Crane. *The Anatomy of Revolution*. New York: Prentice-Hall, 1952.

Brockriede, Wayne C. and Robert L. Scott. *Moments in the Rhetoric of the Cold War*. New York: Random House, 1970.

Broesamle, John J. *Reform and Reaction in Twentieth Century American Politics*. Westport, CT: Greenwood Press, 1992.

Brooks, Thomas R. *Walls Came Tumbling Down: A History of the Civil Rights Movement*. Englewood Cliffs, NJ: Prentice-Hall, 1974.

Button, James. *Black Violence*. Princeton: Princeton University Press, 1978.

Bytwerk, Randall L. *Julius Streicher: The Man Who Persuaded a Nation to Hate Jews*. Briarcliff Manor, NY: Stein and Day, 1982.

Cameron, William B. *Modern Social Movements: A Sociological Outline*. New York: Random House, 1966.

Campbell, Karlyn Kohrs. *Critiques of Contemporary Rhetoric*. Belmont, CA: Wadsworth, 1972.

_____. *Man Cannot Speak for Her: A Critical Study of Early Feminist Rhetoric*. New York: Greenwood Press, 1989.

Cantril, Hadley. *The Psychology of Social Movements*. New York: Wiley and Sons, 1963.

Carter, April. *Direct Action and Liberal Democracy*. New York: Harper and Row, 1973.

Chesebro, James W., ed. *Gayspeak: Gay Male and Lesbian Communication*. New York: Pilgrim Press, 1981.

Clabaugh, Gary. *Thunder on the Right*. Chicago: Nelson-Hall, 1980.

Coleman, William E., Jr. and William E. Coleman, Sr. *A Rhetoric of the People: The German Greens and the New Politics*. Westport, CT: Greenwood Press, 1993.

Condit, Celeste Michelle. *Decoding Abortion Rhetoric: Communicating Social Change*. Urbana: University of Illinois Press, 1990.

Crawford, Alan. *Thunder on the Right*. New York: Pantheon, 1980.

Curry, Richard O. and Thomas M. Brown, eds. *Conspiracy: The Fear of Subversion in American History*. New York: Holt, Rinehart, and Winston, 1972.

Davis, Flora. *Moving the Mountain: The Women's Movement in America Since 1960*. New York: Simon and Schuster, 1991.

Davis, Jerome. *Contemporary Social Movements*. New York: Century, 1930.

Dawson, Carol A. and Warner E. Gettys. *Introduction to Sociology*. New York: Ronald, 1935.

DeBenedetti, Charles. *The Peace Reform in American History*. Bloomington, IN: Indiana University Press, 1980.

Deckard, Barbara. *The Women's Movement*. New York: Harper and Row, 1983.

Denisoff, R. Serge. *Great Day Coming: Folk Music and the American Left*. Urbana, IL: University of Illinois Press, 1972.

_____. *Sing a Song of Social Significance*. Bowling Green, OH: Bowling Green University Popular Press, 1972.

Denisoff, R. Serge and Richard A. Peterson. *The Sounds of Social Change*. Chicago: Rand McNally, 1972.

Dixon-Mueller, Ruth. *Population Policy and Women's Rights: Transforming Reproductive Choice*. Westport, CT: Greenwood Press, 1993.

Duffy, Bernard K. and Halford Ryan, eds. *American Orators Before 1900: Critical Studies and Sources*. Westport, CT: Greenwood Press, 1987.

_____. *American Orators of the Twentieth Century: Critical Studies and Sources*. Westport, CT: Greenwood Press, 1987.

Dunne, John Gregory. *Delano: The Story of the California Grape Strike*. New York: Farrar, Straus, and Giroux, 1967.

Edelman, Murray. *Politics as Symbolic Action: Mass Arousal and Quiescence*. San Diego, CA: Academic Press, 1971.

_____. *The Symbolic Uses of Politics*. Urbana, IL: University of Illinois Press, 1985.

_____. *Constructing the Political Spectacle*. Chicago: University of Chicago Press, 1988.

Eder, Klaus. *The New Politics of Class: Social Movements and Cultural Dynamics in Advanced Societies*. New York: Sage, 1993.

Edwards, Lyford P. *The Natural History of Revolution*. Chicago: University of Chicago Press, 1927.

Fairclough, Adam. *To Redeem the Soul of America: The Southern Christian Leadership Conference and Martin Luther King, Jr.* Athens, GA: University of Georgia Press, 1987.

Feuer, Lewis S. *The Conflict of Generations: The Character and Significance of Student Movements*. New York: Basic Books, 1969.

Fisher, Randall M. *Rhetoric and American Democracy: Black Protest Through Vietnam Dissent*. Lanham, MD: University Press of America, 1985.

Fortas, Abe. *Concerning Dissent and Civil Disobedience*. New York: American Library, 1968.

Gamson, William A. *Power and Discontent*. Homewood, IL: Dorsey Press, 1969.

_____. *The Strategy of Social Protest*. Homewood, IL: Dorsey Press, 1975.

Garner, Roberta Ash. *Social Movements in America*. Chicago: Markham, 1977.

Graber, Doris Appel. *Mass Media and American Politics*. Washington, DC: Congressional Quarterly, 1984.

Griffith, Robert. *The Politics of Fear*. Lexington, KY: University of Kentucky Press, 19770.

Gurr, Ted Robert. *Why Men Rebel*. Princeton, NJ: Princeton University Press, 1970.

Gusfield, Joseph R., ed. *Protest, Reform, and Revolt: A Reader in Social Movements*. New York: John Wiley, 1970.

Haiman, Franklyn S. *Freedom of Speech: Issues and Cases*. New York: Random House,

1965.

Hammerback, J. C.; R. J. Jensen; and J. A. Gutierrez. *A War of Words: Protest in the 1960s and 1970s*. Westport, CT: Greenwood, 1985.

Hampton, Wayne. *Guerrilla Minstrels: John Lennon, Joe Hill, Woody Guthrie, and Bob Dylan*. Knoxville, TN: University of Tennessee Press, 1986.

Hart, B. H. Liddell. *Strategy*. New York: Praeger, 1960.

Heberle, Rudolf. *Social Movements: An Introduction to Political Sociology*. New York: Appleton-Century-Crofts, 1951.

Hoffer, Eric. *The True Believer*. New York: Mentor, 1951.

_____. *The Ordeal of Change*. New York: Harper and Row, 1963.

Holland, DeWitte T., ed. *Preaching in American History*. Nashville, TN: Abingdon Press, 1969.

_____. *America in Controversy: A History of American Public Address*. Dubuque, IA: Brown, 1973.

Horton, Paul B. and Chester L. Hunt. *Sociology*. New York: McGraw-Hill, 1964.

Hribar, Paul A. *The Social Fasts of Cesar Chavez: Critical Study of Nonverbal Communication, Nonviolence, and Public Opinion*. Los Angeles: University of Southern California, 1978.

Huey, Gary. *Rebel with a Cause: P. D. East, Southern Liberalism, and the Civil Rights Movement, 1953–1971*. Wilmington, DL: Scholarly Resources, 1985.

Hughes, Langston. *Fight for Freedom: The Story of the NAACP*. New York: W. W. Norton, 1962.

Jaggar, Alison and Paula Rothenberg. *Feminist Frameworks*. New York: McGraw Hill, 1984.

Jameson, J. Franklin. *The American Revolution Considered as a Social Movement*. Boston: Beacon, 1956.

Jeffreys-Jones, Rhodri. *Violence and Reform in American History*. New York: New Viewpoints, 1978.

Johnson, Chalmers. *Revolutionary Change*. Boston: Little, Brown, 1966.

Katope, Christopher George and Paul Zolbrod. *The Rhetoric of Revolution*. New York: Macmillan, 1970.

Kendrick, Alexander. *The Wound Within: America in the Vietnam Years, 1945–1974*. Boston: Little, Brown, 1974.

King, Wendell C. *Social Movements in the United States*. New York: Random House, 1956.

Kriesberg, Louis. *The Sociology of Social Conflicts*. Englewood Cliffs, NJ: Prentice-Hall, 1973.

_____. *Social Conflicts*. Englewood Cliffs, NJ: Prentice-Hall, 1982.

Lang, Kurt and Gladys E. Lang. *Collective Dynamics*. New York: Crowell, 1961.

Leeman, Richard W. *The Rhetoric of Terrorism and Counterterrorism*. Westport, CT.: Greenwood Press, 1991.

Lens, Sidney. *Radicalism in America*. New York: Crowell, 1966.

Linkugel, Wil A. and Martha Solomon. *Anna Howard Shaw: Suffrage Orator and Social Reformer*. Westport, CT: Greenwood Press, 1991.

Lipset, Seymour and Sheldon S. Wolin, eds. *The Berkeley Student Revolt: Facts and Interpretations*. Garden City, NY: Anchor Books, 1965.

Lomas, Charles W. *The Agitator in American Society*. Englewood Cliffs, NJ: Prentice-Hall, 1968.

Lowenthal, Leo and Norbert Guterman. *Prophets of Deceit*. New York: Harper and Row, 1949.

Maclear, Michael. *The Ten Thousand Day War: Vietnam, 1945-1975*. New York: Dodd, Mead, 1975.

Marable, Manning. *Black American Politics from the Washington Marches to Jesse Jackson*. London: Verso, 1985.

Marcus, Eric. *Making History: the Struggle for Gay and Lesbian Equal Rights, 1945-1990: An Oral History*. New York: Harper Collins, 1992.

McAdam, Doug. *Political Process and the Development of Black Insurgency*. Chicago: University of Chicago Press, 1982.

McLaughlin, Barry, ed. *Studies in Social Movements*. New York: Free Press, 1969.

Meier, August, Elliot Rudwick, and Francis L. Broderick, eds. *Black Protest Thought in the Twentieth Century*. Indianapolis: Bobbs-Merrill, 1971.

Mendlovitz, Saul H. and R. B. J. Walker, eds. *Toward a Just World Peace: Perspectives from Social Movements*. London: Butterworth, 1987.

Michener, James. *Kent State: What Happened and Why*. New York: Random House, 1971.

Miller, Gerald R. and Herbert W. Simons, eds. *Perspectives on Communication in Social Conflicts*. Englewood Cliffs, NJ: Prentice-Hall, 1974.

Miller, James. *"Democracy Is in the Streets": From Port Huron to the Siege of Chicago*. NY: Simon and Schuster, 1987.

Mills, Nicolaus. *Like a Holy Crusade: Mississippi; the Turning of the Civil Rights Movement in America*. Chicago: I. R. Dee, 1992.

Morris, Aldon D. and Carol McClurg Mueller, eds. *Frontiers in Social Movement Theory*. New Haven, CT: Yale University Press, 1992.

Nordskog, John Eric, ed. *Contemporary Social Reform Movements*. New York: Scribner's, 1954.

Oates, Stephen B. *Let the Trumpet Sound: The Life of Martin Luther King, Jr*. Bergenfield, NJ: New American Library, 1982

Oberschall, Anthony. *Social Conflict and Social Movements*. Englewood Cliffs, NJ: Prentice-Hall 1973.

Olasky, Marvin. *The Press and Abortion, 1838-1988*. Hillsdale, NJ: Lawrence Erlbaum, 1988.

Oliver, Robert T. *History of Public Speaking in America*. Boston: Allyn and Bacon, 1965.

Oppenheimer, Martin and George Lakey. *A Manual for Direct Action*. Chicago: Quadrangle, 1965.

Payne, Gregory. *Mayday: Kent State*. Dubuque, IA: Kendall/Hunt, 1981.

Phillips, Donald E. *Student Protest, 1960-1970: An Analysis of the Speeches and Issues*. Lanham, MD: University Press of America, 1985.

Poloma, Margaret M. *The Charismatic Movement: Is There a New Pentecost?* Boston: Twayne, 1982.

Powledge, Fred. *Free at Last? The Civil Rights Movement and the People Who Made It*. Boston: Little, Brown and Company, 1991.

Powers, Thomas. *The War at Home: Vietnam and the American People, 1964-1968*. New York: Grossman, 1973.

Price, Jerome B. *The Antinuclear Movement*. Boston: Twayne, 1982.

Raboy, Marc. *Movements and Messages: Media and Radical Politics in Quebec*. Trans. by David Homel. Bridgewater, NJ: Baker and Taylor, 1984.

Reid, Loren, ed. *American Public Address: Studies in Honor of Albert Craig Baird*. Columbia, MO: University of Missouri Press, 1961.

Rice, Donald E. *The Rhetorical Uses of the Authorizing Figure: Fidel Castro and Jose Marti*. Westport, CT: Praeger, 1992.

Roberts, Ron E. and Robert M. Kloss. *Social Movements: Between the Balcony and the Barricade*. St. Louis: Mosby, 1974.

Rush, Gary B. and R. Serge Denisoff. *Social and Political Movements*. New York: Appleton-Century-Crofts, 1971.

Sale, Kirkpatrick. *SDS*. New York: Vintage, 1974.

Schandler, Herbert. *The Unmaking of the President: Lyndon Johnson and Vietnam*. Princeton: Princeton University Press, 1977.

Schmid, Alex and Janny de Graaf. *Violence as Communication: Insurgent Terrorism and the Western News Media*. Beverly Hills: Sage, 1982.

Scott, Robert L. and Wayne E. Brockriede. *The Rhetoric of Black Power*. New York: Harper and Row, 1969.

Shelling, Thomas G. *The Strategy of Conflict*. Cambridge: Harvard University Press, 1960.

Shupe, Anson D. and David G. Bromley. *The New Vigilantes: Deprogrammers, Anti-Cultists, and the New Religions*. Beverly Hills, CA: Sage, 1980.

Skolnick, Jerome H. *The Politics of Protest*. New York: Ballantine, 1969.

Smelser, Neil J. *Theory of Collective Behavior*. New York: Free Press of Glencoe, 1963.

Smith, Arthur L. *Rhetoric of Black Revolution*. Boston: Allyn and Bacon, 1969.

_____. *Language, Communication, and Rhetoric in Black America*. New York: Harper and Row, 1972.

Stohl, Michael, ed. *The Politics of Terrorism*. New York: Dekker, 1983.

Stohl, Michael and George Lopez, eds. *The State as Terrorist: The Dynamics of Governmental Violence and Repression*. Westport, CT: Greenwood, 1984.

Taylor, Michael and Charles Lomas. *The Rhetoric of the British Peace Movement*. New York: Random House, 1976.

Toch, Hans. *The Social Psychology of Social Movements*. New York: Bobbs-Merrill, 1965.

Tompkins, Phillip K. *Communication in Action*. Belmont, CA: Wadsworth, 1982.

Touraine, Alain. *The Voice and the Eye: An Analysis of Social Movements*, trans. Alan Duff. Cambridge: Cambridge University Press, 1981.

Turner, Kathleen J. *Lyndon Johnson's Dual War: Vietnam and the Press*. Chicago: University of Chicago Press, 1985.

Turner, Ralph and Lewis M. Killian. *Collective Behavior*. Englewood Cliffs, NJ: Prentice-Hall, 1957.

Turner, Victor. *The Ritual Process*. Chicago: Aldine, 1969.

_____. *Dramas, Fields, and Metaphors*. Ithaca, NY: Cornell University Press, 1974.

Unger, Irwin. *The Movement: A History of the American New Left, 1959-1972*. New York: Dodd, Mead, 1975.

Viorst, Milton. *Fire in the Streets: America in the 1960s*. New York: Simon and Schuster, 1979.

Walker, Daniel. *Rights in Conflict: The Walker Report to the National Commission on the Causes and Prevention of Violence*. New York: Bantam, 1968.

Waller, Douglas. *Congress and the Nuclear Freeze: An Inside Look at the Politics of a Mass Movement*. Amherst, MA: University of Massachusetts Press, 1987.

Wardlaw, Grant. *Political Terrorism*. Cambridge: Cambridge University Press, 1982.

Waskow, Arthur. *From Race Riot to Sit-in*. Garden City, NY: Doubleday, 1966.

Watters, Pat. *Down to Now: Reflections on the Southern Civil Rights Movement*. New York: Pantheon Books, 1971.

Westin, Alan. *Freedom Now*. New York: Basic Books, 1964.

Wilkinson, Paul. *Social Movements*. New York: Praeger, 1971.

_____. *Terrorism and the Liberal State*. London: Macmillan, 1977.

Wilson, John. *Introduction to Social Movements*. New York: Basic Books, 1973.

Windt, Theodore Otto. *Presidents and Protestors: Political Rhetoric in the 1960s*. Tuscaloosa: University of Alabama Press, 1990.

Wood, James L. and Maurice Jackson. *Social Movements: Development, Participation and Dynamics*. Belmont, CA: Wadsworth, 1982.

Wright, Sam. *Crowds and Riots: A Study in Social Organization*. Beverly Hills: Sage, 1978.

Young, Richard, ed. *Roots of Rebellion*. New York: Harper and Row, 1970.

Zaretsky, Irving I. and Mark P. Leone, eds. *Religious Movements in Contemporary America*. Princeton, NJ: Princeton University Press, 1974.

Sources of the Persuasive Efforts of Social Movements

Albert, Judith and Stewart Albert. *The Sixties Papers: Documents of a Rebellious Decade*. New York: Praeger, 1984.

Baird, A. Craig. *American Public Addresses: 1740–1952*. New York: McGraw-Hill, 1956.

Bormann, Ernest G. *Forerunners of Black Power: The Rhetoric of Abolition*. Englewood Cliffs, NJ: Prentice-Hall, 1971.

Brandes, Paul D. *The Rhetoric of Revolt*. Englewood Cliffs, NJ: Prentice-Hall, 1971.

Brandt, Carl G. and Edward M. Shafter, Jr. *Selected American Speeches on Basic Issues: 1850–1950*. Boston: Houghton Mifflin, 1960.

Breitman, George. *Malcolm X Speaks*. New York: Grove, 1966.

Burns, W. Haywood. *The Voices of Negro Protest in America*. New York: Oxford Press, 1963.

Capp, Glenn R. *Famous Speeches in American History*. Indianapolis: Bobbs-Merrill, 1963.

Carawan, Guy and Candie Carawan. *We Shall Overcome*. New York: Oak, 1963.

Carmichael, Stokely and Charles V. Hamilton. *Black Power: The Politics of Liberation in America*. New York: Random House, 1967.

Cleaver, Eldridge. *Soul on Ice*. New York: Dell, 1968.

_____. *Post-Prison Writings and Speeches*, ed. Robert Scheer. New York: Random House, 1969.

_____. *Soul on Fire*. Waco, TX: World Books, 1978.

Copeland, Lewis and Lawrence Lamm. *The World's Great Speeches*. New York: Dover, 1958.

Fabrizio, Ray, Edith Karas, and Ruth Menmuir. *The Rhetoric of NO*. New York: Holt, Rinehart, and Winston, 1970.

Foner, Philip S. *American Labor Songs of the Nineteenth Century*. Urbana, IL: University of Illinois Press, 1975.

Glazer, Tom. *Songs of Peace, Freedom and Protest*. Philadelphia: University of Pennsylvania Press, 1953.

Hill Roy L. *The Rhetoric of Radical Revolt*. Denver: Bell Press, 1964.

Hille, Waldemar. *The People's Song Book*. New York: Sing Out, 1960.

Hoffman, Abbie. *Revolution for the Hell of It*. New York: Dial, 1968.

Holland, DeWitte T., ed. *Sermons in American History*. Nashville, TN: Abingdon Press, 1971.

Huls, Mary Ellen. *United States Government Documents on Women, 1800–1900*. Westport, CT: Greenwood Press, 1993.

Jay, Karla and Allen Young, eds. *Out of the Closet: Voices of Gay Liberation*. New York: Douglas/Links, 1972.

Johnston, Kenneth R. *Rhetoric of Conflict*. New York: Bobbs-Merrill, 1969.

Linkugel, Wil A., R. R. Allen, and Richard L. Johannesen. *Contemporary Speeches*. Belmont, CA: Wadsworth, 1965, 1969, 1972.

Malcolm X. *The Autobiography of Malcolm X*. New York: Grove, 1966.

Matson, Floyd D. *Voices of Crisis: Vital Speeches on Contemporary Issues*. New York: Odyssey, 1967.

The Movement 1964–1970. Westport, CT: Greenwood Press, 1993.

Oliver, Robert T. and Eugene E. White, eds. *Selected Speeches from American History*. Boston: Allyn and Bacon, 1966.

O. M. Collective. *The Organizer's Manual*. New York: Bantam, 1971.

Rinzer, Alan. *Manifesto: Addressed to the President of the United States from the Youth of America*. New York: Collier Books, 1970.

Rosen, David M. *Protest Songs in America*. Westlake Village, CA: Aware Press, 1972.

Salisbury, Harrison E. *The Eloquence of Protest: Voices of the 70s*. Boston: Houghton Mifflin, 1972.

Seeger, Pete. *American Favorite Ballads*. New York: Oak Publications, 1961.

Smith, Arthur and Stephen Robb. *The Voice of Black Rhetoric*. Boston: Allyn and Bacon, 1971.

Wrage, Ernest J. and Barnet Baskerville. *American Forum: Speeches on Historic Issues, 1788–1900*. New York: Harper and Row, 1960.

———. *Contemporary Forum: American Speeches on Twentieth-Century Issues*. New York: Harper and Row, 1962.

Index